Praise for Mar
Dancing Sou⏤ ⏤⏤⏤gy

I met Maria Nhambu in 1976 when she came to teach at Central High School where I was principal. With my encouragement, she created and taught an African Studies program. I now understand how much of Africa she brought to her students. Her story is intimately tied to Africa's story, America's story and history. An invaluable book for anyone passionate about Africa and the human condition.

—*Joyce Taborn Jackson, Ph.D., Licensed Psychologist*

We know her times of loneliness, neglect, confusion, and sadness, and we watch as she faces challenge after challenge that could easily have broken her spirit. Ultimately, she suffered racial and religious prejudice and emotional abuse, often from the adults who should have protected her. Her story of resilience and faith will bring hope to many.

—*Marian Wright Edelman, President and Founder,*
Children's Defense Fund

From Tanzania to America, Nhambu's story of determination continues to emphasize the power of education. Nhambu has never forgotten her roots and has had a life-long passion and commitment to the education of Tanzanian children. As a board member for Operation Bootstrap Africa she was able to give valuable insight into the challenges facing families and communities in Africa as they seek a brighter educational future for their children.

—*Diane Jacoby, Executive Director, Operation Bootstrap Africa*

Nhambu offers vivid instances of the dynamic forces, both from within and without, that have shaped her destiny. From the bleak circumstances of her formative years, an evolving woman of substance and beauty emerges—one who embarks on an intellectual and emotional journey of a lifetime.

—*Mitchell Dasher II, President, Omega Psi Phi Fraternity, Inc.,*
Kappa Upsilon Charitable Foundation, Inc.

It has been my honor to know a woman from another continent and immediately become soul sisters for over thirty years. From day one the two of us have traveled side by side in our pursuit of fitness for the whole person by blending *Aerobics With Soul*® with my wellness mission at the Marsh. To hear Maria's truth in every chapter of her life has inspired thousands of us to face discouragement, danger, loneliness, illness and hardship...with joy and love!

—*Ruth Stricker Dayton, Founder, Owner and Executive Director,*
The Marsh—A Center for Balance and Fitness

Nhambu is an amazing woman with a graceful power that emanates from her. Her story is inspirational and motivational. She held to her own light and truth even though she was often in a sea of darkness.

—*Kristen Bomas, Speaker, Author, Seminar Leader,*
The Circle: A Kristen Bomas Company

What a story! What a life! Maria Nhambu makes her soul available to her readers to see and enter into issues of race, identity, love, motherhood, career and creativity. She gives us insights into how she survived a rough childhood of abandonment and mistreatment. Her story exemplifies the power of faith in God, in others, and in oneself. Her memoir series will inspire many!

—*Rev. Toney Jackson, Pastor of Bethlehem Baptist Church, Newark, NJ,*
Spiritual Counselor, Workshop and Seminar Leader

Maria Nhambu's memoir trilogy reveals life's unexpected twists and turns. This series is well-suited for book clubs where readers can talk about abuse, exploitation, inequality, racism, history, culture, politics and survival of the human spirit. Inspiration is in the form of a pervasive reminder that we all are precious and valuable in the eyes of the Infinite. We are loved fiercely by our own internal "Fat Marys" and we have access to the mind of God at all times.

—*Anna Trelc Blangiardo*

Nhambu and I grew up at the Don Bosco Orphanage and School together. **Africa's Child** is the voice of many Kifungilo children who are unable to put into words their experiences as succinctly and honestly as Nhambu has. What inspires me most about Nhambu is her love and passion for Africa, in spite of her heartbreaking childhood. **Africa's Child** is a gift to all of us.

—*Imelda S. Browne, CTA, Senior Travel Counselor, AAA Travel*

I'm riveted by **Africa's Child**. I find the story mesmerizing—transporting to me not only to another time and place but to the contours of the heart and soul of an intriguing and courageous chronicler.

—*Gerry Regan, Editorial Director and Co-Founder of*
The Wild Geese Irish Social Network

Several times I needed to set this profoundly personal memoir aside for a day because of related incidents in my own life that left indelible impressions. Undoubtedly this will happen to all readers of this finely woven portrait. Memories refuse to be stored in cocoons permanently; they have to morph into flight and wing around occasionally.

—*Jane E. Lang*

Africa's Child is a story of a soul that triumphed over odds that appeared insurmountable. Maria Nhambu's recounting of her African childhood both charms and horrifies us. Nhambu showed both strength and growth of unconquerable spirit as she followed God's mysterious plan for her. Yes, Nhambu had a place in the world. Yes, she had something great to share, and yes, there was clearly a force for good at work in her life as she walked the path set before her. **Africa's Child** is a life's adventure that movies are made of and truly a story for our time.

—*Reverend Nancy Norman, Unity of Delray Beach, Florida*

Africa's Child is a profound coming of age memoir. The story is authentic, raw, and personal. I spent many sleepless nights as I tried to process all that occurred to her. It is a story of cultural and religious definitions. It's one of the few books that I have read that questions the way Black people treat one another—all the remnants of colonialism.

—*Rosalind Murray, former President of National Organization for Women (South Palm Beach Chapter), former President of National Coalition of 100 Black Women (Palm Beach Chapter)*

Nhambu has done a remarkable job of recreating the orphan experience in such a way that I truly felt I was there with little Mary and could see the world through her eyes. It was powerful, moving, beautifully written and it gave me a much better sense of what a child can endure and come out of with strength and grace and the perseverance to move on.

—*Margo Hinnenkamp*

Survivor seems too small a word to describe Maria Nhambu but that is the only word that keeps swirling in my head and my soul! She survived and TRIUMPHS from the very beginning. Her story should be OUR story—of strength, perseverance, insight and fortitude. Loved, loved, loved this from the first page to the very end! Through the laughter, pain, tears and pride, it grabs a hold of you and doesn't let go!

—*Ketly Blaise Williams, President, Can We Talk, Inc., Translation Services*

I must say that I had a very strong emotional reaction to reading **Africa's Child**, and I couldn't just put it on the shelf after having read it. I picked it up and thumbed through it and carried it from room to room as if by this process of possession, I could come in closer contact with this story which I think is most powerful as a story of making a life.

—*Brooks Goddard, Regis College and Temple Israel (Boston) Institute of Lifelong Learning, President of Teachers for East Africa Alumni*

AMERICA'S DAUGHTER

Meeting Maria Nhambu (when she was Maria Bergh) and having an African as my high school teacher influenced me and inspired me in so many ways. She awakened and encouraged my interest in Africa that led to five different trips to Africa. She helped spark my search for my own heritage and identity. She planted seeds for my art and community awareness and activism. To read about that time in our lives and learn in depth about her life is a revelation to me. Just as she opened new pathways for me, **America's Daughter**, book two in her incredible life story, will do the same for others as she relates a true American story!

—Seitu Jones, Visual Artist and Sculptor, B.S., MLS
Loeb Fellow Harvard Graduate School of Design

Nhambu's plight is not hers alone; her fight against odds is not hers alone; her right to be free is not hers alone. As "America's Daughter," Nhambu's journey to America becomes for her as well as for millions of others, "the home of the brave." Her quest continues to illumine not only to herself, but for herself. Answers, bold and clear, are within reach for all who purposely, definitively declare: I am who I am wherever I am, daughter, son of the universe. Entitled by birth and by birthright, Africa's child growing in stature and wisdom by virtue of origin, I am because we are.

—Grace Hill Rogers, Retired English Secondary Teacher and Principal;
Recipient of Minnesota Alliance of Black Educators Teacher of the Year

Maria Nhambu's unique writing style...puts the reader face to face with the truth about racism, prejudice, and cultural differences. It asks the question: Is it different today?

—Marie-Thérèse Reed, Docteur d'Etat ès Sciences (PhD)
University of Rennes, France, Officer National Order of Merit

Maria Nhambu's memoir with European colonialism and American racial segregation and its impact make **America's Daughter** a must read. The author brings to readers her own middle passage story as a biracial child brought up in an African orphanage coming to the United States. This second book of her trilogy provides readers with many perceptions and insights. Her struggle with identity in America raises profound questions we would do well to ponder today.

—*Benjamin Mchie, Educational Consultant, Writer, Historian, Founder and Executive Director of African American Registry*

Foreign students are so eager to get on with their education and learn about America, but many, I'm sure, will resonate with Maria Nhambu's description of her adventures and experiences in her new country. The story she tells in **America's Daughter** lets us see ourselves in a new light and creates bridges to understanding diverse experiences.

—*Coventry Cowens, Assistant Director, Multicultural and International Programs, St. Catherine University*

The truths that Maria Nhambu shares with her readers in **America's Daughter** are revealing, but for different reasons to both African Americans and the white community. We have so much to learn from each other and about each other. Nhambu teaches from a unique and powerful perspective and the lessons are of great value to us all.

—*Vera Farrington Founder, The Spady Cultural Heritage Museum*

Reading **America's Daughter** will change my life forever. Nhambu's journey is incredible and filled with adversity that most could not endure. Yet she has been blessed to see and love from the inside out, always redefining who she is meant to become.

America's Daughter is a reawakening of the issue of race and ethnicity in this country. Nhambu lives through the familiar and unfamiliar prejudices in every aspect of her life, and with grace and dignity teaches us how to be better than what we have been taught to dislike about others.

—*Sue Anderson, Retired Director, Office of Equal Employment Opportunity, Centers for Disease Control and Prevention Atlanta, Georgia*

An incredible and inspiring story. Maria shares her continued struggles in the second book of her trilogy. **America's Daughter** tells how she deals with issues of racism and prejudice that still exist in America today. It is full of heartbreak, humor, and determination. Her writing is from the heart. Maria's faith and trust in God continues to give her the strength to endure and not give up. A must read!

—*VJ Jackson, Marketing Manager, Best Print and Design, Atlanta, Georgia*

Maria Nhambu's humor, innocence and determination not to be racially excluded from her surroundings are all part of her maturity. In **America's Daughter**, she becomes the very cultured, savvy traveler and the center of many friendships around the world. I love Fat Mary, Maria's second conscience. Her relationship with Fat Mary had me wishing that I too could talk to her.

—*Dale Breise, Retired Bank Executive, Chairman, Delray Beach Chamber of Commerce*

DRUM BEATS, HEART BEATS

In this final volume of The Dancing Soul Trilogy, we join an ever insightful and passionate Nhambu as she traverses diverse cultures and continents and negotiates a complex and shifting web of mixed identities—African immigrant and African American—through marriage, parenthood, and the search for the father she has never known. Through trauma and triumph, love and betrayal, the "Drum Beats" and "Heart Beats" of her native Africa lead her on an ultimate journey of transcendence that will enthrall and inspire readers around the world.

—*Natasha C. Vaubel, Scholar of African history, literature, and film*

Guests at my Rancho La Puerta fitness spa have long raved about the amazing spirit, joy and soul of Maria Nhambu and her *Aerobics With Soul®* dance program. I expected the same when I settled in to read her **Drum Beats, Heart Beats**, and soon I was laughing, crying, and transported for an entire morning by the thrilling drumbeat of her stories, her passion, her life.

—*Deborah Szekely, Co-founder, Rancho La Puerta,*
A Fitness Resort and Spa

Nhambu's memoir is full of lessons about life for all of us—a child slowly becomes aware of the injustice of her birthright, an adolescent learns to prosper in unfamiliar places and among unfamiliar people, an adult drinks deeply of discovery and disappointment, and throughout it all, a strong girl and then a strong woman keeps faith with herself in the face of obstacles.

Drum Beats, Heart Beats makes clear that Fat Mary is not a metaphor but has been a reliable guide in Nhambu's life. It raises the question for the reader whether such a guiding spirit may not reside deep within all of us, if only we would be open to it. She was deprived of the love of a mother. Yet, she has always had the wisdom and the inner strength to have become a loving mother and grandmother, and the best friend anyone can have.

—*Dr. Margaret M. Wong, Foreign Language Teacher,*
Director of International Education

In **Drum Beats, Heart Beats,** the reader senses the passionate beating of Nhambu's heart as she unveils the details of her challenging and fragile relationship with her birth mother. Despite her husband's betrayal, Nhambu's heart remains strong with love of family. Africa calls and the drumbeat in her soul gives her heart the rhythm and determination to leave no stone unturned as she searches for her African father.

—*Diane Gayes, R.N., Certified Instructor,* Aerobics With Soul®

Drum Beats, Heart Beats completes a remarkable autobiography— certainly unlike any I have ever read. This is a life journey that began by describing a childhood well outside the experience of most readers, continued with life-changing surprises, and now concludes with an affirming story of discovery and self-discovery. But it is more than one person's story. The reader will gain insights into some of the cultural norms that surround us, and into the evolution of our own closest relationships.

—*Walter Graff, LL.B.*

As Maria Nhambu does in her first two books, **Africa's Child** and **America's Daughter**, she continues to share her life's journey with honesty and great courage! In **Drum Beats, Hearts Beats**, the last volume, she writes straight from the heart, telling the good, the bad, and the ugly in her life. Through it all she kept the faith!

—*Carletta Smith, MSW, Retired, Minneapolis Public Schools*

The author of **Drum Beats, Heart Beats** has the literary gift and passion to expose the intimate. While she embraces America and dances to its heartbeat, the essence of her soul remains in Africa. Maria Nhambu is Africa's Child.

—*James M. Gayes, M.D.*

Drum Beats, Heart Beats will forever enhance your view of faith, hope, love and the resiliency of the human spirit. Nhambu is an engaging storyteller who gives meaningful perspective on identity, family, race, culture and the search for love and purpose. Nhambu freely shares her incredible life experiences regarding these timeless issues and compels your soul to feel them. **Drum Beats, Heart Beats** will awaken your perception of our common humanity and teach you something about yourself.

—*Rachel Soffer, Attorney, Certified Instructor,* Aerobics With Soul®

Drum Beats, Heart Beats continues the amazing revelations of Maria Nhambu's soul journey. Written with raw emotions, wit, charm, tenacity and humor, **Drum Beats, Heart Beats** is sure to inspire. We follow Nhambu as she returns to Tanzania to search for her father. Fat Mary, her life-long companion is always present, offering hope, wisdom, comfort and lights on her path. Her marriage is a complex dance between contentment and struggle and proves once more that she is a born survivor.

—*Anna Rachele Fitzsimmons*

Dancing Soul Trilogy ✳ Book Three

Drum Beats, Heart Beats

A Memoir

Maria Nhambu

Delray Beach, Florida

Published by

Dancing Twiga Press
Delray Beach, Florida
MariaNhambu.com

ISBN: 978-0-9972561-6-1 paperback
ISBN: 978-0-9972561-8-5 hardback
ISBN: 978-0-9972561-7-8 ebook

Cover and Text by Bookwrights
Front cover photo by Daphney Antoine
Back cover photo of Nhambu by Daphney Antoine

Printed in the United States of America

To

Jeremiah Manoni Nhambu, my father,
Marshall Lawrence Reiner, my brother, and
Amani, Oskar and Liv, my grandchildren

Dancing Soul Trilogy

Map of Africa Showing Tanzania

Map of Tanzania Showing Locations
Mentioned in Text

Contents

Foreword

"As long as we are not ourselves we will be what other people are," writes Malidoma Patrice Somé in *Of Water and the Spirit*. This could never be said of Maria Nhambu because she is very much an original and comfortable with herself. We continue to meet her authentic self in *Drum Beats, Heart Beats*, as we did in the other two volumes of her riveting memoir.

Raised in an orphanage with only a first name, she knows the importance and weight of names. Toni Morrison wrote in *The Song of Solomon*, "When you know your name, you should hang on to it, for unless it is noted down and remembered, it will die when you do." Today we see so many people doing ancestry and DNA searches to find out who and what they are. It's not an online search we read about in this book but an actual on-the-ground ancestor search.

Maria (the name I knew her by) only learned her father's name at age forty-five. She and her half-brother Larry decided to journey back to Tanzania to look for her father with little more to go on than courage and faith. Larry remembered the names of a few men who had worked for his parents during his early childhood in colonial Tanganyika, and this guided them as they explored the locations and towns where Larry once lived.

When they finally found her father, he had one request—that she take his name to America so it would be known and live on there. She fulfilled her father's request by legally changing her name to include his, as did her children.

To her surprise, an enduring and unplanned honor to her father's name occurred when she donated her African art to Marian Wright Edelman's Children's Defense Fund, and the organization chose to name it The Nhambu Collection.

The large and varied collection is displayed throughout the buildings and grounds at the Alex Haley Farm in Tennessee and the CDF headquarters in Washington, DC. The Nhambu Collection continues to inspire, educate, and empower its viewers to experience the spirit and beauty of Africa through the creativity of its people.

Now those who see this collection will learn of her father's family name. "Nhambu," in fact, is the name she prefers people to use. Before she even knew her name, she lived its meaning, in the Sukuma language, of a bridge person—one who facilitates understanding among differing cultures.

In *Drum Beats, Heart Beats*, Nhambu uses elements of critical race theory to question the relationships of race and class, gender and sexism. A mixed-race person, she taught herself to be an "African American," in part because she was identified as such in American society and in part because the identity thrust upon her gave her the satisfaction of finding a group that she could belong to.

Originally a French teacher in public schools, Nhambu created an innovative program to teach Swahili, African culture, and dance. She drew deeply upon her childhood experiences in Africa to instill in all students love of self and love of culture and heritage.

Nhambu is one of humanity's beautiful women, both inside and out. People young and old love her and are drawn to her. Despite her difficult childhood, she developed a wonderful sense of humor, and her ability to always look on the bright side of every situation makes people around her acknowledge their own greatness and feel that nothing is impossible.

All who work for the ancestors of Africa know grief and sacrifice. Those who were brought to America against their will by people indifferent to their suffering know well Nhambu's burden, and they love her for carrying it and sharing it with such dignity. Her story helps us protect our tattered and torn humanity, soothe our tortured and tormented souls, and reveals that, despite our suffering, we can find ways to see joy and beauty in life.

Nhambu has known the agony of abuse, abandonment, and betrayal, but she realized very early in her childhood that she had the will to survive and discovered the necessity of finding hope and working for a better future. These experiences can make her book hard to read at times.

Abraham Lincoln once referred to African Americans as "thinking machines," as if they had no souls and could be raped, robbed, tortured, mutilated, and cheated without an ounce of guilt or remorse.

Nhambu lets us know that she's been there, and the stories she tells illustrate her understanding of the human condition and offer an introspective examination for self-derived solutions.

She returns to Africa several times and experiences her mother country as an American tourist, discovering a world of luxury and privilege that was previously denied her and other Africans. She also encounters the "ugly American" on safari and suffers the torment of realizing she has one foot in each world.

Nhambu writes about how words spoken to her profoundly affected her thoughts and emotions and her self-image. As Confucius noted, "Without knowing the force of words, it is impossible to know more." And writer Jodi Picoult states, "Words are like eggs dropped from great heights; you can no more call them back than ignore the mess they leave when they fall."

Having grown up with harsh words of judgment and rejection, Nhambu savors the words of encouragement and love uttered along her path, like those of her adopted mother, Cathy, or of her college French professor, Mrs. Reed, who lavished praise on her and called her endearingly *"Mon petite chou."*

She immediately bonds with her white half-brother, Larry, when he tells her that he loves her and had been longing for a little sister. An unbreakable bond of trust develops between them.

For Nhambu, good, kind words healed and protected her, while bad, hurtful words ripped and tore into her heart and played over and over in her mind. Through her story and choices in life, she teaches us how to bear the hurt, learn to forgive, to heal, and to find joy and love within ourselves.

Her biological mother, Dorothy Reiner, earns Nhambu's distrust by refusing to tell her who her African father is and by refusing to acknowledge or relate anything about their life together. Many words are better left unsaid because they can hurt and damage a sensitive human mind more than punches and kicks or lashes from a whip. Through Nhambu's story we see that though much has been taken from her, much endures.

Maria, thank you for reminding us of these profound truths. We love your ability to lay bare our souls to us. Without your books, parts of our souls would be hidden even from our view. Your friendship with my wife, Imelda, and the life you shared in the orphanage has enriched our lives. For these and more reasons, you are my "soul sister."

Dallas L. Browne, PhD
Honorary Consul for Tanzania, St. Louis; Professor of Anthropology Emeritus, Southern Illinois University–Edwardsville; Author of Culture: The Soul of Africa and the Coming Gold Rush

A Note from the Author

I began my author's note for my first book, *Africa's Child*, by stating that it was the personal story of my life at the Don Bosco Home in Kifungilo. I then mentioned my discovery that those of us who grew up there often had different memories and experiences of what we had lived together.

In my second book, *America's Daughter*, I wrote about the complexities of adjusting to American life, especially as a biracial African.

Now, in this, the third and last volume of my memoirs, I again emphasize that this is the personal story of my life as someone who grew up without a family but who deeply longed for one.

Having my own family—a husband and two children—was deeply fulfilling and meaningful for me. It was the promised land, the payoff for having endured such suffering, doubt, loneliness, and misery as a child. Having my own family was one of the greatest and most valued gifts of my life.

Beginning with the first words of my memoir, I have written truthfully from my heart about my experiences and have freely expressed my emotions and thoughts. I continue to do so in this final volume. When the family I valued most was weakened as a result of betrayals that I forgave, it became devastating to realize that living happily ever after with my husband might not be possible.

I had to face the possibility of divorce. People often make light of the breaking up of a family as though it is not a big deal because it happens all the time and life goes on. They point out that "it takes two" as an underlying reason for marital discord but forget to acknowledge that it also takes two to be faithful and remain married. The same people who want to hear every detail about a death in the family avoid talking about the prospect of divorce because they do not see it for what is—the death of the marriage.

In the chapters recounting the difficulties that surfaced in my marriage, I write what cannot be adequately felt and understood unless you have experienced a childhood like mine. I only ask that you understand where I am coming from and that you see my soul, even if it is uncomfortable to read my truth.

As a child, I created Fat Mary because I had no choice. I had no one to whom I could express my innermost thoughts and fears. She is the reason I survived the psychological pain of my upbringing. "Fat Mary," for those who haven't read my previous books, was my detested orphanage nickname that I turned around and used to represent the part of me that is invisible to others—my powerful, true, and authentic inner self. Fat Mary was my counselor and consoler. She loved me unconditionally and kept my traumatic childhood experiences for me until I could process them, understand them, and come to terms with them.

Fat Mary continues to play a role in my life today, but I am older and wiser now and am not afraid to be my authentic self or express all the emotions I experienced as a result of questioning my marriage. I fully understood the enormity of the effects a pending broken marriage could have on me, my children, my family, and my friends.

The mysteries of my life and origins have been revealed along the path I have traveled, but not without great cost and effort. For all those who have participated in my life, my gratitude is great.

Prologue

African drum beats established the unique rhythm of my life from the day I was left as a newborn at an orphanage for mixed-race children. The orphanage, in Tanzania, East Africa, was run by German missionary nuns. Moved by the plight of biracial children who often suffered ill-treatment and outright rejection, the nuns founded the Don Bosco Home and Boarding School at Kifungilo for children like me.

My story began in a country yearning to be independent of British colonialism and eager to forge its own identity. In *Africa's Child*, the first volume of my memoir series, Dancing Soul Trilogy, I recount my experiences growing up, my longings for family and education, and my struggle for identity.

The discipline administered by the nuns was frequently harsh and, at times, brutal. Although our basic physical needs were provided for by the nuns and benefactors, I still had to face my realities: I had no identity, no tribe, no family, and no mother. Most children at the orphanage at least had a mother to visit them. Bullying and cruelty on the part of other children, and especially by the older girls in charge of us, were daily experiences.

My love of learning and longing for further education kept me focused, motivated, and hopeful. It also brought me into contact with inspiring and supportive teachers. One of those teachers, Catherine Murray Mamer, only four years older than I was, took me back with her to America and arranged for a college scholarship. My adventures in learning to be an American, and especially a Black American, are told in *America's Daughter*, the second volume.

Discovering dance and its power to heal my soul played a vital role in my survival. I have always relied on dance to make me feel alive and fill me with joy. In America I created a fitness program called *Aerobics With Soul®—The African Dance Workout* as a way to share the essence of dance and to touch the essence of life. It is also my way of sharing my African heritage. For many years, I taught African dance to elementary school children through the Young Audiences Program in Minnesota.

In America I fulfilled another deep longing by having a family of my own. The blessings and joy I received from my family almost erased the pain of this absence in childhood. I was very proud and happy that, even though it was later in my life, I could experience what family felt like. I loved my husband and children and made up my mind that no matter what, I would never, ever break up our family.

My birth mother came looking for me when I was thirty-three years old, and she introduced me to Larry, my half-brother, when I was thirty-nine. Neither one of them looked like the family I had pictured and longed for when I was at the orphanage. It surprised me that my mother Dorothy was white, since most of the orphans in Kifungilo had African mothers and European fathers. I didn't adjust easily to that fact because I knew that a white person (*mzungu*) in Africa enjoyed privileges I had never experienced and couldn't relate to. It was evident from the beginning that we would not have the mother-daughter bond that blossoms when a mother raises her child. She didn't seem to be interested in me as her daughter, only as someone she had sacrificed for the sake of her family. When her husband died, her curiosity and maybe her guilt led her to search for me.

Dorothy, it seemed, had more trouble establishing a relationship with me than I had with her. When we were alone, she talked to me like I was an African in Africa, using language that was used for servants and subordinates. When we were with company, though, she chose her words carefully and spoke to me as an equal.

On the other hand, my white half-brother Larry, a Boston pediatrician, was delighted to meet me and was convinced that I was his African little sister Judy who was raised by his parents. When he was eight years old, his parents told him that his little sister had died, though he didn't fully believe them.

I am grateful to Dorothy for introducing me to my brother. He loved me at first sight, and we bonded the minute we met. He walked the walk with me and helped me bring the search for my identity full circle. He talked at length about his *mzungu* upbringing in Tanzania and his everlasting love for Africa, and we compared notes. He was very privileged compared to me, but we had our childhood loneliness in common. He was a lonely little blond boy whose greatest happiness came from playing with African girls and boys in the village, which meant he spoke tribal languages almost before he mastered English.

Our mother died without leaving any information about who my father was. Larry suggested traveling together to Tanzania to search for my father, even though we knew it could be a daunting and ultimately futile search.

My marriage to a Norwegian businessman had opened up a whole new culture to me. He was an excellent provider for our family, and we had a comfortable life with travel to every part of the world. Throughout our marriage, every time I prayed, I thanked God for him. However, I couldn't figure out what was happening in our last three or four years together. He said and did things during that time that made me wonder if I knew him at all.

The only certainty in life is change. Come with me as I continue sharing what fills me with joy, challenges my spirit, breaks my heart, and heals it.

1

Into the Past

After my mother Dorothy died in 1986, Larry, my half-brother, and I were sure we would find information she had left us about my father. We searched her house and records. Nothing. Not a clue, even though we both had asked her to clarify that part of my life. Two years passed and then one day Larry phoned me with the suggestion that we travel to Tanzania together. While looking for my father was part of our plan, we especially wanted to share our experiences of Africa with each other. Despite having the same mother, we had grown up very differently in a place we both loved.

Meeting Larry in 1979 was the opposite of meeting our mother Dorothy three years earlier. When I met him, I still hadn't gotten over the shock of discovering that my mother was a white American. The woman who said she was my mother was reserved toward me, distant, stiff even. When I saw her approaching Cathy and me at the airport, I realized I had seen her before at the orphanage. She would meet with me in the convent parlor like other visitors looking to adopt a child. I also remember her visiting me in the hospital when I was seriously ill as a child. If indeed she was my mother, I wondered, why hadn't she ever held me or touched me or spoken a single word during those meetings?

Dorothy didn't tell me I had a half-brother for several years. Our relationship—reserved and cautious for the most part—was fraught with unspoken and even forbidden topics. The first thing I noticed about Larry, on the other hand, was his relaxed and accepting body language. He had joy on his face, and without his saying a word, I felt the love in his heart. How could he be so different from Dorothy who raised him?

He was a practical man who dressed simply and economically in the typical, subdued pastels that, when I was in Africa, I assumed were required of white people. He was eight years older than I was and only a few inches taller with very little hair on his head—most of it had migrated to his mustache. Telling people that we were from the same African tribe would have been more believable than the fact that we were brother and sister!

Larry and I talked almost the entire time on the long flight from Boston to Amsterdam to Kilimanjaro. Whenever our mother came up in the conversation, his voice and body language changed as if he knew he would soon have to face the truth about her life in Tanzania. When I first met him, he admitted that he and his mother were not close when he was growing up. He knew little about her personal life in Africa because he had gone away to boarding school at age seven, and when he came home for holidays, he and his father took extended safaris together to explore different parts of Tanzania. In contrast, he always spoke tenderly of his father. I could tell that he still missed him twenty years after his passing. I tried to imagine what his father's life must have been like, taking into account that he didn't divorce his wife over the birth of her two brown children.

When the other passengers settled down to sleep after our delicious dinner on KLM, Larry and I kept conversing. I asked him if he still knew people in Tanzania.

He shook his head. "Probably not. I haven't communicated with any of the servants we had since I left for college in 1952. I saw a couple of them briefly when I visited in 1960 and 1963. But three of them pop up in my dreams every so often. I'm sure they must be dead, given the average life span of an African male. I remember one man fondly. He was with us the longest, ever since I was a little boy before I went to boarding school, and he was always there when I returned for holidays. He was like my second father. His name is Yeremia. I never knew his last name."

"Wasn't that the name written in the Swahili/English dictionary we found among Dorothy's things when we were searching for information she might have left us?" I asked.

"That's him."

"Dorothy kept that dictionary. Did she ever talk to you about him?"

"We never discussed her life in Africa. Dad and I sometimes talked a little about Africa, but Mom never did. She said she never wanted to go back because it wouldn't be the way she remembered it, and it would be too painful."

"Painful? Seems to me life for her and the other *wazungu* (white people) in those days was privileged! Even nowadays, whites in Africa have advantages and benefits. Maybe she feared that after Tanganyika gained independence, she might have to treat Africans as equals rather than as second-class citizens as they did under British rule."

"The one time I did try to get information from her, she refused, saying she was protecting people."

"Larry, she said the same thing to me. And that led me to think my father might have been an African pastor or a priest or a government official. I wonder whom she was protecting. I knew that white priests sometimes fathered half-caste children, but I had never seen an African priest, and until I met my mother, it had never entered my mind that my father could be African."

"Sis, we might not find your father—whoever he is. What happens if we do find him and he's a disappointment?"

"Something else to consider. If she never intended to reveal anything about my father, are we going against her by searching for him? How I wish Dorothy could have faced her demons about this. Or maybe she really didn't know him. One time when she was in a relaxed mood, I tried again to get information from her. She told me that she didn't remember anything because 'it happened so fast.' I asked her if she was raped, and—you guessed it—she reached into her purse for her angina pills."

"No matter the outcome, let's try to have a great time revisiting our childhoods and making up for lost time."

"Easy for you to say," I told my brother. "But seriously, I feel close to you and sometimes it even feels like we grew up together."

"For me you're replacing Judy, the little sister I had in Africa. I can still remember walking with Mom to her grave when I came home from boarding school the year I was eight. She told me that Judy had died from pneumonia." Larry's eyes filled with tears. "I couldn't stop crying at the grave. She let me cry for as long as I wanted, and when I stopped, that was it. Judy's name was never mentioned again."

The more I learned about Dorothy, the more detached I felt from her, even though she was my mother and her decisions had set me on my life's path. This trip to Tanzania was unlike any other I'd taken before. Was I embarking on some terribly exciting but foolhardy adventure that might lead into a black hole from which I might emerge more damaged than before? I was scared and confused. I recited some of my favorite mantras: There is nothing to fear but fear itself. What doesn't kill you makes you stronger. This, too, shall pass. Behind every cloud there's a silver lining. In the end, everything will be okay; if it's not okay, it's not the end.

Don't forget, I am here with you. We will brave this chapter of your life like we've done every other one. I can still see us repeating Mother Majellis' mantra from middle school in Mhonda: "Nothing ventured, nothing gained." You've always believed in miracles. Look at how many have happened in your life so far. There's no reason to believe that the miracle of finding your father doesn't await you.

My dear Fat Mary assured me that miracles have no expiration date as long as I didn't give up pursuing and believing in them.

2

Larry's Africa

 Larry and I discussed our present lives, and every so often we'd pinch ourselves in gratitude for having found each other and for the blessing of this trip. He had divorced his wife, the mother of his three children, and was living with a woman he hoped to marry. I was disappointed to learn that he had begun his affair with her while he was still married. My husband's affair a few years ago still caused me pain. I visited Larry looking for support and comfort when I learned of Kjell's affair, but my brother seemed indifferent and assured me that I'd get over it. I discovered then that it was difficult for him to talk about personal matters—his or mine. I knew that sharing my marital problems with him would only make me feel more alone.

Our travel plans had us visiting my childhood sites first. I tried to prepare him, knowing that nothing would be as it was when I was growing up in Kifungilo.

"When I returned to the orphanage in 1974 for the first time after leaving for America in 1963, the entire place seemed miniature to me, almost like an architectural model on display at city hall or in a hotel lobby. It was an odd sensation because Kifungilo was huge and practically my whole world as a child. You will see what home was for me the first nineteen years of my life." As I told him about people and incidents from my childhood, I was impressed at his attentiveness and eagerness to learn about me. I shared with him my experiences as a biracial child. Now it was time for me to learn about life in Africa from a *mzungu's* point of view.

"I'm flattered that you have opened up to me and trusted me with your painful childhood memories, Sis."

"You can trust me too, Larry. I want to know everything from the very beginning because, as you know, Dorothy was not exactly a chatterbox. I'd very much like to hear about your parents and your childhood in Tanganyika."

Larry explained that his parents first came to Tanganyika as missionaries, and then worked for the British government. In that capacity, they were transferred to various districts. That meant we'd be visiting several villages in our search. I also wanted him to tell me what he knew of our family's history before our mother went to Africa, because Dorothy had shared very little of her background with me.

"Mom was born Dorothy Ragna Isel in Chicago, Illinois, the oldest of three sisters in the family of Gottlieb and Ragna Knudsen Isel. Our grandmother Ragna was the oldest of seven Norwegian kids and was born in Bergen, Norway. Frank Isel's family came from Hanover, Germany, but he was born in Chicago. You've met Mom's two sisters, Marjorie and Marion.

"When she was six or seven, Mom's family moved to Texas and lived on a farm in what is now Houston. There, Mom learned to ride bareback and to ramble around shoeless. She also greatly impressed her first schoolteacher, a lady named Lulu Raab. When I was a medical student in Houston from 1956 to 1961, we went to visit Lulu and were regaled with stories about Mom's brightness. Then the family moved back to Lombard, Illinois, where her father bought a flower farm and raised peonies. Apparently, he also raised a little hell with a lady tenant who rented his farmhouse. Our Norwegian grandmother accepted it all stoically as 'God's plan.'"

"The Norwegian I married," I said, "is stoic, but God is not in his vocabulary. His idea of 'It's God's plan' is shoving all unpleasantness under the rug and proclaiming 'It is what it is.' How about your father?"

"Well, my grandfather was Albert Reiner, whose family came from Alsace-Lorraine, and my grandmother was Minnie Raynor whose family was Swedish. The family moved to Chicago from Cincinnati sometime before my father's birth. My father met our mother while she was working at Sears Roebuck when she was still in college. They courted for two years and married in 1933. I was born three years later."

"When and why did your parents go to Tanganyika?"

"My dad became a minister in a Christian church. When I was three years old, my parents went to Tanganyika as missionaries with the African Inland Mission, a nondenominational evangelical group from the U.S. I'll never forget how shocked I was when he told me later that part of the preparation for becoming a missionary to Africa in those days was the removal of all his teeth and being fitted with two false racks!"

"Ouch! Now that's taking preventive medicine to the extreme. Do you remember anything about that first trip?"

"Yes! We went by freighter—the SS *Sagadahoc* of the American-South African Line. We were the only passengers on the three-month voyage from New York to Dar-es-Salaam via Cape Town, East London, Port Elizabeth, Durban, and Lourenço Marques. The captain, a doughty old salt, didn't care too much for children, especially an investigative three-year-old. My parents kept me in check with difficulty. Three days out of Cape Town, some thirty days after leaving New York, the ship ran into a major tidal wave. I was sitting in a highchair eating, and it tipped over. As I landed, my nose hit the edge of a bucket. The captain had to radio Cape Town for instructions as what to do about a broken nose (nothing) and what to worry about (nothing). When we arrived in Cape Town, I was taken to a hospital where an X-ray confirmed that I had a broken nose. No treatment needed.

"At a zoo in East London, South Africa, my parents rented a rickshaw pulled by a Zulu in full war dress. I would not get into the rickshaw because I was afraid of him, so I trailed along behind, keeping up because the rickshaw puller took it easy. In the same zoo, I took a ride on an elephant in a little frame saddle that held six kids. The only other event I remember was a ceremony crossing the equator. The crew filled a huge canvas sack with water to make a swimming pool on deck, and everybody got dunked—a ritual that apparently goes back to ancient Greek days.

"The whole trip took three months on the freighter and a week or so by train. In October of 1938, we landed in Dar and took the Central Line train to Mwanza. From there we were carried by palanquin to Kijima. There were no roads. We lived there from 1939 to 1941."

"You have a good memory!"

"With a childhood like mine, you don't easily forget."

I tried to sleep, but the passengers snoring on the plane kept me awake. I thought of Larry and his parents on the large, sparse freighter traveling for three months across a vast ocean to an unknown place to do God's work. I imagined them carrying their trunks and other luggage on the train and being transported by palanquin like I'd seen in history books. I wondered how they felt, trudging over terrain with no roads. They must have been very tough—physically, psychologically, and spiritually.

Larry's breathing was heavy. I was glad he could rest. He was probably anticipating the emotional toll of facing the secret African life of his dead parents and its effect on his own life.

From deep in my heart, Fat Mary appeared.

It was missionaries who brought you up. Their lives in Africa were a lot like your brother's and his parents. They were dedicated to God, and they did what they thought was necessary to convert the Africans from their beliefs and bring them Christianity. The colonizers came to Africa as explorers but ended up claiming and ruling Africa for their own countries in Europe. Your brother grew up with colonizers who looked down on the missionaries. But for most Africans, these two groups were the same.

Fat Mary was absolutely right. Growing up in Tanganyika, I seldom saw a difference in the reasons that brought *wazungu* to Africa. The white-skinned foreigners came to serve and be served. All white people were called *wazungu*, whether they were British, French, German, or American.

The KLM stewardess turned the lights on to serve breakfast, and Larry picked up where he had left off, assuring me that, all in all, he'd had a good childhood in Africa. "Actually, it was a fairy-tale childhood, if you leave out how homesick I was when I went to boarding school at Arusha International Primary School and then to Prince of Wales School in Nairobi."

"Do you still have friends from those days?"

"Life in colonial Tanganyika was not really conducive to deep friendships. Families would be posted to other towns or go back to England. The three-month school terms broke up many school relationships, and we instinctively learned to protect ourselves from close attachments because friends would just disappear. Starting boarding school at age seven gave me somewhat the same feeling about my parents. Teachers just replaced them in the routine. Yet, there was a general friendliness among whites, which made the whole country seem like a single neighborhood. Perhaps the appropriate description would be that we had many acquaintances but few close friends. That pattern has persisted my whole life. But in my case, because at least I had a family to go to regularly, I had privileges galore."

I reflected on how important friendships have always been to me as Larry continued his story.

"The only close friend I remember having was a boy named Roger Whittaker. I met him at Prince of Wales. His family lived near Nairobi. His mother worked as a secretary for the owner of the movie theater chain in town, so we always got Sunday passes to the flicks. He knew nothing of rural East Africa until he came home with me to Kasulu for a school holiday. He was the only kid ever to come home with me. And as usual we went on safari with Dad. Roger was an excellent whistler and spent many hours trying to teach me how to whistle. He went on to study medicine, then sidestepped into biochemistry at Cardiff in Wales. He found the studies too taxing, but he had started singing with a guitar at nightclubs in Cardiff and eventually made singing his career.

"Many years later, I saw a record jacket on a rack at Heathrow Airport. The name on it was Roger Whittaker. I picked it up, read the back, and sure enough this guy had grown up in Kenya. I called the record company and as luck would have it, he was in their office so we talked briefly. I met him again several years later in Boston on tour, but the years had made him a celebrity, and we just didn't click like we had as kids. I went to a concert he gave, sent a note backstage to him, and he dedicated the concert to me with much nostalgia. When we talked afterwards, it was clear that our paths had taken different forks and we didn't see life the same way. More fodder for my theory that friendships in colonial Africa had a way of fading out."

From early childhood, I've reflected long and hard on friendships, so I shared some thoughts with Larry. "Friendships have to be maintained like every other valuable or beautiful thing. They are like flower gardens. You plant different seeds, water them, and watch them grow and bloom. As you inhale their fragrance and beauty, you thank them for being in your life because you know that whenever things go wrong, you can always sit among them, and their presence will help you recover. But then, out of nowhere big, bad weeds appear in your garden, and if you don't pull them out, they will slowly spread and choke the flowers to death. Some flowers will fade and die because their time in your garden has passed. Everything has a beginning and an end. Because I didn't grow up with a family, I take good care of my friendships. They *are* my family, and I'm usually devastated when friendships go sour, which happens."

"I like that analogy. Unfortunately, it's too late for me."

"It's never too late to cultivate and keep friendships. There's a saying we used to sing in high school: 'Make new friends but keep the old. One is silver the other gold.' I love listening to your childhood stories, and I'm encouraged because with your excellent recollection, you probably have an idea who my father might be, based on who was around your family when I was born in 1943. How old were you then?"

"I was eight."

3

Persons of Interest

 "Sis, I've been agonizing about this ever since we met, especially after I proposed coming to Tanzania together. I have no idea how or where to begin the search for your father. I remember three of the servants very well. Yeremia was the *mpishi* (cook) and all-around head boy of the house. Hezekiah was the houseboy who cleaned and dusted, and Klementi was the *dobi* (laundryman). I have a strong hunch that one of them is your father or will know who he is. The more I think about it, it seems that Yeremia is the one. That could be the reason why Mom kept that dictionary all these years."

I recalled sitting in Dorothy's living room and holding in my hands a beat-up Swahili/English dictionary with these words written in a childish and tentative hand: *This book belongs to Jeremia M. Nhambu.* My stomach tightened up when I read that name.

"Yeremia is the Swahili form of his name, right?"

"Yes, but in the dictionary we found, it's spelled with a 'J,' perhaps because our mother was teaching him English."

"Larry, why do you think it was him?"

"Because he was with us off and on the entire time we were in Tanganyika. I also vaguely remember him and Mom spending a lot of time together in the house when Dad was gone for an extended time. Of course, I thought nothing of it as a child. He was much loved by all of us. He was like a surrogate father to me and taught me all the little mischievous things a father or a big brother would teach a little boy. He took me with him to his village, and I played with the Sukuma children there. I spoke fluent Sukuma and actually spoke it and Swahili better than English—to my parents' embarrassment."

11

"How could your dad leave Dorothy alone in Africa for extended periods? That must have been frightening for her."

"As I told you, after Judy was born, Dad took a number of different jobs and went where the jobs took him. He would often be gone for weeks and left my mom in the care of Yeremia, who stayed in the house with her. But Mom was no pushover! The servants, and even I, were scared of her. Let me tell you a story about Mom.

"During the war in 1944, there was a major drought and then famine in central Tanganyika. Some four thousand people came to the famine relief camp that my mother ran. It was situated near a Roman Catholic mission run by the White Fathers, a French Catholic missionary order. The African residents at the Catholic mission were separated by sex. When the Fathers tried to segregate the camp, there was a riot. Mom, a white woman, all of five feet tall, waded right into their midst and simply pointed to a few of them, saying, 'You, you, you, and you—come to my office tomorrow morning. We'll settle this then. Meanwhile, the rest of you go back to your shelters.' Everybody quieted down and did what she said. I have no idea how Mom accomplished it, but the next day the issue was resolved to everyone's satisfaction. Mom was smart and very tough!"

Among Dorothy's papers after her death, Larry and I found a letter praising the work of both his parents during that time.

> *PROVINCER, C.P. DODOMA*
> *POLITICAL, KONDOA 30.1.1945*
>
> *I enclose herewith the Annual Report for Kondoa District for the year 1944.*
>
> *"I should like to acknowledge the debt which the district owes to Mr. and Mrs. M.L. Reiner for their invaluable assistance throughout the year. That the district has made agricultural progress in a year when everything was against it, is due entirely to the indefatigable perseverance of the former, and the latter, I can only say that Kondoa District was extremely fortunate to find in a year of famine, a person so hardworking, efficient and sympathetic."*

The report was signed by the district commissioner of Kondoa.

"Wouldn't most Africans be terrified of romantically approaching such a no-nonsense woman?"

"That's another reason I think that Yeremia might be your father. Mom allowed him full reign of the house and took it upon herself to teach him to read and write. If it's not him, then the only other people it could be are Hezekiah or Klementi."

"Anyone who worked for your parents is a person of interest, even a complete stranger from the village."

"I feel terrible that Mom didn't tell us who your father is. I wonder what demons were tormenting her that she couldn't bring herself to talk about your conception or birth, and for that matter, her life in Africa."

"Judy and I prove she wasn't a saint. Maybe, because she was a missionary, she was ashamed. When she first told me about my Aunt Marion, who along with her husband, Bill Kerr, were missionaries in China at the time, she said, 'She's the woman I wish I were,' but she wouldn't answer questions about my aunt."

"Aunt Marion is in a category all by herself."

"I hope to get to know her better. They came to Minnesota when Dorothy was visiting us. I am grateful Dorothy gave me you, but don't feel you owe me anything because of her. You had nothing to do with it, and when all is said and done, she might have had a good reason for being so tight-lipped, although something tells me it was the Norwegian in her. When I first asked her why she wouldn't talk about my father and what she was afraid of, she said she was only trying to protect me. She must have known what she was protecting me from. If we don't find anything about him on this trip, it has to be *Shauri ya Mungu*—God's will, as Africans say when they're giving up on something."

We were quiet for a while, then Larry said, "It has to be Yeremia."

"How do you propose we go about proving that? The last time you were in Tanzania was in 1963, twenty-five years ago, and you said you haven't seen or heard from him or anyone since. Where do we begin?"

"I remember all the places we used to live. We could begin by going to the villages and asking for them by name and by looking for the houses my family lived in."

"Are those houses still standing?"

"Who knows? But we can't come this far and not turn over every stone. Before I left for this safari, I went through Mom's photo albums from Africa and Yeremia was everywhere! He accompanied Mom on all her travels when Dad couldn't go.

"I remember Mom trying to teach Yeremia English when I was learning Sukuma from him. I mastered Sukuma way before he could speak much English. He always understood well, but he never spoke it around me. Mom admonished me not to speak Sukuma in the presence of other *wazungu*. But I loved hanging out with the Africans."

"Clearly you were, and still are, one of the original colonial flower children!"

"Too bad we can't just enjoy a safari to visit our childhood homes."

"It's overwhelming to admit the main reason for our trip is finding my father. How can I approach some village man and say, 'May I ask you some questions? Are you my father? If you're not my father, do you know the African who slept with a short *mzungu* woman about forty-five years ago in the village of Kijima, Kahama, or Kondoa?'"

"Even you couldn't be that blunt!"

I admired Larry for his calm ways of assessing things, but the task at hand scared me. Leaving America for a distant country in search of a man who could be my father, traveling to remote villages in the bush over nonexistent roads armed only with a list of three people Larry knew forty years ago, was not a lot to go on. It was like a blind man convincing a blind woman that as long as they are headed in the same direction, they can see! But, despite all this, how could we not search for him? And would I ever have another opportunity to make this trip with my brother?

"Do you really want to do this, Larry?"

"You may think the only reason I left my practice for three weeks is because I wanted to bond with you, but actually my plan is quite selfish. I loved Yeremia, and even if he isn't your father, I want to see him again. After we buried our mother's ashes, I wrote to Yeremia. I even mustered up my Swahili to write it, and I don't think I did too badly. I have an old address from the time he worked at the cotton ginnery in Geita. Unfortunately, I never heard back from him. I brought the letter along. I can't explain it, but everything tells me that he is your father, and even if we can't find him, you will at least know that I wanted to make up to you for what Mom didn't or wouldn't do. I wanted to find him, establish that he was indeed your father, and present him to you myself on this trip."

He took out his travel documents and handed me a white piece of paper folded in quarters. I unfolded it slowly and began to read his letter written in Swahili.

Nov. 11, 1986

My beloved brother Yeremia,
I am writing this letter to inform you about my mother's death, in October this year. She went to the hospital to get treatment for her heart, but unfortunately, she passed away.
This Christmastime, I will be coming to Tanzania with my children.
If it is possible for us to see each other while I am there, I would be very happy. I will be at Tarangire Safari Lodge near Arusha on December 21 and 22. Please write me a letter to the above address or you can send it c/o Rev. J.D. Simonson.
I have a sister, and our mother is Dorothy, but her father is an African man. Her name is Mary. She is an exceptional human being. The two of us are looking for her father. We would be very grateful if you can help us. We are waiting for your reply.
Your friend from long ago, and today too.

Lehwee (Larry) Reiner

"Wow! Your Swahili is amazing! Not bad for a *mzungu*! It's not kitchen Swahili, or *wazungu* or Indian Swahili. It's African Swahili!"

"Thank you! That makes me happy. I signed the letter the way my name is pronounced by some tribes. All of our servants called me

Lehwee. Marshall, my father's name, became *Maisheli*, and Dorothy was *Doloti*."

"Of course! Many East African tribes have trouble with 'l' and 'r' in English, probably because those letters don't exist in their own language, and they often switch the letters in words. Even I had trouble with 'r' as a child, but here's a story for you!

"I had a student from Kenya in my African Heritage class at Central High School in Minneapolis. One day she bluntly told me she needed money in dollars. Even though her father was rich, he couldn't get dollars to her, she explained, and assured me that if I gave her the money, the next time my husband and I went to Kenya, he'd pay us back in Kenyan shillings.

"I wasn't alarmed at her straightforward manner. That's exactly how I was when I first came from Tanzania. I understood her financial predicament because in the late seventies, African banks limited the purchase of American dollars. Few American banks accepted Kenyan or Tanzanian shillings, and those that did gave a poor exchange rate.

"We agreed on a monthly stipend for her. That summer, after leading a safari to Tanzania, Kjell and I flew to Kenya to see friends—and collect our shillings from her father, who turned out to be a member of parliament. He met us at the airport with a suitcase full of Kenyan bank notes.

"As we left the airport, we saw crowds of people heading towards a large building. The women, in one line, were dressed in colorful *khangas* and the men, in separate lines, wore bright *kikoi* and *kitenge* shirts.

"'Where is everyone going?' I asked my student's father. 'Is there a funeral?'

"'Oh no,' he replied. 'Today is the day of National Erections!'"

I thought Larry would never stop laughing, but he finally managed to say, "Good one!"

As he put the letter to Yeremia away, he said, "I also have to tell you, dear sister, on this trip I must find out if you and Judy are one and the same."

"You're still thinking that I'm Judy and that she's not in the grave your mother showed you when you were eight years old."

"We're going to find out."

"It means so much to me to learn about your life in Tanzania, but our lives couldn't have been more different—me being brought up in an orphanage by German Catholic nuns, hoping to be adopted or to leave Kifungilo when I grew up, and you being a *mzungu* brought up in a *mzungu* home, by *wazungu* parents employing African servants, eating *wazungu* food, and attending the much-envied *wazungu* schools."

"I never felt like a *mzungu*. I always referred to the *wazungu*—including my parents—as 'they' and to the Africans and me as 'we.' As I've said, my fondest childhood memories are of playing with African boys and girls and trying to act and talk like them. I couldn't wait to leave the house, take off my shoes and most of my clothes, and play in the bush and muddy streams and villages, and then be scrubbed to the bone by Yeremia before my parents saw me when I got home. I still have sweet dreams about my childhood among African children."

I felt close to Larry. All my life I'd heard colonial children speak very disparagingly about their African playmates. Did any of the many other *wazungu* raised in Africa have a relationship with their African playmates as Larry described?

Fat Mary changed the subject. *Don't be afraid of what you will or will not find out. Your hunger to know your parentage is normal. You can admit that you do not need your parents now. Even as a child, you already had within you everything you needed to become the person you were meant to be. The strength, the determination, the persistence, and the perseverance with which you endured your childhood has prepared you for this trip.*

We've come a long way, my beloved Fat Mary. With you still by my side, I know we shall face and conquer the unknown.

4

My Childhood Home

 When we landed in Arusha, it felt like I was stepping on Tanzanian soil for the first time. It was an important first for me because now I had a blood connection to someone in Africa.

Fumbwe, the driver sent by Serengeti Select Safaris, picked us up at Kilimanjaro Airport and drove us to Reverend David and Eunice Simonson's beautiful house at the foot of Mount Meru. They were Lutheran Missionaries whom I loved and admired. Their house took my breath away when I first saw it ten years ago. It was built on land given to them by the Maasai whom they'd served and ministered to ever since they arrived in Tanganyika in 1956. From afar, it looks like a typical African house with thatched roof and light mud walls, but the design is such that it has rooms on several levels, glass windows and many Western-style comforts, beautiful furniture, and African art.

It was good to be back with them. They always received my family and me so graciously. Eunice had a talent for scrounging around her tiny kitchen that had no running water and miraculously producing a meal that was always a feast! We enjoyed many conversations at the dinner table facing the majestic purple, blue, and green 14,980-foot Mount Meru, so close that it seemed to sit at the table too.

It was refreshing to be able to discuss almost anything with them. In my African world, certain topics were taboo for "People of God." Here, missionaries were frequently discussed because David wanted to know my opinions since I was a product of missionary upbringing.

This evening, however, I had no conversation in me. I didn't want to discuss the real purpose of this safari with our hosts. Using flight fatigue as an excuse, I went to bed early. Yet, I couldn't sleep. My mind and heart were just about bursting with excitement and anticipation for what awaited us. For my prayers that night, I put our trip in God's hands.

Yes, be calm and have faith. His will be done. Be positive and everything you ask for will be granted, Fat Mary whispered in my ear. She always understood.

Early the next morning we left Arusha and the Simonsons for our much-anticipated trip to Lushoto and the orphanage in Kifungilo. Larry remembered visiting Lushoto when our mother taught at the European School there. Driving through Same and Mombo reminded me of the trips I used to take by bus on my way to Mhonda for middle school and to Morogoro for secondary school. I relished the scent of the eucalyptus trees, the red-rust color of the soil, and the picturesque villages hugging the slopes of the Usambara Mountains. In the distance, their famous violet blue peaks harboring mysterious rivers and streams that emptied into narrow thundering waterfalls, brought back mixed memories.

Many visitors to the orphanage commented that Kifungilo was situated in one of the most beautiful spots in all of Africa. But my reality was that I lived in an orphanage, and in order to get out of there, I had to get an education beyond the Standard Four the nuns provided for us. That meant long, uncomfortable trips on antique buses driven by erratic, lead-footed, often drunk drivers whose biggest thrill was to see how fast the bus could turn the corners or maneuver along the precipitous roads without tumbling into the valley! The buses had names like "Nearer My God to Thee," "Prayer Time," and "Life is Short."

It would take a whole day on the bus to make it to my boarding schools in central Tanzania. The buses made a few stops where students with money got off to buy bananas, *mandazi*, a deep-fried dough rolled in sugar, samosas, and Fanta. I never had money to buy anything, but we always had a sumptuous lunch of cheese and sausage sandwiches; a pear, apple, or peach; and some biscuits packed by Sister Silvestris. We Kifungilo girls ate quietly in the bus because the others made us feel like we should stay put. Before they got to know us, they felt that as *hafu-casti,* we all thought we were better than the full Africans. Although several of them looked at us with envy as we ate our *mzungu* lunch, I looked at them with more envy, because they had money to buy Fanta or bananas or whatever they wanted. I wanted to be able to buy something—anything!

On this trip with Larry, I had money as well as food, drinks, and chocolate in the cooler. I could also stop when and where I wanted. With personal needs taken care of, the scenery embraced me again and forced me to admit that even though I didn't notice it as a child, it has always been there. Tall, massive eucalyptus trees planted by Germans right after the First World War lined the road that approached the tiny town of Lushoto, built on sloping terraces and dotted with red-tiled roofs you'd expect to see in Germany.

The Germans loved Lushoto because of its mild climate and location at the end of the world. I suppose some of them had fled their mother country because of the Nazis. As we approached Lushoto this day, I looked down into the town from the high road and saw government buildings, cobblestone roads, and bridges supported by stone arches still proclaiming affinity with their colonial masters. Although the surrounding area was sparser than I remembered due to deforestation for charcoal and lumber, there were still vast areas of cultivation that demonstrate why Lushoto with its fertile soil has long been considered the fruit basket of Tanzania.

I spotted the dentistry and St. Joseph's Catholic Church amidst the red-tiled and burnt-brick houses of the quaint little town in what has often been called the Switzerland of Africa. I have since heard of other places in Africa claiming that distinction, but Lushoto will always be my little Switzerland. The dentistry, known all over Tanzania, was started by a German Kifungilo nun; then Sister Eileen, who was Lizzy when she was at the orphanage with us, also became a dentist.

As soon as we pulled in front of the dentistry, Sister Eileen came flying out to greet us. She smiled so broadly that her soft facial features folded into her large tan cheeks. She wore her usual white cotton habit with a short white veil, the front starched and raised on her forehead, and a large silver crucifix hanging from a red silk cord around her neck. I introduced her to Larry and we had a quick cup of tea and homemade scones before she joined us for the short ride to visit Frank and Betty Humplick in Yaegethal, a quiet spot just outside of Lushoto that used to belong to a German farmer. Betty and her sisters weren't orphans, but as biracial children they attended the boarding school at Kifungilo.

Betty's husband, a well-known and much-loved pop singer in Tanzania, was at the Kifungilo orphanage along with his two sisters, Thecla and Mia. At age ten, Frank (he was Francis at Kifungilo) left because boys were sent away to all-boy mission schools in southern Tanganyika, while his sisters stayed on. They were a biracial family and had parents like some of the other children I grew up with.

In the '50s and '60s, Frank and his sisters formed the Pop Music group *Frank na Dada Zake* (Frank and His Sisters) and became one of the most popular singers in Tanganyika. A few years ago in Tanzania, I heard their songs on the radio program *Zilizopendwa* (Favorites).

"How come you never age?" I asked both of them as we sat in their comfortable living room that had the imprint of an interior decorator raised in Kifungilo. The room had the formal, yet practical feel of the Sisters' convent and priests' guesthouse. Every time I reunited with Betty, I saw the Betty of my childhood—formidable, stubborn, hardworking, and strict when it came to defending her rights and those of her siblings. Her younger sister Imelda is one of my best friends from Kifungilo. As little children at the orphanage, we—including Imelda—used to be terrified of Betty. As an adult, she still had that "don't mess with me" attitude, but now it was mixed with the softness, love, acceptance, and appreciation that comes from turning a hard life into a good life.

Sister Eileen, Frank, and Betty accompanied Larry and me to Kifungilo. During the trip Sister Eileen had us in stitches as she told her famous and infamous stories about the bad old days at the orphanage. When Sister laughed or cried, her whole face turned bright red. She was now telling about Teresia, who could pass for a *mzungu*, except for her very curly blond hair. Teresia had stolen fruit and had been told to go down to the convent to confess, but before she went for her punishment, according to Sister Eileen, Teresia gathered the children who had helped her steal and they all went to see Sister Fabiana, the nun in charge of the fruit orchards and vegetable gardens.

Laughing as she spoke, Sister continued, "Teresia and her band boldly stated, '*Sista, tunaomba ruhusa kwenda kuiba matunda.*' (Sister, we're asking for permission to go and steal some fruit.) Of course, Sister Fabiana tried to remain serious. 'So, you want my permission to steal?' she asked. 'Yes, Sister,' the children declared. 'That way it won't be a sin.'

"Sister Fabiana barely kept her composure as she looked at the children with telltale purple around their mouths from having eaten stolen plums and passion fruit. All she could say was, 'If you children are seen near the fruit orchard, I'll have to tell Sister Silvestris, and you know what she'll do.'"

Sister Eileen's story brought back the memory of how we kids would beg for forgiveness when a nun threatened to tell Sister Silvestris about something bad we did, because whenever Sister heard about our transgressions from another nun, we were guaranteed a merciless beating. I suspect Sister was afraid of being reprimanded and belittled by the Mother Superior and other nuns for raising little criminals.

As we approached Kifungilo, I was again struck by how small, beautiful, and peaceful it seemed. Why didn't I ever see or feel this when I lived here? Whether memory is a friend or foe, it is undoubtedly a selective caretaker of the past. It will hand it back when the heart is open to seeing the truth, no matter how much time has elapsed.

At the brick guesthouse Larry and I had one of those delicious convent suppers that almost convinced us we were in Germany! Everything was fresh from the garden and the farm, from the chunky vegetable soup, eggplant, mashed potatoes, bread, sausage, and applesauce to the sweet peppermint tea with leaves floating in it. I was looking forward to our visit with Sister Jacinta, the nun in charge of the kitchen, because I loved watching her round chubby face, with little slits for eyes, as she told story after story about the changes at Kifungilo. She always laughed at her own stories and went from one to the other, not caring if we knew when one story ended and another began.

I think she was trying to give me a message with one of her stories about a young African woman who wanted to become a nun. Sister Jacinta told us how this novice had decided she'd had enough of the trials and tribulations of being Black. After dinner one night, the novice announced that all her prayers and novenas had been answered, and she was "healed" from being Black. For many months, she acted like a *mzungu* nun—imitating the way the white nuns walked and talked, sneezed, ate, drank, and prayed.

This struck us as funny, but Sister Jacinta reminded us that it wasn't at all funny and we should stop laughing. We put on our serious faces as she continued the story, saying that the novice was now often sick and gloomy and was getting progressively thinner. Sister recounted how one night, when the novice was very ill, she dreamt that she had died and that when she got to heaven, God didn't recognize her and sent her to hell. From that day on, the novice spent every free minute repenting, and she thanked God that reverting to being Black came naturally and wasn't as hard as trying to be white. She came to terms with her Blackness, Sister said with emphasis, and the ailments the poor novice had suffered while trying to be white disappeared.

Sister Jacinta finished her story with, "Gott knows how he made us, and ve must like zhe color he gave us also."

Do you know why no matter how hard your life was as a mixed-race child, you never wished that you were a mzungu? Fat Mary asked me. *In the absence of a loving mother, your religion taught you that because God created you, you were his child. You believed that God loved all his children. It is his love that taught you how to love yourself. You learned that loving yourself the way you are was an important requirement for a happy and fulfilling life.*

In the morning, we took a short tour of Kifungilo. Even though it was now a government-sponsored secondary school, in my heart I saw past and through the remodeled buildings and grounds and was back at "my" Kifungilo. As we walked around, I heard the schoolgirls singing as they marched up the hill toward the classrooms, dressed in their uniforms of a blue skirt, white blouse, burgundy cardigan, white socks, and black sneakers. With their close-cropped black hair and shiny brown faces, they lit the path until I heard the words they were chanting. In call and response, they repeated political slogans and independence rhetoric directed against the past colonial government and whites in general. After their compulsory morning "training" for national service, they settled into their prospective classrooms.

In my day most everyone was racially mixed in Kifungilo, but now the students are almost all Black Africans from various tribes. In order to avoid tribal cliques and help students prepare for their exams, they are required to speak only English. Academically, Kifungilo is considered one of the best secondary boarding schools in the country, and only government ministers and the wealthy can afford to send their daughters here. The nuns kept their convent and the grounds, including the farm with all its orchards and animals, while the government, under President Julius Nyerere's nationalization policy, took over the section of Kifungilo that had been the children's quarters and made it an exclusive government-run school where parents pay high school fees.

I noticed the size of the new box-type buildings overshadowed and diminished "my" Kifungilo buildings, sandwiching and hiding my schoolroom, my sewing room, my *nyumba ile* ("that room" used as an all-purpose room) until the whole place looked like an unfinished Rubik's Cube. I had to think hard to recall what was here, what was there, where did they move this or that. I was glad to see that the statue of Blessed Martin (now Saint Martin) was still standing in the exact place on the same tiny lawn full of dandelions where I used to kneel and pray to find my mother.

Most of the furniture we used in the orphanage had been made at Sakarani Carpentry School, a Benedictine Missionary Brothers compound. We spent the afternoon there then went to Gare, the mission school run by Irish Rosminian Fathers. When I was a child, we'd walk the eight miles from the orphanage to this school for picnics on feast days. That day we had tea with Father Kennedy and Father Spillane who again reminded me how I answered him when

I was about three or four and he asked me, "What's your name, little one?"

"Amelican gal," I had answered proudly. I couldn't pronounce the English "r" yet.

Years later when I was living in Florida, I was at a concert in Miami by the Soweto Gospel Choir. On the way out, a lady approached me.

"Your gorgeous outfit tells me you're from Africa," she said. "What country?'

"Tanzania," I replied.

"I'm originally from Ireland, but my favorite uncle was a missionary in Tanzania. I always intended to visit him, but he died suddenly."

I asked her where he was stationed in Tanzania, and she said in the East, she thought at someplace she pronounced "Gayer." As we walked out from the theatre together, a familiar face jumped to mind. "How do you spell the name of the town in Tanzania?"

"G-a-r-e," she answered.

"Was your uncle a Catholic priest and was his name Father Kennedy?"

"Yes! That's my uncle!"

"I knew your uncle. He used to come to the orphanage where I was raised to say Mass and hear confessions when our priest was on vacation."

We both rejoiced in this fortunate and seemingly accidental meeting. She told me her name was Nuala and that she was visiting from San Francisco and leaving the next day. I said we had almost decided not to make the drive from Delray Beach to Miami because of the pouring rain! We hugged as though we were long-lost relatives.

The next morning, I emailed her the picture of Rosa's wedding that I was about to include in my first book, *Africa's Child*. The picture of the wedding party shows Rosa, who was my big girl at the orphanage, her husband, two flower girls (one of whom was six-year-old me), and Father Kennedy, tall and handsome in his black cassock, and several Girl Guides in uniform in the background.

Nuala and I became friends. At a book signing hosted by a friend of hers, I met Maureen, a British woman from the Cayman Islands who had been raised in Kenya and attended Saint Mary's School in Nairobi. My mother had told me that she taught at Saint Mary's for several years before leaving Africa. Maureen remembered a "short, kind of fat and frumpy" American teacher whose name was Mrs. Reiner.

"That was my mother, Dorothy!" I told her.

"Oh my God! It never occurred to me that your mother would be white! But more than that, there is no resemblance. You and Mrs. Reiner couldn't look more different."

Maureen went on to tell me that her parents lived up the hill from the school and would invite my mother for dinner during the holidays because her husband, Marshall, was often away on safari or in the bush working for the British government, and Mrs. Reiner remained at school when everyone was gone.

While visiting in Gare I went to see Lucinda, the Kifungilo girl who had gone to Mhonda Middle School with me. Although we got along toward the end of middle school, in my earlier years at Kifungilo and Mhonda she made my life very difficult because of her bullying. If I did everything she told me, I would be blessed with her friendship and the amenities—sitting next to her or borrowing her sweater—that came with being her friend. I mostly remember the days that for no reason I'd be on her "shit list." She'd isolate me from the other Kifungilo girls in Mhonda by spreading rumors that I was a thief, a liar, and a hypocrite with no personal hygiene. I would do anything—wash her clothes, make her bed, do her homework, steal and lie for her—to get back into her good graces when I was ostracized. She was living a hard life now. Her alcoholic husband had died, and she worked several jobs to support herself and her children. Most of all, the years of hardship had left such harsh, deep grooves on her face that she looked and acted like a grandmother even though we were both about forty-five.

Our middle school history briefly flashed in front of me as she ran to greet me and kissed me three times on the cheeks. I greeted her and made small talk. It was obvious that she had no recollection of her childhood transgressions and cruelty. I always wonder why it is that perpetrators of evil, cruelty, or betrayal are so often blessed with the gift of forgetfulness, while the victims are cursed with eternal remembrance!

Fat Mary smiled at me without judgment saying, *Count your blessings.*

5

Two Goats

 Upon our return Frank and Betty's house, there was a card from the district commissioner Mr. Kilivata inviting us to dinner at a nearby hotel. He had just received several thousand dollars from Operation Bootstrap Africa to help build schools in the Lushoto district. He was thrilled and invited local officials to the celebratory event. As we took our places for the dinner, I noticed two guests sitting at a side table. They looked tired, sweaty, and dust covered, and were eyeing the silverware with curiosity. From my own experience, I knew they didn't have a clue what to do with it. Mr. Kilivata introduced Larry and me, saying that I was on the board of directors of Operation Bootstrap Africa, the organization that sent money to build primary schools in rural Tanzania. He gave a touching speech of gratitude and praise for Operation Bootstrap and then introduced the guests who had caught my attention.

"We have a very special couple with us today. They walked for two days from Handeni to Lushoto in order to meet the representative of the organization that has helped them build the first primary school in their village. Ladies and gentlemen, Mr. and Mrs. Masaine."

All eyes turned toward the couple who slowly stood up. Mr. Masaine thanked Mr. Kilivata for not forgetting the people of the Maasai Steppe who longed for an education but were denied it because of their cultural traditions, poverty and remote location. He was happy and proud because his children now had the chance to go to school—an opportunity he never had. Then, looking at me, he apologized for not having a gift worthy of the sacrifices that people thousands of miles away in America had made in order to build

28

schools for Africans they didn't even know. At that moment Mrs. Masaine left the room and returned with two goats in tow!

"These goats, Mama," he said respectfully, "are for you—a male and female. The whole village pitched in to offer them as a token of our gratitude. As they reproduce, we pray for God's blessings on you and all the good people of America. May his blessings multiply in your lifetimes and extend to your children and grandchildren."

I was touched by their gesture, but I didn't know if I should accept the goats and bring them to the table with me or take them and leave the room. Finally, I knelt down by the goats and stroked their backs. With a goat on each side of me, I gave a short speech of thanks to Mr. and Mrs. Masaine and to all the people of their village on behalf of Operation Bootstrap in America. I was relieved when Mr. Kilivata said that the goats would spend the night at the hotel grounds and would be brought to me in the morning.

I worried about how to handle the delicate situation of not taking the goats back to America with me. Would Mr. and Mrs. Masaine be offended? I decided there was no need to let them know that the goats would remain in Tanzania. I explained my plan to Mr. Kilivata, and the goats were delivered to Betty and Frank the next day. Betty took them to the veterinarian, who gave them their shots, dewormed them, and told her how to care for them. I asked her to breed them, sell the offspring, and give the money to Mr. Kilivata to send to Mr. Masaine and the village to buy school supplies for the children. Betty and Frank honorably fulfilled my wishes until the goats were too old to breed. Then, as is the custom, they were slaughtered and enjoyed by nearby villagers who gathered to celebrate the school supplies the goats had made possible.

To this day I love goat meat. On every occasion that I've eaten it on my trips to Tanzania and the Caribbean, I begin the meal remembering my two goats.

Hidden in one of the many valleys in the mountain slopes that surround Kifungilo was Masange Primary School. I had been to Masange before with Sister Silvestris when we went to visit the *maskini* (poor) in the village to bring them food and clothing, and if all went well, to baptize them. I was grateful for the opportunity to visit the school again on this trip with Larry. When we entered the classroom, the children stood up and sang "Mungu Ibariki Afrika" ("God Bless Africa"), the Tanzanian national anthem. They were so surprised when I joined in, they almost stopped singing!

But it was hard to focus on singing as I looked around the classroom. Huge pieces of plaster hung from the ceiling and walls. Two small warped wooden blackboards stood on the floor in the front of the room. Long wooden desks, weathered with deep cracks, were arranged in four rows, filling the room. The windows had no glass or wood slats, and the once white walls now had dirty brown patches. Pairs of bare feet rested on the uneven ground of what was formerly a smooth cement floor.

On this windy day, few children had sweaters, and those who did clutched them close. The visible poverty clashed with the faces of smiling children who sang song after song to welcome us. I looked at their faded green slates and their hand-bound tiny notebooks arranged with pride on top of the long desks where so many children squeezed together to work, they had to stand in zigzag fashion. This was nothing like the Masange School of my childhood or the place I had shown my husband and children in the early eighties.

A few years after Tanzania gained independence in 1961, primary education was made compulsory for children and free for all, young and old. In Arusha I had visited a Bootstrap school and witnessed seven-year-old children and forty-year-old men and women sitting side by side under a tree, learning to write the alphabet on slates or torn and wrinkled pieces of paper. Would making education free in such a poor country and under such miserable conditions compromise the quality of education to the extent that it did more harm than good? How would graduates of Masange Primary School compete in middle school with city students who had plentiful supplies and more teachers? After four years in primary school, would they just go back to the *shamba* (field) and to the lives they knew? Would they go back to helping their parents raise little brothers and sisters, cultivate the fields, fetch water, search for firewood, and herd cattle, all the while believing that things would be better when they grew up because now they could read and write? How would what they learned in school make a difference in the quality of life for them, the village, and the tribe?

I told the principal, an African Precious Blood Sister, about Operation Bootstrap Africa and its mission of building primary schools. She sang God's praises as if she had already received funds. I promised to talk to Mr. Kilivata, their district commissioner, on her behalf, and hopefully she would get what was needed to fix the school's physical structure. All the children accompanied us to our car, clapping, smiling, waving, and singing goodbye songs until we disappeared down the road.

After Mass the next morning, I walked to the confessional at the back of the church and knelt down. Some of the "sins" of my childhood returned to laugh with me. The nuns endlessly told us that we were all sinners, and we had to perpetually ask God for forgiveness and go to confession every week. Sometimes when I hadn't committed any sins, I made up a few based on the Ten Commandments and confessed them to Father Gatang—a short, roly-poly man who shuffled around, stroking his gray beard that fell from his plump, rosy cheeks to his wide chest like a perfectly round bib. I'm not sure if he had a sense of humor, but he must have laughed when, at age nine, I confessed that I'd coveted my neighbor's wife and committed adultery!

After morning tea, we said goodbye to the Sisters at Kifungilo and left for our trip back to Arusha. Late in the afternoon, we stopped under a familiar acacia tree just outside of Mombo for a picnic lunch that I'd been anticipating all morning. Sister Jacinta had prepared a basket for us—one of those hearty lunches that only German no-nonsense farmers pack. In between two thick slices of home-baked wheat bread slathered with a half-inch layer of sweet unsalted butter were multiple slices of Westphalian ham and slabs of Swiss cheese. There were hardboiled eggs, three kinds of cookies, sliced pears and apples, soft toffee, and two Cadbury's milk chocolate bars to indulge a sweet tooth. I knew Sister Jacinta would find some beer for us, and sure enough, my favorite Safari beer was in the basket. My sandwich was extra thick because our Muslim driver Fumbwe didn't eat pork, so I accepted his share of Westphalian ham, which I stuffed in my sandwich and bit into like a cobra unlocking its jaws to swallow a small goat. I fell asleep thinking about the food I had just gorged myself with and wondering how many children at Masange Primary School would go to bed hungry that night.

On our way back to Arusha, we stopped for a few hours at Finca Coffee Estate in Usa River. Larry met my friends Abdu and Fatima Faraji and visited Fatima's thirty-two-acre farm that had nineteen acres dedicated to Arabica coffee. The first farmer in Tanzania to participate in a program to breed and raise Heifer cows, Fatima made her own cheese and butter; she had goats, rabbits, geese, and chickens, and grew a myriad of tropical fruits, nuts, vegetables, and flowers. She had macadamia nuts, cashews, and groundnuts (peanuts) along with passion fruit, blackberries, lemons, oranges, breadfruits, several kinds of bananas, and avocados. Her vegetables included tomatoes, spinach, cabbage, lettuce, carrots, beans, and corn, and she had every conceivable herb including parsley, sage, rosemary, and thyme! She grew the food she needed to feed her livestock and used cow manure to make biogas, which she used for cooking when electricity was cut off, which frequently happened, and for fertilizing a few acres of organic coffee.

Interspersed throughout the farm were tall flowering purple jacarandas, vibrant orange flamboyant and flame trees, birds of paradise, yellow acacia trees, philodendron, and bougainvillea in mind-boggling hybrids and hues. Roses, orchids, marigolds, daisies, carnations, calla lilies, chrysanthemums, violets, morning glories, and a slew of other flowers whose names I didn't know bloomed everywhere. A gigantic, ancient, plump candelabra tree stood guard in front of the house, overlooking a clearing in the tall trees where Mount Kilimanjaro, sixty miles away, peeped out to greet them just before sunrise and sunset on a cloudless day.

Their farm was like Kifungilo in that everything tropical and temperate grew and flourished side by side. In my eyes, Fatima was the original Earth Woman. In the late 1960s her husband was Tanzania's ambassador to France under President Julius Nyerere. His profession as a diplomat, politician, attorney, and businessman provided the necessary funds for equipment, labor, and supplies. Fatima's intuition, intelligence, diligence, and hard work made Finca Farms one of the most profitable, progressive, and admired private farms in the country.

6

Dorothy in Charge

 If we hadn't had such a hectic schedule and important trip ahead of us, Larry would have liked to stay a few days with the Farajis at Finca Coffee Estate and farm paradise. Back with the Simonsons that night, we mentally and spiritually prepared ourselves for the next phase of our journey: seeing the Tanganyika of Larry's childhood that I knew nothing about.

It took me a while to fall asleep. I was imagining all the possibilities of our secret mission in search of my father. Most thoughts were good, but some were scary and kept sleep at bay. I sensed Larry was probably having an even rougher night.

Sleep well, my beloved, Fat Mary wished me goodnight. *No one on earth understands the meaning and importance of this trip better than I do. Your desire and hunger to know yourself has not abated in your forty-five years on earth. You have subconsciously longed for this search your whole life, and now you are back in Tanzania where it all began. Your faith and hope have led you to this day.*

The next morning, we headed toward Tarangire National Park, where we stopped for lunch, then took off for Kondoa. Although Kondoa was not far from the main road I had traveled many times on my way back and forth from Kifungilo to schools in the Central Region, I had never been there. I had several classmates in high school who were from there, and I remember them as being secretive and keeping to themselves. The terrain and weather of the area couldn't have been more different from the cool temperate highlands of my Usambara Mountains.

Larry was reflective again. What must he be feeling? He's visiting the country he loves with his sister, but he's not sure if she's the one he knew and loved or if she's a new sister he never knew he had. I entered into the conversation I was sure he was having with himself.

"Tell me, my dear brother, what do you remember about your life in Kondoa?"

"Where to begin?" After a reflective pause, he said, "Well, in my day, Kondoa was the district capital, located two miles off the Great North Road. It had been well-established by the Germans. Government housing, left over from German days, had tin roofs, thick walls, and usually a wide screened-in verandah that ran around all sides of the houses. I learned the rudiments of bike maintenance—how to change wheel spokes, brakes, cables, and tires on my bike. The district headquarters, or *boma,* was about a half-mile down the hill.

Along the road between the houses and the *boma* was a huge old baobab tree. An *askari* (policeman) told me that the hollow compartment inside the trunk served as headquarters for the German forces during a battle in the First World War. Indeed, poking around inside the tree one day, I found several rifle shell casings—although I had no idea how they got there. The *askari* described the battle around the baobab tree with sweeping arm movements. Africans fought side by side with the Germans who ruled Tanganyika in those days, but many Africans detested the Germans and refused to fight, hiding instead inside the tree and cheering for the British and South African troops."

I relished Larry's descriptions and his eager sharing of childhood memories. I ardently wished I could have known him as a young boy and as my big brother. We were making up for that loss.

Larry continued with his memories. "Living in this town allowed us the most civilized lifestyle we achieved. Travelers on the highway often needed assistance. Mom and Dad quickly got the reputation of being generous and willing hosts. People would frequently drop in unannounced, especially around dinnertime. The most memorable travelers were a pair of Americans in a brand-new postwar Studebaker, who were driving from Cairo to Cape Town as part of an advertising gimmick to show how well built the car was. Unfortunately, it broke down in Kondoa and they were stranded for three weeks waiting for parts from Dar-es-Salaam. They stayed in our house the entire time. Although they promised to send us newspaper write-ups of their trip, we never heard from them again, so I assume their advertising campaign failed."

"Do you remember who worked for your parents then?"

"Like I said, we usually had four helpers—a houseboy, a cook, a *dhobi* or laundry guy, and a gardener. The servants we had were all Sukuma who had followed us from the mission station in Kahama. I only remember the three I told you about—Yeremia, Hezekiah, and Klementi."

Hearing Yeremia's name, I wondered again why Dorothy kept his dictionary among her books in America all those years. "What did your parents do in Kondoa?"

"Until 1941, when Judy was born, they were with the African Inland Mission. Because Judy was racially mixed, the mission felt it necessary to send them back to the States in disgrace, but my father refused their passage money and decided to earn his own. He took a job with the British colonial government—nationality made no difference in wartime—and booked passage on the good old *Sagadahoc* again. Alas, the Nazis torpedoed the old tub, creating an international incident which was overshadowed by the Japanese attack on Pearl Harbor in Hawaii. With America then entering the war, my parents were unable or unwilling to get passage to the States. From 1941 to 1962, my father worked for the government in various capacities. He was an agricultural officer, famine relief worker, and did resettlement work involving monitoring and control of sleeping sickness.

"When Tanganyika gained independence, my dad was the only white official left in his post. As an American citizen, he was assigned the job of hauling down the British flag at midnight in Kahama. He joked that he felt like an American revolutionary—215 years late! For the next two years, he taught history at Saint Mary's School in Nairobi where Mom was teaching. Then they both returned to Wheaton, Illinois, to take care of Dorothy's mother who was ill."

I noticed that our driver, Fumbwe, was also listening to Larry.

Even though Fumbwe spoke very little English, I was sure he could understand everything, just as in Kifungilo we understood the nuns when they spoke German though we couldn't speak it.

"During the war years, there was a serious manpower shortage, so Mom held various positions in the government. At one point in Kondoa, she was assistant district officer under a seventy-six-year-old official. He was an avid gardener and fell out of a lemon tree he was pruning, breaking his neck. They buried him next to Judy in the white folks' cemetery. Mom was then acting district commissioner. The Africans were upset that a woman was in charge and incidents occurred as they expressed their displeasure. Once, she found two cobras in her desk drawer as well as scorpions in a sugar jar at home. By the time a Mr. Henry Fosbrook replaced her, however, she had earned the respect of everyone and the district was running smoothly.

"For two or three years after the war, she taught English to Polish Jewish refugees in a camp near Kondoa, then to Greek children in the Greek school in Mweka above Moshi—now a wildlife conservation college. She went to teach at the Lushoto school around 1948. After I went back to the U.S. for college, she started teaching at Saint Mary's School in Nairobi."

7

Lion's Breath

Dorothy had often talked about her time at Saint Mary's, originally founded as a Catholic boy's school for the children of missionaries and other white families.

"German nuns taught me at Kifungilo until I was chosen to go to a distant middle school for African girls. Where did you go to school?"

"I went to boarding school at age seven when Mom started working. She pretty much worked the rest of her life, until she retired for the second time in the U.S. The rhythm of our family life revolved around boarding school schedules. Mom and I would be at our respective schools for three months, then home for roughly one month. Whenever I was home, Dad would always have a safari to go on, and the two of us would be away together in the bush for a week or two."

"The time you spent together on those safaris is probably the reason you always felt closer to your dad."

"The safaris were the highlight of my holiday. I recall so many stories from those special times. I'll tell you two. We were sleeping in a big safari tent, each on a camp cot under a mosquito net. At the back of the tent was a turned-down Dietz lamp and rifle, which dad always traveled with. I was awakened in the middle of the night by the horrible smell of rotting flesh and started to sit up. My father's voice cautioned me, 'Larry, be still. There's a lion in the tent!'"

"Oh my God! What did you do?"

"Sure enough, on the other side of the net, some ten inches from my face, was a lioness—the source of the smell being her breath. I froze just as Dad had asked. The lioness sniffed everything in the tent, including the gun, and then left. Dad got up to put his rifle in bed with him. From then on, he always slept with his rifle when on safari.

"The second anecdote involved a meal. In each location we visited, it was customary for the local chief or headman to prepare a meal for the visiting *bwana*. We sat on little stools around the communal pot scooping up *ugali* and making little cups with our fingers, which we then filled with stew usually made with meat saved for a visitor who was considered important. On one occasion Dad asked, 'This meat doesn't taste quite like anything I know. What kind of meat is it?'

"The chief replied, '*Bwana*, never mind what kind of meat this is. Just enjoy it.'

"I remember my father freezing, returning the piece of meat to the pot, and telling me, 'Larry, don't eat any more.'

"'Why, Dad? It tastes pretty good.'

"'I think it's human flesh,' he replied.

"We never learned for sure if he was right. We were in Unyamwezi territory and possibly some cannibalism had gone on during slavery days, but there was no real history of it that we knew of in colonial Africa. The chief continued to eat but said nothing to us."

"You should write about your childhood in Tanganyika. Tell me more stories."

"Are you sure? I fear I'm sounding like the nostalgic Karen Blixen in *Out of Africa*."

"I like your stories better, though I must admit that the romances and shenanigans among the whites of her time added to the appeal and intrigue that made *Out of Africa* such a popular movie. Dorothy could have written a similar book if she had been able to embrace her life in Tanganyika. Sorry. Go on!"

"Mom told me that I was very frustrated when an African arrived at our house carrying his big toe in a jar. He had chopped it off with a *jembe* (hoe) and wanted Dad to glue it back on. Seemed like quite a reasonable request to me, and I didn't understand why Dad didn't do it. Incidences like that made me decide that when I grew up, I would be a doctor and learn how to glue people's big toes back on.

"An old leper woman, blind and missing her nose and most of her fingers, would come and sit by the kitchen steps. I was much taken by her plight and spent hours speaking to her in Sukuma. After some weeks, Hezekiah, one of the workmen, asked her if she knew she was talking to a *mzungu*. She said it wasn't possible. It had to be a Sukuma boy she was talking to. She was only persuaded after placing one hand on my straight hair and the other on my chattering mouth. I grew very fond of that old lady and again decided to be a doctor so that I could give her new fingers and a new nose. I can honestly say I have never even thought of any other career besides medicine.

"Mom would see me going off to play and tell me sternly not to remove my shoes. 'Yes, Mom,' I would promise, but invariably, within a hundred yards or so, my shoes would be abandoned and often lost. I had pretty rough feet and got lots of jiggers as well as a variety of worms from walking barefoot."

"We also had jiggers in Kifungilo," I admitted, "which we dug out from our feet. Apart from the severe itching, they didn't bother us too much. All of us had head lice at one time or the other. Sitting in twos on the steps by the laundry room, we removed lice from each other's hair by making narrow rows with a fine-tooth comb and searching the exposed skin and hair shafts for lice and their eggs. We'd run the comb through a small section of hair at a time, catching all the miserable vermin on the comb's teeth. Then we'd squish the lice dead between our thumbnails. I hated seeing the blood burst out of them. Without warning, every few months Sister Silvestris would initiate a "lice patrol," dipping our heads in kerosene that made our skin burn until we screamed and cried. In a few days, we'd recover and scrape off the scars from the wounds on our scalps. It worked! The kerosene killed the lice on contact, and we'd be lice-free for several weeks. We hated the kerosene remedy so much that we constantly searched each other's heads to avoid Sister's kerosene dunks.

"Worms were another thing altogether. When Sister Silvestris decided that she'd heard one too many distended stomachs growling, she'd resort to her proven method of ridding us of worms—castor oil—and we had to fast all day. Sister would stand near her big girl helpers, who had sticks to hit anyone who ran off when their turn came. The wicked-tasting, thick castor oil was poured down our throats using the same tablespoon for all the children. Our stomachs grumbled and rumbled and heaved until we ran to the toilets.

"We spent most of the day in the toilets. The toilet house harbored individual stalls built along the same drainage trench that slopped down into a large, stinky cesspool. Sometimes we managed to deposit our load of squirming worms inside the stall, but seldom did they make it down the hole where they were supposed to go. Every shape and size of worm came out of us. They crawled on the floor and up the stalls of the toilets and made their way outside. Long roundworms, hookworms, and little square sections of broken tapeworms covered the ground near the toilets.

"Once I helped another girl, Elise, get rid of her tapeworm. As she leaned over, I pulled and pulled and pulled. The tapeworm was at least two feet long when it broke off. We scooped up the slippery, flat, pasta-looking worm in our hands and dumped it in the toilet. I will never forget how Elise's stomach looked hollow after expunging the worm.

"I was so jealous of her being thin. I don't know if I told you that I was very fat and awkward as a child. My nickname was 'Piggy Knife' and sometimes just 'Piggy,' though Sister Silvestris and the other nuns called me 'Fat Mary.' We all knew that tapeworms ate up your food. One day I made a deal with Elise that if she'd give me her tapeworm, I'd give her my fat! I asked her how it felt to have that long worm living in her stomach. She said she didn't feel it. I had also dumped my load of roundworms, and apart from the severe rumblings, gassy, and distended stomach, I hadn't felt them either. Those worms cross my mind every now and then even as an adult, and all I can say is nasty, nasty, nasty! That's the reason I don't eat spaghetti."

8

Larry's House in Tanzania

 Larry chuckled, then said, "We have such strong memories of our childhoods. I remember the day I went off to school for the first time. I was seven and we were living in Kilema. A lorry—Harchand Singh Transport—came from Dodoma with other kids on it. A huge tarpaulin on a frame covered the back of the lorry that made the daylong trip to Arusha School. For the first term at school, my mother went with me. My grandmother Isel had done the typical American grandmother thing and sent me a bunch of new school clothes. When I showed up at school, it was immediately obvious a change of clothes was needed. All the Standard Six girls thought I was an unbelievably cute plaything in my Lord Fauntleroy outfits. I was still into the 'girls are yucky'—especially white girls—stage. I kept trying to get away from them and hide. Mom had to spend a few days with an Indian tailor making me khaki shorts and shirts like the other boys.

"Also, sometime shortly after I went off to school, my father was transferred to Kwa Mtoro, a small town in Kondoa district, which was the main settlement of the Sandawe tribe, an interesting group. They are a relic of the *Hottentots* in a sea of Bantu tribes, click language and all." [Today the term "Hottentot" is considered pejorative and these first peoples of southern and eastern Africa are called "Khoi/San."] There, all my friends were Arab kids, sons of the local *duka-wallahs* (shopkeepers), and I learned a lot of Arabic as well as Kisandawe.

"About halfway on the road to Kondoa was a large overhanging rock. On the underside my father was shown some ancient rock paintings. He was immediately reminded of the cave art discoveries in the South of France, and though he knew nothing of the history or anthropological facts of the paintings, he began a lifelong interest in rock paintings, both in Usandawe and around Kolo, just to the north of Kondoa. He offered ten shillings (about a dollar at the time) to anybody who could show him new paintings, and then he reported the paintings to the Antiquities Department in Dar. Henry Fosbrook was also involved later on, and he, in fact, was given credit for their discovery when Mary Leakey wrote her book on Kolo paintings, some of which dated back almost two thousand years.

"Kwa Mtoro remains, along with Farquar also in Usandawe, a mysterious and dark place in my past. The roads and town were primitive and the people very different. The Farquar area was pagan and animist, and it was there that my earliest memories of witch doctoring occurred. I remember a Sandawe man being healed and another one cursed to die, both by means of a forked-root plant, which I think was mandrake and did the trick for both guys. Farquar was also the site of a large White Fathers Mission that manufactured household items and an excellent brandy. It was a beautiful, well-established station which we often visited, though not just for the brandy.

"I also feel, although I have no proof, that Farquar was where you were conceived, because Mom was on assignment near there for many months with only the servants, while Dad was in Kwa Mtoro. I have a vague recollection of Mom and Yeremia together, holding hands in her tent, which is one of the reasons I feel that Yeremia could be your father."

"Was your mom closer to Yeremia than to the other servants?"

"I think so. After all, he lived in the house for a long time. He followed my parents every place they moved and ended up staying with them more or less the entire time they were in Tanganyika."

"Let's hope he's still alive and that we can find him."

As I finished speaking, we arrived in Kondoa. Larry directed Fumbwe straight to the house he grew up in. This was the house his parents built after the mission authorities ostracized them due to Judy's birth. It was getting dark, but I could see that the dilapidated, unkempt house was once painted mustard yellow with dark green or black wood trimming and a metal corrugated roof.

A Mr. Robert Luambano, his wife, and four children were living in it now, and he warmly welcomed us. We explained to Mr. Luambano who we were and why we were interested in seeing his house. He apologized for its condition and said he had lived there for only two years.

We walked up four concrete steps into the house. Each small room had a kerosene lamp placed on a corner table. In the main room a single bulb hung from the ceiling on a twisted cord. Larry confirmed that the three overstuffed chairs with worn cushions were part of his family's living room furniture. He showed me a little room on the right side of the house. Goat, cow, and chicken feed filled this room, while the adjoining room had piles of charcoal in the corners. When I looked at Larry, I saw that his energy had diminished and his eyes were glassy. He didn't say anything as he wandered around inside and then outside the house.

I let him walk alone with his thoughts. After half an hour, he rejoined us, and I suggested that we find a place to stay and get something to eat. Mr. Luambano took us to the Savannah Hotel nearby. It was a tiny hotel typical for Africans with one big front room that was used as a receiving room, living room, dining room, and nightclub. The outdoor kitchen in the courtyard had two sets of three-legged stone burners with black earthenware pots boiling something over the flames underneath. More earthenware pots filled with dried maize, rice, cassava, beans, and water stood on the far side of the courtyard.

A few steps from these pots by a wall facing the front room were two little sheds. One had a hole-in-the-ground toilet, and the other a four-foot square bathing room equipped with one pail of water. A rusted brass tap with no water stood about four feet above a cement island by the outdoor kitchen. There was no hint that electricity had ever found its way to this hotel. Our tiny rooms had one twin bed each with only a beat-up foam mattress and no sheets, blankets, or towels. We went back to the main room and ordered rice pilau and warm beer. While we waited for our food, I spotted a Sears and Roebuck Kenmore large-load washing machine with its water-stained packing carton partly open.

The owner said it was given to him nearly two years ago in

payment for a debt that a government official in Dar owed him, but he couldn't find anyone who knew how to use it. I wanted to explain to him that along with someone who knew how to use it, he also needed water and electricity, but I didn't. When the rice pilau came, it was bathed in *simsim* oil and full of little stones that we couldn't chew because we planned to keep our teeth!

We were so tired that we didn't worry about cleaning up or changing into pajamas before we threw ourselves onto the bare foam mattresses and slept soundly in our separate rooms. We noticed the next morning that tossing and turning on our disintegrating mattresses filled our tiny rooms with particles of putrefied foam, which we inhaled throughout the night. We both had headaches and sneezed and coughed the rest of the day.

Breakfast was as miserable as dinner had been. As we ate, it finally dawned on us that we were actually where Larry grew up. This place held his fond memories of Judy, his little sister and my big sister. How could I forget this and focus so much on my physical discomfort? I wondered if I had been born here and if it might also have been my home had I not been sent to the orphanage.

We returned to the house and went directly to the nearby cemetery to search for Judy's grave.

"Larry, how did this cemetery come to be here?"

"I don't know why they picked this location. Colonial district capitals usually had a separate cemetery for Europeans, and this was the European cemetery in Kondoa. As you know, Africans are usually buried near their houses in the village and Christians in the cemetery near the mission or church. The one in Kondoa was especially large because there had been a major pitched battle in World War I between the Germans and the British, with Indian army troops on both sides. The English and German dead were buried here—some fifteen to twenty soldiers, if I recall. An old *askari* who fought with the German army lived in Kondoa when we were there. I can still remember his tall tales of the big battle, the carnage, and how the river ran blood.

"The cemetery was about 150 square yards with a four-foot high stone wall that went all around it, as I remember, and the entrance had a green wooden gate set between two cement pillars. But maintenance was discontinued when all the bodies in European cemeteries in northern Tanganyika had been exhumed and re-buried in one location in Dar. Looking at the cemetery now, it doesn't appear to me that anything has been touched—let alone bodies exhumed—in the last fifty years!"

We stared at the jungle that was the cemetery and wondered how to begin looking for Judy's grave when we saw a man running toward us shouting, "Lehwee, Lehwee."

The man, who introduced himself as John Mdasa, was very happy to see Larry. Larry thought he'd heard his name before but had no memory of him. He apparently worked for the Reiners when Larry was very young.

"You used to play with the kids in my village," Mr. Mdasa reminded him, "and when it was time to go home, you hid behind the banana field and insisted we tell your mother that you weren't here. But we couldn't lie to a *mzungu*! We were afraid of your mother."

He then took me by the hand and showed me the banana field, which was quite a distance from the house. He always got into trouble, he told me, because Larry begged for help taking off his shoes and clothes so he'd be like the African children in the village.

"Our Sukuma children loved playing with Lehwee, not only because he shared his toys and everything with them, but most importantly, he didn't think or act like a *mzungu*."

I had my antennae up when I met John Mdasa. Even though his name was not one of those that Larry mentioned from his childhood, I wondered if he could possibly be my father.

9

My Sister's Grave

With the help of Robert Luambano and John Mdasa, Larry and I started combing through the tall bushes and trees of the cemetery looking for Judy's grave. Both men had *pangas*—large, multipurpose, machete-like knives with long blades used for almost everything, from cutting down trees to slaughtering goats, chopping firewood and clearing the bush. We searched the old cemetery for almost an hour before John found the corner of a cement gravestone he thought might be Judy's. I ran to the site and started clearing away the grass and dirt with my bare hands.

Little by little the tombstone presented itself. First we saw DTH . . . 1945 . . . EIN . . . then 941, and then the whole tombstone.

JUDITH ANNE REINER
JAN. 1941 – MAY 1945
R.I.P.

Larry and I squatted in the tall grass by the grave in silence. I didn't look at him because I knew he would be crying. My own heart was beating hard. When I finally turned his way, I saw that Larry was uncharacteristically controlled and composed.

"I really loved her. She's always been a part of my life." That was all he said.

I felt my heart beat in my temples, and I was getting delirious with a myriad of emotions when Fat Mary came to the rescue.

Breathe, she said. *It's all good.*

I was shaking, so she put her little arms around me and tried to rock me. When I calmed down, she took me back to another emotional but happy time in my past when she said, *Isn't this just absolutely magnificent? You now know that you had a sister! She is your blood sister.*

"Yes, it is absolutely magnificent," I affirmed to Fat Mary.

Out loud I said to Larry, "I'm so confused," but he was oblivious to my conversation with Fat Mary and pointed to the grave right next to Judy's.

"Look what we have here," he said. It was the grave of the old man who had fallen out of the lemon tree.

Until Larry actually saw Judy's grave again, he probably wasn't fully convinced that Judy and I weren't one and the same. I could only imagine what memories came to his mind. I felt his longing for a time long gone and a childhood lost. Today his childhood innocence was exposed. Judy was his only sibling growing up. Because he identified so completely with the Africans and was totally blind to skin color as a child, it had never dawned on him that they didn't have the same father. I tried not to interfere with his thoughts, but I feared he would start sobbing in front of the two African men who would be scandalized to see an adult *mzungu* cry.

"Larry, do you remember when Judy was born and when Dorothy brought her home?" I asked.

"Not exactly. I don't even remember Mom being pregnant. I vaguely remember Mom getting heavier and heavier, but she was always rather plump, and no one said anything to me."

"Remind me again, how old were you when Judy died?"

"I was eight years old. I remember it well because I was away at Arusha School the year she died. I had a dream one night that Judy was sick, and Mom was sitting on her bed reading her a story. The dream ended with Judy suddenly falling asleep and Mom closing the book. Several weeks later Mom came to get me at the end of the school term—a most unusual occurrence. I immediately remembered my dream and asked her how Judy was. Mom told me that Judy had died. She fell ill with a bad case of malaria, recovered, then developed scarlet fever right afterward, but in the end, she died of pneumonia. I told her the details of my dream and she said it was exactly how she died—and as best I can remember—on the night of my dream. Judy had been born prematurely and had some sort of congenital heart disease. She was always frail but very intelligent. She learned to speak three languages fluently by the time she died at age four—English, Swahili, and Sukuma."

"You've shown me pictures of Judy, and if I remember well, we don't look that much alike. Do you think our mom had Judy with another man? Why was she buried in the European cemetery?"

"I'm not going to speculate as to whether you and Judy had the same father. I have all I can do to accept the fact that Mom had two mixed-race children while married to my father."

"But why was Judy buried in the European cemetery?"

"Mom and Dad were trying, with no luck, to raise Judy as my sister—as a white child—despite the visible evidence to the contrary. I don't remember there being any overt snubbing of my parents by other *wazungu,* though I was too young to pick up on prejudice, especially with my own very African attitudes."

We remained in silence at Judy's gravesite for another few minutes. Even though I wasn't 100 percent sure that Judy and I had the same father, I believed that Fat Mary's assessment was right. I did feel a longing for and deep bond with my dead sister.

We thanked Mr. Luambano and John Mdasa for their help. Mr. Mdasa insisted that we come to his village to meet his wife and have some homemade millet beer, which we did. In front of their house was a large straw mat with sheaths of millet drying in the sun for making flour and beer. We all drank from the same dish, passing the calabash bowl of just-brewed millet beer from Larry to Mr. Mdasa to his wife and then to me. It wasn't as nasty tasting as it looked.

I asked Larry, "How are we going to find out if John Mdasa is my father?"

"I have a strong feeling that he isn't because he was one of our first servants and left when I was very young. Probably Judy wasn't born yet."

When we asked John Mdasa if he remembered Larry's little sister Judy, he said he didn't, so we had no need to question him further.

I was a little disappointed, although I hadn't expected to arrive in Tanzania and find my father first thing. I reminded myself of Larry's warning before we left the States—that the search for my father would be like searching for a needle in a haystack.

How many years had passed since I was born? Forty-five! When was the last time Larry saw any of his parents' servants? He returned to the United States to go to college in 1952, but then returned to Tanzania for a visit in 1960 and 1963 when all the servants were still alive. It was now 1989. Dorothy died in 1986 at age seventy-seven, and I assumed that my father would be close to that age. But figuring the average lifespan of an African male at forty-eight years, I got depressed thinking about the odds of finding him alive, or even of finding his grave. I prayed for perseverance, strength, and courage to complete my search.

Keep the faith! Fat Mary consoled me. *You know how. Everything will be revealed at the right time.*

Larry and I were emotionally, mentally, and spiritually spent. We hardly spoke during the three hours it took to return to Tarangire. I'm not a swimmer, but after that hotel in Kondoa and the intense emotions at the cemetery, I felt the need to have water cleanse my body and purify my soul. I borrowed a bathing suit from my friend Annette, the manager at Tarangire Safari Lodge, and entered the freezing pool. For the first time in my adult life, I tolerated uncomfortably cold water.

At six the next morning we went with Fumbwe on a game drive. At first, we didn't see much, but then a large number of giraffe came gliding slowly through the tall grass toward us. In the early light of dawn, they looked like sailboats crossing a sea of golden grass waves. I was wearing my *Aerobics With Soul®* T-shirts with the giraffe logo, so I had Larry take a picture of me in the tall grass with the giraffe in the background. They stopped to stare at us and nodded as though they knew us! They stood very near—tall, motionless, and dignified. I chose the giraffe as my symbol for *Aerobics With Soul®* because it's the national animal of Tanzania and because of the elegance and grace with which the giraffe reaches up, up toward the sky, owning the dignity that no other animal can claim.

Elephants, warthogs, ostriches, water buffaloes, zebra and many "little brown jobs"—gazelles, topis, and dik-diks—came out to greet the day. We even saw a lazy male lion on the road wake up and yawn, then roll right back to sleep. Being king of the jungle, he didn't budge. Fumbwe had to adroitly maneuver the Land Rover to avoid him. Larry and I had hoped to see a leopard or a cheetah but we didn't. After breakfast, we left Tarangire for Serengeti and Seronera Lodges on our way to Mwanza.

Along the way we stopped at a town called Mto Wa Mbu (Mosquito River), famous as a tourist stop, to buy and barter for African art and artifacts. I bought some *khangas* and bartered my Riboki (Reebok) shoes for a beautiful, beaded leather Maasai wedding skirt. The woman told me that she would give me her antique beaded neck collar if I had a pair of Nee-kays (Nikes). If another tourist had walked by wearing Nikes, I would have bought them for any price in order to exchange them for the exquisite, multicolored Maasai necklace.

We continued our safari, stopping under a tree a short distance from Mto Wa Mbu to eat the contents of our *lanchi-boxis* (lunch boxes) prepared for us at Tarangire—a cheese sandwich, two boiled eggs, a chicken drumstick, a guava, and Nice biscuits, one of my favorite childhood boxed cookie brands. We washed it all down with a warm Safari beer.

At the entrance gate to Serengeti Park, we spoke only Swahili to convince the park guards to let us pay the Tanzanian national fee rather than the tourist fee, which was substantially higher and had to be paid in dollars. We succeeded, but I think it was because the guard was impressed and happy to hear visitors who spoke such good Swahili.

10

American Tourists

We arrived at Seronera Lodge and drove under the stone canopy leading to the entrance. Seronera Lodge is discreetly built into huge rocks and boulders and is practically invisible amidst the uneven terrain and *kopjes,* or rock hills, scattered throughout the Serengeti. Inside was yet another architecturally brilliant, once posh hotel that was now government-run but had deteriorated due to lack of maintenance. It was the newest, nicest, and the only lodge around for miles, so it was fairly full when we arrived.

My room was adequate, almost clean, but all that was left of the European toilet was the bottom ceramic bowl. The flushing mechanism must have worked once upon a time, but now there was no handle and no water. When presented with such a scenario, I dream of a rudimentary outdoor john or hole-in-the-ground toilet. No flushing and you don't have to sit on or touch anything with your behind. As I put the one towel on the cold ceramic toilet bowl, I heard an obviously American couple with New York accents arguing and swearing in the room next to mine.

"All I want is a fucking place to shit! Is that asking too much? God damn! I tell you, Africans have no clue, but they want top dollars for this dump!"

I could sympathize with them, but when someone puts Africans down—even though I know that from their perspective, they're right—I don't like it. I wondered why they had ever left New York.

"Can't wait for this fucking trip to be over," the woman answered.

"The bastards can't even build a decent road," the man continued. "I tell you when I get home, I'll get into my car, turn on the air conditioner, and drive to nowhere just to feel a damn road, any road, under the car."

As I walked past the open door of their room, I couldn't help but add my two cents' worth of sarcasm and wondered if they would engage with me so I could calm them down.

"You'll probably also have to see a doctor to reorganize the organs rearranged by the bumpy roads and a therapist to help you deal with the injustices you've endured so far."

They turned their heads toward the door, and the man said, "You're fucking right!"

One look at them in their underwear and disorderly room woke me up to minding my own business. I hurried away, wondering if their tour guides gave orientations to prepare them like my husband Kjell and I did before we brought a group on safari to Africa. Back in the States, they probably could get anything money could buy and felt entitled to material comforts wherever on earth they found themselves. The incredible beauty of the land, the animals, and the love and humanity of the people were lost on them here, as it surely must be in the States as well.

Before dinner I took a bath with the bucket of muddy water in the bathroom and felt sorry for the tour guides who had to deal with the couple next door.

Larry and I went for dinner and splurged on a bottle of Zimbabwe Riesling of dubious vintage. The food was quite tasty, and the wine helped me fall asleep and forget the complaining couple from New York.

11

Pastor Yegera

 The stretch of road from Seronera to Mwanza through the western corridor of the Serengeti was without a doubt the worst road I have ever driven on. The narrow two-way path was about five feet across and had giant potholes filled with decomposed trash and dry dirt that swallowed our Land Rover in a cloud of dust every time we hit one. Overhead, trees with long thorns scratched the top of the car, making screeching noises like a car wash that used metal rakes instead of brushes. Even though it was over one hundred degrees in the car as the sun baked us inside our oven, we didn't dare open the windows because that entire stretch was heavily infested with hungry tsetse flies.

We were on that road for about three hours and met only one car, which was driven by a Sikh in his white turban, who offered to take us back to Seronera in his air-conditioned Peugeot. He told us that the road ahead was much worse. We were tempted to take him up on his offer, but there was no other road to Mwanza, and we hadn't come this far to turn back now.

After another hour of misery, we arrived at the park exit. A guard at the gate took one look at us and volunteered, "*Kutoka hapa barabara inatereza.*" (From here on, the road is so beautiful, it glides.) Sure enough, we couldn't believe our sandpaper eyes when we saw a fresh, smooth tarmac road with a bright yellow line down the middle. I thought of the New York man who longed to feel an American road under his wheels. As for my brother and me, nothing on earth could have made us happier than seeing that beautiful road. It felt like we'd entered "the good road" heaven!

Our stay in heaven turned out to be short-lived. A few kilometers from Mwanza, the gliding road ended and a torn-up, once-paved road full of the familiar potholes dared us to traverse its rugged surface. Everything considered, we still preferred this one over the tsetse fly-infested road.

We checked into the New Mwanza Hotel that must have been new once upon a time. It was more neglected and deteriorated than Seronera Lodge without the saving grace of Seronera's architecture. It was located in the middle of town with noise from traffic and construction outside and from guests inside.

I figured that, as is usual on any foreign trip I've taken, we'd be blessed or cursed to meet traveling Americans. Without fail, in the bar was a large group of young Americans who had arrived on an Overseas Adventure Travel (OAT) truck. They were drinking and singing and having the time of their lives. Their conversations assured me that they were a good bunch who appreciated cultural differences and enjoyed laughing at their ignorance and sharing the faux pas they'd made so far in Tanzania with the hotel guests. The young travelers wore T-shirts bought on the trip, and many wore something African, like *khangas*, Maasai beaded bracelets and earrings, or had their hair braided. Larry and I joined them, and by the end of the evening we were just as loud, carefree, and obnoxious as they were. We talked as we made our way to our rooms, being equally inconsiderate of the sleeping guests. After all, we were Americans!

February 22, 1989, is a date I will never forget.

Larry thought that since his parents worked a long time for the AIMC (African Inland Mission Church) in Sukuma country, we should stop by the church headquarters because the chances of finding my father would be better with them. The receptionist at the hotel gave us directions to the AIMC office. There we met an American couple, the Bakers, who were missionaries with the church. We told them in confidence the reason for our visit and asked them for help or leads to someone who might have been in Mwanza District during the time Larry's parents were there. They were kind and sympathetic and suggested that the only person who had been there for a long time was the African assistant to the bishop, Pastor

Thomas Yegera. Unfortunately, he was ill and had been bedridden for three years. Larry and I looked at each other, realizing he could be the only person who might know anything about his parents' former servants Yeremia, Hezekia, and Klementi.

We begged the Bakers to intercede on our behalf to see if there was a chance the bishop's assistant would see us or, if not us, would they present our request to him and be our go-between?

It turned out that they were close to him and so, while we waited with anticipation and concern, they went to visit him to present our case. After about an hour, Mrs. Baker came back. She was smiling and seemed quite pleased.

"Not only will he see you, he and his old friend Pastor N'gwan'gwa, who is visiting him, said that they knew one of the servants—Yeremia. They said that he had become a deacon with the AIMC, but they hadn't seen him for several years, though news of his death hadn't reached them. The last place they heard he lived was in the tiny village of Kasamwa across Lake Victoria."

Before she finished talking, Larry and I were running toward Pastor Yegera's house. In my excitement, the only thing I noticed about his house was that it was small by western standards, but large for Africans. The red brick rectangular house with a green tin roof was an obvious relic of the colonial era. Inside we walked past a dark living room and into a small bedroom, with the only light coming from a partly open window over the bed where he lay.

"*Shikamoo Mheshimiwa*," I greeted him. (Literally: I hold your feet, respected one.)

"*Marahaba mwanangu. Njoo karibu.*" (I am honored, my child. Come closer.)

Pastor Yegera's skin was very dark and a light sweat glistened on his forehead and neck. His shirt was unbuttoned and, like most Africans, he had no hair on his chest. He struggled to sit up, slowly managing to prop himself against two pillows, then gave us his full attention. When he saw Larry, a wide, warm smile spread across his face and his whole body relaxed.

"*Lehwee, Lehwee, umerudi!*" (Larry, Larry, you have returned!)

"I'm so happy to be back and to be able to see you. Thank you for agreeing to see us." Larry responded.

"*Hujambo, Lehwee? Mbona umekuwa mzee!*" (How are you, Larry? Why, you've become so old!)

"It happens to the best of us."

"*Bwana Laina hajambo?*" (How is Mr. Reiner?)

"My father passed away a long time ago."

"*Pole sana!*" (So sorry!)

"*Mama Hajambo?*" (How's your mother?)

"She has died too."

"*Pole sana! Bado unasema Kisukuma?*" (So sorry! Do you still speak Sukuma?)

"Not much, I'm sad to admit. The reason for my visit is that my sister and I have come to Tanzania to search for her father. We do not know who he is or if he is still alive, but we have the names of three servants who worked for my parents, and we're hoping that one of them will be her father. Do you know Hezekia, Kelementi, or Yeremia?"

"I knew them all, but it was a long time ago. Hezekiah moved to the south when your parents were still here, I think, and I haven't heard anything about him. Kelementi passed away a few years ago. The one I remember most is Yeremia. When you were a child, Lehwee, you used to think he was your father."

"I know. He's the one I remember best."

"*Je mzee N'gwan'gwa, umeishasikia Yeremia yuko wapi siku hizi?*" he asked his visitor. (Mr. N'wan'gwa, have you heard where Yeremia is nowadays?)

"*Nilisikia yuko Kasamwa.*" (I heard he was in Kasamwa.)

At that moment there was as knock on the door. "*Hodi Mzee.*" (Knock, knock, Elder.)

"*Karibu.*" (Come in.)

"*Ni mimi, Daudi Kazimoto.*" (It's me, Daudi Kazimoto.)

They switched from speaking Swahili to Sukuma. The whole scene seemed surreal. Here Larry and I were in the assistant bishop's bedroom with three Sukuma men carrying on a long, serious conversation in hushed voices as if they had forgotten we were there. Then, after a minute or so of complete silence, Pastor Yegera spoke.

"You and your sister are very lucky people. Pastor Kazimoto, who has stopped by to visit me, is familiar with Kasamwa village. He doesn't know Yeremia, but he thinks that since it is a small village, you won't have trouble finding his house. I have asked him to take you there himself today."

I remembered how far-fetched our search for my father seemed when we left the States, and now here in this little house with three Sukuma men on our side, everything somehow seemed possible. I was engaging people in my private search who, until today, I didn't know existed.

Suddenly I panicked. Pastor Yegera had just eliminated two people from our list of three persons of interest. What are the chances that the only one left—Yeremia—was alive and that he would be my father? I felt depressed because the odds were not good. I took a long cleansing inhale and exhale and then listened to Fat Mary.

I have been with you since you were a small child. There's never been a time when the mystery surrounding your birth has come so close to being unraveled. Today, there is much at stake. I want you to know that no matter the outcome, you will be all right. If Yeremia is not your father, you will be disappointed, and you will continue your search. Everything in life happens for a reason. Sometimes the reasons are revealed to us, but often they are not. All that has happened in your life was meant to be. Today will be another day of revelation.

12

Ferry across Lake Victoria

 Was it a coincidence that the receptionist at the New Mwanza Hotel knew the address of the AIMC head office? That the Bakers were Americans and friends of Pastor Yegera, who knew Yeremia? That Pastor Daudi Kazimoto, who had just been to Kasamwa where Yeremia lived, stopped in to see his friend while we were there?

I felt the hand of God moving everything into place. Like a symphony conductor, baton in hand, he was orchestrating our journey of discovery, watching all of us in the room play our roles as he directed the music he had composed many years ago.

We went to thank Pastor Yegera, who offered prayers for our journey and blessed each of us, saying, *"Msisahau kurudi kunipa taarifa zote za safari yenu Kasamwa."* (Don't forget to return to give me news about your trip to Kasamwa.)

"Hatutasahau. Asante sana," we responded. (We won't forget. Thank you very much.)

We had tea with the three unforgettable, loving African men, hugged a lot, and cried some before we said our goodbyes.

"Mungu awabariki." (God bless you.) The bishop's assistant blessed us with the sign of the cross, and we headed to the lake. Named after Queen Victoria of England, Lake Victoria is the source of the Nile. Located in East Central Africa along the equator, it borders Uganda, Kenya, and Tanzania, and is the largest lake in Africa and the world's second largest freshwater lake after Lake Superior. I learned about the lake in my African geography classes, and one of my closest high school friends was from an island on the lake.

We drove about fifteen minutes to catch the ferry. As we waited for the ferry from Mwanza to Kamanga, which was forty-five minutes late, I took time to pray. I felt I was praying to find my father for the last time. I reminded God how as a child I'd ask him to find my mother. I told him I knew I hadn't prayed quite as hard or as long to find my father, but I was praying now! Since he had led me here, I asked him if today was the day he had in mind for us to meet.

Fat Mary had a suggestion. *Instead of letting your mind wander from thought to thought, let's you and I pray together in one voice.* I joined my voice with hers as we prayed.

God, I know you orchestrate everything in life. Please give me the courage to accept what today has to bring. If finding my father is in your plans, I'm all for it. If I am not going to find him today, please keep him alive for me until it's time. You remember, God, how you took your time to bring me my mother? I think I have shown patience and perseverance and have followed your decree of "Ask and you shall receive. Seek and you shall find."

After you gave me my mother, I realized that a hunger in my soul still persisted. I am of mixed race, but in my mind and heart I have always felt 100 percent African. There is a reason why you made me and kept me this way, even after bestowing upon me much that is white and American by bringing me to America and giving me two American mothers. Please let me find out why today. As in the past, I promise I will behave, and I will not despair if you're not ready yet. Amen and Amen!

I'm at peace, Fat Mary said. "And so am I," I assured her.

I was so engrossed in my conversation with God that I was oblivious to the chaotic crowd and confusion surrounding me. Lorries and tractors in various stages of breakdown were being repaired at the edge of the lake. They were filled with everything under the sun—from food to fertilizer to livestock. Piled in the trucks were wooden bed frames, foam mattresses, corn-husk pillows, overstuffed baskets wrapped in brilliant *khangas*, plastic bags with dirt or flour; hoes in every shape and size, some shiny and brand new with no handles; green banana stalks, maize, dozens of colorful plastic buckets, charcoal, bags of fluffy cotton, unhusked rice and millet in brown guinea sacks, petrol barrels, vinyl suitcases, live chickens, rabbits in wire-mesh crates, one black-and-white pig, three cows, and a bunch of confused goats.

I watched as they loaded the motor vehicles onto the ferry. Drivers concentrated on their just-repaired vehicles as they backed onto it. The semis, buses, tractors, and lorries were loaded first, and then we got into our Land Rover and waited for a shouting employee to point to us. When the loading was done, there was barely an inch between the vehicles and the rest of the cargo. Humans, animals, produce, and equipment were crammed on top of each other. With thundering noises and severe shaking, the ferry rocked and rolled until it leaped ahead, causing its cargo to lunge forward and the passengers to shriek.

After we composed ourselves, I realized that unless we climbed out the hatch of our Land Rover and sat on the roof, we would suffocate. Claustrophobia was never a problem for me, but I started to hyperventilate. Larry, who was sitting in front, told me not to open the window because the air outside was fouler than the air in the car. I took deep breaths and told myself that I was not going to get sick and I was not going to pass out!

Suddenly, a fear I'd never experienced before took over. I felt like running for my life. I opened the window to escape, but I couldn't open it enough even to stick my head out, so I closed it again. I struggled with the overhead hatch and finally managed to open it. Then I pulled myself up into Larry's forbidden air. Panicked, I gulped in the foul air, believing that my life depended on it. Eventually my heart stopped racing and sweat stopped dripping from my face. I slid back into the car and somehow opened the window. No sooner had I opened the window when a young girl squeezed her baby through it and dropped the infant onto my lap.

"*Naomba unitunzie mtoto. Hapa nje jua kali sana!*" (Please, take care of my baby. It's so hot outside!)

The baby girl was a godsend as a distraction. She was about six months old with very dark-black piercing eyes. She immediately reached for my breast. My motherly instincts made me want to nurse her. Her diapers were layers of rags, wet and full of poop. The smell aggravated my nausea and claustrophobia, and I tried to return the baby to her mother, but she refused. Instead, she climbed over the car from the back, slid down the hatch into the car, and sat next to me. She proceeded to nurse her child without saying a word.

When the baby was satisfied, I played with her and weakly hummed an out-of-tune "Rock-a-bye baby, on the treetop . . ." The baby made happy noises when I hummed and cried when I stopped. I hummed the song until she fell asleep, all the while thinking how ridiculous that song had seemed to me when I first heard it as an adult in America. It occurred to me then that most nursery rhymes were equally ridiculous, but I figured that the end justified the means. As long as they put a child to sleep, who cares that the words made no sense or were outright violent or cruel? But here, in this hot, dark, cramped, diaper-smelling Land Rover on an overloaded ferry on Lake Victoria, in the middle of Africa, it was beyond ridiculous!

Unloading the ferry took a little over an hour, almost as long as the whole trip across. Pastor Kazimoto gave our driver Fumbwe directions, and we were on our way. We resumed the shake, rattle, and roll in our vehicle that had become our signature sensation on most roads during this trip. Although this road also had crater-sized potholes, I ignored them. My head and heart were busy arguing with each other. One was pounding with anxiety and fear, and the other was rationalizing everything. The heart won. I remained a hopeless, emotional wreck for the remainder of the two-hour trip until we reached the outskirts of Kasamwa.

"This is the little village of Kasamwa," Daudi Kazimoto announced. I wondered how he knew since there were no road signs, and the place had only a cluster of four neglected huts. "But I don't know how to find out if Yeremia lives here."

"Let's get off the road and drive down the path. Maybe there's more of the village," Larry suggested.

At that point, I slid into my own world again, and all I heard were mumbled voices coming from Fumbwe, Daudi, and Larry that turned into discordant background noise for my thoughts. I felt I was going to explode. I couldn't think straight. My heart was beating rapidly and I felt nauseated. My hands were clammy and I was sweating profusely. I looked at Fat Mary, but all she did was stare at me.

13

The Unfolding

"Please God, don't let me get sick now," I prayed. "Please let me be present and healthy at this holy moment, at this place, and at this time."

I'm scared of heights and it felt like I was standing on the edge of a cliff, swaying back and forth, trying not to fall off, as I clung to the car window. Something was definitely going to happen today. Could this be the preordained day for me, at age forty-five, after traveling halfway across the world from Edina, Minnesota, to a tiny Sukuma village on the outskirts of Lake Victoria in Tanzania, to find the man who had fathered me?

"You know, God," I continued my prayer, "you and I have come a long way. I knew you were always near, even though at times it felt like you had forgotten all about me. Do you remember when we used to talk every day in front of the statue of Blessed Martin in Kifungilo?"

Fat Mary intervened with a reminder. *Many of your childhood prayers have been answered. You found a mother who loves you like you were her own, and you also found your birth mother. Your prayers will be answered now too. Your faith has guided your life, and your determination has brought you to this place. All is well.*

Everything and everyone was quiet. We had driven several times around what we thought was the village but didn't see anyone to ask about Yeremia. I don't know what made me turn around and look back, but far behind the car, I saw a little boy about four or five years old skipping down a narrow path, coming toward us. He was wearing only a tattered pair of navy blue shorts that were as dirty as his mud-crusted bare feet. He stopped and stared at our car with amazement. I wondered if he was seeing a car for the first time, like so many people born and raised in villages far from the main roads.

"Let's ask that little boy," I said.

"He doesn't look like he would know anything," Daudi answered me in a voice tinged with disappointment and exasperation.

"We have nothing to lose," Larry said. "He's the only living thing around."

We backed up to him. He started running away, screaming, *"Wazungu! Wazungu!"*

Larry and I got out of the car, and I called after the boy, *"Mimi si mzungu. Njoo, nitakupa peremende."* (I'm not white! Come, I'll give you candy.)

The little boy changed directions immediately and approached me with both hands outstretched. I reached into my trusted Le Sportsac purse, hoping I had something resembling candy in the bag that my family called "the pharmacy" because it always produced whatever we needed while on safari. I found a small box of Nice Biscuits, which I gave him.

"Hii siyo peremende." (This isn't candy.)

"Peremende zimekwisha. Kama hutaki biskuti nirudishie." (I have no more candy. If you don't want the biscuits, give them back to me.)

He clutched my biscuits and put his hands behind his back to let me know that he had no intention of parting with them.

"Tunamtafuta mzee fulani. Anaitwa Yeremia. Je unaijua nyumba yake?" (We're looking for a certain old man. His name is Yeremia. Do you know his house?)

"Mzee Yeremia yuko mbele kidogo, lakini anapumzika sasa." (Old Yeremia lives down the road, but he's resting right now.)

Larry and I hugged and simultaneously blurted out, "He's alive! He's alive!" The angel boy in ragged clothes that God planted along our path had just confirmed that Yeremia was alive.

"Naomba utuelekeza nyumbani kwake, au labda utusindikize?" (Please give us directions to his house, or maybe you can take us there?)

"Haya, twendeni." (Okay, let's go.)

We happened to have stopped the car a few yards from the actual entrance to the village of Kasamwa, which lay straight ahead, but we couldn't see it from the road.

The little boy, Larry, Daudi, Fumbwe, and I walked single file past old abandoned huts. A few people were outside; then more people came out of their huts to look at us. Our little angel walked like he was the big *bwana* in charge of an expedition. He marched past the onlookers and took us to a flimsy wooden door, opened it, and pointed to a rectangular house on the far side of the courtyard.

"*Mzee Yeremia yuko ndani.*" (Old Yeremia is inside.)

Larry and I stood speechless as we stared at the house. Had we really reached the end of our search? Could it be possible that Yeremia or anyone lived inside the forlorn and dilapidated rectangular mud hut? As we stood there, I studied the home. It reminded me of the huts I saw when I went with Sister Silvestris to visit the *masikini* in the villages around Kifungilo, except this one showed some signs of having been maintained. It was the largest house in the compound and the cracked, parched beige mud walls reminded me of the edges of Lake Manyara near Arusha in the dry season. It had only one window in front, and the roof was of corrugated metal—a status symbol—instead of the usual thatched roof. A rusty barrel of water stood to the right of the door with a bar of Sunlight soap. Just-washed tin plates, tin mugs, spoons, and a silvery teakettle had been left out to dry in the sun on a nearby table. Three wooden chairs and a well-used blue bicycle leaned against the wall on the other side of the door. Several children in the courtyard left their games and came over to watch us. Our little guide went over and said something to one of them in Sukuma. Then he ran though the wooden door of the house and disappeared inside for an eternity of five minutes.

We jumped as the squeaking door slowly opened. I clearly recall everything around me coming in and out of focus at that moment and everyone moving in slow motion. An old man put one foot over the threshold and then the other. He stood looking around, squinting and yawning widely. He wore lose-fitting gray trousers and a clean, light yellow cotton shirt with a ballpoint pen sticking out of the pocket over his heart. On his feet were well-worn green flip-flops that appeared to be two sizes too small.

Out of respect, we let him take his time to wake up and survey the situation. He continued squinting as he walked toward Larry, shaking his head and looking at him quizzically. Larry couldn't take it any longer. He rushed toward him, gave him a big hug, and started to cry—no, started to bawl loudly and uncontrollably—as they embraced.

"Yeremia, Yeremia, we found you!" Larry said between sobs.

"*Lehwee, ni wewe?*" (Is it you, Larry?)

"*Ni mimi!*" (It's me!) He continued crying without shame.

"*Umekuwa mzee.*" (You've become old!)

"*Na wewe pia umekuwa mzee.*" (You, too, have become old.)

They laughed and continued to hug, pat each other on the back, and high-five over and over. Even though Yeremia was speaking with Larry, he glanced at me off and on, but looked away whenever our eyes met. It was overwhelming to look at him because upon seeing him, I knew he was my father. In my heart Fat Mary was dancing up a storm. The rapid heartbeat, stomach cramping, nausea, and discomfort I had felt for most of the day were now replaced with a feeling of just having exhaled. It was the feeling of knowing that you are about to be rewarded for the fruits of your labor, but you don't want to take anything for granted. I managed to return my focus to the drama between the two men and ignore Fat Mary.

Larry introduced me to Yeremia. "*Huyu ni dada yangu. Anaitwa Maria.*" (This is my sister. Her name is Maria.)

Yeremia shook my hand up and down several times as he struggled for what to say.

I greeted him first. "*Shikamoo Mzee.*"

He quickly answered, "*Marahaba! Karibuni nyumbani. Karibuni sana.*" (I am honored. Welcome to my house. A very warm welcome to you.)

One by one the five of us ducked as we passed through the low door and entered his house. In the main room, two wooden chairs like the ones outside faced several small three-legged round wooden stools of various heights on the dirt floor.

Yeremia pointed to the stools, saying, "*Hivi ni viti vya wajukuu wangu. Kaeni kitako tuwasilimiane.*" (These chairs are for my grandchildren. Have a seat and let's visit.)

Yeremia and Pastor Kazimoto sat on the upright chairs and the rest of us sat on the little stools. Yeremia smiled widely every time he looked at Larry, revealing a full set of teeth, which were partly stained brown.

"*Poleni sana, sina soda wala bia.*" (I'm very sorry, I have neither soda nor beer to offer you.)

I assured him, "*Hamna tatizo. Tumekwisha kula.*" (No problem. We've already eaten.) I lied. In our hurry to find Yeremia, we didn't stop to eat lunch. It was now about three in the afternoon.

Yeremia asked Larry about his father and later in the conversation asked about his mother. Larry told him that both had passed away. Yeremia looked at Larry, lowered his head, and said nothing. After a while he said in a faint voice, "*Pole sana.*" (I'm very sorry.)

Larry started to cry again. I put my arm around him and held him until he composed himself. The rest of us joined him making small talk with Yeremia about everything except what was on our minds. After about half an hour, Larry asked Yeremia if they could have a private talk outside.

They left the room and we waited quietly and patiently inside. I could only imagine the conversation they were having. For the first time, my mind wandered to a topic that I should have addressed before coming here. I was so anxious to find my father that it had not occurred to me whether he would also want to know me. Why did I assume that he would be as eager and happy to meet me as I was to meet him? What if he, like Dorothy, never wanted to discuss me or their relationship? My rapid heartbeat and nausea returned and I felt dizzy.

"Fat Mary, stop dancing and help me! Why am I feeling so sick?"

Your heart is overflowing with emotion! You are relieved to find Yeremia alive, but you are distressed to see this dignified man living in poverty. You believe he is your father, yet what if he isn't? You envisioned a glorious and happy reunion, but you don't know what he feels. So much is happening—how can you be calm? Let's see what will be revealed today.

It seemed like forever before Larry came back into the house alone. After giving me another hug, he proceeded to sit on his little stool and tried to talk. No words came from his mouth, and it seemed like he couldn't hear either.

"Well, is he my father? What did you ask him? What did he say?

Did he remember that he once had a child with your mother? Does he want to be left alone?"

No response from Larry.

"I can't wait any longer. I'm going to talk to him myself."

"Go!" was all Larry said.

I went outside and found Yeremia sitting, looking down, elbows resting on his knees, stroking the sparse gray hair on his head with both hands. He looked up and let me approach him. I sat down beside him. We said nothing for about a minute, then we turned to look at each other. When our eyes met, I tried to talk but no words came out. It was his turn to rescue me.

As he took my hands into both of his, Yeremia said, *"Nimefurahi sana kukuona leo."* (I am very happy to see you today.)

"Je, unanifahamu?" (Do you know who I am?) My voice came out in a whisper.

"Ndiyo, mwanangu. Nimekujua maisha yako yote." (Yes, my child. I've known you your whole life.)

What I remember best about that moment was how quiet and still everything around us was. Our hushed voices seemed to flow into a universe that itself had fallen silent in reverence for our reunion.

Yeremia said to me, "Today we see each other eye to eye for the first time since your birth. The one constant dream in my life has come true. You are seeing me for the first time, but I saw you the day you were born and from that time long ago, I have never forgotten you."

We hugged and held each other in a long embrace that began to make up for all the missed embraces of the last forty-five years.

I still needed to hear him say that he was my father. I gently asked him, *"Je wewe ni baba wangu?"* (Are you my father?) He hesitated for a long time and then began speaking.

"This afternoon I went to bed for a nap as usual, but sleep was very far away. My heart was heavy. I don't remember ever being so restless. I couldn't fall asleep. When I heard the sound of a car and people coming toward my house, I got scared. I knew that something unusual was about to happen. As soon as I saw you, I knew that you were my long-lost daughter. Every day I asked God to keep you safe if you were alive, and to keep you next to him in heaven, if you were dead. Today it is God who brought you to me. Yes, you are the beloved daughter that God gave to me and your mother, Dorothy. Praise be to God! Praise be to God! Let God be praised. All praise goes to God, for he has done a wonderful thing."

We hugged again and I don't know who cried more. At that moment, I thought of the woman who had made this bond possible. I went back to the vow I had made to myself after a conversation I'd had with Dorothy many years earlier when she visited me in Edina. We had been talking about Africa and she was in a good mood. I decided to once again try to get information from her about my father. I asked her, "Dorothy, is there anything you can tell me about my father?"

She uncharacteristically blurted out, "All I can say is that it happened in the dark, it was very fast, and he was gone."

"You were raped?"

"I didn't say that."

She reached into her purse for her angina medication, which she always needed whenever I brought up any uncomfortable subject and especially my father.

Ever since that conversation, I assumed that my father had raped her. I had promised myself that if and when I found my father, that would be one of the first questions I'd ask him.

"Father," I said (I had no problem calling him father right away), "please forgive me, but I have a question that I've waited to ask you for many years. Did you and Dorothy love each other or did you force her?"

He replied without hesitation, "My child, I believe we loved each other. Before you were born, we already had your sister, Judy. The day your mother was going to give birth to you, we went to Tanga hospital together. After you were born, we took you to the Catholic mission in Kibosho. From Kibosho you were taken to an orphanage called Kifungilo. I was very upset. I told Dorothy that you would not be accepted in Kifungilo because you were not an orphan. Because of Judy, the Reiners had problems with the mission and their fellow whites. I think that is why they decided not to raise you themselves and took you to the orphanage. I wanted to take you home to my village so my family could raise you, but it was forbidden, and I was told to never ask about you again. Never! And I didn't. Even though I didn't ask, that didn't mean you were not always in my mind and heart. When I last saw you, you were about three or four days old. Look at you today! Praise God! He has performed a miracle!"

To which I replied, *"Amina!"*

Fat Mary was dancing like her life depended on it! She slowed down long enough to say, *Didn't I tell you that everything that is meant to be will be? You have found your father, and you have learned that he wanted you. He couldn't take you to his village, but he didn't forget about you. Like you, he was a victim of the racial biases of the time. Can you imagine the joy in his heart when he saw you—the forbidden fruit of his union with your mother? Your finding each other will give you both the profound peace you deserve.*

14

By My Father's Side

 The news that Dorothy and Yeremia probably loved each other settled my soul. I hoped this new knowledge would end my nightmares of my mother being raped and attacked by an unknown man. I felt an indescribable feeling of love and gratitude for both my parents. I could see why Dorothy might have found Yeremia attractive. He was a gentle, dignified, handsome, smart, and cultured man. His spirit shone out of every pore of his body, outlining it with a halo of light and energy in sharp contrast to the expected despair and resignation of his life of abject poverty.

After our conversation, I helped him up and we walked toward the house. Before we entered, I half genuflected in front of him, and said, *"Asante sana, Baba."* (Many thanks, Father.)

He put his right hand on my head and said, *"Mwanangu, umerudi nyumbani. Mungu amenijalia, uzeeni. Sasa nitakufa na usalama."* (My child, you have come back home. God has blessed me in my old age. When death comes, it will be peaceful.)

Inside, Larry had stopped crying and was having a conversation in Swahili with Pastor Kazimoto and Fumbwe. As soon as he saw us, he resumed crying. I looked at his wet, red face and wondered how he had any tears left in him, but I knew that this time they were tears of joy. I smiled as I handed him my last Kleenex.

Larry and I knew we weren't going to discuss what had just happened between us and Yeremia with the others. They had just witnessed a miracle—a miracle so big that I doubted if they could fully grasp it even if we painstakingly explained our relationship and our long journey to this house and this day.

Larry reacted like a running faucet that turned itself off and on without warning, while I was like an ostrich egg—hard and strong on the outside, but soft and mushy inside. My egg eventually cracked, and then broke, releasing a thousand emotions. And Yeremia? He repeated his favorite "Praise be to God" over and over.

We moved to the outside chairs as Yeremia told us about his family. He had eight boys and three girls, four including me. His wife was Perisi. Their firstborn Maisheli (Marshall, for Larry's father) was shot when bandits ambushed him on the way to a wedding. Another son was killed in a motorcycle accident near Morogoro. The rest of his children—six boys and three girls—were alive. The boys were scattered all over Tanzania but the girls remained in Kasamwa.

"*Mimi nilikuwa mtoto wa kwanza?*" (Was I your firstborn?)

"You are my second child, counting Judy. May she rest in peace. After you were born, Mr. Reiner searched for a wife for me and brought me Perisi. I had eleven children with her."

"Is Perisi alive?"

"She is, and she's healthy too. She went to the fields this morning, and she will not return until late. What bad luck! The *shamba* (field) is far from here."

I showed him a picture of my husband and our children, Katarina and Karl. He was pleased to see pictures of my children. He laughed and danced with joy as he kissed the photos. He repeated their names over and over, and then when he finally calmed down, he explained the reason for his happiness.

"My grandchildren Katarina and Karl will keep the name Nhambu alive in America. I can see that they are children of Africa. My name will live on in America. Thank you very much."

"*Je, utamwambia Perisi kwamba una mtoto Merikani?*" (Will you tell Perisi that you have a child in America?)

"I will not tell her today. I will wait a little before giving her the news. I know she will be very happy. She loved giving birth to our many children."

He looked some more at the photos, then said, "*Na wewe, lazima uwalete wajukuu wangu Kasamwa. Kasamwa ni kwao. Hapa watao-na mizizi ya familia yao.*" (You have to bring my grandchildren to

Kasamwa. Kasamwa is their home. I want them to know their roots and to see where their African ancestors came from.)

I gave him the small album of family photos, and he put it in an old hexagonal tin with the barely visible words Quality Street Mackintosh Toffee written on it. As a child, I loved that British candy! Visitors to Kifungilo brought sweets and handed one to each orphan. Those who brought Mackintosh toffees ranked high on our list of good visitors. To this day, whenever I'm in Amsterdam Schiphol Airport, I pick up a couple of tins to take back to the States. When my kids were young, I'd hide them. Unfortunately, I often forgot where I hid them and by the time I finally found the toffees, they were either as hard as rock or they had been devoured by my beloved children who had memorized all my hiding places.

The others came out of the house and all five of us joined hands while Yeremia, a deacon in the African Inland Church of Tanzania (AICT), led a prayer of thanksgiving, finishing with his favorite psalm.

"*Mwimbieni Bwana wimbo mpya kwa sababu ametenda mambo ya ajabu.*" (Sing to the Lord a new song for he has done wonderful things.) (Psalm 98)

We repeated the psalm after him several times before we said a final "*Amina!*" On that day, I truly understood the meaning of the word "Amen."

It was hard to leave my father, but he urged us to start back since we had several hours on rough roads to the ferry, then another hour to cross Lake Victoria, and we had to drop Pastor Kazimoto home before retiring to our hotel.

Diesel fuel was very expensive and hard to find in 1989. We were almost out, and the only place we could find some was in Geita, the nearest town. Yeremia said that he would accompany us there because he used to work in the cotton ginnery and knew someone who could help us. All five of us piled into the dusty Land Rover and drove to the cotton ginnery, which looked like a ghost town. Yeremia went to a rusted six-foot rectangular metal shack on the right, which turned out to be an office with somebody actually in it. The occupant was happy to see his old friend. He said that there was enough diesel in the lone gas pump, but it would be difficult to get it out because someone had stolen the pump's hose. He came out with some contraption that was part garden hose, part water pipe, and part soccer ball, and attached one end to the gas pump and the other to the tank of the Land Rover. They pumped and blew, squeezed and groaned for more than forty minutes, siphoning the diesel drop by drop to fill our tank.

Afterward, we exchanged addresses and said goodbye to Yeremia and his friend. As we pulled away, I sadly watched two sets of hands raised above the head in the customary Sukuma goodbye gesture. I looked at my father until he became a blur as we both retreated toward our separate worlds. My heart was full of gratitude, but it was also heavy. America was so far away. Would I ever see him again?

You will see him again. It was Fat Mary. *What happened today was proof of the power of hope. It anchored you in Kifungilo, sustained you in Mhonda and Morogoro, and guided you from America back to the village of Kasamwa. Hope prevented you from ever giving up. We are taught that Faith, Hope, and Charity are the spiritual pillars of life and that the greatest of these is Charity. In your case, Hope was the greatest.*

Today you found out your true name, your birth name—Nhambu. The many surnames you gave yourself in the past did not change who you are, and Nhambu won't do that either. You are who you are from the day you were born. How you live your life is what defines you. I, Fat Mary, am the essence of your being. I am the authentic you!

"Thank you, Fat Mary. I am mindful of the present moment. This is the day I met my father for the first time. This day my father learned that his grandchildren will ensure his name lives on in America."

On the way back to the ferry, Larry was very quiet. I went over the day in my mind to understand why he was so tearful and emotional about meeting Yeremia. It suddenly occurred to me that I had been very selfish about this search. I had been so aware of my desires and expectations that I didn't recognize what this reunion meant to my brother. I put myself in his shoes and imagined how many emotions must have flooded his heart as he saw again the land and people of his childhood. He had told me that he loved Yeremia deeply and that he was like a father to him. I told Larry that he had probably spent much more time with Yeremia than with his own father. Now he is finally realizing how little he knew about his parents' lives in Africa and probably wondering if subconsciously he didn't want to know.

"Larry, do you want to talk about your feelings and today?"

"No, Sis. I won't ever be able to put them into words."

15

Shadow of the Beast

 The drive back to the ferry seemed faster than the trip to Kasamwa, but it was already dark when we arrived at the lake. We decided to take the ferry at Busisi rather than the one at Kamanga—a very good choice after our emotional day in Kasamwa. It was large, quiet, clean, punctual, and carried only passengers. No trucks, cargo, or animals this time. We crossed Lake Victoria just after sunset, which transformed the water into shimmering, silver sheets of liquid that danced around the large granite *kopjes* protruding from the lake floor. My heart was as light as the silver sheets of water, and I, too, did virtual dances around the boulders with joy and gratitude, but mostly in awe of what had happened. I made a conscious effort to be present and not let anything on the ferry distract me. That ferry ride is forever imprinted on my mind and heart, and whenever I revisit that miraculous day, my feelings are as intense as they were then.

We drove to Pastor Kazimoto's home, and since the lights on our Land Rover didn't work, we fervently prayed along the dusty dirt road that we would arrive in one piece, without a pothole swallowing us or animals or bandits getting us. It took us an hour to travel fifteen kilometers, but we arrived without incident. Pastor Kazimoto invited us into his home. His wife had just given birth to a baby girl three days ago. Larry, a pediatrician, offered to examine the baby. Even under the dim light of a kerosene lamp, he could see that she was healthy. We said goodbye and arrived at the New Mwanza Hotel about midnight.

In the morning, when Larry and I met for breakfast, it was obvious that we were both drained. I had difficulty comprehending and identifying my emotions. It felt like I had been carrying the secret lives of Yeremia and Dorothy for years and years. I was unfamiliar with the void in my heart that morning. It was as if I had locked a taunting beast in a closet for years, and then one day, out of the clear blue, I unlocked the doors and faced it because I was no longer afraid.

Several occurrences in my life made it possible for me to release the beast in the closet. The first was when Cathy became my mother; the second was when Kjell became my husband, and the third was when Katarina and Karl became my children. My family, beginning with Cathy, chipped away at the beast, bringing it down to size, but it still remained in my closet.

In spite of the love and care that my family gave me over the years, I sometimes found myself drawn to that closet to see if the beast was still there. It was good to see that it had lost its teeth, but believe it or not, I was often relieved to find it there. I had lived with it for so long, it became part of my self-image and affected how I related to the world around me. For as long as I can remember, I've worked hard on getting rid of the burden—the beast—I inherited from my parents.

Few people, not even my family, know or understand the role this beast has played in my life. I've resolved many times that one day I would open that door and get rid of the beast once and for all. During my visits to the closet, I'd unlock and lock the door, each time thinking that it was for the last time. I had come a long way from the days of letting the beast hold the only key to my true happiness. I'd come a long way from the loneliness of the orphanage. At this stage in my life, I knew the beast that once occupied the closet had been reduced in size and significance, but I also knew it had not fully disappeared because it represented an important part of my unknown past. Shadows of my past will always hover over my present, but I cannot let the past define my future. I am now in possession of the truth about the beast and I am in charge of it, rather than the other way around.

That morning I defiantly took a peek into the closet, and all I saw was the shadow of the familiar beast. The shadow shrank and moved in waves along the floor and walls of the closet until it blended into the light of the rising sun.

16

Larry's Father

 Sitting with my brother at a tiny breakfast table in the New Mwanza Hotel, I was drained from physical exhaustion, but my heart was at peace. Having only the empty space in my heart that the beast once occupied took some getting used to. I would pinch myself and then I would pinch Larry and say, "Tell me, Larry, that this is not a dream! Tell me that we really did find my father. Tell me that he and our mother had a love affair. Tell me that I am living proof of their love! Tell me—"

"Let's not go that far!" Larry interrupted. "When I told you that I always had a hunch that Yeremia would prove to be your father, I didn't say that they had a love affair."

"Maybe they didn't have a love affair, but they certainly had some kind of an affair."

"Well, there you have it. No wonder I loved you the moment I set eyes on you. When Mom first told me about you, I hoped you would turn out to be Judy. Even though you were not her I felt the same way as I did with Judy. You are my little African sister!"

"I have no words to thank you, Larry. You are the one who made this miracle happen. Without you, I would have never found my father or learned anything about my mother's life in Africa. Growing up, I wished I had a sibling—a brother or a sister. If I were given the whole world to search to find someone I'd like to have as a brother, I'd pick you! You! You! You!"

"Same here, same here! I'm going to start crying again. Because of you, I have a better understanding of my mother, and I'm seeing my parents from a whole new perspective."

"It's difficult for me to imagine what was going on in your father's mind. Did he know? Was it okay with him? He must have trusted his wife to leave her alone for months on end in some remote African village with Yeremia."

"My father was the most honorable man I know. He often took blame for things he didn't do just to help someone he loved. Right now, I'm feeling bad for him. He knew that Judy was not his child, yet he raised her as if she were. When you came along, he probably couldn't take the abuse and ridicule from the missionaries and other whites, though I never saw any of it, so he sent you away."

"I can understand that. Do you think your parents were in love with each other?"

"I wouldn't say they were in love. Like all marriages, they started out being in love and ended up liking each other. I know that Dad loved Mom very much. His world revolved around her. There was nothing he wouldn't do for her."

"His acceptance of Judy under the most difficult circumstances a missionary family can find itself in is, without a doubt, proof of his deep love for your mother."

"Unfortunately, she had to give you up, and you had a hard life in the orphanage."

"But then Judy died after they gave me up. My life at the orphanage wasn't bad all the time. The nuns were often kind. What was hard, regardless of what the nuns did to us or told us, was that I felt that my parents didn't want me. That was my lifelong question. Why wouldn't parents want their children? It was easier for me to believe what one of the orphans told me—that my parents were killed in a car accident. I kept wondering if there was something wrong with me, but truthfully, after I met our mother, I knew that it wasn't me who had problems with my life. It was Dorothy."

Fat Mary, of course, would reassure me that I was precious and perfect in her eyes. I wanted to tell Larry about Fat Mary, to tell him that the survival of my soul was in her hands and that she had taught me to love myself and never, ever give up hope, but I didn't.

"I always wished I had a living sister, and here it turns out I had you all along," Larry said.

"Let me tell you something about your father. A few years after meeting Dorothy, I was planning a trip to Africa and would be in

Nairobi. She had taught at Saint Mary's School there for many years, so I asked if there was anyone I could contact to send her greetings. She seldom discussed anything about her life in Africa, but she said, 'There's a Father Harnett in Nairobi and I still communicate with him. I've already told him about you. He knew my husband well. They were close friends. He's with the White Fathers in Kenya.' She gave me a letter to take to him.

"I did connect with Father Harnett. He was very reserved and spoke in monosyllables except when I brought up your father. I can still hear his words. 'Marshall Reiner was the most honorable man you could find in all of colonial Africa. Impeccable of character and a true Christian. There are three people in my life that I admire most—God, my father, and Marshall Reiner.'"

Larry was quiet. I could tell he was missing his beloved father. So much information about his parents and their lives—it must be intense for him. I wondered if he had ever talked about his parents' life in Africa with them or anyone before.

"Larry, we've found my father. I know you took time from work for this. Do you still want to continue our trip and visit the places you grew up?"

"Yes, we planned it and we're here. I'd like to see my other childhood homes again."

We stopped at the front desk to ask for *lanchi boxis* and were told that they had lunches but no boxes. They wrapped our generous lunches of chicken thighs, fried fish—head and all—boiled eggs, cheese sandwiches, fried potatoes, and plantains in newspaper, and we were on our way.

We went first to the AIMC office and the bishop himself was in. He gave us permission to go and say goodbye to his assistant, our revered Thomas Yegera. The American missionary Mrs. Baker took us to his house. When we arrived, Pastors N'gwan'gwa and Kazimoto were with him again.

At the end of our visit, his parting words to us were, "*Ni Bwana wetu aliyeamuru siku hii. Ndiye yeye aliyeamua mambo yote. Mungu asifiwe.*" (This is the day that the Lord has made. It is all as God ordained. Praise be to God.)

I knelt down near his bed as he put one hand on my head and continued, "He has protected you, our child, for all of your life, and now he has brought you back to us. We embrace you as one of our tribe. May you represent the Nhambu name and the Sukuma people in America. We have been greatly blessed."

To Larry he said, "*Wewe ulikuwa Msukuma kutoka zamani. Karibu tena nyumbani!*" (You have always been a Sukuma. Welcome back home!)

After we shook hands and hugged, Mrs. Baker walked with us to the car. I felt only love in my heart for her. She was everything a missionary should be—spiritual, sympathetic, caring, respectful, warm, loving, and firm in her faith. It was she and her husband who had told us about the old assistant to the bishop. It was he who knew Larry's parents and their servant Yeremia. It was he who recognized Larry from years ago and engaged Pastor Kazimoto to accompany us to the tiny village of Kasamwa where a little angel boy led us to a compound off the road and pointed to a house that harbored an old man trying to take a nap. That old man was what this trip was all about. There was no doubt in my mind that God was our Tour Operator and Safari Guide.

I warmly hugged Mrs. Baker from my heart, knowing she'd forever be an important part of my story.

17

Road Drama

 The first ten kilometers of the road to Kahama via Shinyanga were the kind of road adventure one would write home about. Often on this trip I was very grateful to have discovered exercise bras that were my breasts' salvation. Small as they were, they bruised and ached after every road trip. On the outskirts of Shinyanga, we stopped under a shady tree near the road and ate the food from our *lanchi boxis,* which tasted so much better when unwrapped from newspaper. We arrived in Kahama and went straight to the Canaan Guesthouse, the only place to stay. As Larry and I walked to town after checking in, he told me that this was the last place he lived with his family before he left for college in America.

"I remember that the mission station was very small and had a one-room school. The house we lived in had thick, cool brick walls and a huge thatched roof. The kitchen was separate from the main house across a small yard. Behind the house was a hill topped by those tall rocks (*kopjes*) so common around Mwanza. There was often a pride of resident lions on that *kopje,* and I remember frequent, early morning rock-climbing expeditions with Yeremia to watch the lions. They pretty much left when we arrived. No exciting exploits to report.

"But there was one night when a leopard came around the house trying to get a pet of ours, and our night watchman—I think it was Yeremia again—killed it with his big *rungu* (club). The next morning an amazed Dorothy and Marshall couldn't persuade him that he had done something dangerous. It was all part of his job, he said. I think it was also here that a missionary neighbor killed a twenty-two-foot python. I was quite impressed by its size."

"Who wouldn't be!"

"So far, I see only ruins of the school and ghosts of the houses and shops that used to stand right here."

We bought a few *khangas,* and I was thrilled to find a large classroom map with the countries, the oceans and lakes, deserts, and all the mountain ranges written in Swahili. We strolled around a bit and then returned to the Canaan Guesthouse. After a meal of tea and greasy samosas, we made our way by flashlight to our tiny rooms that featured rusty metal beds, tattered foam bits for mattresses, and no sheets or towels. My room smelled so bad that I doused myself with an entire sample vial of Christian Dior Eau de Toilette from my Le Sportsac pharmacy, which intoxicated me into a deep, rejuvenating sleep.

We left Kahama at nine the next morning and drove on another mediocre road for about two and a half hours when all of a sudden, right in front of us, was an American-style road with a dotted yellow line running down the center and solid white lines painted along the edges. We were so excited! We were sure it was built by Americans. We jumped out of the car and started taking pictures of it from every angle as we admired it. Suddenly, three *askari* with AK-47 rifles pointed at us made us walk backward toward our Land Rover. They asked Fumbwe for his driver's license and the car registration papers. In my very best Swahili, I asked them what was going on.

"Don't you know that it is forbidden to take pictures of a police station?"

"What police station?" I asked looking around.

He pointed to a large "P" on a six-foot-high blue and white sign to the left and said that he saw us taking pictures of the sign. He asked for Larry's camera.

"Don't give it to him," I said. I explained that Larry was a tourist, and we were so happy and impressed to see this beautiful road that we had to take a picture of it to show his friends in America that Tanzania had good roads.

"Only crazy people take pictures of an empty road. Why are you lying?"

I insisted we were telling the truth and proceeded to describe the terrible experiences we've had with the roads so far. I asked him who built the road.

"Italians!"

"Italians?" we repeated, dumbfounded.

The *askari* discussed it among themselves and then let us go. After wishing us a good trip, the lead *askari* scolded me, "You're a native of Tanzania. You know the rules. Next time you're caught, you will go to jail."

We couldn't win with roads! We either cursed them or blessed them, and the one time we praised them, we almost ended up in jail! Laughing over our predicament, we continued on to Kahama.

"Okay, Larry, last night we were too tired to talk, but now tell me about Kahama."

"The town is situated about thirty-five miles from the Mwanza line on the Central Railway, in the middle of Nyamwezi land—the land of the Children of the Moon. The language, Nyamwezi. is almost exactly like Sukuma, so I was once again able to speak fluently like a native as opposed to a *mzungu*. Mom and Dad would use their Sukuma to the amazement of the villagers, and I also remembered the Sukuma intonations, which were slightly different, just as a New York accent is not the same as a Minnesota one. I've been told that my colonial-kid Swahili has a Sukuma accent. This was the last post where Yeremia worked for us. Dad made sure that he learned to read and write and finally sent him off to work as a clerk in the cotton ginnery in Geita.

"Our cook here was a colorful, elderly Muslim named Salehe who had worked as a chef at Government House in Dar. Gone to seed and prone to bouts of drinking, he nonetheless still remembered some fabulous recipes from his glory days. Our dinner parties were the envy of all. He told us a tale of a formal banquet at the governor's palace in Dar. There were fourteen guests and fourteen pieces of fish. One of the guests took two pieces of fish and was told by the server, '*Rudisha moja!*'" (Return one!)

I told him about a flight I was on from Dar to Zanzibar when a passenger took two pieces of taffy, and the stewardess slapped his hand, saying, *"Rudisha moja!"* (Return one!)

18

Mr. VIP

Larry continued telling me about his childhood home. "Kahama is the town I remember most but liked the least. It had little to commend it, being semi-desert with few amenities. I do have one strong, treasured recollection of our family life here, though."

I took notice, because it had occurred to me before that Larry seldom if ever referred to his family in Africa. It was always Mom or Dad or "my parents."

"There was a big, old short-wave radio, the size of a present-day TV set, powered by a car battery, around which the three of us gathered every evening at nine to listen to the BBC World Broadcast. 'Eighteen hours Greenwich Mean Time. Eight p.m. South African Time. Nine p.m. East African time. This is London calling. Here's the news.' Between supper and news time, we'd sit together in the living room, conversing on occasion, but usually each reading a book. When we found something of interest, we'd read it out loud. In these days of multiple channels and home TVs, such shared family evenings are regretfully gone forever."

"At the orphanage we knew there were radios in Lushoto and in the surrounding villages, but I hadn't seen or heard one. We got no news of the outside world except rumors brought back by the children who went home for the weekends or holidays. We used to steal the four-inch square pieces of German newspaper that were cut up for toilet paper. One of us would read the German script, butchering the pronunciation, while the rest of us nodded like it made sense. We would then sit in a circle on the grass or on the cement verandah by the school, guessing and discussing the news from old German newspapers we'd rescued from the toilet."

"It's wonderful to remember so much of our childhoods," said Larry. "How lucky we are that we genuinely want to learn about each other."

"We're not only learning about each other, we are realizing that the life experiences of a *mzungu* and an African in the same country were like night and day!"

I was happy to leave Kahama. There wasn't much to see—just scattered ruins of colonial buildings. We left for Kibondo right after our breakfast of tea, a boiled egg, and sliced green tomatoes over a piece of fluffy white bread.

Arriving in Kibondo, we went to the Tanzania Christian Refugee Service (TCRS) guesthouse where the Simonson's son Nate had made a reservation for us. We were told that all the rooms were taken. We showed the manager our itinerary with the dates of our reservation.

"Sorry," he said. "A bank VIP arrived this morning and your room was the only unoccupied one, so we gave it to him."

"May I speak to him?"

"He's out now, but he's already checked in and his belongings are in the room."

An important-looking gentleman came over to see what was going on. We presented our case to him. He asked to see the reservation book, something we had requested but had been denied. He saw that our names had been crossed out. He asked the manager why he gave away the room when we had made reservations two weeks ago and then insisted we be given a room.

Finally, the manager sent someone to remove the bank VIP's belongings from the room. We moved in and returned to the reception room to thank the man who had interceded for us by asking him to join us for the only drink available—a warm beer in an unlabeled brown bottle. As soon as the beer came, the bank official returned and saw his belongings on the chair by the door.

"What's going on? Why are my belongings here?" he demanded.

The hotel manager explained to him that we had reservations and it was our room.

Our friend tried talking to him, but it didn't help. The banker went on a tirade about the ugly, pushy, racist Americans and how the manager was going to pay for what he had done. As he gathered his belongings, he looked at us and spat on the floor in front of us. "Ugly Americans!"

At that point, I stood up and told him in Swahili (which no one suspected I spoke) that he was an "ugly African" for thinking that he was a big deal just because he was a Very Important bank official. I told him that my brother was a doctor in America, and he would never use such language to anyone, especially to strangers!

"And who do you think you are?" he shot back. "Even if you live in America, you're just a woman and a half-caste at that! As is our custom in Africa, you must apologize for talking back to a man."

"Bloody fool!" I hadn't used the old British swear word since I was a child. Larry was getting nervous and whispered to me to let it go, but I couldn't. "You're half my age and there's also a custom in Africa which dictates that you should never disrespect your elders, especially those who are old enough to be your mother! I will apologize to you, but you must first apologize to me."

To everybody's surprise, he reached out and shook my hand and then shook Larry's hand, saying, "It's my fault, my fault. Please forgive me."

I apologized for the language I used, but not for talking back. He bought all three of us another beer and joined us. The three African men in the room wanted to know where I had learned my Swahili and if they taught such good Swahili in America. Before I had a chance to explain, our intercessor friend replied for me, "In America, everything is possible!"

19

African Hippie

 I woke up with a hangover from hell! I felt so bad that I almost stayed at the guesthouse while Larry went to visit a nearby hospital, but I didn't want to miss the hospital. We visited a rudimentary children's hospital called Kabanga. There, Larry examined the very sick children with tears in his eyes. Most were dying from malaria, dysentery, unnamed parasites, or, as Larry suspected, of AIDS, which had been identified in America a few years earlier. Each sick child had a mother or aunt or other female family member sleeping on a mat on the floor by the bed. They cooked their food outside on the hospital grounds and except for administering medication, took care of all of their children's needs—including bathing and feeding them.

A calm and composed older nurse named Severa took us around to the children in their little cots and spoke about the difficulty of caring for her patients. The hospital had very limited, inadequate, and outdated supplies. She said they had to decide which children could be saved and then would give the medicine to them instead of wasting it on those who had no chance. No matter what the children were admitted for, she told us, most were given aspirin as their only treatment. A few got better, but most died. On each cot was a soft, handmade patchwork quilt that Severa said had come from benefactors in Europe and America.

Seeing the sick children reminded me of my own illnesses when I was young. I had been very sick with typhoid and then with malaria. I wondered if I would be alive today if my mother hadn't insisted that I be transferred to the European hospital where treatment was better and medical supplies were available. I will never forget that day in the hospital and how the children tried to smile and look us in the eye as their family caregivers on the mats below thanked us for stopping by and then offered us something—a banana, cooked sweet potato, a tomato, groundnuts, tea leaves, mango, even a safety pin, and a tattered head scarf.

We left for Kasulu early in the morning and arrived just after noon. Larry was looking forward to seeing Kasulu again, so I didn't have to probe for his recollections.

"Kasulu was by far the most beautiful of the stations our family was posted to. It was by a steep escarpment near a wide, lush river valley. A small hill reached out from the escarpment, making a promontory where the government residences and the *boma* were located. The district commissioner's house was an old German fort at the tip of the promontory, complete with battlements and a heavy wooden door covered with metal studs.

"Our house was next in line about a hundred yards away. It also was German-built with thick brick walls. The living room opened onto a large concrete deck overlooking a flower garden on the top of the promontory, with a long-distance view of the *dukas* (shops) and inns along the river in the valley below. In the backyard was a small rondavel, which was my room. My little hut was memorable for its disarray, for I was not a neat child. I remember the piles of junk—from a Meccano construction set to a chemistry toy lab as well as the first American-style bicycle I made. When we left Kisulu, Yeremia inherited it, though I don't think he was impressed by the homemade bicycle."

"Did *wazungu* kids make their own toys too?" I asked in surprise. "It never occurred to me that they would, especially not bicycles! Usually African children made toys from discarded cardboard boxes, bits of wood and twigs they picked up around the village along with bottle caps, tins, and cans found on the road. At the orphanage, Sister Silvestris saved scraps of fabric and thread for us to make our dolls. My imagination went wild as I made dresses, head wraps, purses and other accessories for my dolls because I envisioned myself wearing outfits like those when I grew up. Maybe that's how I acquired my sense of fashion. It certainly didn't come from the nuns who raised me!"

"I learned from the African children I played with," Larry continued. "They made impressive and functional bicycles, trucks, planes and other toys from wood and any material they'd find around their village. All the credit for the bicycle I made goes to their ingenuity!

"That escarpment in Kasulu led to a plateau about 5,000 feet above sea level. At the first small village, within two miles from the Burundi border, there was a Seventh-day Adventist Mission hospital with an American family staffing it. We visited them frequently. They had planted apple, plum, pear, and peach trees, so we enjoyed temperate-climate fruits from them and tropical fruits from the valley in front of our house.

"I remember going to a Christmas party at our next-door neighbor's house when I was twelve years old. In those days, the water we drank was boiled, filtered, and placed in bottles— usually old gin bottles. I was given my usual homemade orange squash but with the first gulp, I knew that someone had diluted the squash with straight gin instead of water. Apparently, a servant had mixed up the bottles, refrigerating the wrong one. With great maturity and stealth, I said nothing and proceeded to drink the squash as I always had. Since I knew nothing of sipping alcoholic drinks, it wasn't long before my mother was eyeing me suspiciously. She asked me to bring my glass to her for what I figured was my downfall, so I drank the remaining half a drink with huge gulps. She smelled the gin and I was banished to my rondavel. The night was horrible, complete with throwing up and a big headache the next day.

"Did you ever try alcohol again as a child?" I asked Larry.

"Of course! I got very creative finding and drinking the forbidden substance and eventually realized that *pombe* (homemade African brews) put me in a happy mood without the morning hangovers. Needless to say, I joined my little friends whenever there was a village celebration."

"Naughty little boy!" I said, playfully shaking my finger at my big brother.

"While on the subject of childhood embarrassments," Larry continued, "the ultimate one for me occurred when I was on my way home from school in Nairobi. The trip took one week. I traveled by train to Kisulu, then by lake steamer on Lake Victoria to Mwanza, an overnight at the Lake Hotel there, then by rail to Tabora with an overnight at the Railway Hotel, and finally an overnight train ride to Kigoma on Lake Tanganyika. I was instructed by my father, who had to drive fifty-five miles from Kasulu and cross a major river by ferry, that if I ever arrived in Kigoma and he wasn't there to meet me, I was to go to the Revingtons' house, the very same district commissioner and his family we knew from Kondoa.

"At age ten or so and traveling by myself, I was somewhat less than perfect in matters of hygiene such as bathing, teeth brushing, and changing clothes. The only time my dad failed to meet the train I had in fact been wearing the same clothes, including socks and heavy boots, for the entire week without ever bathing and never brushing my teeth.

"The DC's house—a large palace built by the Germans before the First World War for the visit of the crown prince of Germany—was one of three such palaces. The others were later used as hotels in Dar and Tabora. You approached the house via an extensive formal garden, with the carriage drive leading up to a sweeping staircase—which to me in those days seemed like the steps of the capitol in Washington, DC—and then a magnificent marble platform at the top of the stairs. Unkempt and accompanied by an equally disheveled porter carrying my trunk, my personal procession was immediately intercepted by the gardener, who frostily instructed me to wait right there at the base of the stairs while he informed the *Memsahib* (woman of the house) of my arrival. Soon Mrs. Revington appeared.

"I still have trouble telling the rest of this. I was sternly told to strip off everything I was wearing and put on a robe, which a servant tardily supplied, before I put one foot on that magnificent entrance. My clothes were collected by a houseboy and carried off to be burned. I was led by one ear into a bathroom and told to take a hot bath. 'Don't touch anything until you're clean. God knows what vermin you might be harboring!' When my father was told some three hours later, he was mortified! And to this day the memory of Mrs. Revington glaring at me from the top of the staircase some thirty feet away still makes me cringe with embarrassment."

"You know what, Larry, you haven't changed much. I don't mean in the hygiene department, but in your personality and character. You were the original African hippie! I can't imagine a little white boy traveling alone for days across so much of Africa without fear. You loved the land and the people, and they loved you back and protected you."

"My love affair with Africa is still going strong. It's so hard to reconcile the beauty of this country and the care I received from its gentle people with the poverty and hard life I see everywhere now. Africa is not just a part of me, it is me and always will be. We cannot be separated. I must find a way to come back and give back."

As Larry reminisced about his childhood in Kasulu, we approached the picturesque little town and went straight to the district commissioner's house. Larry gasped. "It's nothing like I remember. What happened to the long staircase and the marble landing? Where are the flower gardens and the fruit trees?"

"Larry, even if they're no longer here, don't you ever erase them from your mind and heart. Your ties to and love of Africa will never die."

For a long time after Tanzania's independence, tourists were not allowed to photograph villages, towns, or people as they pleased. So, we had to go to the district commissioner to obtain a permit. At the district commissioner's house, the woman who came out to greet us was one of my classmates from Marian College in Morogoro (now Kilakala Girls Secondary School)! Not only did we get permission to take pictures, she personally escorted us on a tour of the town. She took us to see the Kasulu cultural director who was living in Larry's parents' former house. I was just hoping that Larry would hold it together and that this visit to one of his favorite childhood homes wouldn't be as traumatic as his visit to Kasamwa. He walked around his former home, touching trees and rocks that seemed to welcome him back. The cultural director invited us inside for tea. I was happy to see that Larry was doing fine.

In Kasulu, we were invited to spend the night with two expatriate families. Larry stayed with an American couple, and I stayed with a German family whose two children spoke only German and Swahili. They reminded me of Kifungilo and my German upbringing. The food was rich, delicious, and plentiful, the furniture was stern, the cushions starched and upright, and the house simply immaculate! I luxuriated in the Western amenities like warm water, the indoor toilet with soft toilet paper, good hot coffee, clean sheets, and soft towels. As I slipped into the crisp sheets, I remembered making the starch that the nuns used for their habits from cassava when I was in Mhonda Middle School. My friend Paulina would have to fix my lumpy starch so I wouldn't be punished.

20

David Livingstone, I Presume?

 In the morning the American family invited us for breakfast and after enjoying a typical American egg, cheese, and vegetable casserole, we left for Kigoma. We checked into the Railway Hotel, where a relative of my friend from Usa River, Fatima Faraji, was the manager. Fatima had made reservations for two single rooms for us, but they had only double rooms that cost a lot more. Well, the double rooms cost a whole twelve dollars per night! Larry and I decided to "splurge" and get the double rooms.

The only place we wanted to see in Kigoma was Ujiji. Henry Morton Stanley found the lost explorer, doctor, and missionary David Livingstone there and uttered his famous phrase, "Dr. Livingstone, I presume." Ujiji was an important trade terminal for the Arab caravans coming from the coast of Dar-es-Salaam with slaves and commodities. I recalled learning about Ujiji in high school. The town's architecture showed the Arab influence on the Swahili houses, some of which had wooden doors like the famous ones in Zanzibar, reflecting its predominantly Muslim population.

David Livingstone, a Scotsman, had been exploring Africa since 1840, making several expeditions back and forth from Britain. After two decades, he was well known throughout the English-speaking world, but no one had heard from him for a long time, and rumor had it that he was dead. This precipitated a massive search. An American named Henry Morton Stanley, working for the *New York Herald*, led an expedition and found him in 1871, supposedly sitting under a mango tree in the town of Ujiji.

I assumed that the two small mango trees there now replaced the original tree at this unimpressive monument. A curved nine-foot wall made of large cement bricks had the outline of Africa with a cross in the center of the map marking the exact spot where Livingstone was "found." A little museum in the back had pictures of David Livingstone's early expeditions to the area as well as a mural depicting the famed meeting between the two men, complete with them tipping their hats to each other, just as in my history books.

As unimpressive as the monument was, I felt the weight of history and the love and admiration we had in high school for Dr. Livingstone because of his tireless work against the East African slave trade. Africans called this explorer and missionary "The Good One." He was sent to Africa by the London Missionary Society to try to enforce the laws abolishing slavery that had just been passed in England. He wanted to be a Christian missionary but ended up being known mainly as an explorer.

According to historical accounts, Livingstone died in 1873 as he knelt in prayer in a village hut in what is now Eastern Zambia. His faithful Zanzibari servants cut out his heart, buried it under a tree, and then made a nine-month trip carrying his sun-dried remains wrapped in bark to the coast. There, outside the Mission Church, they set down their burden and solemnly announced, *"Mwili wa Daudi."* (The body of David.)

The tale of that journey from the interior is one of the most moving stories in the annals of African exploration. In Africa's heat, Livingstone's body would have deteriorated rapidly and no one would have ever heard of him again. He would simply be listed as "British Missionary—lost in Africa" as so many explorers were at the time. Yet, by one of those ironies that seem inevitable in Africa, the body, in a new coffin of zinc and wood, was transported from Bagamoyo to Zanzibar on board *HMS Vulture*, before it was taken to London and buried in Westminster Abbey. The Africans, whom he came to save, saved him and his legacy by lovingly caring for his body, transporting it thousands of miles on foot to the coast in order to send him back home to England where he became a hero.

21

Lake Tanganyika

 From Ujiji, we went to the tour office to make arrangements to go to Gombe Stream Park in the morning to see Jane Goodall's chimpanzees. We paid for the boat that carried ten people, yet when we arrived the next day, we were told that the big boat was out of service. If we still wanted to go, they had a four-person canoe to take us there. We took the canoe, which had a motor, and embarked on Lake Tanganyika.

Lake Tanganyika is the second deepest fresh water lake in the world. It has over two hundred fifty species of fish and seven species of crab as well as gastropods, mollusks, and crustaceans. I also heard that it has a unique water cobra that fishes at night and lies on the rocks by day. Whenever I looked through a pictorial book of Tanzania, within its pages was always a picture of a beautiful and haunting sunset on Lake Tanganyika. I was hoping that on our way back we would be blessed with one.

Our little motorboat, called "Fifi," quit twice before we got to Gombe, but we were not perturbed. The sun was out, a calm but steady breeze brushed across our faces, the engine was not loud, and all along the shoreline were narrow fishing boats with colorful fishermen at various stages of preparation for fishing in the dark waters of the lake. We asked the guide, who also ran the boat, to take a picture of us on this mysterious, crystal-clear, and incredibly beautiful lake. As I write in my home office, I am looking at the framed photo on my desk of my brother and me in the tiny boat, basking in the glorious sun over Lake Tanganyika.

It took an hour and a half to get to Gombe. When we arrived, we found the same group of Americans that we saw at the New Mwanza Hotel, traveling with the barebones Overseas Adventure Travel safari that these young people enjoyed. Their transportation was a large tarpaulin-covered truck with benches. They pitched tents, cooked their meals around a campfire, and carried on as if they were camping in America. I enjoyed running into them because it was obvious they were having fun visiting Tanzania and learning about African culture. They could give lessons about how to act on safari in Tanzania to complaining tourists on far more posh tours.

After a brief stop at the main rest house we started our hike with another guide up the mountain in search of chimpanzees. About ten minutes into the hike, we saw three chimpanzees who ignored us. They stretched out on a grassy patch and went about their own business as if they didn't know we were watching them. We continued up the narrow, well-trodden path through the thick, dark, and humid rainforest to the waterfall. A nursing chimp glared at us from three yards up a tree. As Larry took pictures, the chimpanzee relieved herself of number one and number two as she watched us. I swear she was laughing!

"You go, girl!" I said to her.

The loud sound of falling water made us quicken our steps as we came to an opening in the dense forest. There the sun's rainbow rays pierced through the canopy of trees above a pool. Sitting on a rock with our feet dangling in the cool water, we took in the beauty and serenity of the tropical forest. The various loud sounds from jungle creatures didn't perturb us. I don't remember ever feeling closer to nature. Nature was in me and I was a part of it. The waterfall, the soft moss over dark boulders surrounding the pool, the individual trees with multi-shaped and multi-colored leaves, the soft and sweet sunshine, and the chimpanzees all acknowledged my presence. After about an hour, we tore ourselves from this paradise and headed back.

Our OAT friends invited us to have dinner with them at sunset at their camp near the Railway Hotel. We met for drinks and watched the famous sunset over Lake Tanganyika. I gave them an

Aerobics With Soul® dance class under a thatched roof rondavel on the lakeshore. My heart melted with joy and love and thanksgiving as we danced. The Americans let themselves go and danced as though they knew what they were doing! I had a hard time concentrating on teaching because the setting of this dance class took my breath away every time I looked up and saw the velvet gold and amber lake become part of our dance.

Apparently, I was not the only one carried away by the magic of the moment. After class the OAT guide told me, "I don't know what was more beautiful—the sunset over Lake Tanganyika or watching you dance!" I knew that what he felt was the beauty of my soul blending with the beauty of nature. He got it!

At the start of the dancing session Larry had been upset because his camera was in the car, and Fumbwe had gone to look for diesel for the next day's drive, so no pictures.

"A beer calmed me down enough to forget about taking pictures," he told me later, "and I let myself get carried away by the spectacle before me. I found myself quietly watching, tapping my feet, sipping my beer, but mostly trying to fight back tears of overwhelming joy."

At the close of the evening, we said goodbye to the OAT group, and the next morning we left early for Kibondo. When we arrived at the same TCRS guesthouse, lo and behold, who was there to meet us but the VIP banker with whom we'd had our run-in and then became friends! We dined together and spent an enjoyable evening with him.

Before we left Kibondo, Mr. VIP warned us that it had been raining heavily, and he'd heard reports that the road from Nzega to Singida was impassable. He advised us not to try to drive back to Arusha in one day and suggested a guesthouse along the way. Larry and I thought *déjà vu*—what road could be worse than the tsetse fly-infested, dust-bowl tunnel we took from Seronera to Mwanza?

We were wrong. Very wrong! We drove past Nzega thinking it wasn't so bad, but a few kilometers ahead we saw that Mr. VIP was right. I kicked myself for ignoring what I knew for a fact—when an African tells you that the road is bad, it means there is no road!

It turned out to be the worst road of the entire trip. There literally was no road. It was washed away and had become part of rivers and lakes we had to drive across. We saw trucks and cars sitting every which way in the water and wondered why we thought we would have better luck. We chugged along in the water aimlessly and desperately until we had a better idea. Catching long twigs floating toward us on the "road," we used them as depth finders. Larry and I took turns wading in waist-high, muddy water with our twigs in front of us, feeling around for solid ground to guide Fumbwe and the Land Rover. He drove three yards forward and one yard back as we zigzagged for hours among debris, mud, and the wading, exhausted animals.

Our trip to Arusha took fifteen hours instead of the usual seven. This was a total anti-climax to what I had already dubbed "a spiritual trip of a lifetime." It took us a long time to physically recover. Our bodies ached for days and we moved in slow motion.

Back in Arusha, while sitting at the Simonson's dining table, I stared at Mount Meru as if I were seeing it for the first time. I was not myself. I was a different person from yesterday and especially from the day before. A week of intense anticipation, anxiety, and euphoria had now left me physically, mentally, and spiritually spent. The fatigue affected my mood. I felt that I held something so very personal and private, and I didn't want anyone to take my story, run with it and turn it into news for public consumption. My heart felt heavier and heavier. I couldn't understand how the euphoria I experienced a few days ago could turn into the depression I felt coming on. I didn't want anybody to ask me anything about my journey and my discoveries. I asked Larry to keep my father and the details about our trip a secret until I figured out what to do with this newfound information.

The Simonsons were anxious to hear about our trip. I love them dearly and they have always been extremely kind and caring to me, but I found myself resenting them for asking if I'd found my father. At first, I hesitated, but eventually I told them that I had, and I shared the essence of our trip. I talked about the village, and I skimmed over the intense sentiments of the reunion. I didn't want to be questioned any further. "It's all so new and overwhelming that it will take me a while to sift through the drama and trauma before I can talk about it publicly."

"We fully understand," Dave said.

"We're just so happy for you that you now know your father. We prayed for this outcome and God answered our prayers," Eunice said with hands crossed over her chest.

22

The Price of Identity

That morning I accepted who I was and was comfortable with the truth. I had been brought up in an orphanage, received the blessing of a lifetime to go to America, had Cathy who loved me as a mother, found love in my husband and children, had met my birth mother, and in the last two days, had encountered the last piece of the puzzle that was my identity.

But why did I feel so hollow today when only a few days ago I was bursting with happiness? Why was I so uncomfortable talking about my father? Why did I feel like some threads and colors were still missing from my life's tapestry? Could it be that I had become so at home with the facts of myself as an orphan that I was now a stranger to my new identity, like people who lose a lot of weight have trouble adjusting to being thin? Maybe I was afraid of having a large extended family that had played no role in my life so far, and now I had to decide how to relate to them. In the discrepancy between our incomes and lifestyles, would I feel responsible for alleviating their poverty? Did I want to play an active role in my large African birth family, or did I simply want to know my father? As a child, when I prayed to find my mother and then my father, finding siblings never entered the picture. I was beginning to understand the saying that urges us to be careful what you pray for, because you might get it.

When I got back to the States, I casually told Kjell, Kata and Karl that I had found my father and that his name was Yeremia Manoni Nhambu. I asked them to keep it to themselves until I was ready to tell others, and they agreed. But based on Kjell's reaction and enthusiasm when I had found my mother and considering how little

I trusted him in matters of the heart, I didn't expect that he would keep his promise this time either. Sure enough, it was only a matter of days before one of our friends called and said that she knew it was a secret but Kjell had told her about my father. "Here we go again!" I said to myself. Whenever I confronted him about breaking a promise to me, he had a convincing answer. Nothing was different this time.

"This is such exciting news," he said. "How can you ask me to keep it quiet? I know everyone will be happy for you."

What Kjell didn't understand—and seemed incapable of understanding—was the pain of rejection and abandonment, and the loneliness of never having had a father, mother, or family to call my own. He didn't understand that it was my pain, my sorrow, my fears, and my story that he was invading and celebrating and claiming as his own to tell to whomever he pleased, whenever he chose. He had no appreciation of or empathy for how I felt sitting at a dinner table or in a roomful of his business acquaintances while he told my story as if I weren't there. It seemed that the only important thing about my childhood for him was the story, rather than the person whose story it was. I wondered why he took so much pleasure telling my story. Did he secretly believe that marrying me gave him ownership of my life story as a marital asset? How come Cathy, Kata, and Karl understood?

They respected my wishes and they instinctively knew that it was *my* story to tell, not theirs. The few friends I eventually told understood it too—but not Kjell! He continued to take my story and make it public, made it his to tell, surprise, and inform whomever he wished to impress with the inside scoop about me. His actions reminded me of the media frenzy we see so often on TV in America whenever there is a sad or bad story to report. He kept telling me that there was nothing to be ashamed of because everybody would be "blown away" by it.

To tell the truth, I was never ashamed of my story but I also never enjoyed telling it. Until I decided to write my memoirs, if you wanted to hear my story firsthand, you'd have to drag it out of me in bits and pieces, and you would have to be a person I considered a very good friend indeed. I have never been ashamed of who I was. I was insecure and lonely and often I felt rejected, but I was not ashamed of me. Fat Mary always reassured me that I had done nothing to be ashamed of.

You are a child of God, and this knowledge along with his grace taught you early in life that you should dwell on your blessings and give your hurts and disappointments to me for safekeeping. Others who have not lived your life and taken your journey may project their attitudes on your story because they have no other frame of reference than their own.

Without a doubt, the biggest blessing God bestowed on me was giving me Cathy at a very critical time in my life at the end of high school. It was a turning point for me. I was ready to return to Kifungilo where I would probably remain until it was time to be married off to the next man who came looking for a bride. Without Cathy, I don't think even Fat Mary, with her deep understanding of me and my uniqueness, could have foreseen my adult life.

Cathy, Katarina, and Karl were big blessings in my life. My husband Kjell, on the other hand, was a mixed blessing. I knew that he loved me, but he also made me feel as though I should be eternally grateful that I was married to him. I often asked myself if someday it would occur to him that he could also be grateful that he was married to me. Did I add anything to his life? Even in my most skeptical moments, I convinced myself that he loved me to the best of his ability. I read that some people can love a barrelful and some can love only a thimbleful. I also often wondered if he loved me for me, or if he loved me for himself.

It took several months before I felt comfortable enough to talk about finding my father. My news was always received with tears of joy, hugs, laughter, and dancing! Whenever I was alone, I would relive the day I met my father over and over again for months on end.

23

My Garden of Eden

 I had a father now—a father who wrote me long, hand-written letters on lined, green notebook paper in Swahili. I pictured him writing to me and remembering our meeting and his lifelong care for me when he was forbidden any knowledge of or contact with his daughter. My connection with him was deeply meaningful and I looked forward to hearing from him. He gave me news of family members and progress on the house we were building for him. Larry, Kjell, and I were sharing the cost. I wrote back and sent photos and money to him via Sister Catherine, a Maryknoll nun now working in Mwanza who was my teacher at Marian College, and she took him to the bank to exchange the money.

Now it was time to take my family to Africa to meet Yeremia. I felt joy and pride that I would finally be able to present Katarina and Karl to the grandfather they didn't know they had. Kata was twenty-one and Karl was almost fourteen. Cathy had just turned fifty and for her birthday, Kjell and I gave her a ticket to return to Tanzania for the first time since she left the country with me in 1963.

In early August of 1991, Kjell, Karl, Cathy, her daughter Eleanor, and I left Minneapolis on a KLM flight for Tanzania. Katarina would join us later. Eleanor was a year older than Karl. Although she was my little sister whom I adored and loved, it took a while before she understood our family connection. As a child she was always humming and singing, especially at mealtime. No wonder she grew up to become a talented singer and musician. I was looking forward to her spontaneous entertainment during the trip.

We were full of gratitude, excitement, and amazement at our good fortune. Kjell didn't mind that Cathy and Eleanor were joining us on our trip, but he warned me point-blank that they were not going to Kasamwa, my father's village, with us. He told me in no uncertain terms that meeting my father for the first time was "a family affair."

Using his frequent flyer miles, Kjell upgraded Cathy and Eleanor to business class. Every time I turned to look at them as we sat upstairs in the Boeing 747, they were so full of smiles, you'd think they were gliding through the heavens on their personal silver cloud. Their happy faces would help me ignore Kjell in case he really meant to exclude them from accompanying us to my father's village.

As soon as we arrived in Amsterdam for our day-long layover, Kjell left us at the Airport Hilton Hotel and went to meet his friends who had flown in to look at a boat they wanted to buy. We had made plans to visit the Anne Frank house, but Kjell somehow forgot what trip he was on and returned too late for us to go into town.

This time, the long flight from Amsterdam to Kilimanjaro seemed very short. Before I knew it, we were in Arusha at David and Eunice Simonson's home having a meal at their welcoming table overlooking Mount Meru.

After lunch we drove to Tarangire on a new and beautiful road. As our Land Rover pulled into the parking lot, we were greeted by the welcoming crew who'd come to carry our luggage to our rooms. Kjell and I stayed in a bungalow, Karl had his own tent, and Cathy and Eleanor shared a tent. After giving thanks for our safe arrival, I bemoaned the fact that we would be in Tarangire for only a couple of nights.

A force propelled me to the platform overlooking the Tarangire River where I stood in awe of the glorious panorama that leisurely stretched on and on in front of me as far as the eye could see. The panorama of rolling hills and valleys—with hundreds of ancient baobab and acacia trees that must have provided food, shelter, and shade to the offspring of the original animals and birds that left Noah's Ark—pulled me into the land. It is one of my treasured pleasures in life to sink into the rugged armchairs under the gigantic thatched roof of the reception area and watch the parade of animals in the valley as they maneuver into position to drink from the river, taking turns and choosing their spots. This powerful Garden of Eden absorbs me into its mystery and history, and at the same time, it can reduce me to a speck, an insignificant grain of sand in the face of its majesty.

Whenever I stay at Tarangire Safari Lodge, I request a bungalow. Like most Africans, I am deathly afraid of wild animals, so sleeping in a tent ranks high on my list of feared activities—right below riding a donkey down into the Grand Canyon! The stone wall of our bungalow separates us from the tents a few feet away. But we might as well be in a tent because we can hear everything going on in and around them, especially the animals' nighttime pursuits and the snores of other travelers.

I recall the nights I spent in a tent before bungalows were built at the lodge. The night air is cool and forces me to enter my tent and slide under the covers, even though I'd rather stay up and attend to the multitude of strange sounds that will keep me awake my first night in Africa. Instead of counting sheep, I start pairing animals with their sounds and wondering if I will be lucky enough to see them on the morning game drive.

I'm wide awake. I realize jetlag is interfering with my sleep, so I tune out the night sounds and take a moment to curse the time difference. Right after, I remember to thank God that I'm awake, because I'm thrilled to hear a lion's roar in the valley. Then my heart starts pounding because I realize the lion is not far away. In fact, it's prowling boldly around the tents. I hold my breath when I hear elephants stomp the ground and fling their trunks as they tear at the baobab tree nearby. They sound like giant saws cutting the trunk as they noisily tear out chunks and rhythmically chew them. When they pee, a powerful waterfall suddenly pours onto the earth outside the tent. Immediately, I smell the pungent urine that cuts a ditch into soft dirt inches from me. No matter that I've experienced lions and elephants by the tents many times and that I know they've never attacked, I fervently pray that this will not be the exception. When

I hear them inhale and exhale so close to me, I tremble under the covers until they move on.

Throughout the night various dramas play out. Hyenas in the valley strut around like gang members, laughing and taunting each other as they patrol the game reserve, challenging each other to brazenly steal another animal's kill. Wildebeests and gazelles nervously prance around the bushes, hoping to see the dawn; baboons alternately snore and copulate all night long; zebras lie in zigzag heaps, keeping each other warm in between the tents. I shake like a leaf because I'm sure a leopard has chosen me for a night meal. From the corner of my eye, I see a pair of yellow dancing eyes peering through the canvas like searchlights. During the day, I'd consider a sighting of the shy animal a blessing, but at night, the stare of a simple serval cat is enough to stop my heart! I promise God that I will do anything for him if he transports me to the land of sleep.

When I wake up, I'm surprised by the lightness and joy in my heart. A multitude of birds compete for my ear as they sing their individual melodies. The sun slowly lights up and warms my tent, and before I get out of bed, I say a prayer of thanksgiving for once again having survived my first scary but blessed night among God's creation.

24

Cathy Returns to Kifungilo

My brother Larry and his girlfriend Carolyn had come from Boston to go on their own safari, so we all were able to spend time together on this trip.

After breakfast our group left for Lushoto and Kifungilo in Eunice's brand-new, powder-blue Range Rover. Kjell drove the entire way and we enjoyed the spectacular Usambara Mountain range. We cut our way along the winding, narrow roads with high escarpments on one side and precipitous drops only inches away from the road on the other. Now I understand why missionary priests who came for their yearly retreats to Kifungilo called this road from Mombo to Lushoto the "highway to heaven." Compared to their own primitive mission posts in remote areas of Africa, beautiful and tranquil Kifungilo—perched high in the mountains with its crisp, pollution-free, eucalyptus-fragrant air and a sky that burst into a dome of fiery stars every night—must have seemed like heaven on earth.

I recalled a conversation I'd had with Abbas, a driver on one of my earlier trips to Kifungilo along this same road. I loved talking to Abbas because he was a wise and gentle Muslim from the Sambaa tribe around Kifungilo. His shiny dark skin lay wrinkled upon his small face and his pupils were hidden behind a gray-white film over his sunken eyes. He was well-respected by all the other drivers because he was old (late fifties), knowledgeable, and very kind. He loved it when I spoke Swahili. He once told me that even though I now had an accent when I spoke Swahili, it was the "Queen's Swahili" not diluted by slang and Africanized technological English words like *kompyuta* (computer) or *rodibloki* (road block) or *kaunta* (counter) that had crept into the language.

"What I like the most about hearing you speak Swahili is your voice. You sound like an angel. You should come here and help our youth discover the beauty and lyrical sound of our language. You should hear how some of them swear nowadays! Their Swahili sounds harsh and angry. Not only have they lost respect for their culture and heritage, they treat their elders as if they are stupid and no longer relevant."

He was not the first one who told me that I sounded like an angel, yet I couldn't help but wonder if most people's voices didn't sound loud and rough to Abbas compared to his own gentle and sweet one.

"Having been brought up in the orphanage where we spoke a mixture of Swahili, German, English, and Sambaa, I had no opportunity to learn swear words. My bet is that the nuns didn't know any!"

He was too respectful of the nuns to smile at my comment. "I've heard of a nun from Kifungilo who walked for miles to bring food and *dawa* (medicine) to villages. I left Lushoto a long time ago, so I never met her. But she's well-known and liked by everyone in my village."

"That was Sister Silvestris, and I was probably with her on her visits when I was at the orphanage. I carried her supplies—aspirin, sugar, hard candy, tobacco, used clothing, holy water, and the Bible. She was often called when someone in the village was dying. She would drop everything and rush to baptize them."

"Even the Muslims would let her into their homes at the time of death," Abbas remarked. "The Muslims called her after the potions and rituals of the *waganga* (medicine men) failed."

"I wonder if they knew that she often secretly baptized them so she could win another soul for God and eternal life in heaven. Pouring water on their foreheads and reciting prayers probably seemed just as mysterious to them as the rituals that *waganga* performed."

"When people are dying, they will accept help from anyone. Whether the villagers understood what she was doing or not, as long as they trusted and believed that she was there to help them, her religion didn't matter."

When we passed the sleepy little town of Soni Falls, the child-hood emotions that lay in my heart and memory resurfaced. I felt fearful, alone, and abandoned at the same time as I felt chosen and privileged to be visiting Tanzania with my family. Now, as an adult, I've come to look at myself as the embodiment of "mixed blessings."

In Kifungilo my family and I stayed at the priests' retreat house again. The food was every bit as wonderful as I remembered. We did our usual walk around the grounds, this time accompanied by Sister Monica, the headmistress of the girls' secondary school that the orphanage had become. We visited the classrooms where the girls just about fell off their seats when I spoke Swahili to them. I told them about my work involving African dance in America, and I did a few steps from several tribal dances I had learned while I attended Marian College Secondary School. They laughed and shouted with delight when they recognized their own tribal dances.

We passed by the dispensary and clinic that provided treat-ment to neighboring villagers. At a well-baby clinic, mothers were taught how to care for their children. Some of the children sang for us as Eleanor passed out chewing gum. They had happy and healthy faces—not the sad and desperate faces often seen in fundraising videos.

On our way to the church, I demonstrated how as children we rang the large bell hiding under a canopy of dense ivy. Our group stopped and prayed in front of the statues that we children had helped Mother Ancilla make. I pointed out where the Nativity scene stood at Christmas in the back of the church, where I used to pray ardently to Baby Jesus to help me find my mother. On this day an old resident priest greeted us. He was wearing the same garb worn in my time over forty years ago—white tunic, black shoes and socks, black braided sash, and huge silver crucifix hanging from a thin red cord over his chest.

Our next stop was the Sisters' kitchen with its huge twelve-burner, wood-burning stove from Germany. Little had changed. Now, as in my time, narrow shelves against one wall were full of jars of homemade jams and preserves, canned peaches, pears, and plums in heavy syrup, pickled onions and cucumbers, and several tins filled with homemade cookies and fudge. In a tiny screened cupboard sat butter vats and aging cheeses in various shapes, sizes, and colors; on the floor stood large containers of milk, fresh from the cows, waiting to be boiled.

We walked along the old irrigation canal edged by blooming white calla lilies and passed by the cows, sheep, goats, rabbits, ducks, chickens, and turkeys on our way to the vegetable and fruit gardens. An A-shaped cabinet of wood and glass held a photo of the priest who founded the Order of the Precious Blood Sisters. Inscribed on it was "*Mit Gott, Fur Gott, Es Geht.*" (With God, for God, so it goes.)

Nearby was a large pond teeming with goldfish and framed by a beautifully landscaped maze of zigzagging paths with multicolored flowers. The main path took us to a quiet spot that was very special for Cathy and me. This tranquil scene was exactly the same as when Cathy and I sat there twenty-eight years before. Tall, slender cypress trees planted close together shaded the circular pond and welcomed us to sit again on the same warped, wood bench like we did in 1962. The ground was soft with fresh green moss and a scattering of dry pine needles and acorns from the trees above. It cushioned our tired feet now as it did so many years ago.

The place where Cathy asked me if I would like to go to America with her is forever engraved on my mind and heart. It is the sanctuary that guards the miracle that brought us together. Little Baby Jesus from the Nativity scene answered my Christmas prayers here. He gave me my mother—not my birth mother, but my mother.

I remember how nervous Cathy was then. She wasn't free to tell me about all the effort it took to make that day possible. She'd spent many months doing her homework, and she knew more about me than I did. Like everyone else, she had believed that I was an orphan with no family except for the nuns in Kifungilo. She contacted Mother Clotilda, a dreaded nun from my childhood, who, as Mother Superior at that time, was uncharacteristically helpful. She told Cathy that I wasn't an orphan at all!

They contacted my mother, Dorothy, who was teaching at Saint Mary's School in Nairobi. This time, after many requests by several families to adopt me during my childhood, Cathy was given permission—even though she was only four years older than I was. The fact that she was an American and would take me to America and put me through college, is perhaps what made the difference. Also, Dorothy was planning to leave Africa for good that same year, and whether she'd admitted it or not, she must have worried a little about what would become of her grown child at the orphanage.

With an American birth mother, I was entitled to an American passport, and Dorothy wrote to the American embassy with proof of her citizenship. Knowing that hospitals at the time did not issue birth certificates, and the colonial government courts did not record African births, I wonder what proof she gave that I was indeed her child and was entitled to American citizenship. Without my mother's participation, it would have been impossible to leave Tanganyika. I am forever grateful and indebted to her that when it really mattered, she stood up and claimed me as her daughter, even though she forbade Cathy to mention a word of her existence to me.

Many years later, Cathy told me that getting me a passport was a nightmare! If it hadn't been for Hubert Humphrey, a family friend of hers who was then the Democratic senator from Minnesota in Washington, I might never have realized my childhood dream of coming to America. It was through Senator Humphrey's personal intervention that I received my American passport as my birthright. Years later, when I met him in Minneapolis, all I could say when I greeted him was "Thank you for helping me obtain an American passport." He remembered Eugene Murray, Cathy's father, as a dyed-in-the-wool Democrat and dismissed his beyond-the-call-of-duty involvement in my case with the declaration, "I'm always happy to claim any new American for the Democratic Party!"

I wondered if Cathy, who worried so much about so many things, had started working to find me a scholarship in America before she even knew if I'd accept her offer to take me away from the orphanage forever.

All the feelings we experienced so long ago came back to both of us as we sat on the bench holding hands, tears in our eyes. Cathy and I had come a long, long way from 1962 and this serene place that witnessed the miracle of our story.

Cathy, Eleanor, Kjell, Karl, and I continued our quiet procession on the shaded path and climbed the road along the Stations of the

Cross that took us to the cemetery, where I retold the story about the nun who cared for me as an infant. Sister Theonesta carried me around in her large apron, and whenever she made the Stations of the Cross, I'd cry every time she genuflected at a station. The other nuns were convinced I was responding to the drama of Jesus' crucifixion until they realized I was hitting the ground at each station! I suppose she didn't notice the bump I felt each time I hit the ground at all fourteen stations! The love and care she gave me was the closest thing to motherly love that I had in my infancy.

In the cemetery we stood at the grave of Sister Silvestris whom Cathy, Kjell, Kata, and Karl had met. Sister Theonesta was buried near her. The founders of the orphanage, Mother Ubalda and Mother Ancilla, were in prominent spots near the ten-foot-tall wood and metal crucifix at the center of the cemetery. Dear old Father Jeakel lay nearby.

At the grave of Zahabu, the woodcutter, I told the story of how when he met Kjell for the first time in 1974, he invited us to the tiny hut that Sister Silvestris had built for him. He was so proud of it because now he had a metal padlock and his possessions would be safe. Once our eyes adjusted to the darkness inside, we saw a bed of wood and straw, a couple of three-legged wooden stools, a tattered blue wool blanket, some green metal cups, a large aluminum spoon, and ragged clothes on a pile in the corner on the dirt floor. His favorite possession, a black felt bishop's hat, full of moth holes, sat in the center of a narrow table. His face glowed in the dark with pride and joy when he put on his hat for us to admire.

"*Nitazame! Nitakapofika mbinguni nitakuwa askofu. Nataka nizikwe na kofia yangu ili niichukuwe mbinguni. Nisipokufa kwa muda mrefu, panya watamaliza kofia hii!*" (Look at me! When I get to heaven, I will be a bishop. I want to be buried with my hat because I want to take it to heaven with me! I must hurry up and die before the rats finish eating the hat!)

He searched his tiny ht for something to give us, then finally gave Kjell two small over-ripe tomatoes and an egg, saying, "*Hii zawadi yenu!*" (This is your gift.) Kjell graciously accepted the gifts and passed them on to me. We shook his hand and thanked him.

He laughed long and loud with satisfaction when he saw that he had made us happy, and I laughed with him in return because his toothless mouth and ancient face was the same one I knew so well from childhood.

As we left Zahabu's grave, Karl said to me, "Mom, I think when someone gives you something even though they need it, that's a gift from the heart and is much more meaningful than buying something from a store."

"You're right. So often, especially among the very poor in Tanzania, I've seen this kind of giving—giving from your need, rather than from your excess."

Next was a visit to the dormitories we children lived in from the time I was ten until I left Kilfungilo at nineteen. When I was little, the big and little girls slept in one large room, with the little ones sleeping two or three to a bed. The little boys slept in the dormitory with the little girls for a few years until they, too, got their own dormitory near the old schoolhouse. When the big three-story building was finished, we called it "the new house." At the time it seemed like a castle. There were separate sleeping spaces for the big and little girls, and each of us now had our own narrow, wrought-iron bed instead of rough, homemade wooden ones. The ceramic Eastern-style toilets were located inside between the two dormitories.

This "new house" had a refectory (dining room) with several long wooden tables and benches, and a recreation hall on the first floor with an old organ that was played on feast days. Sister Silvestris' room was at one end of the big girls' dormitory on the second floor. I showed Eleanor and Karl what used to be my bed.

Because Kilfungilo was a government school now, students had mosquito nets and little cabinets in which to store belongings. When I lived there, the third-floor attic had clotheslines to hang laundry when it rained. That's where we kept our small wooden suitcases and trunks (made by Zahabu) with all our treasures—a favorite dress, a pair of feast day shoes, homemade dolls, crocheted berets for church, letters we wrote to each other on scraps of paper we found in trash baskets, and anything we considered precious—including groundnuts (peanuts), a shilling or two from visitors to the orphanage, a colorful leaf, smooth pretty stones, buttons, ribbons, and hairpins. Despite having padlocks on the boxes, stealing occurred. This inevitably resulted in hunts for the thief, false accusations, and a fight between the thief and the victim—and invariably culminated in a thorough beating with a cane by Sister Silvestris if the crime was reported to her.

On either end of the attic were the rooms where Sister stored the many boxes of clothing and shoes donated to the orphanage from Europe, mostly from Germany. In the weeks before Christmas, she'd take us to the attic so we could choose a dress and pair of shoes as our presents.

25

Blessed Martin's Statue

While the others returned to the guesthouse for a little rest before dinner, I went to visit with Blessed Martin and Fat Mary. At the place where Blessed Martin's statue had stood was a small, nondescript building. I knew it was the right spot because I recognized the dandelions and bits of lawn that remained around the new building and in front of the sewing rooms. I felt empty and asked out loud, "Where is Blessed Martin?" It felt like a big part of my past had been ripped away. I knew Kifungilo was no longer an orphanage, but how could anyone remove the statue that was the most meaningful for the orphans?

I sat down near the building at the spot where I had buried the doll I got from my best friend's mother when I was five. As soon as I did, Fat Mary appeared.

No one can remove Blessed Martin from your life. No one can erase the beautiful memories of the time you spent playing with your beloved friend Elizabeth by the statue. The only constant in life is change. You prayed to Blessed Martin to change your life, to take you away from the orphanage, to find your mother, and to get an education. You, too, have changed. But as long as your inner self—your heart and soul, which makes you a unique human being—does not change, nothing important is lost. You do not need a statue to keep your memories of Blessed Martin. You still have him the way you did when you were a child. Nothing is different except the physical location of his statue.

I hugged my dear friend and companion and went to join the others at the guesthouse. Fat Mary always knew how to cut to the truth about a situation. I walked around the back of the old school building. There was Blessed Martin leaning against the wall of the school! He looked exactly the same as he did years earlier. I took a scarf from my purse and cleaned the bird poop from his cape and continued to dust all of him—his head with its short frizzy hair, his sunken eyes, the short cape over the long one that went from his shoulders to his ankles, his hands with long, thin fingers holding a crucifix, his robe which came down to his shoes in vertical folds, and the foot-high pedestal. It felt good to be close to him, even though he was so compromised. "I guess the students in the government secondary school don't need or want you, or care about the important role you played in so many lives," I said to him as I brushed off the neglect.

Talking to him made my orphanage life come alive, and memories raced back, mostly memories of my beloved friend Elizabeth. She and I and Blessed Martin were inseparable. The last time I saw her was before I left Kifungilo to go to a boarding school two hundred miles away. When I returned at the end of the school year, I was told that Elizabeth had run away and no one knew where she was.

26

Masange Primary School

 After dinner Cathy and I sat in the long living room on the same upright chairs with crocheted doilies that we had sat on years earlier. I asked her how she felt being back in Kifungilo after so many years.

"I've been teary-eyed most of the day, but I held it together," she answered quietly. "It keeps coming to my mind over and over that Dorothy should also be here with us. I feel her presence and the role she played and still plays in all our lives."

"As my birth mother, she should be one of the main characters in the story of my life, yet because of the choices she made, she will forever hover in the background, just like she did when she was secretly taking care of me when I was here. She stayed in touch with the nuns and got reports about my progress and such, but I had no idea she existed. For selfish reasons, I've always wished that she'd written her story about her life in Africa. Can you imagine how fascinating it would be? It would make Karen Blixen's *Out of Africa* seem like a generic colonial fairy tale. I once asked her to write her life story, but true to character, she chose to take her story, which is my story too, with her to the grave."

The next morning, we walked to the little village of Due that seemed a stone's throw away but was about two miles on foot. When we arrived at Masange Primary School the children who had been waiting for us all morning greeted us with a song.

Karibuni wageni wetu wapendwa
Mliotoka sehemu mbali mbali

Hii ndio shule ya Masange
Karibuni mjisikie nyumbani
(Welcome our beloved guests
Who've come from far off places.
This is Masange School.
Welcome and make yourselves at home.)

This was the same dilapidated rectangular building divided into classrooms that Larry and I had visited three years earlier. The physical structure was still in a sorry state. Nothing had been done to fix the gaps and missing parts of the roof, walls, and ceiling that were now wide enough to suck a little child out of the classroom in a windstorm. It was hard to believe that the happy children who just sang for us could learn anything in such an environment. They filed into their respective classrooms, and we visited each, giving the children pencils and notebooks, which made them stand up, sing, clap, and dance with gratitude.

On the front row of the second-grade classroom was a little *zeruzeru* (albino) girl. I wondered if she was related to the family in Mkuzi with several *zeruzeru* children that Sister Silvestris took special care of and often took us to visit. She would provide them with long-sleeved dresses and hats for protection from the sun, and ointments for their open wounds. This little girl was sitting alone on a long desk, looking dejected and bewildered. Sores at various stages of crusting ripped her lips open and some were swollen with pus. Red scabs and large, dark skin patches resembling enormous freckles covered her face and exposed skin.

Without melanin for pigment under the hot African sun, albinos tend to die early from skin cancer and other illnesses that seldom affect the general population. When the children stood up to sing, she stood up too, but I noticed that she was not singing. My heart ached for her. To be an African albino is much harder than being an albino from a country in another region like Scandinavia. Parents loved their albino children, but sometimes they also believed that such children were a curse from God. They would hide them in the huts, not only to keep them from ridicule, but to protect them from the weather extremes of the Usambara Mountains. Albino children live even shorter and more difficult lives in a country where the average life span is brief and a hard life is the norm. Albino children are considered pure and special and are at times sacrificed in rituals to ward off illness and bad luck. Many also suffer because of the myth that having sex with albino virgins protects from or cures AIDS. How brave of this little girl to go to school! Would she live long enough for her courage to pay off?

In Lushoto, we stopped at the dentistry to visit Sister Eileen. We found her sitting outside, under a poinsettia tree, wearing a large plastic apron and surrounded by buckets of water and cotton bags filled with plaster of Paris powder. In several little boxes were mysterious-looking metal contraptions and instruments. She explained that she was making dentures the old-fashioned way by mixing plaster of Paris with water, kneading it to a smooth mixture, and filling the metal denture impression trays. After letting them dry a few days, she would break open the metal trays with a hammer and painstakingly scrape off the excess rock-hard plaster around the impression to leave a smooth set of teeth. She worked on them a little bit every day and finally polished each tooth, finishing up with an enamel coating and preservative. After a couple of weeks, she said, a grateful *mzungu* would come to pick them up. We were fascinated!

27

That's My Mary

It was time to leave. A deep and heavy sadness grabbed me like it always does whenever I have to say goodbye to the region of my childhood.

We said our farewells and then began the long drive to Dar-es-Salaam, the capital of Tanzania. Six hours later we arrived at Bahari Beach Hotel on the Indian Ocean. The rondavels with their thatched roofs gave the hotel the look, but not the feel, of an African village. Unfortunately, as so often happens in African-run hotels, maintenance was not a priority. All of us immediately acknowledged that we'd been spoiled by the delicious food, starched and embroidered bedding, impeccably clean toilets, well-maintained grounds, crisp, clean mountain air, and the deep serenity and isolation of Kifungilo.

It was refreshing to see mostly Africans in the hotel as guests, not servants. In the past few Africans could afford to stay in such a hotel. Tanzania had its political ups and downs during and after *Ujamaa*, a one-party s,ystem established under its first president, Julius Nyerere. Although *Ujamaa* was based on the African concept of "familyhood," it could not survive in its purest form, and in 1985 a most remarkable thing happened in Africa. A sitting president chose to retire, declaring that he wished to pass the reins peacefully to a new generation. The new government evolved into a democratic republic with a multiparty system that brought more development and progress to its citizens. With the majority of the population being Muslim, it was fitting that Ali Hassan Mwinyi, a Muslim, replaced Julius Nyerere, a Catholic, when he retired.

In the dining room the next morning, seated at the table next to us was my orphanage childhood friend Imelda, her husband Dallas, and their four boys from America. I knew they were traveling in Tanzania, but I never dreamt we would run into them. Our two families blended into one, and we spent the day together being tourists, visiting attractions, buying souvenirs, and trying not to complain about the miserable conditions of the rooms, the food, and the service, because we understood the situation.

Kjell had lined up a visit with Mr. Kitomari, the tourism minister. Watching him speak to the minister, I realized again how Kjell would come alive in the presence of someone he considered important. After quickly introducing us, he ignored us while the two of them outdid each other with insincere compliments and exaggerated formality.

We seemed invisible to him. "Why is Kjell so thoughtless and self-absorbed?" Cathy asked. "You never talk about it."

"After twenty-three years of marriage and his admitted affair, I've learned to pick my battles. I've been keenly aware of what you just observed. Once, when I was pregnant with Karl and we were at a car dealer convention in Europe, we joined several dealers at a bar after dinner. Kjell ignored me the entire evening to the point that I was sure he'd forgotten I was there, sitting alone at a table for four. I tried repeatedly to get his attention. He was doing his usual routine of praising himself and bullshitting to impress and influence others. Actually, I was often embarrassed for him. It was obvious that he couldn't see that not everyone admired him as he admired himself. I don't know if it was because I was pregnant and therefore more emotional than usual, but I started feeling abandoned and sorry for myself. After about an hour of this, I became angry. I decided that it made no difference to him whether I was there or not, so it wouldn't matter if I left. I walked out into the cold night, ordered a taxi, went back to the hotel, and got into bed.

"About two hours later, Kjell walked into the room and was fit to be tied! 'What in the world has gotten into you? Why did you leave without telling me?' he sputtered. 'You know these meetings are all about networking, and I have to take advantage of every opportunity to do so while I'm in Sweden.'

"I asked him why he couldn't have taken a minute out of his networking to check on his pregnant wife. He just fumed that I had forced him to walk to the hotel in the cold, because I had his billfold in my purse. Apparently, he couldn't borrow money from his important networking buddies. One of the things that surprised me the most about the incident, Cathy, was it never crossed Kjell's mind that something could have happened to me. He was mad and upset because I inconvenienced him and embarrassed him in front of his new best friends."

"No matter what it looks like to others, those of us who know him, know that Kjell is for Kjell," Cathy added.

"Kjell is a good man and a good father to our children. He has qualities that I like and admire. I keep reminding myself that I am not a saint by any stretch of the imagination, either. I've got to take the good along with the bad. For me, at this point in our lives together, the good outweighs the bad."

"The problem is that the bad is so baaaad!" Cathy sighed.

"I believe he loves me and I know that I love him. But what he wants from me and from everyone is to stroke his ego, and I've never been good at that!"

"He does an excellent job himself. Don't you remember what Dorothy said a couple of days after meeting him? She told us, 'Kjell is very pleased with himself.' That was so perceptive."

"As you know, Cathy, I'm big on counting my blessings. In spite of his flaws, he has contributed a lot to those blessings. I am always grateful for the lifestyle he has afforded us over the years, and he is very generous, not only to me, but to my friends too. I don't think there is anything I have ever asked him to get or to do for me or my friends that he hasn't done or at least tried to."

"Now that's my Mary talking!"

Whenever Cathy said that to me, which she often did, I could never figure out what she meant. Did she mean *That's my Mary* who endured so much as a little girl and who now believes that what she's experiencing with Kjell is so much better that she should just tolerate it? Or is it *That's my Mary* who believes that she's unworthy of being loved because her mother took her to an orphanage and all glory should go to Kjell for loving her now? Or *That's my Mary* who believes that any kindness Kjell has shown her should be repaid with everlasting praise and gratitude?

I'm hoping she meant *That's my Mary* who has survived much harsher humiliation and patronization than what Kjell dishes out and is with him by choice. *That's my Mary* who knows full well that no one is indispensable in her life, including Kjell, and that when the cons outweigh the pros in her marriage, her keen survival instinct will kick in.

In Dar, we went to see the Village Museum, or *Kijiji Cha Makumbusho* (literally "Village of Remembrance"). The outdoor museum covers a large area. Huts of various sizes, shapes, and forms of construction represent the largest of the more than 120 tribes of Tanzania. For some unexplained reason, we were not allowed to take pictures at the museum. Forbidding tourists to take pictures at the only tourist attraction in Dar seemed like bureaucracy gone mad! Not only were we watched very closely as we walked in and out of the huts, but outside the museum Kjell was arrested for taking pictures and videotaping the State House. Two policemen with their AK 47s pointed at him ordered us to follow them to the police station. They had been watching him videotape two majestic Arab dhows on the Indian Ocean, and when he continued with a panoramic view of the harbor, he supposedly filmed the nearby State House.

I explained in Swahili that we did not intentionally take pictures of the State House but were simply photographing the ocean and the harbor. Kjell played what he had filmed for them. After about fifteen minutes of viewing, they realized we were telling the truth. Their mood changed from accusatory to amazement as they saw photos of the places we'd been before coming to Dar. They especially enjoyed the pictures of animals and asked us about the game parks, which they had never been to. Instead of criminals, we were now entertainers and educators. They thanked us profusely for the video show and let us go with a warning about the prohibition against taking pictures of official buildings, which included government offices, schools, hospitals, museums, and airports. Thinking back to what Larry and I experienced on our trip three years ago, I wanted to add "new roads," but I didn't. I wondered how they dealt with satellites orbiting in space that could take pictures of anything, anytime.

We had been invited by my friend Abdu Faraji to visit him at his apartment while we were in Dar, so we set out, vague directions in hand, asking people along the way for help finding his place, which he had said was near the Yeyitch Club. Kjell stopped several Africans and politely asked them if they knew how to get to the Yeyitch Club. They all knew the place very well, but each gave him different directions. After driving around for a while, Kjell got frustrated and decided to ask the first *mzungu* he saw for directions.

"Good afternoon, sir," Kjell greeted him. "Would you know the way to the Yeyitch Club?" The *mzungu* look puzzled and said that he had lived in the neighborhood for a while but had never heard of the Yeyitch Club. Kjell thanked him., As we were pulling away, the *mzungu* called to us, "Do you mean the Yacht Club?"

We burst out laughing! Of course—the Yacht Club! Seems like from Abdu on down, the Africans pronounce the word phonetically. How would they know that "yacht" is pronounced "yawt"?

With Cathy we went to see Mr. Chonya, the director of the Community Development Trust Fund (CDTF), the organization that allocated the monies Operation Bootstrap Africa raised for building schools in rural Tanzania.

After learning that Cathy had come many years ago to teach at Marian College, Mr. Chonya, a good and humble man, thanked Cathy for taking a year out of her young life to volunteer. "Thank you for your work in helping us build the country at a critical time in our history. I beg you not to be disappointed when you see that the fine foundation you laid is practically destroyed. We at CDTF, with help from abroad and especially from America through Operation Bootstrap, are doing everything in our power so that your sacrifice will not be in vain."

Cathy was deeply touched. I could see that she was trying to say something, but when she nodded, the tear drops that had swelled behind her glasses rolled down her cheeks one by one.

Nyumba Ya Sanaa, the House of Art, that the Maryknoll Sisters, including Sister Antonita, my art teacher at Marian College, had worked to establish in Dar was the next stop. It still supported artists and artisans. The Sisters would have been proud. The center offered a great variety of good and reasonably priced African art and artifacts for sale, including ebony carvings, batik paintings, batik fabric, silk screens, woodcuts, caftans fashioned from *khanga* and *kitenge* fabrics, dresses, T-shirts, greeting cards, placemats, and magnificent jewelry made from colorful ceramic and glass beads, local seeds, and brass. Besides serving as an outlet for cottage industries to sell work to tourists, it also employed handicapped people.

From here we went to visit the Ebony Carvers on Bagamoyo Road. Rows and rows of little shacks with corrugated iron or thatched roofs held the fantastic Makonde ebony carvings for tourists and locals to buy. For those who like to bargain, this was bargaining heaven. Tourists traveling with me on safaris have proclaimed me the patron saint of bargainers! I bargain African style for myself and for them.

To be successful in the art of bargaining, it's necessary to engage in back-and-forth banter by joking, ignoring what you want to buy, ridiculing the price, and even walking away so the seller thinks you're no longer interested in the item. He will then lure you back by lowering the price. I usually end up having the upper hand and can pretty much name my price. Luckily for the seller, right after I've won the back-and-forth bargaining, I usually feel really bad when I realize how much the item would cost in America. When I consider how well off I and most tourists are compared to them, I feel ashamed of myself, and I end up paying close to and sometimes more than what they originally wanted. Kjell never understood why I bothered to bargain in the first place!

I explained to my Norwegian husband that it's "an African thing."

Learning Tribal Dance

 In the morning we packed our ever-expanding suitcases and squeezed them into our overloaded car for the trip to Morogoro and Marian College, the high school run by American Maryknoll Sisters that I had attended. Cathy was my Oral English teacher and coach there. The school, now called Kilakala Girls Secondary School, had seven hundred students. Celestina Amri, a former Marian College student Cathy and I both remembered fondly, was the principal. She was happy to see us and we reminisced about everything, especially the plays that the drama club staged each year, since she was quite the actress and Cathy quite the drama coach!

As we walked around the campus, what I saw with my eyes clashed with what I saw with my heart. The buildings were run-down, but some effort had been made to maintain them. The flower beds between buildings that we used to water daily now had nothing but brown twigs in parched soil that couldn't remember once filling the air with sweet fragrances that accompanied us on our walks from class to church, to the dining room, to the library and dormitories. I visited the last dormitory I slept in. It was the closest one to the Sisters' convent. We behaved when we lived there because we thought that the principal, Sister Dolores Marie, whose room faced our building, could see everything we did.

Sister Dolores Marie was a saint in our eyes. She understood so much about her students' hard lives at home. She showered us all with love and gave us plenty of her time to talk about our lives. She left America for Africa with no experience and became an instant and beloved mother to nearly three hundred young African girls from sixty tribes. I have always loved Sister Dolores Marie, even though she discouraged Cathy from adopting me and taking me to America. I now fully understand her reasoning. She was protecting Cathy from the insecure, moody, and troubled teenaged, half-caste girl who might expect more from her than she could deliver, or worse, never understand the mother-daughter relationship, take advantage of her, or never adjust to life in America. I'm eternally grateful to Cathy for listening to her heart on this one. Without her intelligent heart overriding much of the advice from others at the high school, I might never have come to America.

America turned out to be the land that took me the way I was and opened doors that might forever have remained shut for me—doors to education, service, employment, and travel. But the most important door America opened for me was opportunity. Luckily, from childhood I had already discovered the door of faith. Faith in God and in myself. That knowledge sustained me when I discovered that America would not automatically or necessarily heal my childhood wounds. I saw that issues of abuse, self-worth, poverty, race, and hatred were not unique to Africa. I met and dealt with them everywhere in America. Had I not come with Fat Mary in my heart and Cathy as my mother, and had I not experienced unconditional love from her, I seriously doubt that I would be the person of value I know I am today. America gave me the opportunities, but it was individual people who helped me succeed.

That day I sharply remembered Mary Rose Ryan—my former name—of years ago, who spent so much time in the recreation hall we were visiting. It looked nothing like I remembered! Missing was the piano where I played a duet with Sister Mary Ward for the Overture to the *Mikado*, the Gilbert and Sullivan musical that the Drama and Glee clubs staged. It was a major production, complete with brilliant green, yellow, blue, and pink satin kimonos and elaborate wigs made out of dyed black sisal. We formed singing and dancing groups that competed for prizes. In my group, the three of us called ourselves Sunny, Happy, and Smiley. We often sang songs by Elvis Presley ("Hound Dog") and the Everly Brothers ("Devoted to You") that we learned from 45 rpm records. We played the records on a gramophone, trying to decipher the English lyrics, which we belted out with butchered pronunciation and no comprehension whatsoever! I asked Celestina if she knew what became of my posse—Stella and Theresa. She hadn't heard anything about my two friends.

In this hall students from many tribes learned each other's tribal dances, a requirement imposed by the Sisters. Every Sunday evening we danced our hearts out on the large cement floor, imitating students from other tribes and showing off. This requirement shaped my life. Back then I had no way of knowing that our joyful dancing in this recreation hall, where my soul was nourished weekly by dance, would lead to creating one of the loves of my life! Years later, I modified the dances and steps I learned in this hall, commissioned music, got certified by the American Council on Exercise, and created *Aerobics With Soul®*—a fitness program based on African dance. I am grateful to the Maryknoll Sisters for seeing value in African dance and encouraging us to learn and treasure it, while so many other missionaries encouraged Africans to abandon their cultures as they became Christians.

Judy, Larry's half sister, who died at age four. She was Nhambu's full
sister.

Larry, Nhambu's half brother, with his parents, Marshall and Dorothy Reiner, and Judy, Dorothy's daughter with Yeremia.

Grave marker for Judy, Nhambu's sister.

Nhambu meets her father Yeremia for the first time.

Larry and Yeremia, who worked for Larry's parents
as a cook and household servant.

Nhambu and her father, Yeremia, the day they met.

Nhambu and Larry on a boat crossing Lake Tanganyika
on the way to Gombe Stream National Park.

Kjell, Eleanor, Nhambu, Kata, Karl, and Cathy
on their trip to meet Yeremia.

Karl and Kata on the ferry across Lake Victoria on their way
to meet their African grandfather.

Kopjes are a prominent geological feature in parts of
Tanzania. These are in Lake Victoria.

Kata, Kjell, Perisi, Yeremia, Karl, and Nhambu
when the American family met Nhambu's father.

Traditional Sukuma ceremonial pots that Yeremia
commissioned as gifts for Nhambu and her family.

Mlekwa, Nhambu's half sister, one of Yeremia and Perisi's
three daughters.

Nhambu with Yeremia holding the handwritten recipe notebook
he used when working for the Reiners.

Yeremia Manoni Nhambu.

Yeremia and Nhambu in front of his original house.

Yeremia in front of his new house with three of his sons, Perisi, and Nhambu.

Yeremia, Perisi, Nhambu, Kata, and Karl along with other family members.

Nhambu with her father and brother Amani.

David and Eunice Simonson, Lutheran missionaries who worked with the Maasai in Tanzania and founded Operation Bootstrap Africa.

Eunice Simonson in front of their African-style house.

Sister Eileen and Nhambu with
the Usambara mountains in
the background.

Statue of Blessed Martin,
now Saint Martin de Porres.
He is the patron of mixed-race
people and racial harmony.

29

More Malaria

 Our journey continued to Mikumi National Park near Morogoro where we spent the night in a beautiful, fairly new hotel. Karl and Eleanor swam in the pool, watching huge marabou storks and a lone bull elephant pacing around the pool.

On our way to Dodoma the next morning we had to deal with elephants, giraffe, and zebra sauntering casually along the main road that crossed the Mikumi Park. Dodoma, because of its central location, had been named the new capital of Tanzania, but someone must have forgotten to inform the operatives in the old capital of Dar-es-Salaam of this fact. Dar would never concede to playing second fiddle to any other city, especially not Dodoma! Granted, Dodoma was centrally located, but it was a remote, miserable, and desolate town located in a region that qualified as semi-desert. We passed several modern office buildings under construction on our way to the Railway Hotel to spend the night.

Between Dodoma and Tarangire is the little town of Kondoa, where Larry and I found his childhood house and my sister Judy's grave three years earlier. Upon arriving in town, we drove straight to the house and to the overgrown cemetery in the bush, which didn't appear to have been touched since our visit three years ago. I combed the tall grass and bushes with a stick until I found Judy's grave marker. I wished Kata had been there.

Emotionally it was nothing like when Larry and I saw the grave for the first time. Cathy, Kjell, Karl, and Eleanor gazed at the tombstone in complete silence. They looked at me and their unspoken questions about my mother's life in Africa and the secrets she took to her grave met with the quiet surrender I felt about not knowing the whole truth. We were bearing witness to the secrets of my parents' lives at my sibling's burial place.

To change the mood, I asked Cathy about how she felt being back at Marian College, and she said, "Africa feels a little like my life. So much of what I expected to happen has not. It has spread out its enthusiasm for independence and progress all over without being a real success in anything."

"What success do you wish for your life?"

"As I said, I feel just like Africa. I can't verbalize exactly what that means. I define my life as having bits and pieces of what I hoped to achieve, but nothing has been concrete or fully realized."

"You must feel 100 percent fulfilled when it comes to what you were trying to do for me. Look at me! Don't you feel proud of what I've become? How many people would or could do what you did at age twenty-three? I know I disappoint you often, especially on this trip, when it comes to my enjoyment and use of money now that I actually have some. But I could tell you at least twenty other things you have done right in your life so far, and everyone who knows you could too."

Karl was very quiet. I thought it was because he was confused and sad about my whole childhood situation, so I asked him how he was doing.

"It's unbelievable to be able to be here and to actually see the grave of someone who was your flesh and blood. I just wish I felt better. I have this dull headache that interferes with my thinking and talking."

"Have you been taking your malaria pills?"

"Yup."

"When we get to Tarangire, you can rest."

"I can't wait to lie down, but I wouldn't have missed this experience for anything!"

Karl definitely did not look well that night. I touched his forehead and he had a fever. I gave him aspirin and another dose of the malaria prophylactic we were all taking at the time, and he fell fast asleep before dinner.

That evening Kata arrived on the KLM flight, drunk and throwing up. Her fear of flying often incapacitates her, and she will not go near a plane unless she takes tranquilizers or drinks throughout the flight. Kjell picked her up from the airport and she went straight to bed.

When I went to see Karl in the morning, he was awake but not quite alert.

"How are you feeling this morning?"

"I slept well, but my body hurts."

"We have one more day here before we leave for Mwanza. I hope both you and Kata will get some rest and that you'll feel up to the trip to meet your grandfather."

The next morning both kids were ready to go, though Karl still looked gray and weak. We piled into Eunice Simonson's Range Rover and the Serengeti Select Safari's Land Rover and our two cars headed to Ngorongoro Crater. Karl threw up repeatedly most of the way but looked surprisingly well when we arrived. We drove down into the crater—the world-famous volcano caldera teeming with wildlife. Both of my children were feeling well enough to take in the spectacle, exclaiming their amazement with joy and exuberance.

The next morning, Karl didn't look well again, but he insisted that he was ready to travel. When we got to Ndutu, another lodge in the Serengeti where we had planned to spend the night, it was clear he had full-blown malaria. He alternately shook the bed as he shivered from chills, and then perspired from a fever of 103. He was also throwing up and was just generally miserable. I remembered how awful malaria felt from my bouts of it. We decided to stay in Ndutu as long as necessary for him to feel better before traveling on to Mwanza. We ended up staying three extra days. On the morning of the fourth day, he said he was ready to go meet his grandfather, although his skin now looked a bit green and the whites of his eyes were yellow.

Our rooms at the New Mwanza Hotel were something else! For starters, there were used condoms scattered all over the floor in Kata and Karl's room. The once-white porcelain Western toilet was a rusty dark brown with little bugs floating in the putrid water that reached the top of the bowl that had no seat or cover. I went to the reception and told them that the room hadn't been cleaned. They were given another room, which was a little better. We always traveled with toilet paper, washcloths, and towels, but here was the first time we had to use all three.

I stayed awake all night thinking about the next day. My father was coming to meet us at the hotel after breakfast, then we would go to his little village of Kasamwa. I prayed that Karl would continue to feel better and that Kjell would not be on my case about Cathy and Eleanor meeting my father with us. Did he really think I would make them stay in their rooms and then come down afterward? Did he even want them to meet my father at all?

After this trip, you will have come full circle! Fat Mary knew that I was anticipating an argument with Kjell. *You will present your family to your father. What your husband wants is what he wants. That's all! Without Cathy, he would not have met you. She made your family possible. She should have the pleasure to witness the miracle she set in motion with her love. Kjell feels that she is intruding because he doesn't understand matters of the heart. He cannot see the sacrifices she has made for you, him and your children.*

30

African Grandfather Meets American Grandchildren

 Kata and Karl would be meeting their African grandfather soon. This meant so much to me, but how would the communication with their grandfather go? Yeremia didn't speak English and my kids didn't speak Swahili. I thought of Larry, who had made this meeting possible, and all we went through to find the African side of the family.

Karl announced, "He's here!"

Kata, Karl, Kjell, Cathy, Eleanor, and I hurried out of our rooms. Before heading downstairs, Kjell took me aside and said in an exasperated voice, "The kids should meet their grandfather without Cathy and Eleanor butting in. They should wait and come down later."

I so thoroughly disagreed with him about this that I just walked past him and went downstairs. My father had traveled with another man and they were sitting by a table in the lobby. As soon as he saw me, he stood up. After we greeted each other, he looked at my children and said, "*Nawatambua Katalina na Kawal kutokana na picha ulizoniachia, safari ile.*" (I recognize Katarina and Karl from the photos you left with me last time.)

I introduced Katarina then Karl and they hugged. My father smiled from ear to ear when he said, "*Mungu wangu! Watoto wako wanafanana ne wewe na mama wako.*" (My God! Your children look just like you and your mother.)

Kjell was introduced next, and I could tell that my father was uncomfortable when Kjell hugged him. Apart from Larry and me three years earlier, I doubt that he had hugged another white person, male or female, in the last thirty years.

I then introduced Cathy and Eleanor. *"Huyu ni yule mama nilio-kueleza kwamba alikuwa mwalimu wangu, halafu alinichukua Merikani kunisomesha na kunitunza, na huyu ni binti wake."* (This is the lady I told you about who used to be my teacher, then took me with her to America to educate and take care of me, and this is her daughter.)

"Nashukuru sana mama. Wote tunashukuru." (I am very grateful, Mama. We are all grateful to you.) He then introduced his companion. *"Huyu ni kaka yako Joni."* (This is your brother John.)

We shook hands. He was a very thin and very serious man who looked almost as old as our father. He continued to hold my hand, then took a couple small steps back and proceeded to check me out. *"Safi sana! Nimefurahi sana kukuona leo."* (Very nice! I am very pleased to meet you today.)

Glad I passed inspection, I thought.

We sat on both sides of a long table, and Kjell ordered soft drinks for us and a Tusker beer for John. My father continued with the habitual lengthy African greeting, asking about every aspect of each of our lives as I translated.

"I wish so much that I spoke Swahili," Kata said to her grandfather.

"Na mimi, maskini sisemi Kiingereza! Ninafahamu kidogo tu." (And poor me, I don't speak English. I understand only a little.)

When my father was satisfied that he knew as much as possible about Kjell, Kata, Karl, Cathy, and Eleanor, he announced that it was time to take the ferry to his home.

When we arrived at Lake Victoria about fifteen minutes away, Kjell and Fumbwe drove the two cars onto an old tub of a ferry named *Uzinza* while the rest of us walked on, aware that we were being observed with curious attention. Once on the ferry, Cathy and Eleanor climbed back in the Land Rover, while the rest of us squeezed single file along the railing, the only space that didn't have cars, trucks, or cargo. We settled in for the forty-five minutes it took to cross. I stood close to my father. It wasn't every day that *wazungu* took the ferry, and I heard all sorts of explanations from the passengers about who we were and why we were there.

"The old man lives in Kasamwa and is very rich. He is building a huge house with cement, glass windows, and a corrugated metal roof," a well-dressed woman with a child on her back volunteered.

"Wait, one of the *wazungu* is speaking Swahili. Listen," said her friend with beautifully braided hair.

"How can a white lady speak Swahili like us?" asked a tall, thin woman in the group.

"Shhh!" She put her index finger on her mouth. "If she speaks Swahili, she can understand us!"

"She's not a *mzungu*. She's *hafu-casti*. Look, even though she's dressed like a *mzungu*, her skin is quite dark, and she has the telltale signs of a mixed person—dark blotches on her face. And look at her hair. The color is uneven, and the texture is frizzy and as curly as the springs of a metal bed." Everyone laughed.

"She has to be African. Look at the bright clothes she's wearing," said the mother with the child on her back.

"She's African for sure. All mixed up, but African."

The group laughed and gave each other high fives. Their conversation continued.

"Congratulations to us. One of us has made it and passes for a *mzungu*," the woman with braids proclaimed.

"The young ones are the children of the *mzungu* man and woman. They are not as white as their parents. I read in a newspaper that in Europe white people prostrate themselves to the sun for hours and beg God to make them Black. But God never really makes them Black like us."

"I'll exchange my black color for theirs if they want it."

"I think the young ones are afraid," said a very short woman who waited for a turn to speak.

"What are they afraid of?"

"I heard that Europeans are afraid to come to Africa because they think we'll eat them."

"You're crazy! Europeans couldn't be so dumb."

An older woman approached the huddled group of gossipers and in a good-natured voice said, "Why don't you mind your own business?" It was easy to tell that she was related to them because they laughed, greeted each other, and asked about relatives. "I know the whole story. The driver of their Land Rover told me that the one who speaks Swahili is the daughter of the old man and those are her children," the older woman said, pointing to Kata and Karl. "When I asked who their father was, he said he would tell me for a price! Of course, I refused."

"I think their father didn't come."

"I heard that the white couple [Kjell and Cathy] with their one child [Eleanor], who is in the car with her mother, are missionaries."

"It must be. No *wazungu* would take the same ferry to our village with us."

"If you had given the driver your bananas, we would know the whole story."

Well, I thought to myself, the women will have lots to talk about to their families and each one will recount her own version.

When the ferry docked at Kamanga, it was exactly like when Larry and I came—confusion everywhere! A colorful and vocal group of people—gesturing, pushing and shoving, carrying bundles and baskets on their heads while holding the hands of little children and grandparents—tumbled out of the ferry. They dispersed and soon vanished into narrow streets and paths that started at the lake and led to villages miles away.

Our two vehicles were on the road again, with Yeremia in our car.

The roads were worse than I remembered. Pouring rain turned a two-hour trip into three hours. My father laughed when he saw me take pictures of the water-filled, pot-holed road we were driving on.

"What are you going to do with those pictures?" he asked.

"I'll show them to my friends in America, so they appreciate the roads they often complain about."

Our little two-car caravan finally arrived in Kasamwa. Even from the street we could hear hustling and bustling and pounding noises coming from Yeremia's compound.

Women and men dressed in colorful *khangas* and shirts filled half the compound. Their singing was almost drowned out by workers pounding on the roof of the new house that Larry, Kjell, and I were building for Yeremia.

As we approached the compound I had flashbacks to the first time I set foot in this remote village. I briefly felt again the despair in my heart and a sinking feeling in my stomach because this had been the last place left for us to look for my father. If we didn't find him here, our long trip would have been in vain. It's a blessing that we cannot fully re-live past emotions, because when I entered this compound back then I was scared, anxious, and nervous!

My family cautiously followed behind Yeremia, who repeated, *"Karibuni nyumbani, karibuni nyumbani!"* (Welcome to my home! Welcome to my home!) A woman dressed in a light blue *kitenge* with large bright red fish printed on the fabric came running toward us with outstretched arms. She extended her hand to greet my father. They spoke a few words in Sukuma and then he introduced her.

"Huyu ni mama wako. Anaitwa Perisi." (This is your mother. Her name is Perisi.)

"Yes, I am your mother," she said. "Always call me Mama."

"Shikamoo Mama!" I said as we shook hands. Her warm acceptance of me contrasted sharply with the memory of my birth mother who refused to let me call her "Mom."

Perisi didn't wait for further introductions. Turning to Kjell, Kata, and Karl, and then to Cathy and Eleanor, she took each one's hand and, holding it in both of hers, shook it many times. Giving a broad, welcoming smile, she repeated, *"Karibuni, karibuni familia kutoka Merikani."* (Welcome, welcome, my family from America.) When she finished with us, she went to our driver, Fumbwe, and shook his hand too.

Looking around, I saw about sixty men, women, and children sitting and standing to one side of a large house that stood where Yeremia's tiny, thatched roof house had been a few years ago. Workmen on the roof pounded away until my father asked them to stop. He introduced us to the building contractor, who told us that it was the largest house he'd built in the village. When we approached the house, the crowd followed us with smiling eyes, filled with wonder and excitement about relatives from America. They stared at Kjell, Cathy, and Eleanor, but not as much at Kata, Karl, or me.

31

My Father's House

The very first thing my father did was to give us a tour of the house. I assumed that the group of people who came along for the tour was immediate family.

Inside, my father introduced us to the rest of the family. Two aunts, one uncle, other siblings, and fifteen of his twenty-one grandchildren. We first went to the sitting room, which was painted bright blue and had a map of Africa on one wall and a large handmade poster of the family tree on another wall. We settled into the old-style colonial, straight-back wood sofa and chairs, and my father proceeded to tell us who was who in the family tree and where they were now. He told us that three brothers had died and two were unable to come to meet us. From the family tree and my date of birth, I saw that I was the second of my father's thirteen children and Judy was the first.

The house itself was made of cement bricks, and the walls were plastered smooth and then painted in strips of white, pink, and blue. The large square windows had glass slats with iron grates on the outside.

There were five bedrooms besides the master bedroom. On one of the beds in the master bedroom was a medium-sized cardboard box with a flashlight and all kinds of contraptions made of twigs, cloth, and string, and tiny patchwork blankets. This was Perisi's homemade incubator that she used to care for the village's premature babies. She told us that even though she had never gone to school, she was the village nurse and midwife. She couldn't remember how many preemies she had nursed to health in that little cardboard box and given back to the happy mothers. Gently, she picked up a tiny baby girl from the box who was hardly larger than her hand, saying she was one of the smallest she had cared for. But she was confident that after a few months, the infant would be ready to go home.

A storage room was filled with sacks of charcoal, beans, and rice, along with hoes, brooms, empty boxes, plastic bags, piles of firewood, and a lopsided red wheelbarrow. Even though the house was nowhere near finished, the family had fully moved in.

We returned to the sitting room, and my sisters brought in the rice, chicken, pickled tomato, and cooked banana stew along with bottled water, Coke, and Fanta. Yeremia stood up and read from the Bible before blessing the meal. Then Perisi took one item at a time from a large straw basket my sisters had brought in and passed it to Yeremia.

"These gifts are for you to take to America. When you arrive home, you will have a remembrance of your Sukuma family." My father repeated this sentence as he presented each of us with a small traditional Sukuma clay pot. The ritual pots had been made specifically for us and were given with love and pride. The ones for men had cows on the lids and the ones for women had birds. The male ones were for drinking special homemade brew like millet beer; the women used theirs to carry the brew to the men. The bottle-necked ones with no lids were to hold water to wash hands before eating and the wide-mouthed pots were for serving food. We were very moved by the thought that went into commissioning and making these special tribal vessels. They were precious to us and I knew they would bring us back to this room whenever we looked at them in our homes in America.

I was a little embarrassed when it was time for us to present our gifts. Even though most of our gifts were special requests from them, and I was excited when I purchased them, now they suddenly seemed materialistic, insignificant, and superficial.

We had new clothes for them—a pair of trousers, sweaters, a shirt or T-shirts, a dress or blouse, a comb, soap, and toothpaste. The kids jumped with glee when they received their candy, gum, notebooks, pencils, and sunglasses with fluorescent frames. My father loved the fluorescent sunglasses. He took a bright lime green pair from a granddaughter and wore them during the meal. Kjell brought a canvas bag full of his used shoes and clothing for the men, and I gave a bag filled with my clothing, shoes, and bling from Wal-Mart, which the women loved!

Both adults and children tried on their clothes and opened their gift bags with big smiles and a million *"Asante sanas!"* (Thank you very much!)

When the noise level subsided a little, I presented Perisi with the one item she had requested—a boom box! When she saw the box, it didn't matter that she couldn't pronounce anything, she joyfully read out loud: AM/FM/SW/Radio/Stereo/Cassette Recorder! She paraded around the table, laughing and dancing better than any of her grandchildren as she thanked God and us for the boom box.

Fredy, a brother who lived in Dar-es-Salaam, grabbed the box from her and announced that only he knew how to use it since he'd seen many, even bigger ones than this in the city. Luckily, we also brought batteries, and after Fredy installed them, we tried to find a station with dance music, but all we got was some spirit-possessed Christian preacher who said the end of the world was near. He wouldn't get a single convert from our gathering that day! Everyone was in a celebratory mood and some even tried to dance to the radio preacher's rhetorical warnings. My father suggested that Yotham bring his Gospel Choir cassette to see if the boom box really worked for what they needed it for most—to play music cassettes in church. Before the cassette arrived, the box was passed from person to person and everyone pushed or pulled or tapped a button on it. The two-foot rectangular boom box was the biggest they had ever seen—except for Fredy, of course. A grandchild, about six years old, almost flew off the floor when he pushed a button and activated the multi-colored disco strobe lights that pulsed and flashed lighting up the dark room. What joy!

When the cassette arrived, everyone danced to the Christian Choir singing *"Mungu Mkubwa!"* (God Is Great!) with the disco lights flashing. Even Cathy and Kjell danced. We picked up the little ones and danced with them and passed them to each other. The smallest grandchildren were fascinated by and a little scared of Eleanor's lily-white skin. As they danced, they eyed her and kept their distance, even as they imitated her dance moves. My sisters thought that Kata and Karl were good dancers and asked if I had taught them.

"No," I answered. "But they've got our African dancing gene!"

Here in this tiny village of Kasamwa, in a small room packed with family, we danced, knowing that everyone appreciated the joyful and carefree expressions of love and gratitude emanating from mind, body, and soul. When I glanced at Karl, I saw that he had stopped dancing. He told me that his heart was dancing, but his body was still a little weak from the malaria. I thanked God that he was here. I feel my children will forever remember this day and this moment. We are proof that it is possible to be racially diverse, speak different languages, live on different continents, belong to different faiths, and still be One Big Loving Family!

When the dancing subsided, I asked my father if he had anything left from the time he was with my mother.

"*Nina sanduku lake.*" (I have her trunk.)

"Is there anything in her trunk?"

"*Kitu kimoja tu.*" (Only one thing.) He walked from his corner in the room and went down the hall to the master bedroom. A few minutes later, he returned holding a small notebook with a faded red cloth cover.

"*Hiki kilikuwa kitabu chetu. Alinifundisha namna ya kupika kizungu. Angalia! Huu ni mwandishi wake, na huu ni wangu.*" (This was our special book. She wrote down recipes and taught me how to cook the European way. Look! This is her handwriting, and this is mine.)

He gave me the book and the American contingent gathered around me as I flipped the brown, water-stained pages. I saw that my parents had used Swahili, English, and Sukuma interchangeably within the same recipe.

Biscuits *ya* Soda, Pancakes, Chocolate Cake, Love Cookies, Cheese Soufflé, Chocolate Pudding, Spice Cake, Nut and Date Cake (*Keki ya Matende*), Pound Cake, Sugar Cookies, Lemon Whip (pudding *ya Malimau*), Sponge Cake, Doughnuts, Butterscotch Pie, White Cake with Water, Crumb Cake, and God Cake. Several of the recipes were written entirely in Sukuma by my mother.

I asked my father if he cooked only desserts for my mother.

"My cooking was well known among the missionaries because Mama Doloti taught me how to cook European desserts. It was not necessary to teach me African cooking."

He told me to take the book to America and cook the desserts for my family. I thanked him and put the precious notebook in my purse.

Perisi announced that she had something to say. First of all, she thanked God Almighty without whom nothing is possible for bringing her newfound family across the ocean safely to the little village of Kasamwa. For ten minutes she recited all that she was thankful for. The most often named item on that list was the house. She had tears in her eyes when she compared the quality of her life before and after the new house was built. She recited several areas of her life that had changed drastically, including having a place to keep her beloved preemies and having a place for their children and grandchildren to call home and come home to without the shame of poverty.

Yeremia added gravely, "*Mmenipa heshima kijijini.*" (You have given me respect in the village.) He, too, had tears in his eyes. I put my arm around him to tell him that it was okay to cry in front of us. The house we built for him would be considered far below American standards. It had no electricity or running water, and the roof was a single sheet of corrugated metal. Yet, compared to what they lived in before, this decent cement house with several rooms, tiny as they were, was unimaginable and unbelievable. The dignity and eloquence with which they expressed their gratitude humbled us and left a profound impression.

Unfortunately, all good things come to an end and it was almost time for us to leave. My father read from the Bible again and blessed us for our long trip back to "*Nchi iliyopendwa sana na Mungu, inchi inayoitwa Merikan.*" (The country that God loves, the country known as America.)

Before leaving, we went outside to greet the rest of the relatives. I can never remember the names nor do I have any idea of their relationship to my core family. It was also quite confusing because there were many more people gathered in the courtyard than before we went into the house. Some were neighbors and onlookers from near and far who were having mini-celebrations on the spot. We took several family photos, while the many gathered neighbors waited their turn to take photos with us.

My father wanted to accompany us to Mwanza, where he would stay with relatives. Our traveling group eventually managed to cut through the crowds, say our goodbyes, and get into our cars to retrace our way to Kamanga and the ferry. Just before we pulled out, I turned to look at my father's compound, hoping to see the house from a distance. Instead, I saw a sea of beautiful people waving both arms overhead, singing and swaying back and forth, as they watched our car disappear on the pot-holed road to the ferry.

I sat in a back seat of the Land Rover, and as we jerkily made the two-hour drive to the ferry, I connected with Fat Mary about this soul-marking experience.

Fat Mary was waving to the family with the biggest smile I'd ever seen on her face! She slowly but excitedly went over every moment in the house and in the village, repeating most of what was said and imitating each person's dancing style, including the little grandchildren wearing fluorescent sunglasses. She finished with, *Isn't this absolutely magnificently wonderful?*

32

Family Matters

After so much emotion and celebration in Kasamwa, I don't know how Cathy, Eleanor, and I had the energy to go to the Mwanza market to buy *khangas* and other souvenirs, but we did. We all had dinner together, then Yeremia went to spend the night with relatives.

We were exhausted and turned in early, though I wasn't looking forward to going to bed. I knew that Kjell would resume complaining about Cathy and Eleanor being with us when we met my father.

"Thank you for making this trip possible for our family and for building Yeremia a house," I began my conversation with him. "Did you see how much joy we brought into their lives?"

"You're welcome," Kjell replied in his usual monotone. I've often wished that once when I thanked him for something he agreed to pay for, he would say something like "You're welcome, but it's our money, and we're both to thank."

"Wasn't it great to have the whole family there? We can always relive it because you filmed it all." By giving him credit, I hoped he'd be in a good mood.

"It would really have been a great day if I hadn't been so mad at you for ignoring my concerns about Cathy's pushiness this morning."

"Why are you so upset that Cathy wanted to come and meet Yeremia? How many times do I have to remind you that it is she, and she alone, who is responsible for making this reunion possible? Have you forgotten all she did in order to adopt me? She had to work with the nuns at the orphanage to set everything in motion and get permission to take me out of the country. She had to ask my mother to vouch that she was an American citizen and I was her daughter so I could get an American passport, and she had to secure a college scholarship for me and find the money for my ticket to America. Don't forget, she was the one who communicated with Dorothy when she came looking for me. Cathy was present when I met my mother for the first time, and when my mother introduced me to my brother Larry with whom I trudged the Tanzanian countryside in search of people he knew from his childhood in case one of them turned out to be my father. We found him, and this day was possible all because of Cathy. As my adopted mother, she has every right to meet my father when I want her to."

"I can't argue about her role in your life, but Cathy has never known her place. She's intruded into our lives from day one—wanting to join us on family events, inviting herself over, dropping in whenever she wanted, and even letting herself into our house. You always ignored me when I got angry about this. If we'd stopped her then, she wouldn't be here today to intrude one more time into what is clearly a family affair! And she has the gall to bring Eleanor along."

"First of all, you're forgetting that we gave her this trip back to Africa when she turned fifty. Second, I just don't understand why you can't get it into your supposedly intelligent brain that Cathy is family! She loves me as though she'd given birth to me, which is a lot more than I can say for my birth mother, Dorothy."

"I've never considered her family. What she did for you was great and admirable, but it's going too far to pretend that she's your mother."

"I bet you considered her family when she loaned you money for your business early in our marriage. You've always been jealous of my relationship with her, and you've tried to drill it into me that she is not my mother. What's the problem with me loving her as a mother?"

"Facts are facts. You're delusional."

That answer surprised me. I always felt that he was the delusional one—delusional about his own magnificence and importance. "If delusional means that I consider Cathy family, then I'll live with my delusion as a badge of pride and honor."

Underlying Kjell's discomfort with Cathy is the fact that for reasons I cannot explain, he felt superior to her and especially to her husband, John. He often talked down to them or dismissed their concerns as trivial. At times he was outright mean, and when we'd object, he'd come back with, "Can't you take a joke?"

Years later, at Eleanor's wedding rehearsal dinner, family and friends had gathered to watch childhood videos of her and her husband-to-be, Micah. Everyone had an opportunity to say something interesting or funny about them in their growing-up years. We were having a great time laughing along with the young couple, though some of their friends' recollections seemed to surprise them.

When it was Kjell's turn, he said, "Ladies and gentlemen, these childhood videos show the people who raised this couple. Considering the gene pool that Eleanor is from, I think you will agree she turned out pretty good!"

The laughter and happy voices of friends and family died down as the expressions on many faces turned from joy to perplexity and incredulity. Kjell felt quite smug about his "joke" and didn't understand why I was upset and why no one laughed.

"How could you say something that awful?" I was really embarrassed for him.

"It's a joke!" he said with a smile.

"It's not a joke when you're the only one laughing!" To me, that incident summarized how Kjell always felt about Cathy and John.

33

Yeremia's Wish

The next day my father joined us for lunch at the Tilapia Hotel on the shores of Lake Victoria. When it was time for us to leave, he was very anxious to speak to his grandchildren.

"*Malia, tafsiri maneno yangu ya kuagana na wajukuu wangu.*" (Maria, translate my parting words to my grandchildren.)

I waved to Katarina and Karl to come and join us. I was pleased when they knelt to greet their grandfather the Sukuma way. He put his hands over their heads and spoke to them.

"I am asking that when you return to America, remember me, your grandfather. Remember our tribe and our customs. The most important thing is that I do not want you to forget your name— Nhambu. This is the name of our lineage. I want our name to live forever in America. You are the ones who will guard it and give it everlasting life."

"We will. We promise!" Kata replied, holding her grandfather's hand.

"We'll always remember you and our name Nhambu." Karl shook his hand too.

"*Sawa sawa!*" (Very good!) Yeremia pulled both of them to his chest and with a sigh of satisfaction, hugged them. He trusted that his grandchildren would fulfill his request regarding the Nhambu name living on in America.

I made a pledge right then and there that when I returned to Minnesota, I would legally add *Nhambu* to my name. I repeated *Maria Nhambu Bergh* to myself several times and was very happy with my decision. Eventually, I decided to use just Nhambu as my first name.

Again, it was hard to say goodbye to my father this time, just as it had been a few years ago. Tanzania is so far away, and each goodbye felt like it would be the last.

Our cars left Mwanza for Seronera, located in Serengeti National Park, right after lunch. Entering the park, we saw herds of giraffe and elephants, lions, topis, gazelles, zebra, a lone secretary bird, guinea fowl, waterbuck, crocodiles in the river, and many hippos in the hippo pool. I don't know if it was because he was enjoying the animals, but Karl was looking better and acting more like himself. I was glad that he seemed to have finally recovered from malaria.

We arrived in Seronera a few hours later. Karl chased the vervet monkeys and baboons that were playing inside and outside the hotel, and with his dad's heavy video camera, filmed the animals around the lodge. He loved filming the rock hyrax that, with their short dark brown fur, look like huge rats, but actually belong to the same species as elephants. It was wonderful to see him smiling again.

The last leg of our trip in Tanzania took us back to Tarangire, and we spent two more days resting and enjoying leisurely game drives. Before we left for Kenya, we stopped at Usa River to say goodbye to the Farajis and then left for the border town of Namanga.

After encountering a group of Maasai traders and the sales pitches for their wares—everything from beautiful multicolored beaded collars to Maasai blankets, spears, and snuff containers made of horn—we crossed the border and drove to the Intercontinental Hotel in Nairobi. In the morning we went to visit Karen Blixen's house in a suburb of Nairobi called Karen. I had taken tourists here several times before, so I left the family at the house and went shopping for African art at Utamaduni with my high school friend Thecla. Seeing the Ngong Hills beyond Nairobi reminded me of colonial times and of a framed photograph of these hills my mother gave me before she died. It was the view she saw every day while she was teaching at Saint Mary's School in Nairobi.

At the Giraffe Manor we fed the giraffes who ate from our hands, whipping and curling their long black, sandpaper tongues as they picked up the dry pellets we bought there.

While in Nairobi we stopped to see my former teachers from Marian College—Sister Dolores Marie and Sister Mary Ward—and visited with several other friends from Tanzania who lived there. I also managed to give an *Aerobics With Soul*® class at a fitness studio. The clients, who were familiar with most of the music, sang along and thoroughly enjoyed themselves.

Although this was an amazing experience for my entire family, one thing was made very clear to me during our family trip to Tanzania. I knew that Cathy and Kjell only put up with each other because of me, even though Cathy had never told me outright that she disapproved of Kjell. Because I was so in love with him, I wouldn't have heard her, and she respected that. But before we got married, I told her that I sensed she wasn't happy with my decision.

"Is there anything about him that you think I don't see?" I asked her.

"I know that he loves you, Mary. My concern is that he loves you only for himself and not for you! He will take what he can from you—including Africa, at some point."

What in the world did that mean? I wondered at the time. I really didn't understand, so I let it go. But I eventually realized that Cathy felt Kjell was full of himself and controlling to the point of dictating what my relationship with her should be. A dear college friend Jackie, my maid of honor and godmother to Kata and Karl, had a similar perception of Kjell. She was civil toward him for my sake. Still, Jackie told me one day, "Kjell doesn't see your soul, and therefore cannot fully appreciate you. He appreciates you only as you relate to him."

On my part, I struggled with accepting that the beautiful, exciting, and loving relationship we had in the early years of our marriage was gradually changing. Even if he might have been dissatisfied with certain aspects of our marriage, I knew that it would never occur to Kjell that I might be too. He often gave the impression that I owed most of my accomplishments to him and that he was the one who made it possible for us to live the way we did. My contributions did not enter his mind. He was proud of me because in his mind, I brought him glory and praise. During our marriage, I had several conversations with Fat Mary about this and one day she hit the nail on the head.

The husband you adore hurt you very much with his affair, and you have not fully recovered. You forgave him and believed that forgiveness would make your love and marriage whole again. But your trust in him was lost, and you're still trying to find it. Your heart was broken, and you're still trying to mend it. For him, once he said he was sorry, he believed all was over and done with, and your marriage would go back to how it was. He forgets that trust is earned, not willed! His emotional intelligence is limited. You are superior to him in this aspect. You feel deeper. You know deeper. You love deeper. You chose to remain in the marriage. It was the right decision.

34

Royal Safari

 Our many strong ties to Africa led to developing a travel agency. It was a godsend! As tour guides, we led photographic safaris to Tanzania and Kenya for several years. Seeing magnificent and exotic African animals was usually what tourists went on safaris for, but we also made a point to visit the schools and hospitals we sponsored and supported. Visiting these facilities made the biggest impression on many tourists, and they shared as much as they could of themselves and often sent donations after they got home.

What I enjoyed most about our safaris was watching enlightenment, understanding, and appreciation blossom in the minds and hearts of many tourists we brought to Africa. For most of them it was a trip of a lifetime. Their expressions of joy reduced the impact of the one or two difficult people on each safari to insignificance. The complainers on each trip fell into two categories: those who expected Africa to be like home with the same comforts, amenities, and services, and those who felt superior to the Africans, pitying or blaming them for how they live.

One tourist seemed sad as we drove through Maasai country just north of Arusha. Along the road we saw young, newly circumcised males with their ritual ostrich or bird-feather headpieces, painted faces, and long black robes. The woman asked me, "Do you think these people could ever be happy?"

I was taken aback, but had the presence of mind to say, "It depends how you define happiness."

"I mean, look at them!" she responded. "They're walking about aimlessly all day like they don't have a care in the world when they probably don't have a pot to pee in. Why can't they dress like normal people, find a job, earn some money, go to school, and make something of their lives?"

I was stunned. "If that's your definition of happiness, then probably they will never be happy. A happy person usually sees happiness in others, and I think each person has their own definition of happiness."

"I suppose you could be right. I guess I can never know what makes these people happy."

"Isn't happiness subjective?" I persisted. "These Maasai youth know what makes them happy. Happiness comes from within and from the context of their cultural values."

"Well, I can't imagine painting my face and wearing feathers on my head would make me happy. Thank God I know better!" she concluded. I let it go.

In 1996 we took the royal family of Norway on safari. Kjell, Kata, Karl, and I traveled the Northern Safari route for two weeks with King Harald and Queen Sonja, and their children, Princess Martha Louise and Crown Prince Haakon. The royal family had an entourage of Tanzanian and Norwegian secret service personnel accompanying us everywhere, staying in the same lodges and hotels.

Even though I made several mistakes—despite three pages of royal protocol instructions, which I didn't strictly follow—either the royal family didn't notice or they enjoyed my little faux pas and found them refreshing.

My family experienced firsthand that a safari with royalty was a safari like no other. We planned the itinerary, and then everything was done for us. It was luxurious—the food and service were exquisite, and the wine and liqueur brought to every lodge and tent where we stayed was the best—yet we still met with the typical hardships one would encounter on a safari in the African wild.

An unforgettable highlight of the safari was our hot air balloon trip over the Serengeti. Here we were—the royal family of Norway and the "royal family of Nowhere" together—in a balloon gliding high over the vast Serengeti Plains whose rugged roads, scattered hills, and sparse forests cut through the tall grasslands that harbored hundreds of animals we couldn't see at ground level. The complete and utter silence during the outing was transformational. It was almost an out-of-body experience that made me feel like a lone bird who owned the entire sky.

After our bush safari, we accompanied the royal family to Dar-es-Salaam for a state visit with President Benjamin Mkapa and his wife, Anna.

What I remember most about the royal family was their humility and their respect for the country and its people. If it weren't for the required royal protocol, which they tried to minimize, you'd never know who they were. Their warmth and comfort around us almost made us feel like one of them; even so, we knew our place.

After the safari, they invited us to their palace in Oslo where we relived the entire trip, looking at photos and recounting the many funny occurrences during the two weeks. The queen remembered in detail how a group of baboons got into the secret service room and rampaged the place, removing film from cameras and scattering the secret servicemen's belongings. I wanted to tell them—but didn't dare—about another safari when baboons entered a tourist's room through an open window and ransacked it. They took a box of a woman's tampons and holding them in their mouths like cigarettes, sat outside on the ground and "smoked" them.

35

Rancho La Puerta

 Six years after filming *Karibu,* my first *Aerobics With Soul®* video, I realized that even though I had modified the dances and movements, the workout was too hard for the average American. So I created and filmed *Serengeti,* a level below *Karibu.* Two years later I wanted to create a video a level above *Karibu* that retained more of the tribal aspects of African dance and that would challenge advanced students of *Aerobics With Soul®.* My dream was to film it on location in Tarangire National Park in Tanzania. Thus *Kilimanjaro* came into being. Three instructors—Diane, Nedy, and I—came from the States along with an eight-member film crew. Salma, also an instructor, flew in from London, and two male dancers joined us from Nairobi. The makeup artist, Teresa, also from Nairobi, recruited the African men from a fitness studio there. I had sent them an instructional video and the choreography before the trip, so they could practice the moves, but they never even opened them.

It soon became obvious that they needed help learning the moves. Diane, a petite, white Minnesotan with long blond hair, came to the rescue and held daily sessions with them. I'll never forget seeing Diane urging the muscular dancer to move his arms and shoulders and showing the other six-foot-tall, gangly Kenyan how to swing his hips! She was the perfect one to teach them because she was very dedicated to learning and performing each movement authentically. Even today, she loves and faithfully represents *Aerobics With Soul®* and continues to teach it every opportunity she has. When her grandchildren visit her, they all do *Aerobics With Soul®* together.

With videos offering three levels of difficulty, I could now more easily share *Aerobics With Soul®* with a larger audience.

About the same time, a friend suggested that I become a presenter for the International Dance Exercise Association (which later became IDEA: The Association for Fitness Professionals). The fitness craze of the '80s was quickly becoming an industry with instructor guidelines and certification via theoretical and practical exams.

When I looked at becoming a presenter, I didn't think that *Aerobics With Soul®* would qualify, because my values and objectives seemed the opposite of what was required, especially for the theoretical written exam. I was completely lost when I looked at the sample exam with newly invented fitness terms that didn't apply to my class, which is based on and inspired by African dance. My husband encouraged me to get certified, and I knew he was right. For credibility and to be an IDEA presenter, I had to take and pass the American Council of Exercise (ACE) exam.

The anatomy and kinesiology section of the exam reminded me of my schooling in Africa and memorization marathons, so I memorized everything. When I felt ignorant, I asked myself if anyone in the fitness industry at the time would be qualified to certify me to teach *Aerobics With Soul®* —my own creation based on my cultural heritage.

I did pass the ACE Group Fitness exam and then the IDEA exam to become a provider for Continuing Education Credits for instructors seeking ACE recertification. For my efforts, I was invited to be a presenter with IDEA for several years in various cities around the country. I cannot express how enlightening and satisfying it was for me to participate in those international conferences and conventions! I learned about different fun and exciting classes from fellow presenters; from the many lecturers, I gained a deep understanding of exercise, nutrition, and health.

A highlight of the late nineties was presenting at a fitness convention in Acapulco, Mexico. As I finished with the final number of the cooldown, called *Sala*—Prayer, I looked up from the stage floor after doing the straddle stretch to see the huge hotel ballroom packed full of dancers with smiles on their faces. Their arms, open and raised toward the heavens, were silhouetted against the orange and gold hues of the sun setting over the ocean beyond the open doors of the ballroom. The unforgettable sight was intensified by the feeling that nature, too, embraced the moment.

Santiago, Chile, was the site of another unforgettable presentation. I felt almost delirious with joy and amazement when I heard my African music blasting from giant speakers dominating the presentation venue while several hundred convention participants happily danced the free dance portion of *Aerobics With Soul®* socializing, singing, and showing off their unique Latin versions of the African moves.

African American Women on Tour (AAWOT), a weekend-long women's empowerment conference series held in six different cities every year, was founded by Maria D. Dowd. In the early 1990s I participated as a presenter and vendor of *Aerobics With Soul®* videos and merchandise. AAWOT was an eye-opener for me, expanding my vision and knowledge of the accomplishments and diversity of African American women in the United States. Conferences with speakers like Alice Walker, Iyanla Vansant, Susan Taylor, Ruby Dee, Nikki Giovanni, and Maya Angelou were educational and empowering. I was also exposed to beautiful and creative African and Afro-centric clothing, jewelry, art, home furnishing, and cosmetics that I seldom saw in Minnesota. My favorite designer was Ahneva Ahneva, who used bold, bright African fabrics—from mud cloth (*bogolanfini*) to kente cloth—appliqued on Western gabardine, cotton, linen, wool, and silk to create stunning contemporary and functional fashion.

I always wore my fancy African outfits to the conferences because no matter how well I thought I dressed, I couldn't keep up with what the others wore. The women really dressed up, especially for the banquets! I often heard women I didn't know say, "Here comes Miss Thang. Mercy me!" I wasn't sure how to react to this remark, because it wasn't done with malice—they smiled at me as they spoke—but I was a little confused. At a conference with my friend Carletta, I heard someone call, "Hey Miss Thang, how's it going?"

"My name isn't Miss Thang," I said, carefully correcting her. "It's Maria Nhambu Bergh."

"Oh, my clueless African friend," Carletta said, laughing. "When someone calls you 'Miss Thang,' it's a compliment!"

I also found out at AAWOT conferences that despite having many close African- American friends, there was much I didn't know about Black life and culture in America. I had similar experiences when I presented at the National Alliance of Black School Educators Conventions and at Black Expos around the country. I learned more about American Blacks at those gatherings than I had learned the entire time I'd lived in America.

At a cocktail party for IDEA presenters at their International Conference in San Diego, an enthusiastic instructor approached me, saying she had been doing my *Karibu* workout video after reading in *Essence* magazine that my video had tied with Jane Fonda's for first place in the Aerobic Combination category of City Sports Fitness Video Awards in New York. She introduced herself as an instructor at Rancho La Puerta and said she thought *Aerobics With Soul®* would add a lot to the fitness program there. After giving me the phone number of the person to contact, she said, "Promise you will send your information to the Ranch."

"I'll see."

"My name is Coco. I crashed this party to meet you. Don't tell anyone, and please follow up." She waved goodbye as she slipped out of the room.

No way was I going to teach at some ranch. The only image that came to mind when I heard "ranch" was cows, horses, cowboys, and the song "Home on the Range" that the American nuns taught us in high school in Tanzania.

When I returned home and looked up Rancho La Puerta online, I was amazed at its beauty and vastness. Not only did it not look like a cowboy ranch, but it was founded by Edmond and Deborah Szekely in 1940 and was the original destination fitness resort and spa. It looked like paradise! I did send an *Aerobics With Soul®* press kit and *Serengeti,* my beginning level video, to the Ranch. Sunny, the programmer, wrote back saying she liked my program and would keep me in mind, but presenters were fully booked for the next two years.

Three months later I got an urgent call from Sunny asking if I would be interested in filling in for the presenter who taught a dance class called Soul Motion. She said a group of African Americans went to the Ranch every July and Soul Motion was one of their favorite classes. I accepted and was excited that the African-American group would come to my classes.

I put together a forty-five-minute class, packed my animal motif leotards and a couple of African outfits, and was on my way to Mexico two days later. When I stepped onto the bus that transported Ranch guests from the San Diego airport, across the Mexican border at Tecate, and to Rancho La Puerta, I felt euphoric. The landscaping, sights, sounds, and smells of the Ranch took my breath away, even in the scorching heat of July.

The first night I couldn't find my way from the dining hall to my little house in the staff quarters. For two hours I wandered around the immense property of exotic gardens, winding cobbled trails, pools, and individual casitas in total darkness except for the lanterns close to the path and the light from the moon. I didn't regret being lost because I was alone, communing with nature, and she was very welcoming to me. She told me that this was a place where I would relax, renew, and reflect on my life, that I would be recharged with confidence and courage to follow the path that destiny laid out for me. By the time I found my little house, I felt I had been in this place many times before.

Yes, you've been here. That's why it's so familiar! Fat Mary reminded me. *Not physically, but you've been imagining this place ever since the orphanage. You used to chase butterflies and grasshoppers and tried to imitate the singing of the birds. You loved to wade barefoot among the calla lilies along the stream near the cemetery. You often fell asleep among the rose bushes and dreamt you were a flower in God's garden. Your childhood has prepared you to recognize and appreciate beauty everywhere you find it. Nature is God's gift to humans—all humans, rich or poor. In spite of your hard life, you did have an awareness of the beauty that surrounded Kifungilo, even though you could seldom stop to experience and celebrate it. You instinctively knew that nature nourishes and heals the soul.*

I slept soundly and when morning came, I was ready to teach my class. I taught six very full classes that week, and I was convinced that I had created *Aerobics With Soul®* for a place like the Ranch. The guests "got" the "soul" in *Aerobics With Soul®* which doesn't always happen. Two numbers into the warm-up, I could see and feel inhibitions melt as the sweet African music was internalized and expressed in each person's movements. Throughout the aerobics section of the class, I saw happy, smiling faces, and by the time we got to the free dance, Kuchumaa gym was alive with free spirits energetically dancing their own unique interpretation of the African song. The beautifully harmonized South African singing of "Give Us Power" by Mbongeni Ngema combined with the reverence of the dancers taking in and expressing the words of power in their own ways brought tears to my eyes. Everyone is usually quiet when this song plays, but on this day it was especially serene. I opened my eyes to see if everyone had left the room. They were all there and I saw that most of them had tears in their eyes too.

In my teaching I have proven over and over again that you don't have to be African or of African descent to dance the African way. Our way is natural and innate. With a few exceptions, all humans are born with the ability to walk and to dance. There is a Zimbabwean proverb that says, "If you can walk, you can dance, and if you can talk, you can sing." How we walk and dance, and how we talk and sing are influenced by nature, nurture, and environment, but it is always possible to tap into our natural movements. In my years of teaching dance in America I've found that most westerners have a hard time relaxing enough to not care how they look to others while dancing. I finally understood the American saying "Dance as though no one is watching." At first, that saying didn't make sense to me at all! Why dance if no one is watching? As I see it, we dance to express our emotions and to communicate with other dancers and spectators, not with walls in empty rooms.

Rancho La Puerta has a special place in my heart and in my life. *Aerobics With Soul®* has been affirmed, embraced, and enjoyed in this setting of exotic beauty, peace, joy, and rejuvenation. It is one of the biggest blessings of my life that every year since 1996 I have shared my creation with the guests at the Ranch and have, in turn, received from them an indescribable sense of joy, gratitude, and affirmation. My experience there reminds me of an African saying about participation in community activities, especially dance: "You bring who you are and what you have to offer to the group and take what you need."

36

Zeb the Dog

 Kata graduated from Tufts University in 1992. Her college years flew by fast and were relatively smooth. It seems like one day I just looked up and she was on her own, working for Harvard Translations. It was only after she had graduated that she told me what it was like being a fair-skinned, African Norwegian at the university.

Having come from a home with a Black mother who emphasized her African heritage and was raised in Tanzania, Kata knew more about Africa than many of her classmates. She told me that some of her Black classmates welcomed and encouraged her attendance at Pan African Society meetings, while others resented her presence. That she understood. What frustrated her was the way white people always needed to precisely break down and understand her heritage, and then proclaim her one thing or another. She said she often felt like a spy in the white world, or a double agent. She decided she was functionally white because she looked so white and because she never suffered discrimination. But she was not at ease, and there were only a few individuals here and there with whom she shared her complex heritage. Her closest friends around that time were from Uganda, Iran, Iceland, and a few from the U.S. She always seemed to get along best with people from other countries.

It really hurt to know that she was confronting issues I had also dealt with, not only as a child but throughout my life. Times had changed and I didn't want to project my experiences on her or try to predict what racial attitudes she might encounter. Maybe I should have discussed race with her when she was growing up and especially before she left for college. Instead, I let her find her own way to handle the issue. I have never been sure why, but during her college years we were not as close as we used to be when she was home.

The summer that Cathy turned fifty, Kata brought her college boyfriend home to Minnesota. He was the life of the party when we "roasted" Cathy by auctioning her treasured old-time clothes, jewelry, and accessories stored in trunks in her basement. The auction was to raise money for the Peace House Community, a place of daytime hospitality where Cathy volunteered working with the homeless. Her daughter Eleanor and I served as auctioneers, and friends modeled the vintage wear. The bidding went wild when Kata's tall and handsome boyfriend modeled a skirted bathing suit. Amidst the fashion show, the eating, drinking, and dancing, John and Cathy's beautiful garden resembled a rose garden party in England at the turn of the century. Not only did we enjoy ourselves, we raised two thousand dollars for Peace House.

A few years later, friends had a fiftieth birthday party for me at their Lake Minnetonka home. Then the *Aerobics With Soul®* instructors, who knew I never had a birthday party as a kid, threw a children's party for me at Nedy's apartment, complete with paper hats, noisemakers, nursery rhymes blasting from a CD player, and party favor bags. The party made up for all the birthday celebrations I didn't have as a child.

King Harald of Norway was visiting Minneapolis and the banquet to honor him happened to be on Kjell's fiftieth birthday. With all the Norwegians who would undoubtedly attend the banquet, I saw an opportunity to have the 800 or so attendees sing "Happy Birthday" to him during the king's banquet. I asked the emcee, whom I knew well, if we could do this and he looked at me aghast.

"This is not done! Not in the presence of a king, Maria," to which I replied, "There's always a first time."

"I'll do what I can, but I promise nothing."

The banquet was over and everyone stood up when the king and his entourage left the hall. I was disappointed that my plan had failed, but while everyone was still clapping, the emcee returned to the podium, grabbed the mike, announced that it was Kjell's birthday, and led us in singing Happy Birthday to him! The next day I had a formal dinner catered at our home in Edina with twenty-five of our close friends and continued with the celebration.

"How did you pull it off?" was the question I got most during the dinner.

Speaking about the improbable, I wondered how Kata pulled off bringing a dog home for Christmas. Yes, a dog! After arriving in the United States, one of the first things I wrote about to my friends in Africa was seeing with my own eyes that Americans kept dogs and cats in their houses—and even slept with their animals! My African friends said that if it were true, Americans must not be very civilized, but I suspect they thought I was making it up.

I am petrified of dogs. Dogs at the orphanage were German shepherd guard dogs, trained to chase and bite any African they saw. The *wazungu* around the orphanage also had ferocious dogs, which they used for protection. Kata knew I don't like pets in the house, so she and her father conspired to just do it! Puppy Zeb looked like a big rat to me.

"What brand of dog is it?" I asked Kata, trying not to show how upset I was.

"Mom, it's what 'breed,' not what 'brand.' He is a Schnoodle—a mix of schnauzer and poodle. Isn't he cute? I love him!"

I looked at the object of Kata's love and wondered if there could be a more pathetic-looking puppy in the whole wide world. But then I remembered something that happened when she was three or four. We were riding in the car when Kjell happened to mention that Buster, the Norwegian elkhound who was the family dog in Norway and had helped Kata learn to walk, had died. Kata burst into tears and between sobs talked about how much she loved Buster. I listened to her crying and sympathized. Even I cared about Buster and recognized his gentle intelligence. I had known him since I first went to Norway. He accompanied Kjell and me halfway on our hike up the mountain to that doomed boathouse honeymoon. So I was taken aback when Kjell turned to Kata and brusquely said, "Stop crying now. That's enough."

The current object of Kata's canine love had protruding eyes that seemed too big for his face, and his scrawny little body was covered with inch-long curly, salt-and-pepper fur that reminded me of worn-out Alaskan seal slippers. He became even more ugly in my eyes when he proceeded to poop and pee in the middle of the living room, as if to tell me that the feeling was mutual.

"Oh Mom, he's so scared and so small, and he just made a long trip on the plane. Dad said it was all right to bring him. I hope you're not too angry with me."

"Of course! Why should your dad care whether I like dogs or not?" At this stage of our marriage, I wondered in my heart whether he cared about anything going on in the house or in my life.

37

Buddhism

When we went as a family to meet my father in Tanzania, Kata was finishing her studies in Boston and Karl was a freshman at Edina High School. They were both deeply affected by the trip, especially Karl. I think the living conditions and the poverty they encountered, and the fact that their newly found African relatives lived so far away, saddened and depressed them. Karl said he wished we had taken one of the young African cousins back to the States with us.

Soon after we returned, Karl took up skateboarding seriously and crashed frequently until finally he said he had had enough falls and gave it up. He was also profiled and frequently stopped by the Edina police who asked him what he was doing in our neighborhood. In those days, racially mixed boys were not often seen in Edina. Once he and his white friends from the neighborhood were skateboarding on the grocery store parking lot despite the "No skateboarding" sign. They were all arrested for trespassing, but only Karl was taken to jail. When his white father arrived to claim him, the police were visibly shocked that Kjell was his dad. After all, Kjell was well known in the community! Who would have guessed that his son was Black! The police apologized to Kjell and let him take Karl home without further discussion.

Karl formed a music band with four others called the Totallies. We suffered through their awful-sounding rehearsals in our basement. His band members would walk in and say "Hi, Mrs. Bergh," play for hours (it seemed), and then I'd hear, "Bye, Mrs. Bergh."

I couldn't figure out their outfits or style. Karl wore a Mohawk, which he dyed bright red, and others had hairstyles that looked like glorified John Travolta-style in *Grease*, while a couple seemed to carry bird nests in various stages of completion on their heads. For a time, he had a girlfriend who had purple and green hair, wore black lipstick, and dressed in bright red tights under a short yellow skirt. She'd sit upstairs with me while the band rehearsed. We would look at each other as though we knew we should say something, but neither of us did. Most of my son's friends were very respectful toward us, but one time I physically threw out one of them, heavier and taller than I was—because he called me a "Big Black Mama"!

During his band days, his grades suffered so we enrolled him in Sylvan Learning, a tutoring service, but after a year, nothing had changed. We were worried about his school performance and tried to switch him to a private school for his senior year, but he would have had to repeat the eleventh grade. He refused to switch. His grades got worse his senior year, but I was determined that he would graduate with his classmates instead of getting a GED. I approached Azell Smith, my dear friend Carletta's husband, who was a school principal in Minneapolis, for his advice. He enrolled him in an after-school class and became his personal advisor and friend. With Azell's help, Karl did well and received his diploma with his classmates.

He decided not to go to college right after high school, so he worked for his father at the travel agency for a bit, got odd jobs here and there, and concentrated on his band. In 1998, two years after finishing high school, he was ready for college and decided to go to the American Intercontinental University in London. He lasted one year and then returned home.

About this time, Karl discovered Buddhism. It was not a surprise to me because Karl is a gentle soul, kind and generous to a fault and sensitive to the needs of others. Material possessions mean little to him, and his happiest moments are when others are happy.

He pursued his Buddhist studies at the Tubten Kunga Ling Buddhist Center in Deerfield Beach, Florida. He loved his teacher Geshe Konchog Kyab, who took him under his wing and nurtured his spirituality. In him, Karl found a spiritual guide who loved and accepted him unconditionally.

I now understand why Kjell found it difficult to bond with his son, and why he equated fulfilling his parental duties of providing abundantly for his children's material needs with bonding. From Kjell's humble beginnings in Veitvet, Norway, he pursued a capitalist way of life where talent, hard work, opportunities, and rewards made him an indisputable example of the American dream. Geshe-La, on the other hand, was the living embodiment of compassion, detachment from material belongings, and unconditional love and respect for people, the earth, and all living things.

In contrast, Kjell and I were given an award for having achieved the American Dream by the Center for the American Experiment, a Minnesota-based think tank that promotes conservative and free-market principles. The ballroom in a in downtown Minneapolis hotel was packed because the keynote speaker was Judge Robert Bork, nominated in 1987 by President Ronald Reagan to the United States Supreme Court but rejected by the Senate. Kjell surely regretted insisting that I join him at the podium and say a few words as we accepted the gilded bald eagle trophy. I spoke truthfully: "I do not agree with most of what has been said here today, but I thank you for acknowledging that we have achieved the American Dream."

One morning after we had Norwegian waffles, which I made for Kjell every Sunday throughout our marriage, Karl announced that he wanted to study in Nepal because he intended to become a Buddhist monk. I didn't like the idea because he would be farther away from me than when he was in London, and I didn't think he was cut out to be a monk—he loved his girlfriends too much! I tried to discourage him and told him I couldn't wholeheartedly support him in this particular venture because I thought that, at this point in his life, traveling halfway around the world wasn't the right thing to do.

All hell broke loose with his father, though. "What a cop-out! You're running away from your responsibilities and expect the rest of the world to take care of you! What do Buddhist monks do anyway? Don't they just go around begging? Stupid, uneducated people offer them their meager possessions so they can live in luxury."

Karl was madder than I'd ever seen him. He jumped from his kitchen chair and yelled at his dad, "So you think that all I want is to mooch off you and others? Well, let me tell you something. You can live ten lifetimes and you will never be as rich and happy as the poorest monk! You will never understand. It's not all about money. I am tired of putting up with you and your ideas just because you're my dad. I'm out of here!"

Before we knew it, he had stormed out of the house and started running and screaming down the street. Both of us followed him, but he was running so fast that Kjell decided to take the car while I continued after him down the street. After a minute or so, I went back home and prayed. Karl got to a main street and continued running against the traffic. Kjell came roaring up in his car and drove past him. Then he stopped, got out of the car, and begged Karl to get in. I don't know if Kjell apologized or what convinced Karl to get in the car, but he finally did. When I heard the car in our driveway, I ran outside, relieved to see Karl and Kjell both safe and sound.

Geshe-La arranged for Karl to go to India that spring to visit Buddhist holy places and shrines, where he was taken around by his teacher Geshe Lhakpa Tsering. Kjell was more receptive of this idea and gladly paid for the trip. Karl was fortunate to attend the Dalai Lama's teachings in Dharamsala while he was there. He came back a changed person. I knew that Buddhism had handpicked him, and at long last he was at peace with his spiritual direction. He pursued Buddhist studies at Naropa University in Boulder, Colorado, and eventually got his BA in Religious Studies and later his master's in Buddhism from Maitripa College in Portland, Oregon. While in college he spent a few months at two monasteries in Nepal. The first monastery of Kopan is associated with Lama Yeshe, Lama Zopa, and the Dalai Lama who have all taught extensively in the West. The second, Pullahari monastery, is associated with the Buddhist denomination that founded Naropa University in Colorado.

38

Enough

We had been in Delray Beach for less than a year when Anna Mkapa, the first lady of Tanzania, came to Florida to raise funds for her Equal Opportunities for All Trust Fund, based in Dar-es-Salaam. We arranged to have several fundraising dinners with Palm Beach County dignitaries, business leaders, educators, and concerned members of our community. As a result of the first lady's visit, Kjell and I helped launch the Sister Cities exchange program between Delray Beach and Moshi in Tanzania.

After our move to Florida in September of 1998, I noticed that Kjell seemed distant and absentminded whenever he was home from his trips to Minnesota or abroad. He worked hard with me to unpack everything, but was otherwise not involved in settling in.

Before we moved, we had an estate sale and got rid of household furnishings and art, except for our African and Norwegian art. We were going to make our Florida home African, and we planned to buy a small condo in Minneapolis and make that Norwegian. We still had several businesses in Minnesota, and Kjell continued to travel back and forth, as he did when we opened the car dealership in Florida.

I shopped at discount and department stores in order to stick to the budget he had given me for furnishing the house, only to witness him splurge and buy whatever he wanted when he returned. I had drooled over some African-looking bamboo and marble furniture in Boca, but it was way beyond my budget. I showed it to him the next time he was in town. The minute he walked into the store, the furniture caught his eye. "Gotta have it! It's great!" he said.

"Before you get too excited, check the price tag."

"I don't care how much it is. Let's get it."

Without further ado, we bought a sofa, two love seats, a coffee table, a sideboard, two end tables, a four-post king-sized bed, two dressers, two nightstands, and a large mirror.

I was delighted to have the furniture I wanted, but it bothered me that Kjell put me on a home furnishing budget but not himself. I realized that since he handled our finances, he knew what we could or couldn't buy. Suddenly, I wanted to know that too.

"Overall, how much money do we have?" I asked him

"Enough," was his answer.

When we married, we agreed that I could keep my teaching paycheck and he would give me a monthly check for our home expenses such as groceries, children's clothes, my personal needs, and smaller household expenses. I don't think there was ever a time that I stayed within the budget. He gave me duplicates of his credit cards, and I used them whenever my monthly check didn't cover expenses. He seldom complained or asked me to give him an account of how I used my money.

There came a point, many years into the marriage, when I realized that we must have more money than I thought. He bought a small plane; he regularly sent money to his parents and relatives in Norway, helped build a house for my father in Africa, and he would do anything for our children—Montessori schools, piano and flute lessons, trips to Norway every year and to Montserrat for Christmas, and travels in the United States whenever possible. He brought presents for me and the children whenever he traveled without us, and he frequently bought me lavish jewelry and gifts.

Every gift from him provoked two emotions. First was gratitude and love for him, and the second was the wish that I could also buy the same kind of gifts for him, our children, my family, and friends. There were times I purchased whatever I wanted just because he had that power, and I thought he would scold or lecture me when the bill came. More often than not, he said nothing!

Throughout our marriage, every now and again I'd get curious about our net worth and I'd ask him how much money we made. His answer was always "Enough." I gradually realized that no matter how much he bragged to others that we owned everything together and that my name was on all our businesses, he didn't treat me as an equal partner.

I have since figured out that in his mind, it was all his money. I had what I needed and he would buy me whatever I wanted, so how can I have a problem with that? The truth is that I did have a problem with it. It was his way of controlling me. It was all his money. He patronized me and tried to make me feel indebted to him. He often succeeded. He acted like a big *bwana* being magnanimous to his wife and children, who in their turn should remember how lucky they were.

It was sad that he felt he needed to make more and more money. I wondered if he equated our bank balance with his worth. I could have told him that he was great, and I did tell him many times, especially in the first fifteen years of our marriage. I told him how lucky and blessed I was to have him as my husband, and I truly meant it. I told him that from day one—when all we had was fifty dollars between us.

After we'd settled in Florida, when Kjell went to Minnesota for business, he stayed away for longer and longer periods of time. He was the one who had wanted us to move to Florida. He began pitching the idea a few years after he'd built the dealership in Delray Beach, but as much as I didn't like Minnesota winters, the thought of leaving my friends and starting from scratch made me say, "No way!" But he didn't let it go. He said he was tired of the winters and he loved the beach, and we could have a boat right at our doorstep. There was so much to do all year round, and life in Florida would be exciting and new. Once I did agree to move, I was looking forward to his being home and doing more things together as a couple, since the kids were on their own.

One day I reminded him of the hard-sell speeches he used to give me about Florida and asked him why he was going to Minnesota so often. He had told me that once we moved, he'd only make periodic visits because he had great people running the Minnesota businesses for him. That didn't happen.

"It's not my fault that there are so many banquets, meetings, and seminars in the Norwegian community scheduled year-round."

"I thought you'd cut down on the number of events you were attending."

"I can't skip these meetings."

I always knew when Kjell wanted the subject closed, so I left it alone, even though in my heart I knew there was something he wasn't telling me.

39

Writer's Block

 I continued writing my story off and on. Sometimes I'd write every day for weeks on end and other times I'd go for months without writing a word. But at one point I began having a particularly hard time getting back to my story. I'd sit at my computer, look at my notes and outline, write a little, and then delete a lot. Up to now, I had been writing my life story, paying little regard to structure, spelling, or punctuation. I was striving to get content out from deep within me. Since I couldn't write anything new, I'd go back to fix and clarify my manuscript, but I couldn't even do that! I did a mediocre job of editing and finally gave up.

Why was I having such severe blockage? Why was my memory empty? Even though I'd make myself sit down and write or rewrite every day, at the end of the day, I deleted all new material. It felt like the book didn't want to be written at that moment. It was telling me to take time off, and when it was ready, it would let me know. The last week of May 1999, I put my manuscript away and didn't care if I ever revisited it. I wondered what had happened to the enthusiasm I felt when I began writing in 1992.

I remembered what Kjell had said when I announced to my family that I was finally ready to start my book. We had just visited my father and were all gathered at Ndutu Lodge when I took out a small traveler's diary and started jotting notes about our visit to my father's village. As I did so, I said, "You are witnessing history. Maria Nhambu Bergh actually has pen and paper in hand and is finally jotting down the first lines of her autobiography."

"It's about time! Everyone you know has urged you to write your story," Cathy said.

"Please, please do, Mom," said Kata. "Do it for Karl and me."

Karl added, "You have to write everything we experienced in your father's house and in the village. I was blown away,"

"What a story! I'll be the first to read it," Eleanor assured me.

"I'm sure it will be made into a movie," Kjell chimed in, "and I want Robert Redford to play me."

"And whom have you chosen to play me in the movie, may I ask?"

"Oh, I haven't gotten that far."

Cathy wryly commented to me, "I hope you know who the main character in your story is, even though Kjell might not."

From that day in May 1999 nearly ten years passed before I resumed writing.

40

My Father's Death

 In August of 1999 my father died. I had stopped writing in May and wouldn't begin again until 2008. Maybe the universe wanted me to put off writing about my father's death until the sadness was raw again, and I felt it in the present. I thought it was avoidance on my part because I was not ready to revisit the fact that his passing made me an orphan for the second time—this time for real. It wasn't a coincidence that Miriam Makeba's passing happened as I was recounting the devastating death of my father. It was then I realized I couldn't write about my father's death until I had said goodbye to Miriam.

Miriam, when I created Aerobics With Soul®, it was your honest voice that propelled the movements and filled them with feeling. It was the pain and hope in your soul that enabled me to share my pain and hope through my creation. When I listened and danced to your music, I could feel my African heritage as though I was holding it in my hands. Having been brought up in a German orphanage, I knew next to nothing about the beauty and awesomeness of my heritage.

In the sixties, during the height of the civil rights movement, I'd listen to your songs and believe, just as I did as a child, that one could still sing and dance in the midst of suffering and betrayals. I'd listen to the truth you sang about and knew that one day, justice and equality would prevail. Just a week ago, the first Black president of the United States of America was elected! A president with the same roots as I have—an East African father and an American mother. Miriam, you had a lot to do with it. Had you lived, I'm sure you'd be invited to sing in the White House just as you were received with honor by Mandela in South Africa after thirty-one years of exile from your beloved country.

You educated many through your words and music and you showed us that we are all God's children. You taught me to be proud of and grateful to my native country and to my new country. You will never die for me nor for all those who have taken Aerobics With Soul® or those who have listened to your music with their hearts.

A lot of what is good in my life today I can attribute directly to you. Thank you for your role in the quality of my life and in the lives of my children, Katarina and Karl. They grew up with your voice filling the living room and calling them to dance with their mother who was hopelessly addicted to you.

Sleep in love, beloved!

I received an email from my friend and former high school teacher Sister Catherine with the news that my father, who had been ill for several months, had passed away. Sister Catherine, a Maryknoll Sister, was now stationed in Mwanza on the southern shore of Lake Victoria. She was always very kind to me and had been instrumental in keeping medicines, financial help, and communication flowing between me in America and my father who still lived in the tiny village of Kasamwa, across the lake from her residence in Mwanza.

She didn't know the exact cause of death, but she thought he had had a stroke after struggling with a bout of malaria. For days after I received the news I felt restless and hollow. I printed every email I received from Sister Catherine and clung to every word, hoping her descriptions would bring what was actually taking place in the little village into my life in America. Her emails made me feel present in the village, as if I, too, were helping my relatives lay Yeremia to rest. She described the scene at my father's house when she arrived there two days after his passing.

Dear Maria,

As I'm sure you remember, all furniture is removed or put together in one corner of the house and mats are put on the ground. Relatives and close friends will spend three days sleeping and eating during the day, and at night they "kesha" i.e., sing and pray. Yeremia died on Saturday and this was Monday, so people had been there for two nights. They had done a good job of local embalming. They got something from Sengerema hospital, which they injected and then put salt on his body. He was on a bed covered with a "shuka" (sheet), then a curtain was hung around the bed. They were waiting for the coffin to arrive, originally supposed to come on Sunday. They didn't want to wash and dress his body before the coffin came, as they didn't want to wash off the salt. I saw his body and he looked very peaceful. I visited with Perisi (his wife) and the family and neighbors, sitting, even sleeping on the mats, while we waited for the coffin. We all had a meal—village women cook for three days for these occasions. They were preparing the grave—made of cement blocks, in the backyard of the house. They had scheduled the funeral for 3.00 p.m. and the villagers started arriving from early morning. The yard was just packed! You could hardly walk around. Well, we waited for the coffin—but it didn't come! Finally they decided that the funeral couldn't take place until the next day, as it would take some hours to prepare the body, say their goodbyes and prayers, etc.

As much as I hated to leave, I had to return to Mwanza, so I left around 5.30 p.m. I left with some others who also had to return. I was sad not to be there for the funeral, but I took some pictures and left my camera with your sister Mlekwa to take many more. I was happy to see the family, Perisi, the gravesite, and visit with the people. Your sisters Eva, Marita and Mlekwa were there. They told me that when I arrived they thought I was you! Many had never seen you, and they knew you were in America. And of course, I was the only mzungu there. Would that I looked like you!! When I left, none of the three sons had arrived. Yotham was there in his usual condition that Yeremia used to complain about—not too sober! Fredy had phoned from Dar and said that the funeral had to wait for him. En route to the ferry we passed the pick-up truck with the coffin. They said they were late because the coffin wasn't quite ready, and they had to buy insurance for the pick-up truck, ferry broke down and got stuck in the mud. Where else would this happen?

So, I returned to Mwanza Monday evening.

It is now the next week. Mlekwa didn't return until a few days ago, and last evening she and her husband Otieno came to visit. They brought the camera and I'll take the film in today and I hope she did a good job. She told me the details of the burial.

On Tuesday around 11.00 a.m. they started to prepare the body, washed it and got him all dressed up in his best clothes, best shoes AND his glasses! Then around 1.00 p.m. the actual ceremony began and it took four hours. First each person must file by the coffin and say their farewell. The whole village was there and this took four hours, Mlekwa told me. Then prayers by the pastor, then bringing the body to the grave, more prayers, more farewells and then they put the coffin in the grave. She said it was very nice. Fredy arrived on Tuesday around noon and was so thankful that he made it. I hope this gives you a good picture of it and hopefully there will be some good photos. Your father was a dear, dear man and I will miss his visits. He was surely well loved by everyone. One thing more! Mlekwa told me that the family was furious with Yotham for being drunk on the day of the funeral. They have fined him 50,000.00 Tanzania shillings (about $22.00 dollars) and given him until the end of October to pay! Good for them!

> *Pole sana! (So sorry)*
> *Sister Catherine*

The Sukuma burial rituals that Sister Catherine described were foreign to me. The only funerals I'd attended before coming to America were Catholic rituals imprinted on me at the orphanage when the nuns buried one of their own. Because of the somber atmosphere of those funerals, I have made it a point not to attend funerals in my adult life if I can help it. I would say that three quarters of the nightmares I've experienced in my life originated from the crippling fears I had when I saw the blue, stiff bodies of dead nuns, dressed in their full black and white habits, clutching black rosaries with silver crucifixes as they rested in homemade coffins.

I wished I'd had the opportunity to see a tribal burial ceremony. From Sister Catherine's description and pictures, I think my father's funeral was natural, with women audibly mourning and commiserating with each other as they sat on the ground of the compound in large and small groups, wearing their best and brightly colored *khangas* and *vitenges*. I imagined the well-dressed children quietly and respectfully sitting on their mothers' laps, and a few goats wandering among the gathered mourners, thankful they hadn't been slaughtered for the occasion.

My sister Mlekwa, who was my father's main caregiver in his final years, wrote me a long letter in Swahili describing everything that happened from the time he took a turn for the worse until after the burial. "You must not cry, my beloved sister," she wrote. "I made sure that he was buried in his best suit and best pair of shoes and his valued glasses. You made his last years on this earth very good. He loved you so much and was very proud of you. Now he is happy next to your mother in heaven!"

I wondered what she knew about our father and my mother. When I took a close look at the picture of my father lying in the casket, I noticed that the favorite pair of shoes he was wearing was a used pair that had once belonged to my husband and that Kjell had given him back in 1992 when our family went to Kasamwa to meet him for the first time.

Sister Catherine wrote me this note after sending the burial photos:

Dear Maria,

Just a PS to my email about the "kilio" (mourning) and funeral. Mlekwa did a good job of taking pictures of the actual burial. Only one little problem—she didn't pay any attention to how many snaps were left, and I guess kept on taking them to the very end of the ceremonies. Unfortunately, the film ran out as they carried the coffin out of the house, so there are no pictures of the actual burial. I took one of the grave as they were preparing it, and you will see it when you come. You'll just not *see all the many beautiful people, the flowers and the sincere respect and love written on the mourners' faces.*

Sorry.
Sister Catherine

It is a Sukuma custom that all immediate and extended family not present at the funeral travel to the clan's main village to pay their respects at the gravesite and to the remaining relatives within a year of a death. I was dreading the trip back, because I knew it would be hard to be there without my father. Without him, I had little motivation to make that long trip from America. Yet, apart from having to pay my respects, I had to go for another very important reason.

41

My Father's Will

 About five years before my father died, he asked me to help him write his will. He wanted my youngest brother, Amani, and me to be the executors, and now Amani begged me to come home as soon as possible because his older brothers were pestering him to read the will. I knew very well that no matter what was written in the will, the brothers would distribute everything the way they wanted. All members of the immediate family had been waiting patiently for my arrival from America for my father's "wealth" to be distributed.

On November 28, 1999, three months after my father passed away, Kjell, Sister Catherine, and I went to Kasamwa so I could fulfill my duty. When we walked into the compound, I saw more relatives than I thought I had gathered in anticipation under a makeshift awning outside the house. I tried to take it all in, knowing that many were relatives I'd never met and that I'd never see again. Even before my father's death, three of his sons (my half-brothers) had been eying the house that Larry, Kjell, and I had built for him. They had wanted to make money renting rooms in the house even while Yeremia and Perisi were still living in it. That was the main reason my father wanted to write a will. Written wills, registered at the courthouse, were unheard of in his little village.

In his will Yeremia said he wanted the house to always remain in the family. He didn't want it sold or rented to strangers. To this day I cannot understand what on earth the gathered relatives thought they would inherit from my father. They knew him, and they knew where and how he lived, but somehow, they believed there would be plenty of money or land to inherit. One brother had already made plans for his share of the inheritance.

I had the will in my hand, and after the long customary greetings and drinking of a Coca-Cola, Fanta, or Safari beer, I got down to business. The will was a typical stuffy British document written in stupefying legalese that sounded like gibberish to me, but my relatives were impressed at how official and respectful the legal sheet of paper was. Kata and I had helped my father with some of the wording regarding the house and the family plot he had in Chabulongo, a few kilometers away. Apart from that, I knew of nothing else he owned. I opened the will, which Amani had picked up just that morning from the courthouse, and to my surprise, it was still in English and there were three pages instead of the one I had helped with. I asked Amani why it hadn't been translated, and he said that our father wanted it left in English because it would be more official and intimidating.

My father's will in its entirety:

I, Yeremia Nhambu, a Tanzanian of Kasamwa, Geita, HEREBY REVOKE all testamentary dispositions heretofore made by me and DECLARE this to be my last will and I further declare that I am domiciled in Tanzania.

I HEREBY APPOINT my daughter, Maria Nhambu Bergh of Minneapolis Minnesota, U.S.A. and my son Amani Yeremia of Arusha, Tanzania to be executors and trustees of my will and I declare that all trusts and powers reposed and vested in the executors shall or may be exercised by the survivor of them.

I HEREBY appoint my son Amani Yeremia to be the guardian of my estate.

I DIRECT the executors to first pay out of my estate all my just debts, testamentary expenses and funeral expenses and also all other expenses.

I DIVIDE AND BEQUEATH all my immovable properties described in Schedule 'A' hereto to my sons and daughters and grandchildren described in Schedule B hereto for their life only without any power to sell, mortgage or charge any interest in the said immovable properties.

I DIVIDE AND BEQUEATH my movable properties described in

Schedule 'A' hereto to the beneficiaries described in Schedule 'B' hereto without any power to sell same.

SIGNED by the said YEREMIA NHAMBU of Kasamwa, Geita, after the contents hereof having been fully interpreted and explained to him when he appeared perfectly to understand same, who at his request in his presence, and in the presence of each other have subscribed our hands as witnesses:

Enos Kibendela [our cousin] and Lukas Mashamba [whom I do not know]

As mentioned above, Schedule 'A'

LIST OF PROPERTIES
One house situated in Kasamwa, Geita
One uncompleted house located at Kasamwa, Geita
7 Head of Cattle
2 Goats
The following furniture and household items to be found in the house
18 Beds
14 Stools
15 Chairs
1 Sofa set
1 Water filter
1 Lamp
7 Tables
1 Torch (Flashlight)
4 D batteries

There was nothing about the family land and burial ground in Chabulongo. I figured that family ground is sacred and could not be disbursed as property. The above items were to be distributed among his children and grandchildren, including Kata and Karl.

The will was executed and signed with an illegible signature by a representative of the Tanzania Legal Corporation, Mwanza. After the reading of the will, there was rejoicing and *kigelele* (ululation), and someone put on a cassette of gospel songs and they started to dance. I couldn't bring myself to celebrate with my relatives—it was all I could do to hold back the tears. My father was considered a rich man because he had a house made of cement. I shook hands or hugged the few relatives I knew and approached Perisi, my father's wife and mother of his eleven children (three deceased), but she was avoiding me. At that moment I realized she was sad because her name was nowhere in the will.

I put my arms around her and whispered in her ear that nothing would leave the house without her permission while she was alive. Then I interrupted the rejoicing and announced that our father had told me his will would be effective upon the passing of Perisi. I asserted that he had left everything to his wife and nothing would change hands until she died or chose to distribute it herself. I lied. Yeremia had parted with tradition by spelling out what was to become of his property upon his death, and I was now stepping on another forbidden tribal custom!

Traditionally when the man of the house dies, everything goes to the eldest son or is distributed equally among his sons. The wife and daughters get nothing! I had lived in America for too long to accept this.

I told them that she, and all of us, would honor the one important directive in the will, which was that the house would never be sold. It was always to remain within the family as a home for all to come to.

Without further ado, I bid my farewells and didn't acknowledge the disappointment on the faces of a couple of my brothers. One of the reasons that my father went to all the trouble of writing a will was because two of his sons were pestering him about renting out the rooms. They would get the tenants, they said, and would share part of the rent with him. When I was working with him on his will, Yeremia told me that these two sons seldom helped him and wanted to get him out of his own house so they could make money renting it. They told him that the many rooms would bring a lot of money, and he could rent a place for himself somewhere else and live very well. I suspected they also had plans to sell the cows and goats and furniture and keep the proceeds because that's the way it has always been done. I knew.

I told them that I would return to the village from time to time to visit my father's grave and knew I'd always be welcome in his house. I made a brief farewell speech, thanking all the relatives for traveling for days to come to this meeting at this time to accommodate my schedule. I asked my brothers and sisters to protect and take good care of mother Perisi now that she was alone. How could anyone have issue with that? Even my greedy siblings nodded in agreement. By the time we left, I sensed a genuine feeling of gratitude and love for me from my relatives.

I had one more thing to do for myself. I wanted a tangible memento of my father. Before I left, I asked Perisi to come into the house with me. I asked her if there was something he had used and loved that she wouldn't mind parting with, something I could take back to America with me.

"He really didn't keep anything for himself. He shared everything with family and friends. But let's see. There could be something in his private corner of our bedroom."

She brought out a small dark brown wood trunk with Y. M. NHAMBU written on it in yellow paint. It had no lock, so it was easy to open. In it we found only two objects—two black leather-bound Bibles, one in Swahili and one in Sukuma.

"Can I have these?" I asked Perisi.

"I cannot read, so what good will they do me? What use will you have for these old books? Don't they have Bibles in America?"

"I have a Bible in America, but I do not have these Bibles. You can see how much he used them. They have notes and folded pages and little dried leaves throughout. They will bring meaning to me when I hold them in my hands, just as they did for him. Is there anything else in his private corner?"

She dragged out an old basket wrapped in a *khanga*. When I unwrapped the *khanga*, I found a round hard object full of dents and covered in dust and mold. On the outside, there was a rusted silver handle that looked familiar.

"What's this?"

"It's my husband's singing box. I think your mother gave it to him when he stopped working for her. He used to play it all the time, but nowadays no one knows what it is, and we didn't need it anymore after you brought us the big cassette player."

"A singing box?" It looked too big to be a music box, and it was so covered with mold I hated to touch it.

"Open it!" she said.

I pried it open with my Swiss Army knife. It was a gramophone! The original red velvet interior was in shreds, but a vinyl 78 rpm record, warped from the heat, was still on the turntable. I could barely make out the singing dog on the loudspeaker logo and the red Victor label, which had also succumbed to the heat and moths.

"Can I have this too?"

"What will you do with such an old useless thing?"

"When I was a child, I used to love the gramophone. I often asked the nun in the orphanage if I could be in charge of it and 'make the music.'"

On our way out of the house, I saw his cane leaning by the door.

"Can I have his cane?"

Perisi looked at me with a puzzled expression. "It's just a piece of rough wood that he made himself, but he preferred it to his store-bought walking sticks. You can find a beautiful cane in America when you get old."

I took the gramophone back to Arusha with me and asked my brother Amani to keep it until I found a way of getting it to America. A few months later, a friend from Florida retrieved the gramophone from Amani, carried it on board the plane as his hand luggage, and delivered it to me. It was the one item that my mother and father had enjoyed together. I gave Yeremia's Bibles to Kata when she graduated from Harvard School of Divinity. The cane I gave to Karl when he graduated with his master's degree in Buddhist Studies from Maitripa College, and I kept the gramophone.

42

No Itinerary

 A trip I dreamed of was to travel extensively in Europe without feeling rushed. I'd been to France, the Soviet Union, Italy, Germany, the United Kingdom, Hungary, Greece, Austria, and all the Scandinavian countries, and had seen most of the tourist attractions. Except for Russia, Norway, Denmark, and Sweden, my time in Europe was usually short and rushed. I seldom had a chance to see what I really wanted to see. I was thrilled when Kjell told me that our good friends Wayne and Velora and Terry and Kathie wanted to travel with us to Europe. "I hope this time we'll stay long enough to actually see, participate in, and enjoy what Europe has to offer," I said.

"Not only are we not going to rush, we won't even have an itinerary!"

"Now you're talking! How long of a trip will it be?"

"How long do you want it to be?"

"Long enough to see everything I want to see. A few months?" What's going on, I wondered. Kjell actually wants my input.

"We can start in Norway because Wayne and Terry want to look for their Norwegian relatives. Then we'll go to Germany, Italy, France, and Spain."

"In Germany, I want to see the concentration camp at Dachau."

I had imagined it ever since I'd heard about it when I was small, maybe eight years old, at the orphanage in Kifungilo. The nuns and priests frequently mentioned it, speaking freely in German in front of us children, thinking we didn't understand them. We didn't understand everything, but we remembered the word Dachau, and from their demeanor and tone of voice, we knew it was a bad place.

It wasn't until my early twenties in college in America that I finally learned the awful truth about what the nuns and priests so gravely discussed.

I did see the Dachau concentration camp, and I wished I hadn't. After seeing it, I had nightmares featuring Kifungilo orphans and me kneeling in prayer around the ovens, waiting for our turn to be shoved in. We prayed loudly to Blessed Martin in the dream, but he couldn't hear us because his statue was already in the oven. The nightmare usually ended when I saw all of us children dressed in white, hiding under the blue cloak of the extended arms of the Virgin Mary.

The trip to Europe turned out to be all that I had hoped it would be. Terry and Wayne did find their relatives in Norway, and even though they were several generations removed, their reunion and celebration reminded me of when I met my mother for the first time when I was thirty-six and my father at forty-five.

We enjoyed the spectacular tourist attractions of Europe like the Cinque Terre in Italy, Mont Saint-Michel in France, the beaches of Normandy, the Prince's Palace in Monaco, the Alhambra Castle in Spain, the vineyards and wine tasting chateaux of Bordeaux and Tuscany, Portofino's pastel-colored houses, the towers of San Gimignano in Italy, the fortressed medieval town of Rothenburg in Germany, the magnificent Côte d'Azur, and the decadent shopping in Saint-Tropez.

In Norway we hiked from Kjell's parents' cabin, located along Batnfjord, to the three lakes up the mountain. It was to one of these lakes that Kjell took me on our honeymoon thirty-two years earlier when we slept on a decaying cornhusk mattress on the rugged floor of a forsaken boat shack. Although in the years that followed we had frequently hiked up to these same lakes, I hadn't spent a night there since. From what I hear, the boathouse hasn't improved much. After all, Norwegians like to be admired for roughing it!

On this trip to Europe we also took the Hurtigruten, a cruise ship that hugged the Norwegian coast and ventured in and out of breathtaking fjords. Norway is one of the most naturally beautiful places I've ever been to. I could understand Kjell being so proud of it, but what I didn't understand was how he never got tired of bragging about it—as if he took personal credit for what God created. Presumptuous, I'd say, for a self-proclaimed atheist.

He was more relaxed at his childhood farm than at any other place on the trip. We often found ourselves sitting together by the fireplace in some romantic little country hotel, B&B, or chalet in Switzerland, but rather than sharing the amazing scenery outside with me and enjoying each other, he'd start a conversation with a local stranger. We were surrounded by majestic snow-topped mountains and green velvet grass slopes dotted with wooly sheep and cattle click-clacking their wooden cowbells as they peacefully grazed in front of us. I longed to walk out into that romantic setting with him, but Kjell would be focused on chit-chatting with our traveling companions. The unique beauty surrounding us as we sat in our exquisitely decorated loft overlooking a magically lit, cobblestoned, medieval market square in Rothenburg seemed to escape him. I wondered, at times, if he knew I was there.

Soon after our return, Kjell's father, Kristian, fell ill. He had been sick off and on for the whole of 2001, and Kjell spent more time in Norway than usual. I actually admired him for being so attentive and caring about his father, though from experience, I had my doubts that his father's illness was the only reason he traveled so much.

That March, Karl returned from India totally committed to Buddhism. He hung his *thangkas*—Tibetan Buddhist paintings—in his room, made a little altar, meditated, prostrated, and chanted every day. Every opportunity he had, he wore the maroon and gold monk robes that Geshe-La's teacher had made for him. He took Refuge (became a Buddhist) from a visiting Lama in Fort Meyers and was very involved in helping Geshe-La at the Tubten Kunga Ling Buddhist Center in Deerfield Beach.

Around the time we were supposed to join Kjell in Norway, Karl seemed very depressed. He didn't want to go to Norway, but Kjell insisted that it was very important for all of us go because his father was very ill and it might be the last time we'd see him. Kata traveled alone from Boston while Karl and I would be flying from Florida. The morning of our scheduled departure, I noticed that Karl hadn't packed.

"I don't want to go!"

"What's the matter?"

"I just don't feel that's where I want to be right now."

"But your dad and Kata are already there waiting for us. It's important that we all go and see his father."

Until the cab was at our front door, Karl still hadn't packed or budged from his bed. He was staring straight ahead with a blank glassy look.

"Karl, please get dressed and come. We need to be together in Norway."

"I'll come, but I'm not packing."

I was pleased he got in the cab. It wasn't until we reached Fort Lauderdale that I realized he was wearing his bright Buddhist monk robes. He carried only a cloth bag with some books in it. Karl didn't say a word to me for the entire trip from our home in Delray Beach to Miami, to Newark, to Amsterdam, to Oslo and to Kristiansund—a total of fifteen hours, including the six-hour delay in Amsterdam. I was so relieved when we finally arrived in Kristiansund and saw Kjell and Kata. By this point, I was stressed out and tired. When Kjell asked me how I could let our son travel in his Buddhist robes, I snapped back, "Just thank your lucky Norsk stars he's here!"

43

Surprise!

 We drove in relative silence through the three-mile underwater tunnel to Batnfjord, the little town at the mouth of the fjord. As soon as we saw the familiar and charming little town, we all brightened into a better mood, especially Karl. We stopped to get Kjell's favorite foam car candies, a box of Kong Haakon chocolates for me, and a variety of snacks, including the Freia chocolate bars and bottles of Solo soda for Kata and Karl. Karl did not go into the store. He walked around the area to stretch his long legs, looking like a dancer on stilts as his bright gold and maroon Buddhist robes blew in the breeze. When we left the store, we saw three blond, blue-eyed kids running toward him, hands folded, bowing their heads to him, singing "Hare Krishna, Krishna, Krishna," and then running away, laughing.

On the last stretch to the cabin, I had a glimpse of the good old days when we happily made this trip together with little or no drama. Karl was talking and laughing again.

We drove up the narrow road and approached *Berget*, my in-laws' cabin—a small, unassuming cabin they had built and added onto over the years. Kata and Karl usually slept in a loft on top of a detached garage while Kjell and I stayed in the main cabin. When Kjell drove past *Berget*, we all pointed out that he had missed it. He ignored us as he drove along a newly excavated dirt road that opened up to a clearing in the woods.

"Holy fucking shit!" Kata and Karl screamed simultaneously.

"Oh my God!" I said. "What's this?"

"Damn!" said Karl.

In front of our eyes was a huge, newly built log cabin with a green sod-thatched roof.

"Welcome home!" Kjell proudly said.

He was beaming and beyond pleased with himself for having completely surprised us. Kata and Karl jumped out of the car and ran from window to window looking inside. I was delighted because we hadn't had a cabin of our own since we sold Tussebo many years ago. Although I liked staying at his parents' cabin, it was cramped and being a light sleeper, I seldom slept, because someone invariably snored.

Kjell unlocked the doors and we raced to the windows, where we saw beautiful views of the mountains and countryside that cradled Batnfjord and, in the distance, the long, graceful suspension bridge.

The kitchen was state of the art with a dishwasher, stove, microwave oven, and a side-by-side refrigerator that dispensed ice. Cabinets were painted farmer's red with green trimming; a little breakfast nook overlooked the fjord. Kata and Karl each had a bedroom downstairs on either side of a hallway; upstairs was the master suite, complete with a sitting room and a cubbyhole corner that could be used for an office. The master bath had a jacuzzi, a toilet, and a shower with both hot and cold water, plus ample storage space.

"The jacuzzi is just for you," he told me. "And something else just for you—the bathroom floor is heated."

"Heated!" My eyes popped. Norwegians love to rough it out in their cabins, but not me!

"Not only heated, but I can turn the heat on remotely from Oslo for instance, or even a day before we arrive."

"A warm floor in the bathroom to step on with my bare feet—almost as amazing as the heated toilet seat I had in Minnesota!"

"Don't say I'm not looking out for you."

"I'm impressed and touched. Thank you, thank you, thank you!"

In spite of the euphoria about the cabin, we could not deny that our family was somehow disjointed, unhappy, and distant that summer.

Kata noticed that I was not myself and she asked, "Mom, is everything okay?"

"Yes and no," I replied. "I am really happy that your father built this cabin, but it irks me that he could do it in complete secrecy. If he can build an entire house from scratch across the ocean behind my back, how many other secrets can he keep from me?"

"Dad really wanted to surprise us. Though I guess if I were his wife and we're supposed to own everything together, I would be annoyed if he spent thousands of dollars without discussing it with me."

"It's hard for me to see things his way. He believes that as long as he provides for everything I need or want, I shouldn't be concerned about how much we have, or what he does with our money. I suspect he believes it's his money, and he's being generous sharing it."

"I think you should talk to him about that. Something else I've noticed," Kata added. "You seem depressed. Is there something wrong, like are you sick or something?"

"I'm not really sick, but I have been having the worst insomnia and bad stomach pains for a long time now. I should see a doctor when I return."

"I think we should have a family meeting while we're together in Norway. Too much is out of sync," Kata said.

We did have a family meeting and each of us had a chance to talk about what was bothering us. Kata felt that I didn't support her enough and didn't involve myself sufficiently with what was going on in her life. Karl said he felt that we were not respecting his decision to become a Buddhist, but he was serious and wanted to bring some people to the cabin for retreats in the future. I said that I couldn't put my finger on it, but I had been depressed ever since we moved to Florida.

"I hadn't noticed," Kjell said.

"I think it's because I feel so alone."

"We're sorry, Mom," Kata and Karl both said.

"I feel alone even when Kjell and I are together. He often makes me feel like we aren't equal partners in this marriage."

"How can you complain when I've done and am still doing so

much for you?" Kjell responded. "Are you forgetting the extra pains I took to build this cabin for you and the kids?"

"She's not complaining," Kata said. "We're having a meeting because it's obvious that something is wrong. It's your turn, Dad."

"Well, I have no complaints. Everything is fine as far as our family is concerned. Of course, I've had to travel to Norway many times to build the cabin and to see my father. I had to be distant and secretive because I wanted to surprise you. I'm done with the meeting. Now, what are we going to name the cabin?"

"We're not done," Kata said.

"Well, I'm done. Who has a name for the cabin?"

"HFS for 'Holy Fucking Shit!'" I suggested, because that's what both kids blurted out when they saw it.

"Yes!" Kata and Karl agreed.

"No one has to know what the letters stand for," I said.

"You know that won't work," Kjell said. "The Norwegian contingent has come up with a name. We think it would be proper to call it *Storberget* for 'big hill' since my parents' cabin is *Berget*, 'little hill.'"

"I don't like that at all, or those huge flags outside," Kata said. "It feels kind of flashy, and the cabin is majestic enough. I don't feel we need to broadcast it. Let's just enjoy it."

"I thought you liked the cabin?"

"Dad, we're very happy that we each have our own space now, but we love *Mor* and *Far's* cabin just as much," Karl said.

44

Everything Norwegian

 Back in America, my friends just chuckled when I mentioned the cabin because most of them already knew.

"Kjell said he was building it as a surprise for you," my friend Dale told me.

"A cabin in Norway as a surprise for me? Really!"

Every Monday at 7 a.m. Dale and I walked six miles along the ocean in Delray Beach. Together we solved many of the world's problems, but more importantly, she helped me heal by being a trusted friend. At a critical time in my life, Dale held my hand and listened to me from her heart.

"I worked in a bank," said Dale. "Maybe it's none of my business, but how could Kjell take so much money from your bank account without you knowing?"

"Kjell handles the finances and pays the bills. I have credit cards and a checkbook. He gives me a check every month, and I buy what I need for myself and the kids."

"He can spend thousands of dollars building a cabin in Norway, he can buy a boat and business buildings, and you don't know?"

"He usually tells me after the fact. He'll say we've bought something and that I need to go with him to the bank to sign papers. I trust him fully with our money. I must admit that it bothered me when he built a dance studio in our house in Edina without discussing it with me and then built a cabin halfway around the world, again without my knowledge or consent. It makes me feel unimportant and taken for granted."

"But he wanted to surprise you, so how could he discuss it?"

"You're sounding just like him! He has an answer for everything.

Whenever I ask him how much money we make, he always says 'Enough'—like what else is there to know? The next time he wants to surprise me with something big, he should buy land in Tanzania and build us a house that would cost much less than the cabin. If he really had my best interests in mind, he could buy us a condo in Minnesota—something I've always wanted since we moved to Florida.

"One of his first surprises for me—it was the year Kata was born when we literally had nothing—was a four-volume, leather-bound set of books on Norway in Norwegian! That should have been a red flag. Don't get me wrong, though. Kjell has bought me many wonderful gifts of jewelry, clothing, and African Art. He justifies his extravagant purchases for himself, like the plane he once bought and his big and bigger boats, by telling me those items are for us. I never got inside his plane, but I did eventually start enjoying his boats."

"Whenever I ran into Kjell, he'd update me about the cabin," Dale tole me. "It seemed like he really wanted me to know how lucky you were and how wonderful he was to you."

"That's Kjell! I've often told him how lucky I feel being married to him."

"Do you think he feels lucky being married to you?"

"I don't know, because he hasn't told me. Maybe he did indirectly when we were first married, but not as the years have gone by."

Now that we had our own cabin in Norway, I did something I'd always wanted to do—have two traditional *rosemåled* Norwegian bridal trunks painted for us with our marriage date written on them, like those I'd admired in several homes. I also admired the *rosemåled kubbestol* (high rounded-back chair carved from one piece of wood) with beautiful scenes of Norwegian snow-covered mountains and blue-green fjords. An artist who lived near the cabin painted two trunks and *kubbestols* for us, one for the cabin in Norway, and one for our Norwegian room in Florida. They turned out to be more beautiful than I expected.

I also had a *bunad* made for me at the Husfliden in Oslo, the national chain of craft stores. A *bunad*, the traditional Norwegian rural costume, is different for each district. Designs are typically elaborate, with embroidery, scarves, shawls, lace aprons, handmade silver or gold jewelry, special embroidered purses, and leather shoes. The *bunad* from the Kristiansund region was plain, so I chose the one from Telemark with bright red colors against black. I convinced Kjell to get the male version from Telemark, too, and wondered why no one in his family owned one. Ever since my friend Mary Johnson had loaned me hers to wear when Kjell was inducted into the Scandinavian Hall of Fame in 1997 I wanted one for myself.

I wore my beautiful *bunad* for Crown Prince Haakon's visit to Minnesota. My Norwegian friends loved it, but I got questioning and outright contemptuous looks from several guests at the celebration.

45

Money Tub

 When we returned from Europe to Florida in 2001 out of the clear blue, and out of character, Kjell told me that he was planning to sell our car dealership in Delray Beach to his partner.

"How can you sell this dealership when we just moved here? You've always wanted to sell the Minnesota dealership. This is your chance if you need to get rid of one."

"I promised my partner, who relocated to Florida to run the dealership, that one day it would be his. I want to keep my word."

"I don't understand. We live here now, and we've always looked forward to having more time together instead of you going back and forth to the dealerships. If you sell the Minnesota one, we could do that."

"All the papers are drawn, and we'll have the signing in three months. We'll be making an obscene amount of money, and we can buy a yacht and travel wherever we want. My idea is for us to be at sea for most of the year and dock our boat only at interesting places in the Bahamas or elsewhere. That's what I've always wanted to do."

"The papers are drawn? There's no way I'll spend most of my time at sea!"

"You don't have to. You can come and stay for three weeks or a month at a time, and you can fly back home. I'll stay on the boat. You can come and go as you please."

"And you would have any woman you want with you when I'm gone! Somehow your plans are starting to make sense."

"I have no idea what you're talking about."

I wondered why I continued to believe that Kjell would listen to me and sell the Minnesota dealership. Despite the fact that he insisted I was an equal partner with him in our marriage and business, he kept me out of important decisions that directly affected me.

The sale of the dealership proceeded as planned. On September 13, just two days after September 11, amidst the fear, doom, and uncertainty of the terrorist attack on the Twin Towers of New York, we signed the papers.

With proceeds from the sale, Kjell did buy a seventy-six-foot yacht, a year-old Lazzara that was by far the most luxurious and modern boat he'd ever owned. It had three floors with four staterooms, four heads, a state-of-the-art galley, a huge salon with dining area, two washing machines, and crews' quarters that were posher than the staterooms of previous boats. He told me that "money was no object" when it came to decorating and furnishing it. It's really true what people say: a yacht is a bottomless tub in the water that you pour money into.

Since we named it *Serengeti*, I decided to have African-themed décor and hired a pair of decorators with exquisite taste. They made beautiful quilted bedspreads with different colors and animals for each stateroom, window dressings for the salon of bold African designs, and hand-painted throw pillows for the couches in the salon and in the aft deck.

Since I had no budget restrictions for furnishing the yacht, I bought Riedel crystal glasses and Lynn Chase Jaguar Jungle china that I'd always wanted for our house. I commissioned a friend from South Africa to make a large ceramic platter with scenes from the Serengeti for the heavy glass coffee table and matching mugs for the galley. Carvings of African animals graced the tables and dressers, and colorful batik, *tinga tinga,* and oil paintings of African scenes covered the walls. I bought a collection of CDs and DVDs and the best wine and liqueur I could find. I was waiting for Kjell to say something about the cost of all this, because in my opinion, I was going way overboard, but he didn't complain. He was very proud of the boat and bragged to anyone who listened about the great job I did decorating it. As soon as we had everything in order, we invited groups of friends to sail with us to the Bahamas. I recall those trips with fondness. It was a very nice boat and I enjoyed it more than I thought I would.

Along with his generosity to himself in buying the exquisite yacht, Kjell was also very generous to his family. He gave a large sum of money to his parents and everyone in his immediate family—including Cathy and John. I, too, was given the same amount of money. I found this very disconcerting. As his wife, didn't the money he was giving away belong to both of us? Shouldn't I have been consulted?

That July Kjell's father passed away and we all went to Kristiansund for the funeral. Kristian Bergh, whom we called *Far*, had always been good to me. I mostly remember enjoyable times with him because he was funny and a little eccentric. He would read the paper, listen to the radio, watch TV full blast, take notes, and carry on a conversation simultaneously. He spent a lot of time keeping track of Kjell's progress in America and would brag about him often. For Kjell's part, he seemed to want and need his father's approval and praise. Sometimes their conversations were like bragging matches or arguments about who was right on various issues that were insignificant to anyone else. *Far* and his wife Liv, Kjell's mother, took a trip to Tanzania with us and visited us a few times in Minnesota. He took many pictures and subjected any unsuspecting soul who asked about his trip to endless photo-viewing sessions.

The year before, when Kjell revealed his secret cabin to us, *Far* was already quite ill and had come to see *Storberget* in a wheelchair. Although he was uncomfortable, he relished every aspect of the cabin, pointing out all the bells and whistles. It was obvious that *Far* loved and admired his son and was living vicariously through him. At his father's funeral, Kjell was subdued and distant. I felt for him because, of all the children in his family, he was the one most like his father.

A few months after we returned to the States Kjell was still not himself. He was pre-occupied with something he wouldn't discuss with me, no matter how often I tried to broach the subject.

One evening he announced that we had been invited to go to Africa. I couldn't believe my good luck! I was guaranteed to have my husband back, even if only for the duration of the trip. He loved Africa. No matter what was going on in our lives, in Africa the man I married always returned, and I knew he would be playful, full of joy and wonder, and very loving. He told me he had official meetings to attend in Tanzania and Botswana, and he wanted me to accompany him.

Karl with his Buddhist teacher Geshe Kunchog Kyab in front of an African sculpture in Nhambu's backyard.

Cathy and her husband John at Karl's graduation.

Cathy, Kata, Karl, Nhambu and John at Karl's graduation from Naropa University in Colorado.

Matt and Kata.

Kata and Nhambu at Kata's wedding.

At Kata's wedding (front row): Eleanor and Cathy.
Back row: John, Eleanor's husband Micah, Matt and Kata, Nhambu, Karl, and Kjell.

Kata and Matt with their son Amani.

Mandy and Karl.

At Karl and Mandy's wedding (front row): Matt with son Amani, Mandy and Karl.
Back row: Kjell, Nhambu, and Kata.

Karl and Mandy with their children Liv and Oskar.

Nhambu with grandson Amani and the Mama Africa statue.

Oskar and his grandmother.

Nhambu with granddaughter Liv.

Nhambu with first grandson, Amani.

Nhambu with her children Karl and Kata.

John and Cathy Mamer.

Nhambu with her sister Eleanor,

Nhambu with Aunt Marion,
Dorothy's sister.

Ebony Nativity scene carved in Tanzania.

Nhambu's Christmas tree decorated with beaded African ornaments.

46

South Africa Revisited

We hadn't been to South Africa since the early 1980s when it was under apartheid rule, and we were both eager to see the changes that came about after Nelson Mandela was released from prison in 1990 and became South Africa's first democratically elected president in 1994.

It was now three years after he stepped down from the presidency and Thabo Mbeki, the second president, seemed to be following his leadership in working for truth and reconciliation concerning the apartheid regime. We stayed in former whites-only hotels, ate in former whites-only restaurants, and went to a formerly exclusive whites-only private club where Cedric, Kjell's Black friend from Minnesota, was a member. We visited vineyards and tourist attractions filled with people of all races and colors. Kjell's friend lived in a substantial compound in an upscale neighborhood and had servants. His enviable wine cellar displayed South African wines I'd never heard of.

Cedric was generous with his coveted wines, opening some vintage bottles for us to enjoy. He gave us his special tour for wine connoisseurs, though Kjell was clueless about wine and I was almost as bad. He asked what year we got married. We told him 1968, and he went to the cabinet with his special stash of liquors and took out a bottle of 1967 tawny port.

"A gift for you for remaining married for so long!"

"How thoughtful and generous," I said. "We actually met in 1967 and married in 1968, so the port is from the year we met."

All the wine bottles in his cellar were meticulously clean and labeled. Pulling out twelve bottles from his stash of unique and vintage South African wines, he gave them to us to take back to America.

We couldn't refuse his generosity, even though we knew we couldn't haul twelve bottles of wine and one tawny port with us on our three-week trip to several African countries. We thanked him profusely and took the bottles back to the hotel.

Cedric introduced us to several African art galleries. My favorite was a ten-acre outdoor Shona sculpture park. I was open-mouthed with awe from the moment we entered and saw the stone sculptures of people, herds of animals, individual animals, flocks of birds, and nature scenes that beckoned us to stop and look. Tall serpentine stone giraffes thrust their necks into the huge flamboyant trees or stood with spread legs reaching down to us, asking to be touched. The talent of the mostly uneducated men who produced the large, powerful stone sculptures gently spoke to me and told me that they knew how I felt in the presence of their majestic art. An enormous statue of an African woman with a pumpkin on her head and a baby wrapped in a *khanga* on her back stopped me in my tracks. This statue was carved for me! I instantly named it "Mama Africa." She reminded me of the vision I had of an African woman carrying a basket on her head that accompanied the plane as I left Tanzania for the first time. I looked at the $25,000 price tag and couldn't believe it! I knew the sculptor hadn't set the price and that he would receive only a fraction of the selling price.

I was not born in Africa for nothing—I knew the rules of bargaining and I played the game well! I found the African salesperson sitting in a small shack at the edge of the compound and motioned for him to come.

"Do you really believe that anyone, even a rich and gullible American, would pay $25,000 for that statue?" I had to pretend I was not interested.

"Oh yes. Several Americans and Europeans have purchased here, and they didn't even bargain. They paid the asking price."

"You mean the first price?"

"Oh, you've been to Africa before?"

"Not only have I been to Africa, I was born in Africa. In Tanzania.

"I hear that it is beautiful up there. You have Mount Kilimanjaro."

Since I knew what to do if I really wanted to get a good price on the statue, I proceeded to ask him all sorts of questions about his work, his family, his children, his tribe, the village he came from, and where he was living now. While Kjell and Cedric continued walking around in the sculpture park, I managed to bring the price down to $15,000.

"You must not want to sell the statue."

"Of course, I want to sell it. If you don't buy it, someone else will."

"Why don't you call your boss on the phone and tell them that I'm offering $3,000 for the statue." I knew that some white man probably owned the sculpture park and the art too.

"Oh, my sister, he will not agree," he said.

"Just call him!" He called his boss.

"He said $12,000."

At that point, I decided to walk away, as if to imply he was out of his mind.

"Well, I guess I'll have to go to that park down the street," I said. I wanted the statue, and knew I would get it, but I wasn't willing to pay more than $5,000. I rejoined Kjell and Cedric, and we all walked together in the park for an additional forty-five minutes, admiring the art, discussing the AIDS problem in South Africa, and commenting how Mbeki denied how bad it was. All the time, I was waiting for the salesperson to run after me. Sure enough, he did.

"What's your last price?" I asked him.

He ran back to the phone to talk to his boss while I put on my sweater, pretending I was getting ready to leave the park.

He came running to me with a grin on his face. "The final price is $5,000."

We both knew that it was a steal, even if it was five feet high, weighed 2,300 pounds, and had to be shipped to Florida. Before I agreed, he shook my hand saying, "I am happy for you and for the statue."

My bargaining job was not done yet. Now I had to convince Kjell that we should buy the statue. I told him that it was for our house, our art collection, and for all of our friends who would enjoy it. We walked toward it and he looked at the price tag.

"What on earth? Have you lost your mind? Did you see the price?"

"Yes, but I bargained and we can have it for $5,000."

"You should be a buyer for the business. How are you going to ship it back?"

"The salesman said the boss would do it all for us."

Within twenty minutes, a white, very friendly boss came, and Kjell used a credit card to pay for the statue and the cost of shipping it to Miami.

It turned out that the statue arrived in Miami from Cape Town in eight weeks. It took two months to get it from the shipping docks to our house in Delray Beach fifty minutes away.

When it came time to leave for the next leg of our journey Kjell said, "You know we're allowed to take only a total of twenty pounds of personal belongings on the helicopter to the Okavango Delta in Botswana. Let's just leave the case in the room." He didn't care about the wine because he doesn't drink.

"No way! If I can't figure out how to get it back to Florida, I will give it to someone. Maybe the maid or bellboy." I carried the case of wine downstairs to the reception and asked if there was a way to ship it back to the States. The receptionist said they didn't ship, but a shipping company might take care of it.

Considering we were leaving Cape Town early in the morning, I was about to give the wine to the receptionist when out of the corner of my eye, I saw the friendly bellboy who had carried our luggage to our room when we checked in two days earlier; he seemed to be calling me with his eyes. His body language told me to follow him down the hallway.

"I can help you," he said.

"Can you take care of shipping the wine to the States for me?"

"Technically no, but practically yes."

"What do you mean?"

"We are not allowed to take the responsibility of shipping anything for tourists, but I can do it for you from my home."

I was so excited that my wine would be shipped it didn't occur to me that this trustworthy-looking man might enjoy it all himself, and I would never see it again.

"How much would it cost?"

"Give me thirty dollars."

Without further ado, I gave him fifty dollars—thirty for the shipping and twenty for his trouble.

"It shouldn't be too difficult, because each bottle is already wrapped in packing foam," I told him.

He smiled broadly and told me he would take it to his wife in the village, and she would repack it and mail it to me.

When I told Kjell what I had done, his expression told me he couldn't believe my gullibility. "You just said goodbye to the best South African wine you'll never taste."

"Would your suggestion of leaving it in the room have a different outcome?" In my heart, I felt that Kjell was wrong, but I said, "At least I'll know the face of the person who drank it!"

Then one afternoon, about three months after we returned to Florida, I found a strange box wrapped with newspaper with my name and address written in pencil on the side of the box. I had completely forgotten about the wine. Nothing about the package indicated there was anything breakable inside, so I brought in the heavy box and dropped it on the floor.

Inside the box were the twelve bottles of wine and the one bottle of port rewrapped in straw, wood chips, newspaper, and sisal string. The first thing I saw when I opened the box was a yellow, legal-size sheet of paper on which was written in pencil: "My dear God, please make this parcel to be safe in the hands of the African lady in America. Thank you very much. Amen."

After leaving Cape Town we took a helicopter from Gaborone, the capital of Botswana, to Chobe National Park. As I looked out the tiny window, I was surprised to see how barren the land seemed. We went for a late-night game drive—the first I had ever taken. Even though they were the same animals I'd seen in daylight, they seemed more exotic when illumined by the headlights of our Land Rover.

Once on a daytime game drive we came across a lone lion. Our guides asked us whether it was male or female. It was hard to decide because it had a mane, but also the elongated body and genitals of a female.

"We call her Martina," one of the guides volunteered. It took me a while to realize that they had named it after Martina Navratilova, the gay tennis player.

It was Kjell's birthday, so I asked the cook if they could make a cake for him. At the end of dinner that evening the cooks and waitresses started singing "Happy Birthday" from the kitchen. We watched as the candles on the cake burned and melted. The other tourists sitting at their tables joined in the celebration. One of the employees serenaded us on a traditional one-stringed instrument that produced a hauntingly beautiful sound when he held the string in his mouth and guided a bow across it, much like one would play a violin.

This trip to Botswana was a great contrast to the 1981 trip. At that time South Africa was still under apartheid and I was constantly aware of it. I was told that the only way I could accompany my white husband anywhere was if I were declared an "honorary white."

47

Maasai Camp

After Botswana we stopped in Arusha, Tanzania. We attended the Tanzania Tourist Investment Forum at the Arusha International Conference Center where the International Criminal Tribunal for Rwanda had convened with hearings on the 1994 Rwanda genocide. Tanzania's president and first lady were in attendance and invited us for dinner at the Arusha State House.

A highlight of this African trip was our two-night stay at the Maasai-run camp in Sinya at the invitation of William Chambulo, a young mixed-raced man we met at the conference who was passionate about tourism and especially the tented camp he ran on the western side of Mount Kilimanjaro. We had been in the same orphanage in Kifungilo and had heard of each other but had never met, since I was much older.

We arrived from Arusha in the late afternoon during the season of the short rains. Crossing the half-mile from the end of the road to the tents was both a challenge and a relief. The moist red soil around the tall savannah grass cushioned our feet with warm clay, which we found soothing.

A dignified, handsome Maasai man dressed in traditional clothes rushed over to greet us. His is one of the most original and proud cultures in East Africa. Several layers of checkered fabric in brilliant red, blue, white, and black made up his attire, topped by a blue-and-red-checkered swath of wool tied over one shoulder like a Roman toga. At his waist was a walkie-talkie attached to a narrow, beaded leather belt. Tucked in the belt were his long knife in a rugged leather case and an ebony *rungu* (club). Beaded white, blue, and yellow five-inch-wide cuffs adorned his wrists and ankles. Around his neck was a matching wide, beaded collar, which pleasantly contrasted with his friendly and handsome black face. His well-worn sandals, made of old car tires, barely supported his feet.

"My name is Kipululi. I am your guide and I will take care of everything you need or want," he said in perfect English. "You will be very happy with us." He grabbed my Le Sportsac and put it on his shoulder.

At that moment three porters dressed almost like him but without the walkie-talkie greeted us with orange juice, waited for us to drink it, and then motioned for us to follow them as they led us down the narrow path to our tent.

This tented camp was different from most other tourist camps in that it was owned and run by the Maasai themselves. It was one of the most rugged places we'd stayed and gave us the sense of Africa before European colonialization. Tourists seeking the Western comforts offered by most tourist hotels and luxury camps would not come here. The few large green and beige tents were scattered far from each other and the mess tent was in the center, well hidden by lush umbrella trees and wild foliage. This camp offered an experience of Africa—raw Africa, mysterious Africa, natural Africa, teeming with the animals that God created to wander freely and live their lives without fear of being displaced and having their home partitioned into game reserves to enrich government coffers both in Africa and abroad.

Some tourists and well-meaning people wish all of Africa would remain like this camp, available for their consumption whenever they want to escape their civilized world. They resent the development and progress they encounter on visits to contemporary Africa, because they are looking for an Africa that no longer exists.

Although this was the natural Africa, it was not the "deepest, darkest" Africa that early explorers described in their books and diaries, coloring their descriptions with their personal fear of the unknown continent they were exploring. In his book *Heart of Darkness*, published in 1899, Joseph Conrad planted unease and distrust in Europeans and others about the land and people of Africa by portraying it as dark, evil, dense, primitive, ignorant, and hopeless.

Their sensationalized writings and drawings prejudiced the rest of the world and hurt the African continent to this day!

After we cleaned up, we gathered for Safari beer and soft drinks around a campfire. We were sure we were the only people for miles. We had seen many animals on our previous trips to Tanzania, so we decided to stay put, resting in this wilderness, basking in the sweet and refreshing solitude.

Our reveries were interrupted when we heard the sound of a lorry at a distance. It was without a doubt the ugliest sound possible to hear in this peaceful place. As the lorry approached, we saw that it was overflowing with Maasai men, women, and children in their colorful clothing and magnificent beaded neck collars. When it stopped, they jumped from the lorry and surrounded us at the fire. For an hour they sang and danced and performed for us. The little children were beyond belief. They were dressed the prettiest, sang the loudest, and danced with all their hearts! I was worried that it was late and they should be in bed, but then I reminded myself that tourism was an important source of livelihood that they depended on.

In the morning we toured the rest of the camp and saw how spread out and remote it really was. The cook invited us to his kitchen, a small tent. On one side was a narrow wooden table filled with cardboard boxes used for food storage. It was hard to believe that the delicious dinner of vegetable soup, barbecued chicken, fried potatoes, and a medley of fresh fruit that we had the night before was created in this tiny place and cooked on traditional, three-stone fires on the ground. On the other side of the same kitchen tent was the dishwasher—a young Maasai boy who washed the dishes in a basin of sudsy hot water and set them upside down on a white plastic table to dry. With his bare hands, he scrubbed the blackened aluminum pots and pans using ashes from the fire. He wasn't satisfied until the pots shone brightly and insisted that we look at our reflection in their shiny finish.

I asked Kipululi if he would do us a special favor and show us his *boma* (family homestead). I wanted to see his *boma* because it would be real, as opposed to the staged *bomas* and *manyattas* set up near hotels for tourists to see a traditional Maasai compound. Apart from the commercial aspect that benefits the government, tour operators, and the Maasai themselves, these *manyattas* are a vital educational opportunity for tourists. It had always bothered me that most tourists to Tanzania only wanted to see the animals and unique sites like Mount Kilimanjaro, Ngorongoro Crater, and the Olduvai Gorge, but seldom wanted to see how people lived.

Like all traditional *bomas*, Kipululi's had several houses scattered in a circle and along the edges of the compound. A thick fence made from branches of the thorny acacia tree surrounded it. In the center of the compound another circular six-foot-tall straw fence sheltered his cows, sheep, and donkeys. The Maasai coexist with their semi-domesticated animals in the same territory shared by wild animals and move with their herds and possessions in search of water and better grazing when necessary.

Kipululi told us that he had only one wife because he couldn't afford more at the moment. His mother, sister, and three of his children, dressed in their finest clothes and weighed down by layers of colorful beaded collars, bracelets, and earrings, came out to greet us and invited us into their homes. Women seated outside the main house, beading and singing, gestured to us to come see their work. Kipululi told us not to buy anything because he already had necklaces made for us. The proceeds from the sale of their beaded work and handicraft was shared among all families in the *boma*.

Among the Maasai house building and maintenance is done by women. When we arrived we noticed a woman, dressed in her beaded finery, squatting on top of her five-foot house fixing the mud roof.

We crouched and maneuvered every which way to squeeze ourselves through the narrow passage from the door into the one room house. Once in, we had to stay still for a minute because it was smoky and pitch-black inside. After our eyes got accustomed to the darkness and the smells, we saw that there was a stone fireplace for cooking on the ground with an earthenware pot sitting on top. It was only the flash from our cameras that revealed who and what else was there. Sitting on layers of cowhide on a wooden bed just a foot off the ground near the fireplace was a young mother nursing her baby.

"This is my wife and our fourth child." Kipululi introduced us and went to sit next to her on the bed. I took a photo of them together and when the flash went off, I noticed that Kipululi was wearing blue denim jean shorts underneath his magnificent traditional robes. At the foot of the bed were two boys, about five and seven years old, sleeping on a straw mat on the uneven dirt floor. There was a scattering of earthenware pots, a few tin cups and plates, several gourds and elongated milk calabashes, wood for the fire, walking sticks, tattered clothes, and faded photos of President Mkapa torn from a magazine.

Their lives were simple and their needs few compared to mine and those of everyone else I knew in America. Probably living close to the earth gave them a satisfaction and understanding of the meaning of life that might escape the rest of us.

Before we left the next morning, Kipululi gave us a white beaded necklace that his family had made. He told us that white is the color of friendship, and we would always remain friends until we meet again in another place. I felt the same way and lamented the fact that it was improbable that we would ever see him again.

As was always the case when we visited remote parts of Africa, I again got back the Kjell I married. He once told me that rural Africa made him feel like Vasco da Gama, one of the original European explorers, or the missionary David Livingstone. In this place, he was not complicated. He was present and he was happy.

48

Ulcers

 For most of 2002, the year after our trip, I did not feel well. I slept even less than usual, had constant headaches, and for months on end suffered from a stomachache. The cramps went on all day and night. Every time I expressed this to Kjell, he'd tell me to see a doctor and then go back to reading his magazine, watching TV, or doing whatever was more important to him at the time.

I lead a healthy life and always try to figure out what's wrong before going to a doctor. Maybe I wasn't drinking enough water, or maybe the new wine I'd been buying after being educated at wine tasting parties didn't agree with me. I decided to drink more water and less wine and to stick with the brands I knew. Every time I eliminated or added something to my diet, I felt like it worked, but after a few days the cramps and fatigue returned. I finally went to see the doctor. No wonder I couldn't guess the problem—I had stomach ulcers!

Ulcers? Me? No way! My friends' image of me was of Maria the dancer, the fun-loving party girl with a relaxed and direct way of expressing herself, and someone who had no idea how funny she was as she kept them in stitches most of the time. I, too, believed that at this stage in my life I had a very happy body!

I had always thought that ulcers were associated with a stressful life, depression, and an acidic diet. So, I asked myself, what was stressful or depressing about my life in the last year? It took me a long time, but eventually I acknowledged things I had been refusing to face. I could be depressed because I felt alone and isolated in Florida.

I could be stressed because I was trying to figure out why Kjell was usually so distant and robotic around me. I had the distinct feeling that he was barely aware of my presence and didn't see me, even if I was sitting next to him. As usual, I thought my husband's behavior had to be connected to something I was not saying or doing. I also thought that he was bored because he had sold the business in Florida and had nothing much to do now. I had always encouraged him in his pursuit of a diplomatic appointment during the Bush administration, and now I encouraged him to take the graduate course in diplomacy that he'd been talking about for many years.

It was obvious that Kjell was not the same Kjell I had known and loved for so long. There was something seriously wrong and I had no way of finding out what it was. Throughout our marriage, we seldom discussed anything of consequence regarding the two of us. Whenever a difficult topic came up that demanded further discussion, Kjell would change the subject, make fun of it, or walk away, and I too was eager to drop it rather than feel dismissed. I had long ago come to accept the fact that we did not discuss anything unpleasant in our marriage. The Norwegian method of solving problems—shoving them under the rug—was the rule of law in our marriage.

I replayed in my mind his infamous and perpetual brag to me: "Don't you know, I'm Norwegian and we sweep everything under the rug?" It always amazed me that he truly believed that when he ignored things, they were gone! To use his own metaphor, I once asked him what he would do when he finally lifted the rug and discovered that everything he'd shoved underneath it for years was still there. His answer was more of the same: "We don't think about that."

In spite of my worries, I convinced myself that he was one of the best things that had ever happened to me and that he still loved me. When I told Kjell that the doctor said I had ulcers and that I was to take a fourteen-day treatment and follow a special diet, he responded, "I'm glad you know what's wrong." End of discussion.

In my heart, I hoped that my diagnosis would give us an opportunity to talk and find out why I had ulcers and why things seemed so disjointed in our lives, but no luck. Instead, that Norwegian rug bulging with unpleasant secrets and other stuff just opened its big mouth and took more nourishment into its bottomless belly.

For months I felt like Kjell was an empty "shell." The way Americans pronounced his name fit him at this time of his life.

My thoughts proved accurate when we had our second annual Safari Dinner to raise money for Moshi, Delray Beach's Sister City in Tanzania. In the invitation we asked attendees to dress in safari-inspired outfits, and I was amazed and entertained at what some Americans felt was safari gear—a silver sequined blouse with Anne Klein's logo of a lion's face, a sombrero, skirts printed with African-American sorority Greek letter symbols, and black patent leather evening bags with a metal elephant clasp. Best of all, one man wore a Native American feather and animal horn headdress!

I came as a Maasai woman dressed in the traditional bright red wrap skirt decorated with beads and wore a beaded red, white, and blue headdress, wide beaded bangles that wrapped tightly around my wrists, and of course several large beaded collar necklaces, which usually decorated the wall in our living room.

Kjell, having been appointed honorary consul from Tanzania to Florida, was the master of ceremonies. I was sitting by his side in my regal Maasai attire as he welcomed the crowd and introduced those sitting with us at the head table. He introduced everyone except me. At first, I assumed that he'd just forgotten me, but then I thought he must be planning to introduce me later since I was the connection to Tanzania in his life. When things were wrapping up, someone handed a note to the person sitting at the end of the head table. She passed it to me and said it was for Kjell. I checked it out before I handed it to him to see if it was appropriate at the gathering. The note said: "People in the audience want to know who that beautiful woman sitting next to you is. You forgot to introduce her."

I slipped the note in my purse without showing it to him. Kjell was exhausted. He had just flown from Norway with an overnight stop in Minnesota and then rushed to Florida for the fundraiser. But why did he have to go to Minnesota first?

At home that night, I told him, "Tonight you proved what I've suspected for a long time."

"And what is that?"

"You don't see me anymore. I am invisible to you."

"What are you talking about?" he asked impatiently.

"In spite of all my bright clothes, you somehow managed to forget that I was sitting next to you when you introduced everyone at the head table but me."

"Oh, for heaven's sake! I was exhausted and had a lot on my mind. Give me a break!"

"You were so tired, yet you saw and introduced at least ten people not sitting at the head table, including a waiter you knew."

"Do you think I did that on purpose?"

"No, you did not do it on purpose. That's the problem! You really didn't see me!"

"You can think what you want. I'm exhausted and I'm going to bed."

Another opportunity to talk with my husband about us was again shoved under the rug. What infuriated me was that he often bragged, "We never argue."

Kjell's trips to Minnesota didn't ease up even when Kata and Karl came home for Christmas. Everyone who knows me knows how much I love Christmas. I know it's a sentiment from my days at the orphanage when the nuns were very good and kind to us. They gave us presents, clothes and shoes, and had us perform Christmas plays and sing Christmas carols in German, English, and Swahili. We looked forward to Christmas all year.

With a family and a home of my own, I continued that tradition. I went overboard decorating the entire house, including the bathrooms and outside. I put out our set of Christmas dishes the day after Thanksgiving and used them for the entire month. I bought Christmas gifts for family and friends and sent out Christmas cards with photos of our family. This year our card had a photo of Katarina and Karl at *Storberget*, our cabin in Norway, and Kjell and I standing underneath two towering elephants and their long tusks during our Walk with the Elephants Safari in Botswana.

No one was really interested in helping me decorate the house or trim the tree, but Karl often obliged and helped with the tree as long as we put on the *Winter, Fire & Snow* CD and turned up the volume when Julia Fordham sang "December 24th." We'd sing as loud as we could with the refrain "You don't always get back what you give." Kata usually joined in, and we'd play the song over and over. It's actually a sad song about unrequited love, but in the spirit of Christmas, we applied the refrain to gifts. Kata and Karl loved this because it was the opposite of Buddhist teachings in such a hilarious way.

For the second time in our family life, on Christmas Eve, Kjell announced that he had to leave us on Christmas Day to go to a very important meeting in Minnesota taking place on December 26.

"That's what you did last Christmas. Who in their right mind would schedule an important meeting on Boxing Day, the day after Christmas, two years in a row?" Kata asked.

All three of us looked at Kjell for an answer.

"I thought it was strange too, but the regional Volvo VIPs are coming to Minneapolis and I have to be there to host them."

"Geez, Dad," Karl said. "Do you have to go? We're home for so few days before we have to leave again."

"Believe me, I don't want to go, but I have to."

"Will you be back before we leave?' Kata asked

"Sure, I'll be here for your last two days."

"Tell your dealer people how your family feels about these meetings. Aren't those VIPs upset about the timing of the meeting? Don't they have families?" Kata asked.

"They haven't mentioned it."

The three of us looked at each other, and for a moment I had a queasy feeling. It hurt to see that Kjell didn't mind not spending Christmas Day with us. His visits to Minnesota didn't let up. In all of May 2003, Kjell was home a total of eight days.

"What's going on?" I finally asked him. "Did you move me from Minnesota so I could live alone in Florida?"

"You know May is the busy month in the Norwegian community with all the celebrations before, during, and after *Syttende Mai*—Norwegian Constitution Day. The Norwegian consul general in Wayzata depends on me to help."

I wished I could catch him off guard, and he would unwittingly tell the truth about whatever was going on. He always, always had an answer. Yet those answers, while plausible, were not making sense to me. Had he become such a good liar that he believed his own stories? Had we all accepted being brainwashed rather than face the humiliation of dismissal as we watched him shove yet another deceit under his rug?

49

Norway for the Last Time

 That spring Kjell applied to graduate school for diplomacy and was accepted into the program. I was relieved! I fooled myself into believing that the reason he was so off was that he was bored with all the free time he had. After an orientation, his coursework would be mostly online, but he'd occasionally have to attend two-week classroom sessions with his professors in different parts of the country.

In July we went for our annual family vacation to our cabin in Norway. One of the highlights for us was to attend the International Jazz Festival in Molde. Since 1961 this week-long jazz festival has attracted the best and brightest and most promising jazz musicians from all over the world as well as from Norway. We heard Paul Simon and Diane Reeves that year.

Most of the Bergh clan gathered at Batnfjord to celebrate the birthdays of Kjell's siblings. His brother Einar was turning sixty and his sister Ellen would be fifty. We celebrated by drinking magnums of champagne, exchanging gifts, and listening to Einar play his trumpet around the large fire pit. *Mor*, Kjell's mother, cooked her famous or infamous *baccalau*, which inspired mouthwatering anticipation for some and anxious trepidation for others. *Baccalau* is salted cod, potatoes, onions, vegetables, untold spices, and lots and lots of oil. The dish originated in Portugal and was made famous in all of Norway by *Mor*, according to Kjell. I personally liked it a lot and admired *Mor* for cooking it again and again for company and family. *Baccalau* was to visiting guests what waffles were to anybody who set foot in the Bergh household. The waffles were served with butter, whipped cream, dark *gjetost* (goat cheese), various kinds of berry jams including the much revered—by the Bergh clan—cloud-berry jam, and Lyle's Golden Syrup.

The relatives' visit to *Berget* ended when they returned to Oslo, Kristiansund, Stavanger, or Molde. Einar was the last to leave, after Kjell left for the States to attend his orientation session. Before Kjell and the kids left, we visited his ancestors in the cemetery behind the quaint and picturesque Øre Kirke. Ever since Kata was a teenager, she'd say she wanted to be married in the church whenever it came into view from across the fjord or when we drove past it.

Was it a premonition? This time, when Kata said she'd like to be married at the church, I announced, "I'd like to be buried here."

Then Karl spoke. "Mom, that's really deep! How wonderful that you'd like to be buried with the family here!"

"That's really nice, but are you sure, Mom?" Kata asked.

"I hadn't thought about it before, but somehow today it's feeling right to me. Yes! I'd like to be buried with the family because the majority of the people who became my family are buried here."

I knew that I had most certainly lost my mind! I was surprised at how sure I was about my burial site at that moment. What was I thinking? In my right mind, I would never even consider living in Norway, much less being buried there! I could only conclude that my worries about my husband, my marriage, and my future had invaded my brain and caused me to utter such nonsense.

"How about Cathy? Will she be upset?" Kata asked.

"If she outlives me, she'll be upset. I'll discuss it with her when we get back to America." There wouldn't be a discussion. I had already come to my senses.

"Are there laws and rules about who can be buried in Norway?" Karl asked.

He directed the question to Kjell, since he was the authority on everything Norwegian, but for some reason, Kjell didn't say a word.

"Dad, what do you think?" Karl asked.

"About what?"

"About what we're discussing."

"What are you discussing?"

"You tuned out our whole conversation about Mom wanting to be buried here?"

"Of course not! Oh look—a fox just crossed the road! Did you see it? It was big, and I think there were others with it."

If any of the rest of us saw the fox, we said nothing. We drove the last five minutes to the cabin in silence.

Only *Mor*, Einar, and I were left at the cabin. It was without a doubt one of the best times I'd spent with *Mor*. Einar, the fishing addict, caught and cooked fresh fish for us every day. Ellen, living down the hill in the original family farmhouse where Kjell's grandparents had once lived, joined us for dinner and a movie on the plasma TV, hidden inside a farmer's red Krogenes cabinet.

I was the least technologically challenged of those still at the cabin, and I knew that it would be on me to run the TV. Before Karl left, I insisted that he write down step-by-step instructions on how to play a DVD on the new TV. He complied, and these were my instructions:

1. Open the cabinet door.
2. Push the power button on the remote and then push DVD.
3. Click Play.
4. If after you've done numbers 2 and 3 and the movie doesn't start playing, STOP for two whole minutes, and curse our President!

Poor Mr. President! He was cursed more than once.

Some days Einar sacrificed his hobby to take *Mor* and me hiking to one of the nearby wild and beautiful spots abundant in Norway. We basked in the sun as we spread a blanket on soft grass or moss, ate *smorbrød* (also known as open-faced sandwiches), and drank wine and coffee. Ellen and I did the hike of our lives up Reinsfjell in Torvikbukt. The previous year we had enjoyed spectacular sunsets from the cabin. I took hundreds of pictures because the colors and hues of the sky and water changed in front of my eyes every minute as the sun sank deeper into the fjord. From the breathtaking shots of these sunsets and the help of Photoshop, I made a 2003 calendar for everyone in the family in Norway and in America for Christmas.

Mor had always been very cordial and gracious toward me, even though my straightforward style of talking, voicing my opinions, dressing, walking, and dancing sometimes surprised her. As I represented the exact opposite of her cultural beliefs and upbringing regarding female roles and behavior, she sometimes looked at me as though I were from another planet. The relaxed and casual way I expressed my emotions, speaking raw and honestly from the heart, were foreign and maybe even scary to her. Yet, over the years I noticed that she had become more and more relaxed around me, and I didn't see as often that uncomprehending stare she used to fix on me when I was being me. I must say that this vacation was the first time my mother-in-law and I truly bonded. After thirty-five years, it seemed that she had finally decided maybe I was okay! I had always loved and respected her, but until this point she would let me get only so close before she'd put up her guard. She didn't want any confrontations.

This summer we talked about everything under the sun. She even talked about her life with her husband Kristian, who passed away in 2001, and how glad she was that we all went to visit his grave in Kristiansund. When I said goodbye to her a few days later, she hugged me long and hard and cried. On my part, I was filled with trepidation and worry that something bad was going to happen because those last few weeks in Norway with *Mor* had seemed too good to be true.

You're thinking too hard, Fat Mary said to me. *Live in the moment. I will hold all the joy, beauty, and intimacy you've finally found with your mother-in-law and your Norwegian family.*

Kjell returned to *Storberget* for a week after his orientation before we both left for America. He was more distant than ever. The first night, when it was time to go to bed, he changed into his pajamas, came into the bedroom where I was already in bed, grabbed the *dyne* (Norwegian down puff), and said, "Since I snore so loud, I'll sleep downstairs instead of keeping you awake."

"But Kjell, don't you want to get into bed with me first? You left me here with your relatives for a long time, and we haven't made love for ages!"

"You have a poor memory. We just had . . . .ahh, we've been having sex all along."

"If you have been having sex all along, it wasn't with me. Believe me, I would know!"

I sat up in the bed and was about to ask him if he was having an affair, but on his face was the most horrible, angry, and hateful look I'd seen in our entire thirty-five years of marriage. His intense glare stopped me mid-thought and made me hide under the covers. At that moment, I was afraid of him. His message was written on his face: "I am no longer in love with you." But instead of telling me what was really going on, he simply took his *dyne* and his snoring and marched downstairs.

In the morning it was business as usual. No mention of the previous night's conversation or lack thereof. He spoke to me with the same robotic voice and superficially amicable gestures he'd perfected over the years. He looked empty to me. The more I looked at him, the more I realized that he was wired differently than most people. He was a stoic man, a man who kept the peace and appearances at all costs, a man who hid his problems under the rug, a man who never, ever forgot he was Norwegian.

50

It's Time!

This chapter is about what didn't work in our marriage. It's about what went on behind closed doors, inside closed minds, and inside closed hearts that no one—not even our closest friends—knew. We've all heard that "it takes two" to divorce, meaning both parties are at fault. That's often true. But why don't we also say "it takes two" to remain married? We bring all that we are to a marriage, including our baggage and our dreams. "It takes two" to openly discuss the baggage and find a way to help each other realize our dreams. Despite my faults and imperfections, I knew I possessed good qualities that Kjell loved and admired. I felt the same about him. I don't think it occurred to either of us to walk away from our long marriage until "it takes two" became a bad thing. It took two people not married to each other to end our marriage.

As can be expected, Kjell and I did not sing each other's praises during the divorce process. It seemed he believed that each uncomplimentary statement I made about our life together should have been prefixed with "You've been so wonderful to me!" I always told him that he was an excellent provider for our family. He gave us a lifestyle we could only dream about. Many times during our life together, I'd stop and pinch myself for my good fortune. Once when the kids were little and we were all sitting in KLM's business class on our way to Africa, I actually pinched my upper arm so hard I had a bruise that lingered for two weeks.

I have also always known that he was a good, though not great, father who would do anything for his kids. What only I could know was that he was a very average husband.

Did he really believe that bad things done by otherwise good people should be overlooked and have no consequences? He sometimes gave me the impression that he should get a gold medal for not physically or verbally abusing me. I thought everyone knew that in a marriage husbands and wives are good to each other. Mistreating one another, though it happens, is the exception to the rule.

After years of swallowing and hiding what I considered emotional and psychological abuse from him, the divorce gave me an opportunity to express myself. Just as all the stuff that Kjell had shoved under the rug would still be there for him to face once the rug was lifted or moved, Fat Mary had held onto my secret pain so I could face it at the right time.

It's time! Fat Mary told me. *Your survival instincts will rescue you again. You know how to appreciate what is good in your life rather than dwell on the bad. You know how to write your hurts in the sand and carve your blessings in stone. All your blessings are intact. They will take you where you need to go.*

From the outside, it looked like I had everything—an adoring husband who sent me a dozen long stem red roses every week of our long marriage and spoiled me with extravagant material gifts; beautiful, intelligent, socially conscientious children; good teaching jobs; an exercise program that kept me in touch with my heritage; a house in the suburbs; travels to exotic places, and many loyal, loving friends. While all of the above was true, what others didn't know is that I had come to realize, and eventually accept, my husband's true priorities in our marriage. His priorities were himself, his work, his children, and then his wife. Our family was my number one priority, and for many years I thought it was his too. It was hard to accept the truth that our family didn't mean as much to him as it did to me. If it had, he wouldn't have jeopardized it with his extramarital affairs.

Over the last few years of our marriage, divorce had crossed my mind several times. Fat Mary kept telling me *It's time* whenever I felt alone and unloved. I pretended not to hear her and kept on keeping on, taking one day at a time, believing there would be redemption if I persevered. After thirty-five years of marriage, you just don't wake up one morning and announce, "I want a divorce today!" The writing was on the wall for a long time, but I kept erasing it.

Kjell, in spite of his marital indiscretions, didn't see it coming. I am sure that if the thought even crossed his mind, he reassured himself by asking, "Who in her right mind would divorce me?"

As soon as we returned from Norway, in August 2003, Kjell left on one of his many trips to somewhere. I had stopped paying attention to where he was going and just tried to keep track of when he would be home. When he first started traveling extensively for business, he'd call me when he arrived at his destination, check in with me during his absence, and often bring home presents for me. Since moving to Florida, his presents had become spur of the moment, rare, or nonexistent. The last present I got from him after a trip was in May 1998 when he returned from a journey with the Minnesota National Guard to visit bases in Florida, Alabama, and Panama. He gave me a tourist T-shirt and a bandana saying "Welcome to Panama."

He usually didn't share much about his trips, but that time he told me there was only one woman in that National Guard delegation from Minnesota, and he was very impressed by her. The way he talked about her I knew he had slept or was about to sleep with her. I cannot tell you how or why, but I always sensed when Kjell was having an affair, and I was always right, whether he admitted it or not. After this trip, he went out of his way to avoid conversation and paid even less attention to me than usual.

When I asked him why he was always in such a bad or non-committal mood at those times, he dismissed or ignored my concerns, telling me that I was too sensitive or too defensive. Instead of showering me with gifts, compliments, or taking me out to romantic dinners and going overboard with his attention, like cheating husbands often do, he'd snap at me at the least provocation and remind me how lucky I was and how far I'd come from my beginnings in Tanzania. One incident during this period still shakes me up.

Kjell read profusely and he'd often put magazines or articles from the paper he thought would interest me on my chair to read. We were in the family room in Florida when he came over to me and showed me an article he had circled in *Time* magazine.

"Here, you should find this interesting. You were way ahead of the game. You got your *mzungu*."

I had a pile from him to read, so I didn't get to this article until the next day. It was an article about prostitutes in Nairobi and how they hoped to catch a *mzungu* as a husband or lover. The prostitutes, the article said, showed up at bars and nightclubs frequented by *wazungu* and brazenly hustled the white men in hopes of being taken home for the night. The article went on to say that the prostitutes believed that a *mzungu* could mean a ticket out of Kenya and their hard lives and that foreign white men would treat them better than their local men.

I read the article over and over, and each time the hurt in my heart felt worse. Could he be referring to that time in 1981 when we were at the Intercontinental Hotel in Nairobi and we entered the elevator together when a security guard stopped me? The guard wanted to know why I was going upstairs. I told him that I was going to my room with my husband, to which he replied, "You will have to show proof that he's your husband."

Kjell then told him that I was his wife, and the guard said, "Very sorry, sir, we have problems with prostitutes harassing our guests."

When he told me "You got your *mzungu*," was he telling me that I married him because he was a white man? Why was it important for me to read this article now? Was it another attempt to make me feel like I owed him everything I was and had become? When he came home that night, I tried several times to ask him about the article, but I choked on my words.

Whenever I confronted him about having an affair, he'd make me feel like I had nothing better to do but sit at home making up stories. His favorite expression before sweeping any uncomfortable topic under the rug was "Everyone should have it so good!" It hurt me when he said that. What comeback could I have? He was right about my good luck and fortune in my adult life. Had the gratitude I expressed to him gone to his head? Had he convinced himself that I would be nothing without him? Sometimes he was so boastful to me about his role in my life that I began to doubt that I'd contributed anything at all to my success.

I was baffled when people who knew us told me how highly Kjell spoke of me and my virtues to them. He admired me, respected and adored me, and was so much in love with me, they'd say. Well, if he was so in love with me, why had it been so long since he touched me in bed or hugged me and told me sweet things like he used to do? If he adored me, why, when I once felt particularly alone and unwanted, did I have to take his arms one by one and put them around me and ask him to hold me?

When it came to affairs, I realized that short of catching him in the act, he would deny everything. Little did he know that the more he denied it, the surer I was that it was true. Fortunately for him, but unfortunately for me, when he pushed his problems under the rug, he believed they were gone. He was able to continue with his affairs because he apparently figured that if he denied them, they didn't happen.

After living in Florida for five years I had made a few good friends who kept me from going insane. Before inviting me to something they'd ask me, "When will Kjell be in town?" I sometimes felt there was more to their question, and then one day a friend asked me, "Why don't you travel with Kjell?"

"We travel a lot together," I said defensively. "We used to go on vacations two to three times a year. We took that long European trip; we went to South Africa, Botswana, and Tanzania; and we go to Norway at least once a year. I travel a lot with him."

"But why don't you go with him each time? Most semi-retired couples I know go everywhere together. That's the point of working hard when you're young, retiring early, and enjoying the golden years together."

"To tell you the truth, some of the cities he goes to for business are boring. There's nothing for me to do while he's at the meetings. It's just a coincidence that every time there's a function in Delray Beach, he's out of town."

"Nhambu," my concerned friend said, "he has another life! Have you thought about that? He has all the signs."

I thought about what she said. Another life? What other life? Does she know something? Instead of asking her where this idea came from, I said, "No way! Not Kjell. He's just busy being Kjell!"

"Sorry if I offended you."

51

Net Worth

I was in my office at home, preparing for my annual two-week residency teaching *Aerobics With Soul*® as a specialty instructor at Rancho La Puerta in Mexico, when Kjell came into my office, gave me his usual peck on the forehead, and said, "When we sold the dealership two years ago, I had to prepare a net worth statement. I thought I'd give you a copy."

Net worth. Is he finally, after thirty-five years of marriage, going to tell me how much money we have? Is that what net worth means? He handed me a two-page document and I gave it a quick glance. It had all sorts of categories, columns, and figures, and looked quite boring, so I put it in a nearby drawer.

"Thanks. I'll look at it later."

"You should look at it now. It's something you've wanted to know for many years."

"You decided now is the time to tell me instead of when I wanted to know?"

"It wasn't necessary before, but I think you should look at it."

I looked at the paper and saw that it listed all of our companies, properties, life insurance policies, bank accounts, IRAs, and a whole lot of other things I didn't understand.

"Look at the bottom line. It will tell you how much we're worth," Kjell said.

"One more time, what made you decide that I need to know this right now when before you've always answered my questions with 'Enough'?"

"I just wanted you to know."

This answer didn't satisfy me. I wondered why it was time now and not before. Only God knows how frustrated and patronized I felt in the past with his responses. He was always very proud to tell everyone that everything he owned, we owned fifty-fifty! He bragged to me that he knew other men who did not put their wives' names on all their properties, but he wasn't one of them.

If I was an equal partner with him in the marriage, and he said we owned everything fifty-fifty, why hadn't he told me our net worth before this moment? Why did he make so many financial decisions on his own and tell me only after the fact? As his partner, I should have had the opportunity to discuss building the cabin in Norway, selling the dealership in Florida, or buying the yacht, or handing out money to family. But I never had a chance to offer my opinion. He simply told me after everything was negotiated and agreed upon. He was in charge of our money and paid all the bills, but I should have been consulted before and during the decisions, not only after the decisions were made. I put the paper with our net worth back in the drawer and continued burning my music disks for *Aerobics With Soul*®.

About a week later, we went out for our last meal before I left for Rancho La Puerta. Kjell was extraordinarily quiet and stiffer than usual. Anyone seeing us probably thought we were sharing an unspeakably tragic event. I once again told him how happy I was that he was going back to school to get his degree because he seemed to be depressed and lost without his business in Florida. He spoke quietly and in short sentences. It had occurred to me, based on his behavior that year, that maybe he was gravely ill and didn't want to tell me. I was worried about him, although I noticed he was that way around me, but never missed a beat when it came to things he had to do for himself or places he wanted to go. I concluded that his absentmindedness had something to do with my presence because he seemed fine around everyone else. Despite these worries, I convinced my mind that everything was fine, though in my heart I felt that something was very wrong.

52

You of All People

On the evening of September 20, 2003, we returned from dinner. Kjell pulled into the driveway, got out of the car, and came around to open the door for me like he always did. He said nothing until we got inside.

"Are you almost finished packing for Mexico?" he asked.

"Just a few last-minute things. Why?"

"Let's sit down. I'd like to talk to you."

"Oh? Okay!" I went to sit on one of the love seats in the living room. He sat far away on the edge of the couch on the opposite side of the room.

"There's something I've been meaning to tell you for a long time, but I just couldn't bring myself to do it." He sighed audibly. "Well, here goes. I have a friend in Minnesota who is about forty-two years old. She always wanted a child and felt that her clock was ticking. She wrote me two letters asking for my sperm, but I refused each time. She even sent me all the literature about donating my sperm at a sperm bank. She insisted for a long time. Finally, one day, I realized that it was up to me to give her the gift of life. I couldn't refuse her request."

"You donated your sperm?"

"Not quite. I didn't want to go to the sperm bank because people know me in the Twin Cities and running into some clinic to donate sperm was too cold and impersonal. I decided to help her the old-fashioned way."

With each word that spilled out of his mouth, my heart beat faster, and a million thoughts began pounding my brain until it went blank. But something he said begged to be addressed right away because it infuriated me.

"Did you just say, 'I realized that it was up to me to give her the gift of life?' Did I hear you correctly? Do you really believe that you can give life, that you can create life? Many women want children. Being so magnanimous with your sperm, you should put a billboard on the freeway announcing, 'Kjell will be giving life today. Come to his boat this evening.' I suppose being the atheist that you are, you wouldn't know or admit that only God gives life. You, my narcissistic fool, couldn't have it more wrong!"

Having said my piece, my heart sank to my knees. I felt I was in a twilight zone where all I could hear and feel was the loud beating of my heart and the throbbing in my head. I couldn't believe his arrogance! Did he really believe that he had the power to give life? I looked at Kjell, the man I had loved for so long, and realized that he was the man that Cathy had tried to warn me about. His voice seemed to come from somewhere far, far away, like an echo from a deep, dark cave under Batnsfjord, Norway. He looked and spoke like a figure in a hologram.

"Don't worry! I'm not going to leave you! At any rate, she's engaged, and her fiancé might adopt our child. I'm tired of sneaking around and just want to see my child. I'd like to have this out in the open so I can have not only visitation rights but participate in raising her."

"What in the world? My husband has an out-of-wedlock child and then tells *me*, 'Don't worry, I am not going to leave you'?" I was choking! I couldn't deal with his patronizing arrogance.

"You're acting like it's the end of the world, for heaven's sake. Bill Cosby and Jesse Jackson also have children out of wedlock. It is what it is."

"And what do those two men have to do with us? Is it because you think I will accept this better if other adulterers are Black?"

"I assure you that I will not leave you. I do not want a divorce. I mentioned Bill Cosby and Jesse Jackson because this kind of thing happens all the time. It is what it is. Their wives didn't divorce them, and we can continue just like them."

"Lately I've come to suspect that you're a closet racist. Of all the men in the world who have out-of-wedlock children, you mention two Black men. I bet they didn't begin their confessions to their wives with, 'Don't worry, I'm not going to leave you, but I have a little something to tell you . . .' I also bet they didn't insist on publicly raising their out-of-wedlock children while remaining married."

I started shaking. My mouth was watering because I was about to throw up, so I got up and went to the bathroom. I was in the bathroom for about a half hour, almost choking from the knot in my stomach, but all that time Kjell didn't come to check on me. He sat in the same spot until I returned. His voice picked up strength and self-righteousness as he continued where he'd left off. "You of all people should understand why I want to raise my child."

"What does 'You of all people' mean? Are you telling me that because I was born out of wedlock, I should jump up and cheer you for wanting to raise your child? Are you telling me that I shouldn't feel betrayed, humiliated, and rejected? Are you telling me that my feelings don't matter? That *I* don't matter? That's as abusive as you've ever been to me. I should be the one saying, 'You of all people, you, who knew my history, should have protected me from further hurt and never repeat what was done to me.' But over and above, you of all people should never have done it to another innocent little child. And now you have the gall to use my birth to justify your despicable behavior!"

"What I meant was that your mother did the same thing."

"Leave my mother out of this!"

"You hated your mother because of what she did to you, and I am not going to do the same with my child."

"And in your opinion, what did my mother do to me?"

"She abandoned you to an orphanage. I'm not going to be a deadbeat dad."

"Not at any time in my life have I hated my mother. I said that she was cold and insensitive and maybe ashamed that she had me, but I have never, ever said I hated her, because I do not! What she did was the flip side of what you're doing. Like you, she made a mistake. When she realized that she could not raise me, she did the next best thing to protect her family. She took me to the orphanage precisely because it was rumored to be the best place for children of mixed race.

"Although I paid a high price for her choice, unlike you, she did a noble and difficult act. She put her family before herself. Don't you think she wanted to raise me, like she raised my sister Judy? She could have had my father take me to the village to be raised by his wife, and my life would have been much, much harder than at the orphanage. She wanted what was best for her family, not what was best for her! Don't you ever compare yourself to my mother! You don't hold a candle to the dignity and character with which she handled a bad situation. For your information, in my eyes, she did the right thing, not only for her family but for me too! I had a difficult childhood, but I like who I am today, and I have the orphanage and the nuns to thank. You're the most selfish person I know."

"Selfish? If I were selfish, I wouldn't be fighting for my child. I don't see why I have to be divorced in order to raise my child. I really don't want a divorce."

"Kjell, if I don't divorce you, please give me a preview of what our life will be like from now on. Wait, I know! When you and I and your child are in public, I, of course, would be explained away as the nanny or maid."

"While you're in Mexico, I'll fly to Boston and tell Kata, then I'll go to Boulder to tell Karl. Nothing much will change as far as the rest of the world is concerned. It's just that I would like to see my daughter more often and have her join our family on vacations. We could treat her like a child from a previous marriage."

"Oh, my God! But she isn't a child from a previous marriage! Stop the lies! You obviously would have no trouble living with that lie. To paraphrase you, she is who she is—your out-of-wedlock child, and nothing can change that. You sit there telling me how I'm supposed to handle it, but I wonder if somewhere in your plans you've once thought of our kids. You've set out the best scenario for yourself, and, of course, we'll have to oblige because it's all about you!"

"You can do what you want, but I don't think divorce is in your best interest. Don't get hysterical."

"I have a brain and a heart, and I am perfectly capable of deciding what's in my best interest, thank you! Do you love the woman?"

"Oh no! I'm with her only because she is the mother of my child."

"I am the mother of your two legitimate children. Are you telling me that you love me the same way you love her?"

"You are the one I've always loved and still love."

"Stop the lies! How old is your child?"

"She's four and a half. She'll be five in May. She's so beautiful! She has blond hair and blue eyes and is so intelligent. I'm definitely going to pay for her college education. I'm happy when I'm with her, and—"

"Stop it!"

He was stunned that I was screaming for him to stop. He should have been grateful that I am who I am and that I had already experienced unbelievable pain in life. The average wife, especially a Black one, would not tolerate his bragging about his child. She would hit him over the head with a cast-iron skillet and then flatten his balls, rendering him incapable of ever fathering another child.

"What makes you think I want to hear details about your blondie?"

"I'm sorry. I know I've hurt you. I never meant to do that."

"Really? You're so sorry you've hurt me that instead of sitting next to me, holding my hand, and begging for forgiveness as you give me the worst news a wife can hear, you're sitting a mile away on another couch, talking like you're announcing the newest trend in cars and patting yourself on the back that you've finally let it out! You can get lost!"

I started crying quietly at first but then loudly and uncontrollably. Would he come over and hug me, kiss me, and let me cry on his shoulders and tell me how sorry he was? Oh no! He didn't even look at me! He sat there like the emotionally deprived mummy that he was. I guess he was looking for his rug. Unfortunately, the rug had rotted from harboring thirty-five years of his garbage. There was no rug big enough to cover this betrayal.

"Should I sleep upstairs today?"

I didn't believe my ears. His reaction to my loud sobs was just like his mother's reaction years earlier when she offered me a cup of coffee after I had a meltdown in their living room.

"You sleep wherever you please. You will never, ever touch me again!"

"I know you'll feel better in the morning."

I know he probably slept like a baby and snored the night away because he was so pleased with himself for finally having spilled the beans, thinking that once he told me, everything would be fine by morning.

But Kjell didn't think about the beautiful tapestry we'd woven together over the years that told our family history. The only important tapestry for him was that floor rug—the rug that gladly accepted anything and everything he didn't want to face. He brutally shattered my dream of growing old with him and playing with our grandchildren. He couldn't see further than himself.

I went to the bedroom and lay down, hoping I would fall asleep. I shut my eyes and hugged myself tight, and when I did, I felt a pair of tiny arms hug me too.

Let's cry together, Fat Mary said. *It seems like the love you so deserve is once again unattainable. You must listen to your heart and let it guide you from this day forward. Your future awaits you. Obey your heart. Do not let your past define the future. There is no truer or more sacred love than the love of self. You have that. You will continue to build on the firm foundation you put in place at the orphanage. You are loved by many, but your children's love will fill the empty space in your heart that was reserved for their father. Take the time to see if your marriage has brought you closer or further away from your true self. You will now have the opportunity to create a new life that is truly your own. Above all, keep on dancing.*

I asked my shaking body and nauseous stomach to calm down. I told my tears that they could flow only until I fell asleep, because tomorrow was an important day. I asked God and my guardian angel to watch over me so I wouldn't do anything irrational during the night—like going upstairs with a scissors and cutting Kjell's balls off. The thought had actually crossed my mind when he began his confession. I would spend the rest of my life in jail, but so what? Could jail be worse than what I was feeling? But my children—how could they live with the fact that their mother had maimed their father?

53

Embraced by Mount Kuchumaa

 When the alarm went off, I jumped out of bed and fell by the nightstand. My eyes were swollen shut from crying. Since this wasn't the first time in my life I'd cried myself to sleep, I knew what to do. I felt my way around the bed, turned on the light, waited a while, but I still couldn't open my eyes. Putting one foot in front of the other, I made my way to a cupboard in the kitchen and took out two chamomile tea bags, wet them with warm water, put one on each eyelid, and stretched out on the couch in the living room. As soon as I could open my eyes, I walked toward the shower and bathed with the coolest water I could tolerate. My body woke up and my mind came back to focus on my agenda for the day. I had a one-hour drive from Delray Beach to Miami, a 6:25 morning flight for San Diego, a one-hour bus ride from the airport to Tecate, Mexico, and then a few miles more to Rancho La Puerta.

Kjell drove me to the airport. Although he was talking to me, I heard very little. I was only vaguely aware of a stick figure performing driving gestures.

It was a rough trip across the country. I couldn't control the tears that repeatedly filled my face during the five-hour flight, and by the time I arrived in San Diego, my eyes had swollen shut again. A kind passenger helped me get on the escalator down to the luggage carousels where my friend Diane, a veteran *Aerobics With Soul®* instructor who would co-teach with me, was waiting. After we hugged, she asked, "Are you all right? What happened to your eyes?"

"My eyes? Oh, I had a rough time sleeping last night and then couldn't snooze on the plane either."

"Are you sure?" Diane, who was a registered nurse, knew better but didn't push me. "At least you don't have to teach until tomorrow."

"I'll be okay. It's good to see you, and we'll have a good week." I wanted it to be that way and I believed that as long as I was still standing, I would teach *Aerobics With Soul®*.

It took everything I had, and then lots of help from the Universe, for me to teach my forty-five-minute class on Sunday morning. Tears welled in my eyes the entire time I was teaching, and I was afraid I would break down and sob uncontrollably in front of a full class of enthusiastic students who came to dance and have fun. I managed to keep it together until we did the last number of the cooldown called *Sala* (Prayer). Even without the unimaginable sadness I had in my heart, the song almost always moves me to tears. The pace, melody, harmonizing voices, instrumentation, and lyrics soothe my soul. It is a moment in class when we're in touch with our divine selves and that divinity seeps from our souls to our bodies and flows over our faces as warm, cleansing tears. When I arose from the floor after the dance, I saw that I left a puddle where my face had rested on the floor during the dance. But I had taught my first class, and I knew that I would survive the next two weeks.

Try as I did to go on as usual, I knew Diane was concerned. "Nhambu, is anything wrong?" she asked me when we were having lunch after class. "Is it me? Did I do or say something? I know something's the matter. You just taught a beautiful class. Everyone seemed to be right there with you as they smiled, perspired, and danced their hearts out."

I finally had to ease her worries and fears. I revealed what Kjell had told me the evening before I left for the Ranch. I told her everything, and when I came to the part about him having a four-and-half-year-old daughter whom he wanted to raise, her demeanor changed.

"I had heard that rumor, but I could not for one second believe it was true! Oh Nhambu, please don't judge me for not telling you!

"What did you hear? How?" I got dizzy and had to hang on to my chair.

"The wife of one of Kjell's salesmen works with my husband at the hospital as a nurse and she told him. Her husband said Kjell's out-of-wedlock child often comes to visit the dealership and that the child's mother comes with her, usually dressed like G.I. Jane."

"I don't believe you didn't tell me, Diane. When was this?"

"About a year ago. I didn't tell you because the nurse has a reputation for gossiping. I did not want to tell you something so shocking that in my mind could not possibly be true. Nhambu, you must believe that I only had your best interest at heart. Obviously Kjell painted a false picture of a loving husband and father so how could he have a child outside your marriage? It's so hard to believe it's true!"

"Diane, I know how you feel about me, and I know that if you were sure Kjell had a child, you would tell me. I appreciate that you didn't jump on the rumor wagon to spread stories you didn't know were true."

Early every morning we vigorously hiked below Mount Kuchumaa, separating ourselves from the other hikers as I expressed my devastation to Diane. On the first day she said to me, "Nhambu, your energy and intensity are different this time. Your strides are long and your arms seem elongated as though you're reaching for the top of Kuchumaa."

I talked my heart out, and Diane listened. After class, I'd go to the Villas Health Center, get into the outdoor jacuzzi, and wonder how I could have so much pain in my heart when such beauty surrounded me. Mount Kuchumaa, the sacred mountain for the Kumeyaay Indians, with its overwhelming spiritual presence, watched over me like a loving ancestral elder, gathering, teaching, protecting, and loving its offspring. From the spa, I'd go for lunch even though I had no appetite. I had to eat to be able to teach my high-energy classes. After lunch I'd go back to the room, get into bed, and try to sleep. I slept so little both day and night that I had to take a sleeping pill at night. Diane, who shared a room with me, watched me like a hawk. She was afraid that I was so sleep-deprived I'd inadvertently overdose.

By the third day, we hooked up with my beloved Sista-friends, the twins Coco and Connie, who are permanent fitness staff at the Ranch. They insisted we go for a little fresh air, so Diane, the twins, and I went for a short walk up the mountain. The twins had visited me in Florida and had been very well received by Kjell.

"Hard to believe!" Connie said when I finally got the whole story out.

"He was so charming, gracious, charismatic, and accommodating to us," Connie said. "He seemed to be genuinely pleased that we were there, and when I heard a little about your childhood story, I said to myself that at least you'd found a good man. A man who adored you and who would never hurt you. He certainly fooled me!"

"Along with many! Kjell was always gracious to our guests. The only ones that he wasn't consistently pleasant to were John and Cathy, my American parents. Of course, they were not guests. They were family—my family, though Kjell never viewed them as such. They were not politically important, nor were they rich and well connected. He couldn't show off as much to them because they knew him well. Kjell was always uncomfortable around Cathy. I thought it was because he was jealous of my relationship with her, but in the end, I realized it was because Cathy saw through his self-adoration and narcissism!"

"How could you stay in the same house with him and not bash his brains out or hurt him so bad he could never get it up again?" Coco asked. "You're a better person than I am!"

"So, my friend, what's going to happen now?" Connie asked.

"I haven't made up my mind whether I should divorce him or not." In my heart, Fat Mary repeated *It's time* every opportunity she had. "I know I will never live with him again. I'm leaning more and more towards divorce. How can I live with a man who has been leading a double life for so long?"

"In order to lead a double life, you have to be a big, smooth liar!" Diane said.

"That he is," I agreed.

"If there was a way of measuring emotional maturity, you my friend, would have a PhD, and Kjell would be in kindergarten," Coco added.

"How do I go about finding a lawyer?" I asked.

"Rachel!" Diane said. "Rachel is a lawyer. She's corporate law, but I bet she could help you find a lawyer."

"Yes, Rachel! When I've made up my mind, I'll call her." Like Diane, Rachel was an *Aerobics With Soul*® instructor, and they alternated weeks coming to the Ranch to co-teach with me. It would have to be a lawyer in Florida, but I knew with her *savoir faire* and professional connections she'd find me one.

Almost every day of my stay at the Ranch, I received frantic, sorrowful, sobbing messages from Kata. I had to go to the administration building and wait for the phones to be free before I called her back.

"Mom?"

As soon as I heard her voice, I started to cry. We cried over the phone for a while and were unable to talk. Those long-distance tears cost me a small fortune by the end of the week.

"Mom, I'm so sorry! I just can't believe it! Please go back home to Florida. How can you teach? They'll understand!"

"Kata, I'm having a hard time, but somehow Mount Kuchumaa and this place are healing, and my teaching isn't affected."

"How could he tell you when he knew you had to be in front of people, dancing and teaching for two weeks? There's a lot about what's happened that's hard to believe, but I can't get over his timing!"

"I asked him why he couldn't wait to tell me until I returned, and he said he knew I loved the Ranch and that I had good friends here whom I could talk to."

"Does he think that all you do as a specialty instructor is have massages and sit around the pool? I don't see how you can do it. Mom, please just go home, and I'll come as soon as you arrive."

"Believe me, Kata, teaching is going well. I actually think it's good for me. I'm using this time to decide what to do."

"Are you going to divorce him?"

"I've thought about it a lot. I'm leaning towards divorce. The only deterrent is you and Karl. I'm worried about you."

"Mom, please don't worry about us! Do what is right for you. I don't see how you could continue living with him."

"You wouldn't forever blame me for leaving your father?'"

"Not at all! In fact, I think I would lose respect for you if you didn't leave him. Does he imagine he can have two wives and two sets of children?"

"It helps me a lot to know how you feel."

"How can you live with a husband you can't trust?"

"I know! I'll call again tomorrow. You won't believe the story he told me about how this child came to be."

"You and me both if he told you the same story—that a friend of his asked him for his sperm because her clock was ticking, and so he helped her. I am really embarrassed for him."

"You wanted to know why he waited to tell me until the evening before I was leaving for the Ranch. The only reason I can come up with is that he's a coward. He wouldn't have to face me again for two whole weeks."

54

Damage Control

 The next day I received a notice in my villa that there was a FedEx letter for me from Kjell that I had to go to the border to pick up. I left the letter at the border for two more days, then brought it to the Ranch, where Diane and I stretched out on the loungers outside our little villa to read it.

I opened the FedEx envelope and then another cream-colored envelope with our company's logo on the upper left side. Inside the second envelope was a four-page letter, handwritten on gray-lined notebook paper. After reading each page, I twirled it around a few times then tossed it to Diane.

"Well, well, well! Quite a different tone from when he told me in person a few days ago," I said to Diane. "Yet, change the date and year and the fact that this time there is living proof of his affair, the letter is the same as the one he wrote after the last big affair in 1986. At that time, like now, he professed his love and promised me the moon—and I believed every word he said." Diane handed the pages back and I read over them again.

"If he loves me as much as he says he does in his letter, why don't I feel it? Why didn't he kneel at my feet and deliver his 'Come to Jesus' apology—which a betrayal of this magnitude warrants? Why did he sit across from me, giving me the bad news like a carefully prepared report on his business deals? As far as I am concerned, he left out the most important aspect of a confession—the contrition. I think my reaction gave him a hint that maybe this time everything was not going to turn out the way he planned. He had his memorized script, and it didn't look like I was going to follow it. This letter is damage control."

"He probably thinks that he poured out his heart to you, but as an outsider, I find it dry, impersonal, and self-serving," Diane said.

"Precisely! He tells me he loves me and how bad he feels in the same letter where he discusses money, his exams, and a package that arrived. I was so insulted when he told me 'Don't worry, I'm not going to leave you' right after he told me about his secret life with his out-of-wedlock child and baby mama. I should have said no, I'm not worried that you're going to leave me, but you should be worried that I am going to leave you! This whole long letter is about him and his fear that if I leave him, everyone will know that he isn't the man he thinks or says he is. It has little to do with me."

It's time! It was Fat Mary again.

Cathy, like Diane, came to the Ranch as my guest for my second week. Diane was co-instructor with me for her week, and Cathy came to spend time with me, take some classes, and enjoy the beauty of the Ranch. It didn't even cross Kjell's mind how his timing would affect their stay with me. He stole our precious weeks together by his late-night revelation before I left for the Ranch. They were both sad for me, but very angry with Kjell.

After two weeks of love and care at the Ranch, my constant communing with Mount Kuchumaa, the understanding and support of my children, and the insights and encouragement of Cathy and Diane, I decided to divorce Kjell. Before Diane left the Ranch, I asked her to contact Rachel when she returned to Minnesota.

Kjell came to the Miami airport to pick me up. He leaned over to plant his usual dry peck on my cheek but I pulled away. It was eleven at night and for all the fifty minutes it took to drive to Delray Beach, I looked out the window at the full moon and counted the few stars that still shown for me. When we got home, I told him I was tired, but we would talk first thing in the morning. Before he went upstairs, he told me about all the repairs he'd made in the house while I was gone—home maintenance jobs to fix things like the water pressure in the shower, CD player, fans on the deck, and a whole slew of other items that I'd asked him to work on since we moved in five years ago.

55

The Hardest Decision

 Fat Mary's advice, *"It's time,"* gave me the courage to ask Kjell a few more questions before I told him my decision about the divorce.

"What made you decide to tell me now?"

"Two reasons. First, I was tired of leading a double life with my two families. I was getting so confused that some days I wanted to jump off a cliff. The second and most important reason why I had to tell you now is because I want my child to meet her grandmother. *Mor* is getting old, and she'd be delighted to have another grandchild in her final years."

I couldn't believe my ears.

"What makes you think that, at eighty-four, your mother would be delighted to meet an out-of-wedlock grandchild? She has great-grandchildren who are that old."

"At any rate, my daughter needs to know her grandmother."

"Does she know that you're her father?"

"Of course. She calls me Daddy."

"So, it's true what Diane said. When I told her about your child, her response cut through me like a razor blade—that when your offspring came to the dealership, she'd run upstairs to your office calling 'Daddy, Daddy.' Didn't you tell me that nobody knew?"

"Well, I never told anybody."

"And you actually believed that everyone working at the dealership couldn't put two and two together? When I called Carletta from the Ranch, she told me her son who worked at the dealership reported rumors you had a little girl whose mother dressed like G.I. Jane."

"That's what I get for giving him a job."

"He was telling the truth, wasn't he? He and Carletta always appreciated everything you've done for their family over the years and, like so many people, thought the world of you. He felt it was disrespectful to me that everyone knew and I didn't. Being the good Southern woman that she is, Carletta told her son that she'd wash his mouth with soap if he ever repeated such a vile rumor. How often do you see your child?"

"I refused to see her for about six months after she was born. But once I saw her, I couldn't walk away from my own flesh and blood. I had to do my moral duty to a child I fathered."

"There you go again talking about morals. What about your moral duty to your wife of thirty-five years and your two children? Tell me, have you thought about your moral duty to us? Do we matter at all in your life right now? The last time I checked, Kata and Karl are your own flesh and blood too. How can you walk away from them in the name of doing your moral duty to your outside child?"

"Kata and Karl are grown."

"What do you think you've been doing as you led a double life? Isn't that walking away from us all? I know that in your mind I am not your own flesh and blood, so what you do to me probably doesn't matter much!"

"Of course, you matter. That's why I don't want a divorce. Even if it turns out that you want one, I hope it will be amicable and that we will always remain friends."

"Oh, and we can still send each other Valentine cards? You can never see beyond your own comfort!"

I was getting more and more convinced that Kjell had never been truly hurt in the heart. How could he betray, disrespect, and humiliate me in such a public manner and expect us to remain friends? Is he that clueless?

Could cluelessness also be the reason that he thought his mother would be delighted to meet his child? That he could be the father in his new family at the same time he was the father in ours? That everyone would believe him and admire him for helping a friend in need by donating his sought-after sperm? That we would accept his child as if she were from a former marriage?

"How did you meet your woman?" I asked. "And how often did you see her?"

Kjell was happy to oblige. "We met when I was a guest on a trip sponsored by the military. We hit it off and when we returned, I saw her off and on. As I said, I didn't see her for six months after the child was born. After that, I saw them whenever I was in Minneapolis. Often it was at her house, but sometimes we came to our apartment. We went to Disney World together and to the Black Hills in South Dakota. I also took them out on our yacht in Florida."

"You've spent more time with them than you've been at home with me since we moved to Florida. You left out leaving Kata, Karl, and me in Florida and spending Christmas with them in Minnesota under the guise of an important car meeting. You didn't fool me! I've known for a long time that you were having an affair, no matter how much you denied it when I asked or hinted about it. I just had no idea the extent of your deceit. You were leading a double life with another woman and child, doing all the things families do together, while I was alone in Florida worrying that you might be seriously ill.

"I could forgive an affair again, but it will be hard to forgive the extent to which you premeditated deceiving me. Your life with me since we moved to Florida was a series of lies, one after the other, culminating with the biggest deceit of all—starting a second family! If you were unhappy in our marriage, why didn't you tell me? Why didn't you ever bring it up? You pride yourself on avoiding arguments, but this was our marriage! Thirty-five years of history together. Couldn't you find it in your heart to somehow save our family when you felt unfulfilled? Did you have to go and start another family?"

It was probably useless to ask him about affairs I didn't witness, but I did ask about two other affairs I knew he had with women who were our so-called friends.

Kjell denied them both and screamed angrily at me, "You get an idea about an affair, and you don't believe me when I tell you you're wrong!"

"You're talking like you've never given me a reason not to believe you. Do you remember when you had the affair with your employee in the eighties? And do you remember what you told me when I asked you what was going on when you came home late at night, all disheveled, full of lipstick, makeup, and long brown hairs over your unbuttoned shirt?"

"How am I supposed to remember little details like that?"

"You told me that you were helping a friend move late that night and some of the paintings you were carrying were still wet and they messed up your clothes. Jesus Christ, Kjell! What kind of a fool do you take me to be?"

"I didn't say that."

"Oh yes you did! And I suppose if it turns out that you made up the sperm story, you'll deny that you said that too. You'd better come up with something better when you explain your out-of-wedlock child to your mother. Nobody in his or her right mind—except maybe you and your partner in crime—could believe such a ludicrous lie."

"I don't know how else to tell you, but that's exactly what happened."

It's time! Fat Mary was tugging at my heart.

"This is without a doubt the hardest decision I've had to make in my entire life. I want a divorce."

Kjell looked at me dumbfounded. I suspect that up to this point, he had been counting on my Catholic upbringing and marriage vows that proclaimed "til death do us part," and on the value I put on our family, to convince himself that I would never, ever file for divorce. I left the couch and he continued to sit there. I was done with him.

Yes, it's time! Fat Mary was proud of me. *Bravo!*

From the time I made up my mind at the Ranch to divorce Kjell, I was tortured by my decision. I felt the same pain I'd had in my childhood when I realized that my mother did not want to raise me. Again, I felt rejected and unloved. But this time it was by someone who had told me I was the love of his life. After reading the letter he sent me at the Ranch, I knew that Kjell would always say that he was not the one who decided to leave the marriage. In my heart, I'd known for a long time that he had already left me. It was up to me to make it official. Maybe now that I knew I was not imagining things,

I'd find some peace, and the puzzling schizophrenic life that gave me ulcers would end.

I felt an awkward sense of relief after announcing my decision. My omnipresent and faithful Fat Mary started speaking.

Your husband's betrayal is complete and irreversible. Your pain is indescribable, yet familiar. Your husband loved you, but not enough to protect you from himself. People have different capacities to love. The same love you had for yourself as a child will eventually mend and heal your broken heart. Do not be afraid. You're much stronger than you think.

56

To My Children

The first thing I had to do after my decision was to write to Kata and Karl. It was daunting. I looked at the computer and keyboard as if seeing them for the first time. Deep sadness engulfed me as I saw the image of my two children in front of me.

My dearest Kata and Karl,

This is one of the saddest and most painful days in my adult life. I have asked your father for a divorce. We agreed that it will be uncontested and hopefully amicable. We will do everything in our power to avoid a court settlement. Tomorrow I will call Rachel. She will be my legal counsel throughout the divorce proceedings. She will help me find a Florida family practice attorney, and we'll take it from there.

Tears are rolling off my computer as I write. I'm sorry to have to tell you this via email, but I am in shock and a mess. I know that hearing your voices on the phone at this moment would almost be too much to bear! I want to be strong for you and for me. You are my life, and I love you with every cell of my body. I wish I could wipe away the hurt in your hearts. I can't tell you how sorry I am to have to give up my husband of thirty-five years and to have to make you children of divorced parents. I didn't foresee this day. I did EVERYTHING in my power to keep our treasured family together.

But I failed. Please FORGIVE ME.

As far as you are concerned, nothing has changed for me. I'm sooooo grateful to have been given the time on this earth to love you. I can feel your love for me and that's all I need right now.

At moments like this, I remind myself, and I'm reminding you too, that "What doesn't kill you, makes you stronger" and "This, too, shall pass." We will one day be strong and happy again.

I will call as soon as I get myself together. Please continue to email me. Talking on the phone in the next few days will be hard.

I love you with my whole heart.

Mama

The next day Kjell simply said, "If divorce is what you want, and there's nothing I can do to change your mind, I'll respect your wishes, but can we try counseling first?"

"Counseling? At this stage of the game? You who have always pooh-poohed the idea? I'm afraid it's too late. You've already made another family. You want to raise your child. I will not knowingly share my husband."

But out of nowhere, maybe from the force of habit, I found myself telling him that there could still be hope under certain conditions.

"If you're serious about not wanting a divorce, I have a few conditions. You will have nothing to do with the woman. You will have nothing to do with the child, except support her financially. You will move out. You will start long-term counseling, and when the time is right, you will start courting me just like you did when we first met. If at that time I feel you have done the work, are truly repentant, and have really changed, I might reconsider."

"Thank you. I'll think about it and let you know."

He got back to me a few days later. "I can easily leave her, see a counselor, start dating you again, but I can't walk away from my daughter."

It was unfortunate that Kjell knew me and my soul so little. The condition I gave about his having nothing to do with his child was cruel and unrealistic. I knew it. I was not so stupid to believe that he would agree to it. After all, wasn't he on the verge of giving us all up for her? Could he ever be trusted or expected not to see his child again, even if he promised?

What I was doing with that request was testing Kjell to see if he really loved me as much as he said he did in his damage control letter. I needed to know if he loved me enough to give up raising his child to save our marriage and keep our family intact. I needed to know if he could do what my mother Dorothy did for her husband and family. Was he willing to protect us and stay with us, though it might mean he would not be with his child whenever he wanted? Of course, his child would not be sent to the orphanage like I was. She had a mother who wanted her so much that she did whatever it took, even destroying a family of four and a thirty-five-year marriage.

I honestly believe that if Kjell cared for our family as much as my mother cared for hers, I would not have divorced him. Unfortunately, he made it perfectly clear that when push came to shove, he would rather leave me, our children, and our marriage than leave his child. There was no turning back.

I compared his dilemma of wanting to remain married to me while also wanting to raise the child he had with another woman to the Old Testament story of wise King Solomon. Solomon was confronted by two grieving women who each claimed to be the mother of the same baby. He suggested that he split the baby in two and each mother could have half a baby. While the imposter mom thought it would be a good solution, the real mother couldn't bear to see her baby divided and killed. She agreed to let the imposter mom have the baby. Her love and concern for the child told Solomon that she was the real mother.

In our case, I was the real wife and I'd rather give my husband to his woman than suffer the heartbreak and humiliation of sharing him. From another point of view, it consoled me to give him to his child rather than having the child know she was sacrificed to save our marriage. After all, she is innocent. I know firsthand the pain and misery of growing up without a father or family. Even though the existence of the child ripped our family apart, I was a bit comforted to know that at least she will grow up understanding how much her father loved her. This might come as a surprise to Kjell, but not for people who know me.

He told many people that the reason for the divorce was because I wanted him to give up his child. In his eyes, we were getting a divorce because of me. He didn't ask for it. He downplays his many betrayals and the serial adulterer's lifestyle he led throughout our marriage. He thought they had little to do with the divorce. According to his script, it was his desire to carry out his "moral duty" to a child he fathered that led me to file for divorce.

Kjell continued to live in the Florida house and stay in the Norwegian room, and we had little contact with one another until I told him I wanted him to move out.

"Please, let's wait a little longer. I'm seeing a counselor, and she said that you're rushing things."

"Who is your counselor, and what right does she have to tell me that I'm rushing things? What kind of counselor, who hasn't lived a single day in my shoes, has the gall to tell me to go slower and try harder?"

I continued, "It's too late, Kjell. I'm finished with this marriage. There's nothing left in it that I want."

"I had many dreams for this time in my life," he answered me sadly, "and now they're all down the drain."

"Has it occurred to you that I had dreams too? How about my dreams? I had big and wonderful dreams for us after the children left home, but you've systematically destroyed them. You can do what you please with your broken dreams, and I will do what I want with mine. You've always been a big part of my dreams, but let me remind you in case you've forgotten—I was not born in Africa for nothing! I am a survivor and I will continue to pursue my dreams, except you won't be part of them."

"Ever since I met you, I've watched you grow and blossom and transform your dreams into reality. I felt like I was a part of them too, but at some point, I began to realize I could no longer keep up with you."

"You've always been part of my dreams, and I acknowledged your support and encouragement to anyone who would listen," I said. That he felt left behind was a revelation, but that he would admit it was a shock!

Oh my God! Is Kjell looking down at the floor, wiping away tears? Yet I felt he was probably not crying for me, or for Kata or Karl, or for our families and friends that the divorce would affect. He was crying for himself.

My life so far had taught me that I possessed the two most important and indispensable characteristics of a survivor. In order to be a survivor, you need to have the ability to both melt like butter and be as hard as nails when necessary.

In the early months of the divorce process, along with the nightmares, I had good dreams of Kjell telling me that he loved me and me alone and that he was ready to give up everything, even his child, to keep our family intact. I often woke up with dreams that were a complete denial of what was happening. One time in the middle of the night as I walked to the bathroom, the dream continued uninterrupted. In the dream, I whispered to Kjell in the darkness, "I don't think you understood that when I insisted you give up your child if you didn't want a divorce, I was just testing you to see how much you really loved me. It wasn't even one of the original conditions I had. I threw it in at the last minute because my deflated ego needed to be stroked. It was hard to accept that one more time I was being sacrificed to protect others. Since I have practice, I think I will be okay. We can make plans for when and how you can see your child, and we should also ask Kata and Karl."

By the time I got back to bed and pulled up the covers, reality kicked in, and my heart sank to my stomach. I knew that I had to face my real life in the morning, but I took comfort in knowing that, at least in my dreams, I could still find love and forgiveness.

I was very sad that I'd let myself down. I had truly believed that no matter what happened, I would never leave Kjell. Breaking up our family had seemed impossible! I knew and accepted the fact that no one was perfect, and I was sure we could always work things out, because love would keep us together.

Maybe the test of love I gave Kjell was too hard? Was it so hard that no one with the exception of my mother could pass? After she'd had yet another child with an African, she put her husband and family first and me last. But no matter how I looked at it, Kjell sacrificed his family for his child.

One of the reasons I was able to forgive Kjell's first admitted affair, apart from my strong desire to keep our family together, was that throughout our marriage whenever I was disappointed in him, I reminded myself that I had my quirks, made mistakes, and most probably disappointed him and embarrassed him several times too.

In the period leading up to the divorce, I found myself thinking a lot about our life together. It was hard to accept that we were now ending it. Images of our children when they were little and how lonely I felt back then brought tears to my eyes. I had been overwhelmed by motherhood. I felt it was so unfair that with the birth of our babies, my life drastically changed, yet Kjell continued business as usual—going to work in the morning, traveling in and out of the country, pursuing his interests here, there, and everywhere without missing a beat.

I was engorged and that caused beads of milk to seep from the deltoids on my shoulders and from the swelling under my arms. I had a colicky baby who cried all day and night plus an older child who needed care and attention. I was so tired that whenever Karl cried—screamed actually—I'd pick him up, sit in the recliner, and cry along with him until we both fell asleep. Unfortunately, he'd wake up five minutes after nursing. We repeated this scenario three months straight! I was frazzled, fatigued, lonely, and at my wit's end. In early motherhood, I was physically and emotionally miserable. My state of mind would nowadays be diagnosed as postpartum depression.

What I needed more than anything during that time was my husband to love and comfort me, attend to me, and tell me that I was still beautiful and that this, too, would pass. Instead, I felt ugly, unneeded, and unwanted, and I believed that my child would never get over his colic and we would both be miserable for the rest of our lives. It took months, even years, to come to grips with the fact that in my hour of need, a networking meeting in Sweden and other engagements had been more important to my husband than tuning into what was going on at home with his wife and his brand-new baby.

57

Chicken Hat

 It might seem as though Kjell got his way throughout our marriage, and I did whatever he wanted. Far from it! He did whatever he wanted, but he couldn't always make me do what he wanted me to do. I spoke up, argued, and presented my case as well as he did. We often did not see eye to eye, no matter how he bragged about us never arguing.

Once we were invited to a banquet honoring Thor Heyerdahl, the world-renowned Norwegian explorer and archeologist, at a fancy downtown hotel in Minneapolis. I found the perfect hat to go with my long white-and-black flowered halter-top dress. It was made of several shades of black, brown, red, and white bird feathers, which hugged my head and forehead. On the back, the feathers covered my neck at different lengths.

"You're not going to wear that thing on your head!"

"Oh, the hat? I love it."

"You look like a chicken with its head cut off!"

"I think it's stylish and fun."

"Take if off! Wear something else or change the whole outfit."

"This is what I planned to wear to the banquet, and either I wear it or I don't go."

"I'll be in the car."

"See you."

After ten minutes Kjell came to get me. "Let's go!"

The next day there was a picture in the paper from the reception for Mr. Heyerdahl, and guess who was talking to him? Yours truly—chicken hat and all.

Norwegians, or should I say Norwegian Americans, are not

generally known for their sense of style or fashion. I think they're limited by *Janteloven*—the set of social rules governing behavior in Scandinavian countries—and the dictates that define to the last detail their traditional *bunads*. That attitude extended to dress worn at public occasions. Once I attended a Norwegian function with my hair braided African style. A lady dressed in an elaborate *bunad* asked me, "How could you come to our function with your nigger hairdo?"

Another woman at the same function said to me: "You know, you could pass for white." When I asked her why I'd want to do that, she answered, "Life would be so much easier for you."

I received glares and stares whenever I was at these functions. Body language said it all. A few folks were thrilled with my sense of style and told me they even admired my self-assurance and lack of concern about judgment and gossip. Overall, my outfits were one of a kind (because as far as they were concerned, no one in their right mind would wear them), stylish (they didn't know), and flattered my size-six frame (could they be jealous?).

Another behavior of mine that Kjell repudiated occurred when a group of car big shots came to town and we invited them to dinner at an exclusive restaurant. I ordered the New York sirloin steak, but what I got was something that looked like glorified hamburger. I told the waiter that I had ordered a steak and gestured for him to take it back. He left it at my place and went to the kitchen to check.

"For heaven's sake, why can't you just eat it? What's the difference? These are important people, and I don't want you to be difficult." Kjell was exasperated.

"Being difficult is far from my mind. I was looking forward to the juicy steak, and what's in front of me doesn't look like it!"

"Just eat it!"

The waiter came with my correct order and apologized for the mix-up. I only ate a third of the large steak, so I asked the waiter for a doggie bag.

"Are you crazy? You're not taking a doggie bag from a fancy restaurant like this and especially not in front of our guests."

I had had enough of Kjell's concerns about appearances. The doggie bag came, and as we left, I sauntered out of the restaurant, swaying my African hips every which way with the doggie bag on my head African style! As usual, there was no "after discussion" thanks to that rug!

Kjell parents, Liv and Kristian, were visiting us in our home in Edina, and we were having breakfast at the kitchen table. Suddenly, I was startled by cold water on my bare skin. Kjell had just washed his hands and instead of using a hand towel to wipe them, he splattered the water from his hands on my back. As soon as he sat down, I threw my full mug of hot coffee in his face, right in front of his parents.

"Maria!" His mother looked at me in disbelief! She went to help her son wipe the coffee from his white shirt, gray suit, and red tie.

"Does it hurt? Are you burnt?" she asked him in Norwegian, as she caressed his face.

Kjell diffused the situation. "It's my fault," he told his parents. "She hates cold water. I'll just change."

Without missing a beat, Kjell's mother asked me, "Would you like more coffee?" Before I could respond, his father said, "I'd like more coffee." End of subject.

58

Divorce Business

 Kjell moved out and made our boat, *Serengeti,* his head-quarters and home. A couple weeks later, Rachel, who had been researching family practice lawyers in South Florida came to Delray Beach to help me with the interviewing process. I insisted on finding a female lawyer because I honestly didn't think I could look another man in the eye without wondering how many of them had done what Kjell did while being admired and envied by the rest of the world for their generosity and accomplishments as righteous, model citizens. Unfortunately, many people like that forget that charity begins at home. The good they've done will not erase the bad they did to their families.

Rachel and I interviewed three lawyers. I was disheartened to realize that for them, divorce was a business. We had only one lawyer left to interview and were pretty discouraged.

"Don't worry, Nhambu," Rachel assured me. "If it turns out that we don't like this last one, we'll start over. I won't stop until I find the right lawyer for you. I have a feeling that we'll get lucky because she's the sole female partner in a firm of eleven males."

Rachel, twenty years my junior and a law firm partner in Minneapolis, was one of those rare attorneys who was as sensitive and loyal to her clients as she was brilliant. I should know because she was my student at Central High School in 1982. Our mutual admiration and interests helped us bond in a way I can only describe as magical. She loved everything African, especially the music, dance, and food that I often brought to her class in high school. Although we didn't see each other for several years while she was at college and studying in France, we always stayed in touch. She trained to be an *Aerobics With Soul®* instructor and taught in my dance studio and elsewhere while going to law school. I couldn't have found a more perfect person to handle my legal search.

We arrived at a posh, well-organized suite of offices with magnificent views of the Intracoastal Waterway and canals full of extravagant pleasure boats of every size. Before we could sit down in the reception lobby, a dark-haired woman in her forties dressed in a tailored black suit, red silk blouse, opaque black hosiery, and red heels walked toward us from the conference room down the hall.

"Hello! My name is Roberta Stanley, but you can call me Bobby."

She shook hands and asked us to follow her into the conference room. As soon as we sat down, she proceeded to tell us about her professional background and training, and she even talked about some of her interests—African art among them. She described her role, if she were to be my attorney, as well as the role her firm would play when necessary. She asked me to tell her about myself and listened attentively, asking many questions.

"Divorce is one of the hardest things you have to go through in your life," she told me. Tears swelled in my eyes and dropped on the table. When I looked up, I saw that Rachel was crying too.

What a difference from the other lawyers who began by warning me—as they looked over the financial statement Kjell had given me—that divorce was a business and emotions would have to be put aside. It could be because I was very relieved to find an attorney who saw me before the money, I found myself pouring out my heart to her.

"I was raised in an orphanage in Tanzania, and one of the longings I've had, ever since I was a child, was to have a family. I don't believe I am here to start the process that will end the family I finally had."

"I'm so sorry!" Roberta said.

"I have no idea what is involved and I think I am a little scared."

"I see here that you are sixty years old and you've had a long marriage. It is scary, but I will tell you and show you all you need to know and do. This could be the right decision for you."

She then went on to tell us what usually happens when you decide to divorce, from filing the petition for marital termination to signing the final papers in court. She laid out possible scenarios in case Kjell was uncooperative in producing documents or agreeing with the amount and value of our marital assets. Although I knew that she earned her living as a divorce lawyer and had already screened our case to make sure it was worth her time, I was impressed that she didn't mention money and assets until the very end of our two-hour initial meeting.

"I assume he's the one who handles the money in your family."

"I wanted him to since he's a good businessman, but he took it to extremes because he wouldn't tell me how much money we made even when I asked. If it weren't for him giving me our financial statement a few weeks ago, I'd still have no clue."

"Men like to keep it that way! It's a control issue. He presented you with a financial statement, but that doesn't mean we will divide what's on this paper in half. Part of my job is to find, evaluate, and prove that what we're splitting is all of your assets, not only what he says they are. This is my job. I'm not doing charity work here, but I really feel for you, especially after hearing your history. If you let me, I'd like to be your attorney. I know men like your husband—self-made, self-assured, self-righteous, self-admiring, and self-worshipping! That doesn't mean he's a bad man. He's just full of himself. He's also the kind of man who would want the divorce to be amicable, would take care of you and help you with the house if you needed him. But from experience, I know that divorces based on infidelity and double lives are seldom amicable, regardless of the couple's initial intentions. In your case, with a child involved, it's next to impossible. But maybe you'll prove me wrong."

At that point she excused herself, saying she'd be right back. As soon as the conference door closed behind her, Rachel and I jumped from our seats and hugged each other, almost hurting our hands with several hard high-fives as we danced behind our chairs, whispering, "Yes, yes, yes!"

When Roberta returned, she found us seated quietly in our chairs. I told her that I was very happy to have found her and that I'd retain her as my lawyer.

"I will do my very best to represent your interests, work closely with you, and together we will decide the best course of action."

November 24, 2003, I filed for divorce at the courthouse in Delray Beach, and Kjell was served the papers. After a few weeks without a response from him, my attorney pushed the issue. Kjell actually asked me if I could give him the names of the lawyers I'd rejected from the list Rachel had put together.

One of the first things he did after finding a lawyer was to write me an angry email demanding that I "expunge" an item from the divorce petition, seeking reimbursement for everything he'd spent on his daughter and his woman.

"I'm applying for a diplomatic position. I've already told you that I'll reimburse you for what I've spent on them. You have nothing to gain by spelling it out."

"It was my lawyer who wrote the petition, and I'm sure she has her reasons for wording that item the way she did. I trust her completely and I stand behind her judgment."

"All your lawyer sees is money! I demand that you remove that statement. At the very least she should reword it."

I recalled my attorney's predictions about the improbability of an amicable divorce.

"Remember the evening you told me about your child? You repeated numerous times that 'It is what it is,' and that I had to find a way of dealing with it, because you couldn't change it or turn back the clock."

"If you ask her to change it, she will. All you have to do is explain why her wording would be detrimental to me," Kjell replied.

"Of course, I forgot! It's all about you!"

I did talk to Roberta about that item of the petition. Her response was, "He should have thought about his diplomatic pursuits before he created the situation, but I'll change it if you want me to."

I thought about it for a full second. "N-a-a-a-h. It is what it is."

As far as his asking if I'd forgotten that he was seeking an ambassadorship to Tanzania or Norway, how could I forget? In his briefcase he carried a dossier full of letters of recommendation from senators, congressmen, presidents of colleges, business tycoons, and a roster of who's who in the political and civic arenas, including one from Jesse Helms, proving what I'd suspected all along—that he was a closet Republican, despite his noncommittal political stance when talking to me and my friends. He'd sit in his recliner in the family room and read his recommendations over and over every opportunity he had. At times he'd read them out loud to me. Even though he hadn't held any political office or risen up the ranks in the diplomatic corps, he really believed he had a good chance for an appointment based on the sheer amount of political contributions he'd made.

Roberta went to work on our divorce. In my whole life I have never had to read and sign so much paperwork. We had meeting after meeting. Divorce-related emails filled my inbox every day and my mailbox outside was stuffed daily with large envelopes.

During this time Kjell and I communicated only via email. I did not want to see him or hear his voice. Throughout the divorce procedure, I experienced every possible emotion. Sorrow, fear, despair, and indescribable grief emanated from every cell of my body. Each emotion tore through me, leaving me filled with pain and at times paralyzed. I eventually found one I could act on—anger.

Fat Mary was a hundred percent on my side. *People who do not know you well, and your husband is at the top of the list, will be surprised at the anger you're expressing toward him. They will be surprised by your choice of words and how fearlessly you fight for yourself. From childhood, you have swallowed your pain and given it to me. I am the equivalent of Kjell's rug, but instead of hiding unpleasant issues, I safeguard them for solving at the appropriate time. I have absorbed a lifetime of disappointment, sorrow, and hurt. I am full and overflowing. It's time! Time to put yourself first. Time to face, label, and verbalize the myriad emotions that will surface during your divorce. Time to take charge of your future. Above all, it's time to love yourself like you've never loved yourself before. This time, it's really all about you!*

Fat Mary's understanding and support emboldened me to express all my emotions—the good, the bad, and the unfiltered ugly! With each new day, an anger bordering on rage kept building up in me and eventually consumed me. Thanks to the hallways of Central High School, four-letter words and colorful cusses that have never been part of my vocabulary were stored in my brain, and now they fought to be uttered and hurled at my husband. They burst out of my mouth like fiery boulders tumbling down the mountainside, aided by the pyroclastic river of smoldering ash spewed out of an erupting volcano. It is indeed true that "hell hath no fury like a woman scorned." That anger is what made me fearless with my questions and responses to the man I once loved. I needed that anger to keep me focused on the divorce.

The letter he sent me in Mexico right after he confessed had a totally different tone from the matter-of-fact, take-it-or-leave-it arrogant delivery of his confession. When he suspected that I was going to leave him, the tone of his communications went from self-righteous arrogance to damage control. I read and reread the letter he sent to me in Mexico. It had everything I wanted to hear during our marriage, but seldom heard. Unfortunately, this time, his love and devotion fell on deaf ears.

I think I have finally figured it out. Because we were husband and wife, he took me and my love for granted. It's because he really believed that I couldn't live without him. It's because he had convinced himself that he was one of the greatest men on the planet and anyone, especially me, should be so lucky to have him as a husband. It's because, from his humble beginnings in Veitvet, Norway, he prospered in America but eventually got stricken by two diseases often diagnosed in wealthy, self-made men—entitlement and narcissism. It's because it never occurred to him that I would leave him.

Above all, it is because Kjell underestimated me. He underestimated my brain, my heart, and my spirit.

59

Sex, Lies, and Tales

 As the divorce process progressed, Kjell became more and more furious with my attorney. He accused her of being less than professional and said that some of the things she did and required were outright illegal, and even suggested that she should be barred from practicing law. To me that was good news because if Kjell liked my lawyer, she probably wouldn't be doing her job!

My attorney and I did not take Kjell's hurriedly prepared document of our assets to be Bible truth. By now we'd already established that he regularly lied, so in order to get to the truth, we realized that a deposition was in order. She prepared a long list of business-related questions for Kjell, several of his employees, his accountant, his attorney, and his woman.

I wanted to see Kjell's woman this once, at the deposition, and then never again. Roberta said I could attend the deposition held in Minneapolis, as long as I didn't participate in the proceedings in any way—not even with body language.

I hoped the deposition would reveal the truth. In the end, I don't know if I learned the truth and nothing but the truth, but I did learn much about our legitimate business ventures as well as his monkey business. I wanted to look into Kjell's eyes as he answered the same questions I had once asked him. I hoped that under oath he'd finally be honest. At times it was painful to see how he struggled with his answers. Under oath he did reveal the truth about the length, breadth, and depth of his premeditated deception of me, both before and after his child was born.

In general, his woman's deposition was boring. Her appearance evoked a character from *Little House on the Prairie*, a TV series about a family living on a farm in Minnesota in the 1870s and 1880s, and her testimony was accusatory, defiant, and non-apologetic.

I was surprised to find out that Kjell's name was not on the child's birth certificate. For someone who was so keen on doing his "moral duty" to a child he fathered, he didn't want to claim her as his daughter on the most important document of her life!

It also was made clear that his story about receiving letters from the woman asking for his sperm was a total fabrication. Their affair began long before she conceived his child.

When my attorney asked her about Kjell's reaction when she told him that she was pregnant, she reported that he was devastated and asked her to consider her options. He also wanted her to sign some legal documents stating that she would never reveal his identity or file a paternity suit or tell his family.

Kjell confirmed the above and said he knew that she had wanted a child but could not prove whether he was trapped into becoming the father.

At the deposition I also found out why Kjell had an affair to begin with. He said it was because we had problems with intimacy in our marriage. This was partly true. My one problem with our marriage interfered with intimacy. It was a problem of trust—I didn't trust him! After I forgave his previous two-year affair, it took everything I had to feel loved again. I gave it my greatest effort. In time, it did get better, but it was never the same. After I said I forgave him and wanted to work on our marriage, he went back to business as usual as if nothing had happened. He didn't acknowledge my struggle to get back to normalcy, nor did he see how insecure I felt in our marriage.

To top it off, there was no way to talk through any misunderstandings or problems in our relationship. He taught me well that I couldn't discuss or confront him about anything unpleasant concerning him, especially some abstract concept like trust or insecurity. Whenever I tried, he dismissed me with his usual "Everyone should have it so good."

When my feelings and emotions are regarded as irrelevant, it hurts. In my opinion, I did a pretty good job of dealing with my dilemma, because deep down I loved my husband. I was forever telling myself that our family was worth all the swallowing I did. But ever since that first admitted affair, our relationship irrevocably changed.

When asked in the deposition why he didn't want a divorce, his response was that because of my upbringing, he knew family was very important to me and he had promised himself that he would never, ever divorce me for any reason. He said that he had a great deal of respect for me but he only loved me as a person.

I can take someone's disgust, anger, scorn, cruelty, jealousy, and even hatred of me, but pity is in a category all by itself. So Kjell would not divorce me because he pitied me due to my upbringing! Couldn't he have just said that he loved me like he did over and over in his damage control letter he sent me in Mexico? "You are the one I love. You are the one I have always loved and will always love" were his words. Here, in front of the attorneys and accountants I find out that the way he loved me was not the way I believed he did. Does any man marry a woman, raise two children and remain married for thirty-five years because he loves his wife "as a person"? What does loving me as a person even mean?

When would his lies end? I know why he didn't want a divorce. It wasn't because he still loved me (albeit as a person) nor because he felt sorry for me. He didn't want a divorce because a divorce would tarnish his stellar reputation as a husband and father, his exemplary character, his aura of respectability, and the image of the magnificent human being he believed he was.

Last but not least, no matter how much he protested that money had nothing to do with it, he didn't want a divorce because he would have to part with half of his money. Is there a man out there who doesn't feel bitterness and resentment when he has to split with his wife the wealth that he had considered strictly his own? It took my attorney and Florida's no-fault divorce law to make him understand that any assets acquired during our marriage were marital assets and belonged to each of us fifty-fifty.

At the deposition, in spite of Kjell having told me repeatedly over the years that we owned our companies fifty-fifty, he admitted that until recently he was the sole owner and shareholder of all our companies. I owned nothing. Nada! I eventually learned that all those business documents I signed during our marriage were only in my capacity as a glorified secretary-treasurer!

My lawyer insisted on finding all our marital assets and ascertaining how much money we really had. Kjell couldn't simply say "Enough" as he'd so often said to me.

We discovered that Kjell had added his out-of-wedlock child as a beneficiary in the irrevocable trust fund we'd established in 1981 for Katarina and Karl. Where applicable in the document, he inserted "and any other offspring of the guarantor" after the names of our two children.

We also discovered that Kjell had donated thousands upon thousands of dollars to the Republican National Committee and numerous Republican candidates. When he reached the maximum amount set by law, he gave money in my name without informing me. If it suited his objective, he'd also donate to Democrats, but the money he gave my political party was minimal compared to the endless stream of money he poured into Republican coffers.

Kjell protested ad nauseam throughout our divorce proceedings about the sheer number of documents requested or subpoenaed from him. He said he felt crucified because in his mind, he'd been very cooperative and had given us all the documents he considered important. I had to remind him how often since our divorce began he'd been less than truthful. My attorney and I didn't have confidence in much of what he said because we didn't trust him.

I told Roberta that when it came to dealing with Kjell, an African saying says it well: "When the head of the fish is rotten, the whole fish smells." We couldn't take the fisherman's word that once we cut off the head, the rest of the fish would smell fine.

The last few months leading up to the divorce were awful! We were accusatory toward each other, with me furious at Kjell for stalling the divorce process and him furious at my lawyer for demanding more and more documents. We agreed or compromised on several disbursement issues, except Kjell refused to pay for the divorce as he had promised. He said my lawyer had taken advantage of my state of mind and had ordered too many unnecessary and duplicate documents because she saw dollar signs. The more adamant he was about rescinding his promise to pay, the more I dug my heels in and refused to budge. There was no way I'd let him get away with causing the end of our marriage and then making me pay for it. You break it, you fix it! It might not be the way most divorces are paid for, but he promised, and the principle of it made me angry! I produced the email where he assured me that if I wanted a divorce he would pay for it, and I held him to his word.

I don't know if Kjell has ever been deeply hurt before, but I know for a fact that parting with huge sums of money to pay attorneys hurt him. He had one condition for paying my lawyer's fees: that I tell Kata and Karl about his generosity in paying for the entire cost of the divorce. I kept my promise and told our children.

60

Broken Vase

As hard as the months of our divorce proceedings were, some very beautiful things happened during this time that confirmed without a doubt how much I was loved. It was ironic that I felt more loved and appreciated by others at this time than at any other point in my life. I received many letters and cards that lifted my spirit and kept me strong.

To many of my friends who had trouble comprehending how someone who loved his wife could betray her in such a terrible way, my explanation was: There was a major disconnect between Kjell's mind and his heart that caused him to speak from both sides of his mouth. On the one hand, if he valued his wife and family as much as he said he did, he wouldn't take such risks, and on the other hand, if he'd made a mistake, you would expect him to do whatever necessary to make amends and keep his family together!

My French college professor, Mrs. Reed, wrote to me:

"I detected a very deep sadness in the bottom of your dark eyes. You confided in me that Kjell had a long affair that year, but had promised to break it up, never do it again, and take the rest of his life to make it up to you. I remember like it was yesterday how tears rolled down your face when you told me that after his first big affair that you decided to remain in the marriage even though you felt like a beautiful vase that had been dropped, cracked and glued back together. Looks like this time the vase is not simply cracked, it is broken into a thousand pieces and no glue can hold it together to smooth the uneven surface and hide the damage. You will mend your heart with the loving help of your children and your many adoring friends. I am one of them."

Other friends wrote as well:

"I'm beyond shocked! Kjell seemed to be so much in love with you! He sang your praises every opportunity he had. He was so proud of you, and I believed there's nothing he wouldn't do for you!"

♦ ♦

"How could he do this to you when he knew your painful history?"

♦ ♦

"Nhambu, you never said anything! You didn't wear your marital difficulties on your sleeve. I was a little jealous that he sent you a dozen red roses every week for over thirty years, though I must admit there's something weird about those roses. Who sends roses to their wife every week?"

♦ ♦

"He gave you beautiful gifts and was eager to take you everywhere, especially to meet his famous people, and to formal occasions. I did notice that whenever you were together in public he was proud to show you off, though he didn't himself pay attention to you. He stepped back and gloated at all the attention you were getting from others as if to say, 'look but do not touch, she's mine.'"

♦ ♦

"The way he talked about you, you'd think that the Sun and Moon rose around you!"

♦ ♦

"The parties you and Kjell gave were the best. We looked forward to your invitations, especially to the New Year's Eve party. Those were such happy times. We can't believe they're over."

♦ ♦

"I believed that there really was justice in this world. You'd found a husband who made up for your loveless childhood. You're one of the strongest women I know and you will get over this and, in the process, teach us all invaluable lessons."

♦ ♦

"I suppose no one knows what goes on behind closed doors. I always believed you were the luckiest person in the world to have a husband like Kjell, but unfortunately he may have believed that too."

◆ ◆

"Great woman of courage. Fierce woman! I'm proud of you, girl! Your liberation is mine. I feel freed from the web of untruth as well. And the picture that emerges for me is that he isn't and was never 'up to you.' He never really understood you and isn't of your size morally and mentally. Where there's an element of untruth in a relationship, it festers and eventually blows up. You will move into your new life with great energy—and it will be a life truly of your size and scope. I'm watching! Stay strong, as I know you will."

61

Cancer

 In February of 2005, fourteen months into the divorce process, the emotional roller coaster I was enduring and mountains of legal paperwork I had to read and understand took a toll on me. I was exhausted and felt ill without being able to pinpoint the location of my physical pain. A friend suggested I see her gynecologist. I did, and after a complete physical, the doctor ordered an ultrasound of my uterus. She then suggested I get a D&C and a mammogram. I was not happy about the mammogram because I had had one only ten months before, and I knew my insurance company would probably not pay for it. I also wondered what a mammogram had to do with spotting, but I got one anyway.

That evening, Pam, a good friend and a tour operator from Montserrat, called about a cancellation on a trip that she and her husband were leading, and asked if I wanted to take a break from the divorce and go on a three-week cruise to Australia and New Zealand.

What a godsend! I called my lawyer, who told me to go because we could communicate via email if necessary. I scheduled the D&C for the week after I returned from the cruise and started packing. My frail physical and psychological condition justified paying for the only space left on the flight—a first-class round-trip ticket.

I'd always wanted to visit Australia and New Zealand, and I thoroughly enjoyed the trip. Highlights for me were the Sky Tower in Auckland, the Wellington Botanic Garden, the Te Papa Museum emphasizing the rich and varied Maori culture, the breathtaking Fiordland National Park that reminded me of Norway, and Tasmania—the place that so many Americans with poor geographical knowledge confuse with Tanzania. I also relished seeing the Great Barrier Reef I had learned about in high school from a helicopter; the Outback with the multihued and glorious sunrise on the sacred Uluru—Ayers Rock; and all the aboriginal culture and history including the Stolen Generation of half-caste children with whom I have much in common. The Royal Flying Doctor Service base and museum in Alice Springs brought me back to the time I flew with the Flying Doctors in Tanzania, but I didn't know the medical service had originated in 1928 in Australia. I also visited the scenic old Railway and Skyway near Katoomba Falls, the Opera House, and the Nelson Mandela Museum in Sydney.

Throughout the three-week cruise, I was not feeling my best but was determined to see as much as I could and do everything on the itinerary. Pam and others on the cruise who knew me thought it was strange that I wasn't up dancing and partying till the wee hours of the morning, as is my custom. I told them I wanted to conserve my energy for the following days' events, but in truth I was exhausted at the end of each day, and I had a low-grade fever the entire time. I didn't cancel my helicopter ride over the Great Barrier Reef, even though that morning I had a temperature of 102. I remembered that I'd had temperatures of 105 with malaria or typhoid as a child, and so I figured I'd be all right. The evening we left Australia I was especially ill, and I thanked God I was flying first class and could sleep the entire way back to the States. I had a nine-hour layover in Los Angeles that I'd tried desperately to change before I left but couldn't.

Another godsend! Once the plane landed in Los Angeles and I got through customs, I took the shuttle to the airport hotel. Then I set the alarm and slid under the cool, fresh linens that soothed my burning body until it was time to catch my next flight. When the taxi eventually dropped me at my house in Florida, I asked the driver to help me in, because I was weak from having nothing to eat or drink since leaving Sydney. Apart from the fever, my back ached and I felt an overall dull muscle pain, which scared me a little. I got into bed almost fully clothed and quickly fell asleep. The next day when I woke up, I felt surprisingly well, though still weak and dizzy. I was relieved! So nothing was wrong after all, I thought. My body was probably just done in from all the stress of the divorce and the physical exertion of the three-week cruise. I was feeling outright great as I retrieved my messages from the answering machine.

"This is the doctor's office. We know you have an appointment for a D&C next week, but she wants you to come in as soon as you return from your trip."

I didn't think too much about the message. Probably something came up and she had to go out of town and wanted to do the D&C before she left. I listened to the rest of my messages, decided to call her the next day, and went to the grocery store.

When I called the doctor's office in the morning, I was told I could see her that afternoon. She was waiting for me in her exam room, and after a few inquiries about my cruise, said, "I know you think that you're here for your D&C prep, but we have something more important to take care of today. Your mammogram came back and you have breast cancer."

She walked over to me and held me for a long time.

I went blank. The doctor stood quietly beside me and looked at me. I felt like my brain had just melted and spilled out, and she was peering into my empty skull.

"Because the cancer is quite spread out, I've made appointments for you to have a biopsy, another mammogram, and to see an oncologist. She handed me a piece of paper with names on it, which I put in my purse. My mind was still blank and I couldn't seem to feel my body.

"Are you okay?" she asked.

I nodded because no words came from my mouth.

"I know you're in the middle of a divorce, and I'm really sorry that you should have to hear this news at this time, but we must take care of it right away."

I wanted to disappear. I wanted to run far, far away where no one, not even cancer, could find me. Instead, I stood up slowly, reached for my purse, and walked toward the door.

"Are you alone? Will you be okay to drive home?"

I nodded, said thank you, and walked to my car.

I don't remember starting the car, but my body felt like a hollow drum each time the tires hit a seam on the tarmac road. My head was numb and blank. A zombie might as well have driven me home. I think I was holding my breath, because I started to get dizzy. I pulled off to the side of Federal Highway in Boca, turned off the motor, pushed the car seat all the way down, and let my body fall backwards. I felt like an empty caterpillar cocoon after its beautiful butterfly took flight. I figured this is what being in shock was. When I looked at my watch, I realized I had been on the side of the road for over an hour.

When I got home I called Stacey, a friend nearby who came over right away and stayed with me for a long time. She wanted to spend the night, but I told her I would be okay.

62

Drum Beats, Heart Beats

After Stacey left I felt really weak. I was lightheaded when I stood up, so I sat down until the feeling passed. I walked to the kitchen, passed through my dance studio, and climbed up the many steps to the Norwegian room, stopping on each step to catch my breath. I went to the cupboards against the wall and took out my favorite Colleen Waterford crystal goblet. I turned the beautiful glass in my hand, feeling its weight. Hearing Cathy's admonition to use my finest things only for "special occasions," I wondered if today qualified as such an occasion. I went down the stairs carefully, stopping on each step to balance. I walked past the dance studio and back into the kitchen. I opened the pantry door and then the small wine cooler, picked the best Saint-Emilion red wine I had, uncorked the bottle, and poured myself a glass. I lifted the glass to eye level, swirled it a little, and tasted it. Ahhhhh! Good!

I toasted the bas-relief picture of African copper dancers and drummers hanging on the wall facing me, and I watched them observe my every move. I lit the three crystal oil lamps on the coffee table, found my iPod, and searched under "African." I stopped at a playlist with Miriam Makeba and Harry Belafonte singing a duet of "Malaika," pushed the play button, doubled up the large pillows adorned with Ndebele and Zulu women in their national dress, and piled them on one side of the couch. I put one hip down, then the other, and slowly stretched out the carcass that was my body on the couch.

With each sip of wine I felt better. I started to feel myself again and became more aware of my surroundings. I had nothing on my mind except the goodness of the wine and the beautiful etchings on the crystal glass.

Little by little, the zombie that had inhabited me the last few hours faded away, and I was left alone with me. I started looking around the living room. I stared at the walls, taking it all in: the African masks, paintings, tapestries, and batiks; Kente and Ewe wall hangings; Maasai beaded collars, intricate Bedouin silver necklaces, Ethiopian Coptic crosses; Kuba and Guru masks, contemporary metal and clay sculptures of African women and wild animals, the six-foot-tall Ujamaa ebony carving; and the curio cabinet that displayed mostly antique traditional art with some contemporary pieces.

Living surrounded by African art, I'd developed a habit of audibly wondering how, by whom, where, and when each piece was made. I'd picture the artist seated under a tree in the village, creating this beautiful object, but who wouldn't have the luxury of admiring it as often as I did. I'd ask the art piece questions and sometimes it answered me. Today I looked at the art as though I were seeing it for the first time. Certain pieces came alive and told me about themselves even before I asked.

I took a Maasai collar from the wall, put it over my head, and felt its weight on my shoulders as I walked to the kitchen for a second glass of wine. On the way back to the living room, I heard some commotion. I looked out the window but saw no one. It was too late for anyone to come by anyway. I sat down on the couch again, but the noises didn't stop. They were coming from inside the house—from inside the living room. Suddenly, I felt movement all around me. I saw that the masks were starting to move and dance, and the reflections of the Benin bronzes shimmered on the oil lamps on the table. A Maasai man, bowing his head as he asked female relatives for the hand of his beloved, rose from the large red, orange, white, and blue Laban oil painting on the wall; he was followed by the women who leaped from the canvas, flapping their neck collars up and down on their shoulders. I touched their necklaces and showed them the collar around my own neck. The long Kuba cloths shimmied up and down the wall, accentuating their intricate geometric designs and subtle root colors of various shades of brown.

The next CD on the iPod was Wasis Diop's "No Sant," and I couldn't wait for "African Dream," the first song on the CD. Wasis Diop has a deep sexy voice like Barry White's. No matter where I am or what I'm doing, when I hear the first words of any of his songs, I have to steady myself, but then I give my imagination free reign to run with him anywhere he might want to take me. I couldn't remain on the couch. This song is hauntingly beautiful to listen to, but it's the instrumentation and rhythms that touch my soul and make me dance with such a spiritual force that I am totally unaware of my body. I danced with the art, and we talked to each other and to the ancestor spirits they manifest. When "African Dream" ended I turned up the volume and danced for another three songs. Could this be happening? Are the ancestors here?

Not only were they dancing with me, many were also playing musical instruments. Drums of every shape and size softly played in the living room. Beautiful and haunting melodies from the kora, marimba, mbiras, and balafons accompanied the drums, and they all came closer to me, trying to harmonize and synchronize with the rhythm of my heartbeat. The dancers in the room clapped to the rhythms as the music gradually became softer and softer until all I heard was the deep alto of the goatskin drum I had brought with me from Tanzania forty years ago. It had come from the same village that called me to join in the festivities when I was trying to sleep at the orphanage. The sound of that drum was the sweet echo of remembrance and took me back to that long-ago time when I was surrounded by three loving African village women who soothed me by telling me they were all my mothers. Everyone in the room bowed their head and paid homage to the little girl who went to dance in the village. That day was like no other. That day was my salvation. That was the day Fat Mary was born.

After a long silence, the dancing and celebration in the living room resumed in earnest. Fat Mary stepped into the center of the circle of dancers, talking so loudly that she drowned out nearly every other instrument, but no matter how much she tried, she couldn't silence the drums. She couldn't silence them because they were beating the rhythm of her own heartbeat. All I could hear at that point was the familiar strong, assuring, and soothing beat of her heart.

The man beating the village women's drum stepped inside the circle to join Fat Mary. Although he looked familiar, I couldn't make out who he was right away because he was beating the drum with his whole body. Then he stopped the drumming and solemnly walked toward the side of the room, lifted the heavy wooden Sukuma throne that was part of my art collection, put it in the circle, and sat on it. I then recognized him. He was my father.

Mwanangu, my child, I have watched over you from the day I accompanied the Reiners to the Kifungilo orphanage when you were a few days old. I wanted to raise you in my village, but you were forbidden to me. I was told that you would be dead to me, that you were not born for me. They took you away from me, but they could not take me away from you. You have been part of me and have lived in my heart from the day our eyes met. In the orphanage I watched over you and guided you and prayed for you. I wanted you to always remember who you are. You are the daughter of a Sukuma man. The African blood flowing in your veins could not be emptied by white nuns no matter how much they tried.

He reached for Fat Mary's hand, lifted her, and sat her on his lap. My father looked at me with his all-knowing, gentle eyes. *I have come to reveal myself. My spirit speaks through Fat Mary—the voice that always reminded you of how precious you are. Your ancestors have accompanied me here today to recharge Fat Mary with everything she will need to guide you on the long road ahead. She will show you all the truths about cancer. Cancer's journey has no beginning and no end. It stops at regular intervals to inspect its surroundings. It will linger only where it is invited. The best thing to do is acknowledge its presence, but you must not let it take advantage of your hospitality. Take a firm grip of its hand and direct it back on the path of its endless journey. When it is fully out of sight, you will discover the blessings and gifts it left for you.*

The instruments resumed playing once again, and the ancestors began dancing and discussing my cancer diagnosis. Each came up with an idea of how to gracefully send cancer on its way. They agreed that dancing was the best medicine for me. They told me that they would always dance with me. I danced the longest with the BaKuba elephant helmet mask. He let me hold on to his trunk as he swirled me around saying, "See, see, you will never stop dancing." The other dancer that didn't stop dancing was the exquisite red, gold, black, and green silk lady's kente cloth. It placed itself around my hips below my belly to exaggerate the fast and furious movements of my hips.

I was saving the best for last, and now I went to dance with my father. But Fat Mary was sitting alone on the Sukuma throne. I searched for my father among the dancers, but he was nowhere to be found. He had become Fat Mary.

Now we were having a typical village dance party with discussions and disagreements, jealousies and showing off. There were words between the kente cloth and the beaded leather Mbulu wedding skirt. The skirt argued that it should have been worn before the kente cloth. But the kente cloth claimed it had jumped into the dance first, while the skirt was still hanging on the wall, deciding what to do. "Besides," the kente continued, "my colorful and flowing silk fabric is more attractive, graceful, and sensual than your stiff skirt of leather and inflexible beads."

The skirt came to me and demanded that I dance with it before I covered it up with the kente cloth. Just when it looked like there might be a fight, all the dancers came together on the living room floor and encircled the quarrelling pair. With the elephant mask playing referee, it was decided that the skirt was right. I caressed the rolled-up kente cloth as I carefully removed it from my hips and put on the Mbulu skirt. Fat Mary and I danced a few songs with the skirt and were amazed at how supple the leather was and what beautiful sounds the hundreds of beads on it produced as we did a tribal dance. The party continued way into the morning with every piece of art having the opportunity to do a solo dance to show off its beauty.

Toward the end everyone formed one big circle around me, and Fat Mary spoke.

These dancers in your home have come alive in order to assure you that you will not fight the cancer alone. Your life has always been surrounded by your African roots and ancestors who have been watching over you and will continue to do so. You already possess two of the most important components of healing—your persistent faith and your love of self.

Doctors heal your body. Only you can heal your soul. Divorce cannot diminish your soul. Cancer cannot diminish your soul. You must dwell in the realm of the divine and continue the dance of your ancestors. They are the true healers of the soul! Their drum beats are the heart beats that have kept you alive. They will beat for you until the day you join them.

Gratitude for belonging to this rich heritage overwhelmed me as, one by one, I accompanied each piece of art back to its designated place on the wall, cabinet, or shelf. When all were back in place, I finally understood that my passion for everything African—especially African art—was the companion of my passion for survival, which was a gift from my father.

63

Mayo Clinic

 When I woke from my African dream that morning, I was still on the couch. Even without fully comprehending what happened while I slept, I knew I'd had an extraordinary healing session with the ancestors. I noticed that the oil lamps had burned themselves out, the iPod was playing song number 906 out of 2,760, and I hadn't touched my second glass of wine. The best part was that I didn't feel like the hollow, discarded caterpillar cocoon of yesterday. I felt strong and determined to keep on dancing and knew in the center of my being that the ancestors would be involved in my recovery and healing.

On my way to the kitchen I remembered there was something I needed to do that morning. Oh yes. I almost forgot. I have breast cancer and there were some people I needed to call.

I called the biopsy doctor and was told the earliest I could get in to see him was in two weeks, and then it might take a week to ten days to know the results. I called Kata, Karl, John and Cathy, Eleanor, and a handful of close friends to tell them about my diagnosis. I sent a copy of the mammogram to my brother Larry, and to an oncologist who had been Kata's classmate in college. I asked my friend Dr. Jim Gayes if I should wait two weeks for the biopsy, or if I should try to get one earlier with another doctor.

"Nhambu, if I were you, I would take the next plane out of Florida and go to the Mayo Clinic in Rochester. I will start checking around for doctors for you."

"My friend Mary is a physician there. She's the daughter of one of my *Aerobics With Soul*® clients. I'll call her."

"Good, but call right away," Jim said. "You could probably have all the tests and be done with the surgery by the time you wait two weeks to get a biopsy and the results. I've heard it said that the first thing to do when you're diagnosed with a serious disease in Florida is to make a plane reservation and leave Florida!"

I called Mary's cell and was lucky to get her on the first try.

"I'm so sorry, Nhambu. I'm not with the breast cancer clinic, but I know a good doctor. I'll contact her and get back to you."

Two hours later the phone rang. I saw Mayo Clinic on the caller ID.

"Hello, Nhambu? My name is Dr. Lonzetta Neal with the Mayo Breast Cancer Clinic. Mary told me you were just diagnosed and had some questions."

Without a doubt, the dancing ancestors in my dream sent her from heaven. Hers was the gentlest, calmest, sweetest, most soothing and empathetic voice I've ever heard from a doctor.

"Thank you for calling back so quickly."

"Tell me everything you know about your diagnosis, the timetable, whether or not you want to come here for treatment, and I'll take it from there."

I told her as much as I knew from the mammogram report. It showed tumors on several locations in the left breast that appeared to be encapsulated, whatever that meant. I read some more of the report before I realized it was all Greek to me. She told me to fax her the mammogram results, and she'd get back to me as soon as she could.

Early next morning, we were on the phone again.

"When can you get here?"

"Probably in a day or two."

"Good. I'll go ahead and make all the arrangements to admit you. You can bring your records, but we will redo the mammogram, the biopsy, PET scans, MRI, and several other tests before surgery. From what I can see, you will definitely need a mastectomy, but we can't decide if you'll need a bilateral one until after we see you and have all the test results. I will schedule surgery. In the meantime, I know how scared you must be. Try to stay calm and know that you will be in good hands. I'm looking forward to meeting you."

Once more, I was reassured by Dr. Neal's soothing voice, along with my memory of the dancing feast I had had with the ancestors. I told myself that I would be fine and not to be afraid. I told myself that many people have had cancer, and now it was my turn.

On Sunday, March 13 of 2005, I took an evening flight from Miami to Minneapolis. Diane and Rachel, *Aerobics With Soul®* instructors, met me at the airport and drove me straight to the Mayo Clinic, ninety miles away. Later that evening Carletta, one of my closest friends, came to be with me for a whole week of tests and for the surgery.

The registration process at Mayo was out of a fairy tale. Everything ran as smoothly and reassuringly as Dr. Neal's voice. In spite of the number of patients checking in, the process went like clockwork right down to the minute. I was handed a six-page summary of all my appointments and tests for the next week up to and after surgery.

I reported to the contemporary, impressive Gonda Building at the heart of the Mayo Clinic's downtown campus. I couldn't keep my eyes from the internal and external architecture and landscaping. Everywhere I looked there were sculptures, paintings, multicultural artifacts and photographs, antiques in every category. I made a practice of going to appointments early just so I could enjoy the art. I couldn't pull myself away from the extensive glass art exhibit of Dale Chihuly's work, which confirmed for me that beauty and love can coexist with pain and loss.

Sitting in the comfortable chairs while waiting to be called, I observed something that made me feel a tinge of sadness. In the breast cancer wing, the majority of patients were women of course, but most had their husbands sitting with them, often holding their hands. If there ever was a time I needed my husband to be with me, to tell me that I will always be beautiful to him even when my body would be disfigured, this would be it! The one time in my life I really needed him, he was not there.

You do not need your husband. You only need yourself to believe that all will turn out well. You will get the best care from your doctors and your children and friends. And I, of course, am always by your side. It was Fat Mary, and she was right.

As I looked again at the couples grieving and supporting each other, it dawned on me to count my blessings and snap out of my self-pity. I was at the Mayo Clinic, for heaven's sake, one of the best medical facilities in the world. I could have breast cancer and be somewhere in a village in Tanzania receiving little or no care. Later, when Kata and Karl came to Florida to see me during my recovery and I was describing my Mayo Clinic experience, Kata pointed out something I knew but had a hard time accepting.

"Mom, I know that it has been extra hard for you because Dad is nowhere in sight, but you're better off this way. Dad wouldn't have been there for you like those other husbands were for their wives at the clinic. He really can't figure out how to do that."

"You're right. The contrast between him and other husbands would probably have hurt more."

Dr. Neal was as cool, calm, and gentle in person as she was over the phone. I liked and trusted her right away. We talked for an hour before she gave me a complete physical exam. I began my week of appointments meandering in and out, up and around a maze of walkways and tunnels that linked the various Mayo buildings and campuses. From beginning to end, all my appointments were on time, and in spite of seeing several doctors in several buildings, everything went seamlessly.

On March 18, a team of doctors removed both my breasts. Before the surgery, I was shown several videos of my options after the mastectomy, and I decided to wait for the reconstruction until after I had healed. While I was under anesthesia, they also performed the D&C, which was to resolve the problem that initially led me to see the gynecologist who discovered the cancer. I remained in the hospital for three days. The day I checked out, I learned that a dear friend of mine, Barbara Knutson, was at Mayo Clinic at the same time, but unfortunately, she didn't survive. She had lived in South Africa, and was a well-known, accomplished artist and author of children's books, several of them with African themes. She played an important role in *Aerobics With Soul®*, designing my logo, illustrating my basic moves, and creating the artwork for my brochures and publicity.

Carletta drove me back to Minneapolis, where I spent a night at her house, and in the morning another friend, Carol, came by. They packed me up—draining tubes and all—and then the three of us left by plane for my home in Florida.

For a whole month Carletta and Carol nursed me like I was their own flesh and blood. They measured and emptied the tubes collecting post-op blood and liquids seeping from the breast wounds. They cooked for me, bathed me, changed my dressings, answered and screened calls before handing me the phone, drove me to my doctors for checkups, and gave me the tender loving care I needed to heal, both physically and psychologically. I was, after all, in the middle of a divorce, and I had to get back to that nightmare as soon as I was able.

My attorney called often to see how I was doing and didn't mention the divorce unless I brought it up, and when I did, she told me there was time enough for the divorce. It was my time to heal.

I was under the care of an oncologist in Florida for the first weeks of my recuperation, but then flew back to Minnesota where Cathy drove me to the Mayo Clinic to see Dr. Neal and other doctors for my six-week checkup. One of the alternative doctors I saw at the clinic assured me I would beat cancer because, "You've been actively getting rid of 50 percent of the probable cause of your cancer by leaving your husband. Medicine, along with a less stressful life, and the love of your family and friends will do the rest. You will be just fine!"

She was right. Friends from all five continents called, wrote, or came to see me. I have a trunk full of cards, letters, books, and presents from this time. For several months after I returned to Florida I was never alone. So many friends wanted to come to me in Florida as soon as they heard about my illness that Rachel set up a "Time with Nhambu" schedule so visits wouldn't overlap.

64

New Dimensions

 I saw a breast reconstruction specialist at Mayo Clinic. We agreed I should have this type of surgery done in Florida not only because I lived there, but because Florida has some of the best plastic surgeons in America. I also had a consultation with an oncologist at Mayo who prescribed Arimidex, a tiny chemotherapy pill, but it gave me intolerable, incapacitating hot flashes. I was then put on Aromasin, and I tolerated this medication better, even though the weight gain it caused was most unwelcome. All went well with subsequent checkups and after a couple of months I got clearance to go ahead with breast reconstruction.

Karl was graduating from Naropa University in May, only a week after my last checkup at Mayo. There was no way I was going to miss it. I bought breasts prostheses and a bra to put them in and wore one of my African outfits to the graduation. Kjell was supposed to go, but his appendix ruptured on the way to the airport. Cathy, John, Kata, her fiancé Matt, and I went to Boulder for the ceremony. We agreed it was a blessing that Kjell could not come. We were in the middle of a divorce, and I was in the middle of breast cancer treatment. We didn't think we would have enjoyed such a celebratory time had he been there. More importantly, it was Karl's day to shine, and the divorce would have been a distraction.

I interviewed several plastic surgeons and chose Dr. Hilton Becker from Boca Raton. He is best known as the inventor of the adjustable breast implant called the Becker Expander Mammary Prosthesis. The Becker Expander implant functions as a tissue expander and then converts to a breast implant once the tissues have been expanded sufficiently. He came very highly recommended. When I met him I found out that he was from South Africa. We had much in common, from travels to culture, music, and sense of humor.

We scheduled the three-hour reconstruction surgery for June, and Dr. Becker implanted the expander in each breast. My friend Stacey took me to the hospital, stayed for the surgery, and left late at night after I was returned to my room.

About an hour after Stacey left the anesthesia wore off and I was in pain. I slept off and on, but the horrendous pain in my chest area kept waking me up. I had slid way down in the bed, was hooked up to the catheter and drip, and was so constricted by the bandages around my chest that I could only take shallow breaths. I couldn't reach for the phone and I couldn't reach the cord to call a nurse. I tried to move, but blood had caked around the draining tubes on my chest and the slightest movement made my whole side sting like someone was cutting me with a knife. I had a throbbing headache and the pain in my chest was now unbearable. At times it was so intense, I was afraid I was going to die. Other times the pain was so bad, I was afraid I wasn't going to die! No one checked on me for the whole night or if they did, they said nothing and did nothing. I was in the bed near the window and the curtain was drawn between me and my Black roommate. She was quiet most of the time, but once she asked me, "Are you okay?"

"No, not at all!" I managed to say. Finally, early in the morning I heard her pull her call string. After what seemed like an eternity, a nurse came to our room and my roommate told her that something was wrong with me. The nurse came over to my side of the curtain and asked, "Can I help you?"

I just nodded.

"Would you like a painkiller?"

I nodded again with as much strength as I could muster.

"When was the last time you had one?" She looked at my chart and said, "My God! You haven't had a single painkiller since you got out of surgery? I'll get your nurse."

In about half an hour a jovial, tall, unkempt male nurse came to see me. "So, we want some medication, do we? Who doesn't? I've got just the thing for you."

He pulled out a syringe and without a word, jammed what looked like a foot-long needle into my upper left arm.

"That should do it!" he said and then left as quickly as he'd come. He didn't prop me up, or straighten out my bedding, or pick up a pillow that had fallen on the floor. He didn't check my vitals or catheter.

I tried to move myself up the mattress, but any movement caused severe pain. I was sure that the position I was in aggravated all the pain in my body. Fortunately, the shot worked fast and I fell asleep.

When I woke up a few hours later, I was in a worse position than I'd been the night before. My whole upper body was hanging off the side of the bed. The drip had ripped off my hand and I was feeling nauseated and feverish. When the nurse came to check on me in late morning, she set a clean nightgown and some washcloths on the bed and told me I could change if I wanted to. After she left, I tried to sit up but found my body was glued to the nightgown and sheets by my dried-up blood and fluid. I managed to pull the cord and another very nice nurse with a Caribbean accent came and took me to the bathroom. She bathed me and gently cleaned my wounds. As she washed my face and combed my hair, she asked me where I was from.

I told her I was originally from Tanzania.

"Do you have relatives here? Are they coming to see you?"

I explained that I had family in America, but not in Florida.

This nurse, who couldn't have been a day older than Karl, said to me, "You're so brave, baby girl! I'm off tomorrow but since you have no relatives, I'll come by and check on you."

I was sure she was an angel from heaven who came down to earth just for me. She did come to see me the next day and said I looked happier. Actually, I was happy to see her, but I had a very high fever. It turned out that when the male Nurse Wretched jammed the needle into my arm the day before, he put it on the side where I had lymph nodes removed. I almost instantly got an infection, which caused a fever and my arm to swell up. It wasn't enough to have to deal with the reconstruction pain. Now I had a fever, and I couldn't move my arm or fingers! When Dr. Becker came to see me in the morning, he was furious.

"Who did this?"

"Nurse Wretched," I replied. I told him about the previous night's nightmare of neglect. He made excuses for the hospital and nurses, saying they were short-staffed and overworked.

Kata and Karl, whom I had told not to come for the surgery since I felt I was in good hands in the hospital and had friends nearby, tried to call my room, but I couldn't reach the phone. Kata was beside herself when we finally connected in the morning.

"Why did you tell me not to come? Everyone needs family or an advocate when they're in the hospital. If anything happens to you, I'll never forgive myself for honoring your wishes."

I had told her that it would be more painful to see her and Karl sad and distressed about me, and I was sure I could handle it. I was planning to see them soon after I left the hospital.

A dear friend, Ngozi Mensah, and his mother Gladys took me home from the hospital. Gladys stayed at my house with me and took care of me for several days until Cathy arrived from Minnesota and Kata and Karl came. Surrounded by the love of family and friends, I realized my lifelong habit of doing for myself led me to believe I could handle surgery alone.

Ngozi's Jamaican parents had been Lutheran Missionaries in Tanzania, and he had attended the Rift Valley Academy High School in Nairobi. Being with them gave me so much comfort because they spoke Swahili, and we indulged in the language and culture we all missed. Gladys is one of the most beautiful and kind people I know. She was the mother I had envisioned for myself when I was in the orphanage and believed that my mother was African.

A few months after the reconstruction, I got a copy of my records from the hospital and seriously considered suing them for negligence. That I even thought of suing made me realize that I had indeed become an American! I decided to wait until I healed and was done with my divorce before I exposed my poor being and psyche to another traumatic experience. The idea of suing scared me. Would I be able to take on the hospital—an established institution with limitless financial and legal resources—and survive? No, it wasn't worth it. At this point, and throughout my life, I was fighting for myself—for my rights as a human being, and for my dignity. I concluded that the process of suing a mega hospital would diminish me.

Dr. Becker installed a port in my breasts and for several months after the initial surgery to insert the implants, he injected saline into the implant to expand it and grow new skin. A week after the first injection, I went for a checkup.

"How's my African today? Let's take a look."

I took off my top so he could see my wounds.

"Wait a minute! What did you just do?" I had no idea what he was talking about. "Did you just pull your top off over your head?"

He seemed alarmed, and I wondered what I had done wrong.

"Do you know it usually takes patients several weeks to be able to do what you just did?"

"It hurt, but how else was I supposed to remove my top?"

"The instruction packet sent home with you from the hospital says to wear a front-buttoned blouse to doctor's appointments, and we'll help you remove it. The booklet shows rehabilitation exercises to start as soon as you can after breast surgery. You obviously don't need them but take a look at them anyway."

When I got home, I opened the hospital discharge folder and found a series of upper-body exercises I was supposed to begin after the stitches were removed. Well, I had no trouble with any of them because almost all were *Aerobics With Soul*® moves that develop strength and flexibility, which I had not lost even though I hadn't exercised in several weeks.

By my last saline injection, my breasts were so large I could hardly hold my chest up and commiserated daily with Dolly Parton. I had several infections and mini-surgeries along the way that prolonged the reconstruction process. When the doctor made nipples from my own skin and attached them on the new breasts, they too decided not to cooperate and fell off. Instead, Janet, Dr. Becker's wife and professional partner at the office, tattooed an areola on each breast, and I was good to go.

During our talks together, Dr. Becker shared with me one anecdote that was outright amazing. On his office computer he showed me part of what inspired him to invent his expandable breast implant. They were photos of Maasai men and women. Dr. Becker pointed out that by inserting large wooden objects into their ear-lobes to stretch them, which they regarded as a sign of beauty, they were not only adorning their ears, they were creating new skin. He used the same principle to stretch the tight, post-mastectomy surface on a woman's chest to make new skin where there was none before and to hold an implant in place. Here's to Dr. Becker's brilliance and Maasai ingenuity.

65

The Art of Loving Art

Around this time Kata became engaged to Matt Minier in Boston. That news gave me an emotional boost during the reconstruction phase of breast cancer treatment. Matt was the first man I thought was right for Kata. They met at work and still worked for the same company. Two days after a saline injection, I surprised them by attending an engagement party that their generous employer hosted for them.

The next day I returned to Florida and resumed the divorce proceedings with my attorney. We were spelling out the distribution of assets and the divorce conditions in the marital agreement. Roberta had gathered all the information she needed to split all our assets, except for our African art collection. Over the years Kjell and I had collected African art and now had a substantial collection.

Because of our limited income when we first married, we started out with store-bought, mass-produced pieces that in Tanzania we called tourist art or airport art. We developed our sensibility by visiting museums and studying the immense depth and variety of African art, upgrading or replacing pieces as we could and purchasing items wherever we found them. Most of our art was bought in Africa, but about a quarter of it we found in galleries or in antique and specialty shops on our various travels. The last few years we concentrated on museum-quality pieces and sold or donated the earlier art.

I, of course, was passionate about my art and requested in the divorce petition to keep it. Kjell had no problem with that, so our lawyers agreed that we should each get experts to appraise the market value of the art collection to determine what I should pay for it. My attorney suggested that I should set a certain amount above which I would not pay, because she suspected Kjell's appraisers might value it high. I planned to get appraisers who'd do just the opposite and hoped that through this process we'd come to a middle ground agreeable to both. I decided that if my share came to some crazy, exaggerated amount, like five hundred thousand dollars, I'd let Kjell keep the art, and I'd take the money and start over. But I knew Kjell didn't have much use for the art and that he'd probably let me have it for what I was willing to pay.

"Whatever you do, be there when his appraisers come and stay until they leave. Don't help them do their job in any way," Roberta instructed me.

That evening when I got home I looked at and touched the art on every wall and in every room of my home, including the bathrooms, wondering if I might have to give it up. Kjell's appraisers—a woman and two men from a reputable art appraisal firm in Florida—came the following week, carrying volumes of books on African art, a camera, and tape measures. They were cordial but they meant business; they spent a couple days measuring and photographing each piece and taking notes. When I saw the number of books they had and how often they referred to them, I knew they were not at all familiar with my art and that African art didn't have much value in their eyes.

My lawyer suggested that I wait for the results of Kjell's appraisers before bringing in my own. It was several weeks before we heard back from them.

"Nhambu, are you sitting down?" Roberta asked me on the phone one afternoon. "I have in front of me the value of your art collection."

My stomach clenched and I felt dizzy, but I sat down and took a deep breath.

"According to the appraisers, your entire seven-hundred-piece art collection is valued at one hundred thousand dollars."

"And that means I'll have to pay $50,000 for Kjell's share?"

"Can you believe it? There is justice after all! Today you should celebrate."

I did open a bottle of champagne, got a crystal flute from the cabinet, and sat down on a low three-legged African stool. While warm tears of joy swelled in my eyes, I toasted my ancestors and thanked them for their love and protection. Then, after one glass of champagne, my mood started changing. I felt angry, hurt, and disappointed that African art was worth so little to these "professional" art appraisers!

To my amazement, Kjell never said a thing to me about the art except in passing a few weeks later. "The price quoted for the art was ridiculous!"

To which I replied, "I thought so too."

66

Signed, Sealed, and Delivered

 On July 12, 2005, my lawyer picked me up at my house and we went to the Delray Beach courthouse to sign the divorce papers. I had had another surgery for an infection in my implants the week before, and I was not in good shape. She had told me that only one of us had to be present to sign the marital termination agreement, and in case I couldn't go, Kjell could do it. On the date of the signing, Kjell was nowhere to be found. I was told later that he'd gone to Norway. Roberta helped me up the long flight of stairs to the courthouse and I signed the divorce papers. I was exhausted from the eighteen-month divorce proceedings punctuated by cancer treatment and ongoing breast reconstruction. When Roberta dropped me back home after the signing, we found three of my dear friends waiting for us with dinner and champagne. After they left, I sent an email to Kjell.

July 12, 2005

Dear Kjell,

I signed the Marital Termination Agreement today.
As I fade into the sunset of your life, please think about this.
There is something in your soul that is very beautiful to me. That is the part of you I fell in love with and the part of you I believe will never change for me. If you would only look inside yourself, you would see it too.
In spite of the many hurts throughout our marriage, I had the wisdom to realize that you were not all bad, and I was not all good. I concentrated on what was good about both of us—and

297

there was plenty about our life together to love and cherish. In doing so, I manifested more of what was good about me rather than what was not. Unfortunately, in your heart, you didn't know you were a good man, even a great man. You defined your greatness by your successes, the important or famous people you knew, your wealth or your possessions. When you're in pursuit of success rather than happiness, you will never be satisfied because there will always be another achievement, another person you want to conquer and impress. Happiness cannot be pursued from without because it exists within you. You are good the way you are. You are enough the way you are. Look at yourself uncritically and be satisfied. You have the GOODS! Confront your insecurities once and for all. They have already done enough damage to your innate goodness.

Nhambu

Fat Mary reassured me, *You are finally free to become the person you were born to be.*

Later, my lawyer brought a financial advisor to the house for me to interview. I liked him right away. He came across as professional and organized, seemed to know his stuff, and was respectful and humble. One of the first things he helped me do was buy a townhome in Minnesota.

When we moved to Florida in 1998 Kjell promised me we would find a townhome in Minnesota so we could go back each summer. It was now apparent why he couldn't find a place no matter how much I pleaded with him—my being there would have interfered with his second family.

I found a townhome in Minneapolis within walking distance of the city lakes, including Lake of the Isles where Kata used to play as a child. I furnished the townhome with furniture from our home in Edina that was left in the Minneapolis apartment Kjell used after we moved to Florida.

During my "hell hath no fury like a woman scorned" phase of the divorce, I told Kjell that I needed to get my personal belongings from that apartment. Along with clothes, shoes, purses, cosmetics, and other miscellaneous items, my "personal belongings" included most of the furniture we'd bought as a couple over the years. I hired a moving van and took the beautiful hand-painted Chinese armoire. I dumped all of Kjell's papers and files on the floor and took the teak desk. I pulled out the books from the bookshelves and wall units; I took mirrors and stools, paintings and sculptures. I took every appliance, dish, and piece of silverware. I did leave him his favorite Norwegian Ekornes Stressless leather recliner and everything Norwegian that was in the apartment. I loaded the truck and put my belongings in storage until I eventually found a townhome.

When Kjell returned to his apartment after my rampage, he was furious! He told me that all I had to do was ask, and he would have given me anything I wanted from the apartment. To which I replied, "Kjell, the days of asking are over."

At the time, I had no idea when or if I'd ever use the stuff. It just felt good and right to take it. Later, I was happy I did. Apart from saving me money, even today when Kata and Karl and my many friends come to visit me in the townhouse, the familiar things remind them of our home in Edina where they had many good times. I like my townhome. In spite of having so many items from my life with Kjell in it, I feel peace the minute I walk in the door. During the divorce, his presence gradually faded from my life and space until it was completely gone.

67

Katarina's Wedding

In April of 2006, Katarina and Matt married. I had been in the midst of breast reconstruction during her engagement and felt bad that I couldn't be with her more to help with the wedding preparations. I did go to Boston as often as I could and went with her to check out reception and ceremony venues, and to look for a wedding dress and bridesmaid dresses. Apart from the little help I gave her when I was in Boston, Kata planned her elaborate, meaningful, and unconventional wedding on her own. Knowing little about American wedding traditions and protocol, I read Martha Stewart's wedding planning book from cover to cover and offered suggestions along the way.

Because Kata had received her master's degree from Harvard School of Divinity, she was able to secure the Harvard Memorial Church for the ceremony and booked the Charles Hotel for the reception. Kjell's family, including his mother and siblings, and our friend Steinar and his grandchild Vilde came from Norway for the wedding. Kata and Matt gave a party for visiting relatives and close friends at their home. It wasn't as tense and awkward as I'd expected, even though it was the first time we were all together since the divorce.

I was dreading seeing Kjell's relatives again after four years and wondered how we would all behave. In spite of years of experience, I still had difficulty dealing with the Norwegian phenomenon that once you hide something under the rug, it goes away and you could go on with business as usual. I also knew that "blood is thicker than water," and his family would side with him. They would stoically accept the changes in the family. During the divorce proceedings, in order to protect myself, I requested that we stop communicating until after the divorce. I had all intentions of picking up where we'd left off when the divorce was finally over and building on the good relationship I had with the family before 2003, but it didn't happen. I heard from none of his siblings when I was diagnosed with cancer or any time after the divorce, except for the short thank-you notes I received after my annual New Year's email.

Even though it had been a year and a half since I was diagnosed and I didn't get any radiation or chemotherapy except for the pills, for some reason my hair started falling out in huge clumps about two weeks before the wedding. I woke up one morning and discovered that I'd left most of my hair on the pillow! I didn't worry too much because I was planning to wear my gold and silver African outfit with a matching wrapped crown that covered my head to the wedding. As long as I also wore my dignity, grace, and attitude, I knew I would look good. I always felt beautiful in my numerous African get-up-and-go outfits. I covered my few remaining patches of hair with a curly, dark-brown wig and received several compliments for my new hairstyle at the party at Kata and Matt's house and at the rehearsal dinner the next day.

The party went very well. I acted as welcoming and friendly and loving as I really felt, and the Norwegian relatives did the same. Not a single question or comment about the divorce or my illness came from Kjell's family. They exuded happiness for the special occasion that brought us all together again.

As soon as Steinar saw me at the party, he told me that he wanted to talk to me and could we please have breakfast together in the morning.

When I speak about Norwegian reluctance to deal with any unpleasantness, I am talking about the Norwegian family I once belonged to and knew well. Although Norwegians are generally known for their humanitarian and charity work in developing countries throughout the world, they are also known for being stoic, nonconfrontational, and having a strong desire to keep the peace at all costs. But like everything else, it is the exception that proves the rule.

Steinar was the exception. The next morning, I had breakfast with him and his granddaughter. Steinar and his wife Elsebeth, who had died several years earlier, were our close friends in Norway. He said that he'd heard several stories of what caused the divorce and wanted to hear my version.

We talked about everything, beginning with the years leading up to the divorce, the divorce process, my cancer, prognosis, treatment, and the ongoing reconstruction. I told him that after I was diagnosed, there were only two things I feared—one was chemotherapy and the other was leaving Kata and Karl with Kjell as the only parent if I died. The cancer hadn't spread to the lymph nodes, so I didn't need the traditional chemotherapy. I told him that I was feeling pretty good and was very lucky and blessed to be present at my daughter's wedding.

Steinar was visibly sad and emotional as he listened to me. At times his eyes filled with tears. When I was done, he said, "Maria, I cannot tell you strongly enough that you did not deserve this. I love Kjell. He's been my dear friend since childhood and that will never change, but I do not condone what he did. What he did was wrong, and I am sorry for him too. It's good you had the courage to take care of yourself this time. You couldn't and shouldn't continue to be with such a hurtful man. Remember how Elsebeth wanted you to leave him the last time he had that long affair? Remember what she said?"

"I remember very well what she said. She told me, 'Maria, once someone gets away with having an affair, they will do it again and again unless there are severe consequences. Do you want to find yourself in this situation over and over again?'"

"I feel very, very bad that it was my good friend who did this to you and your children," Steinar said. "I miss Elsebeth. She's the only one with whom I could discuss something like this, and she loved you like a sister."

"I know. I miss her too. She was so helpful to me. I hope she's resting in peace and not worrying about me again!"

"I worry about you every time I think of you."

That afternoon I had a long talk with Liv, Kjell's mother. She told me she was still in shock, and she didn't understand Kjell. She told me that marriage was not always easy, but she had really believed that Kjell could never do such a thing.

She continued, saying, "I've spent many sleepless nights thinking and worrying about you and my grandchildren. I am sorry for our family that you are not with us any longer. To me, you will always be the only Mrs. Kjell Bergh no matter what he does in the future. It is very hard for me. I wish he had waited until after I died before telling anyone. This is too much for me. Please forgive him. In my heart I know he still loves you and he will regret it one day."

I hugged Liv and felt her pain—the pain of a mother who loves her son but was slowly coming to terms with the fact that he'd hurt her entire family.

Kata and Matt's wedding was a celebration like no other! It was meaningful, diverse, joyful, and inclusive. I had thought that both Kjell and I would give her away, but she wanted her dad alone to do it. As they walked down the aisle for the processional, the organ played an old Norwegian wedding march, "Brudemarsj fra Øre," written by one of her Norwegian ancestors. Her brother Karl, a practicing Buddhist, co-officiated along with a female Unitarian minister. He recited Buddhist prayers for them. The minister named all the ancestors and family members from both sides who had passed, asking them to be present and to bless the couple. Kjell read a poem in Norwegian, and I gave a Swahili wedding blessing and the following speech:

When I was a young girl, every time I saw a mother and her little daughter walking hand in hand, I said to myself, "I wish a had a mother's hand to hold on to. Someday I will hold the hand of my own little girl." Little did I know that the reverse would be true when God created Katarina.

When you were old enough to know that I also needed you, you were always aware of the times when the sun forgot to shine on me. You held my hand in both of yours and squeezed faith, hope, love, and encouragement into my heart.

Raising you, I was afraid that I was going to spoil you and so make life on your own more difficult. A few years ago, you said to me, "Mom, I know I am spoiled, but if it wouldn't be for you, I would be spoiled—rotten! I want you to know that you were the one who spoiled me with the gift of your presence in my life."

I remember many precious times when you educated me and showed me the way—like the time when we were watching Sesame Street and you asked me, "Mom, who is Mother Goose?" and I said, "I don't know her, we'll have to ask Gramma Cathy," and you said, "My Gramma knows everything!"

As I watched you grow, I asked God for so many things for you that I was afraid he would say I was asking too much! I asked him to keep you healthy, safe, and happy, to help you do the things you have a passion for, to keep you proud of your heritage, to live your life in a way that would honor your ancestors, to be a woman of action, to surround yourself with good friends who would attend to you when I was far away.

Throughout my life I've offered little prayers every day that your wishes would be fulfilled, that you would always have what you needed, and that you would respect and celebrate all life. I prayed that if you chose to get married, your love for your husband and he for you would last forever.

Today, I pray that you will always remember that your union is precious and sacred. I pray that you will be blessed with a little girl just like you and a little boy just like Matt for me to spoil—rotten!

I want you to know that whenever I think of you, I feel love, pride, and the highest admiration for the beautiful, clever, sensitive, caring, funny, respectful, courageous, global, and spiritual woman you've become.

My final prayer for you today is that you will always know the love of God, the love of Buddha, the love of your parents, the love of Karl, the love of your family, extended family, and friends—those who have passed on, those who are here today to witness and celebrate your marriage, and those who could not be here.

May you feel my love within your heart, at this moment and always.
Your Mama

Matt's father read from the Bible, and his mother and I lit the wedding candle on the altar. Matt and Kata exchanged the vows they'd written for each other, and then for the recessional, the chapel was filled by the sound of live African drummers beating their drums loudly, rhythmically, and joyfully while guests filed out of the church. People danced down the aisle, clapping to the drum rhythms as they cheered the drummers.

Spirited dancing continued at the Charles Hotel in Harvard Square as wedding guests greeted each other to the rhythm of the music the DJ was playing in the banquet hall. Tall, exquisite flower arrangements graced the hallways and the center of each table. Guests in their formal attire danced to their seats at the tables. Several guests from Kata's side wore magnificent, brightly colored African outfits with masterfully tied head wraps that could only be described as crowns. The guests weren't interested in sitting down; instead they formed spontaneous conga lines going every which way. It was a unique and exhilarating spectacle of young and old dancing together.

When Kata and Matt finally made their entrance, they were accompanied by Zeb, their dog. Zeb is the one and only dog I truly love. He endeared himself to me forever by nestling at my side on the bed and caring for me the wedding anniversary I spent alone a few months after I filed for divorce. Thankfully, he didn't hold a grudge against me from his first visit when I wasn't very welcoming to him.

Everyone eventually sat down but following dinner the dancing got serious. After the bride and groom dance, we had a mother-daughter instead of the traditional father-daughter dance. I danced with Kata and then Karl called out the names of people, one by one, who had been like mothers to Kata as she was growing up. Each made her way to the dance floor, placed hands on her head to bless her, and then danced with her. The group of mothers formed a circle around Kata and blessed her with more dancing, singing, hugging, and kissing as a send-off into her new life. I think that all the two hundred-plus guests—including party crashers from a class reunion upstairs—participated in the mother-daughter dance because in the end everyone was on their feet cheering with joy!

68

Saved by Swahili

 After recuperating from the wedding, I heard Africa calling. It had been five years since I was last there and I knew I needed an Africa fix. I needed to see Tanzania, my family, friends and visit the orphanage where my life began. For the first time since I left, forty-four years ago, I'd be traveling solo.

Early in the morning of February 17, 2007, I began my trip, arriving at Kilimanjaro airport around 10:30 the next night. As anyone going to visit relatives or friends in Africa knows, traveling light is not an option! I had two duffle bags, a suitcase, a carry-on, which included my laptop computer and a huge Le Sportsac purse weighing over twenty pounds. The customs officials at Kilimanjaro airport, noting all the luggage I brought in as a tourist, asked me to take it aside and made me wait until most of the other passengers had passed through before opening my luggage.

As they were inspecting luggage, I overheard a comment in Swahili by the porter to the customs official checking my bags. "Today we are in luck!" the porter said to the customs man who took my passport and asked me in English, "How long will you be here?"

"Six weeks," I replied.

"Where will you be staying?"

"I'll be traveling around the country, but my home base will be with friends at Finca Estate in Usa River."

"And who are your friends?"

"Abdu and Fatima Faraji."

"Are they here to pick you up?"

"They should be waiting outside."

At his request, I opened all of my luggage, and the customs guy touched my items, digging with his hands into the duffle bags and feeling everything.

"You're bringing too many things into the country. Are these gifts for your friends?"

Knowing full well that if I told the truth that most of the items were for friends, he would confiscate them, I said everything was for my personal use because I would be in Tanzania for a long time.

"She's a liar!" the porter commented in Swahili.

Without telling me which items I had to pay for, he said he would let me go, but I had to pay two hundred dollars duty. I started to ask him what the problem items were, but he spoke to the porter again in Swahili, "As soon as you receive payment, let her go. I know the Farajis. If we delay her on this side, they will enter to look for her."

I asked the porter what I was paying duty for. He told me in very broken English that I had many items that were illegal to bring in the country, but if I gave him two hundred dollars, the customs guy would let me go without confiscating them. I asked him why I was paying him instead of the customs official. I knew exactly what was going on because, after all, I was born and raised in Tanzania. Like several other countries in the world I'd been to, Tanzania struggled with rampant government corruption, especially among mid-level employees.

When he saw that I might make trouble, he went to speak to the head customs official. Returning, he told me that I would have to go back to the same customs line, and this time unpack all my luggage and put everything out for him to see.

At that point, I had had enough of their scheme, so I pulled out my trusted weapon, which always disarms corrupt officials. When the porter started rolling my luggage to the custom post, I grabbed the cart and said in Swahili, "Stop right there. I am going to the customs office to report you!"

"Ala!" His eyes were as big as saucers. "Unasema Kiswahili?" (You speak Swahili?)

I answered, continuing in Swahili, "The customs official is quite stupid! Didn't he see in my passport that I was born in Tanzania? Of course, I speak Swahili. Now give me my luggage and let me go!"

I wasn't so lucky when I got outside. I was the sole tourist from the plane left at the airport. It was dark because the lights in the customs hall were being turned off one by one. To my horror the Farajis were not there! I told myself not to panic and tried to call them on my cell phone, but it didn't work in Tanzania. Out of the corner of my eye, I saw three men watching me and pointing to my luggage. I made up my mind right then and there that if the luggage was what they wanted, they could have it. I saw a man by the pillar using his cell phone and asked him in English if I could use it. He was very kind and let me call the Farajis. By then it was 11:30 p.m. and they were in bed. Abdu picked up the phone.

"Nhambu? Is that you? Both Fatima and I will be at the airport to pick you up tomorrow night! We're so looking forward to your visit." They were horrified to learn that they had the wrong date.

Fatima started shouting at her husband in the background, "I told you it was today!"

"Take a taxi and we will be at the gate to meet you."

"She can't take a taxi! Don't you realize what kind of danger that is for a woman traveling alone at night on that isolated, thirty-mile stretch of road? There are no streetlights until the outskirts of Arusha. We have to go and pick her up!"

Although I was scared, I told them that I would take a taxi. With that, I hung up and handed the phone back to its owner.

Then I looked around and realized there was no taxi in sight! The man who lent me his cell phone was gone. A poorly dressed man who appeared to be about twenty-five years old approached me and told me in English that he had a car and he could take me. I was skeptical, but I had no choice. As we were putting my luggage in the car, I saw the same three men squatting with their heads huddled together in conversation. My heart stopped! One of them came up to me and said, "Not to worry, Mama! My friend is good driver! He know house of Faraji."

I heard the man but could barely see him, it was so dark. The only light came from the lone headlight on the ancient Honda station wagon. I said a little prayer and got in the front seat since the luggage took up all the space in the car.

The minute we left the airport, the driver called someone on the phone and spoke to him loudly in Swahili.

"Nimpeleke wapi?" (Where should I take her?)

I started praying again. It crossed my mind that the driver and his friends were going to take me somewhere, steal my luggage, rape me, and possibly even kill me. I saw my dead body lying behind some trees outside a village for days before anybody found me. The only consolation I had was that if I had to go that way, at least my ashes would be in Africa.

The rusted car was literally traveling six miles an hour, and it sounded like parts were falling onto the road with each mile. When he was done with the phone, I asked if I could use it. I called Abdu, gave him the number of the phone I was using, and asked him to call it every ten minutes and ask how far away we were.

About ten minutes after I spoke to Abdu, the phone rang. I was relieved because I thought that at least the driver knew that someone was keeping track of me. To my horror it was one of his friends. *"Tunakaribia barabara kubwa."* (We're approaching the main road.)

At that moment, I reached over, grabbed the phone from the driver, and spoke in Swahili to the man on the other end. I told him that I was aware of what they were doing, and my friend Abdu was on his way and had already called the police. I said that if I wasn't at Usa River in fifteen minutes, they would be arrested!

"Mungu wangu-weeeee!" (Oh my God!) is all the man could say when I pulled out my Swahili secret weapon!

"Don't worry, Mama, he will take you straight to Usa River!" He continued talking but I hung up on him. I told the driver that I would return the phone to him after I arrived at the Faraji farm. Abdu called several times during the trip, which took an additional half hour. I made the driver give him our location each time.

The driver was visibly shaken when I broke out my Swahili. He tried to speak several times, but no words came. He eventually managed to compose himself enough to ask me where I had learned Swahili.

"I was born in Tanga and raised in Lushoto," I told him. He

was shaking so much, I was afraid he'd forget how to drive, so I tried to calm him down by making small talk in Swahili until we arrived at the Finca Farm gates, where Abdu was waiting for me in his pajamas.

In the driver's rush to get away as quickly as possible, he must have forgotten that we hadn't paid him. I ran after the car with the money and his phone, but he drove away even faster.

As soon as we got into the house, I had an overwhelming urge to call my children. Abdu gave me his phone and told me to talk as long as I wished. It was 2:30 in the morning Arusha time when I got ahold of them. All I said to Kata and Karl was that I was safe in Tanzania with Abdu and Fatima.

That night, Fat Mary sat on my lap. *Remember when you had typhoid and received the last sacraments at age seven, the time you almost died from malaria in 1957, and the ectopic pregnancy in 1974, and recently when you were in so much pain after breast reconstruction surgery? Your time has not yet come. Rejoice and live your sacred life to the fullest.*

Family around Yeremia's grave.

Yeremia's trunk.

Gramophone given to Yeremia by Dorothy.

Church at the Sukuma Museum and Cultural Center near Mwanza.

The pulpit with the altar in the background inside the church
at the Sukuma Museum.

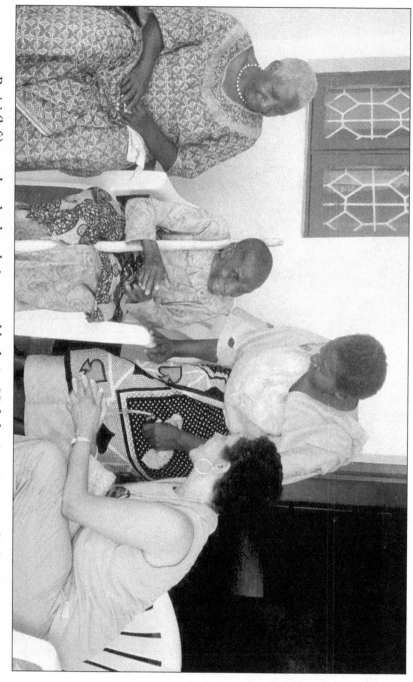

Perisi (left), one-hundred-and-six-year-old relative Njebele, Aunt Loisi, and Nhambu.

Fatima and Abdu Faraji.

Salma Faraji and Claire at their wedding in Ireland.

Nhambu and Thecla, a friend from Marian College,
now Kilakala Secondary School.

Salma, Nhambu and Nedy during the filming of Kilimanjaro, the advanced level of *Aerobics With Soul®* video, on location in Tanzania.

Rachel, Nhambu, and Diane, *Aerobics With Soul*® instructors at Rancho La Puerta, Mexico.

Nhambu and Imelda, a friend from the orphanage.

Nhambu's friend Stefana, who created a school in Uganda for children whose parents are AIDs victims.

Betty with her husband Frank Humplick. Frank and his sisters were popular singers in Tanzania. They were all at Kifungilo with Nhambu.

The Cultural Heritage Center in Arusha, Tanzania, has the largest
collection of traditional and contemporary African art
and artifacts in Africa.

African art in the family room of Nhambu's home.

Surrounded by African art in the living room.

Nhambu wearing beaded Maasai collar.

Nhambu saying goodbye to the statue of Mama Africa as it is crated
for the journey to the Alex Haley Farm in Tennessee and
the Children's Defense Fund.

Elephants passing by tourist tents at Tarangire Safari Lodge.

Nhambu at her favorite spot—the terrace at Tarangire Safari Lodge in Tarangire National Park, Tanzania.

69

Solo Trip to Africa

 The next day, as is the custom when celebrating an important occasion, Fatima slaughtered a goat for me. I braced myself and watched the entire procedure from selecting the goat in the pen, digging a hole in the ground, slitting its throat and draining the blood into the hole, skinning and cleaning the hide, cutting up the goat, and cleaning the entrails to making rice pilau on the small tin stove on the ground in the courtyard. I didn't think I could eat the goat after participating in its demise, but the pilau was out of this world. Fatima and Abdu fought each other for the delicately seasoned entrails or chitterlings, and their three grandchildren smiled with pleasure as they ate their food.

The day after the feast, Fatima and I went to Tarangire Safari Lodge for four days, going on game drives, reading, and enjoying Safari beer in this Garden of Eden. All through our first night, Fatima sang passages from the Quran in Arabic. When I woke her up to tell her that she was singing and I couldn't sleep, she said, "Oh really? Didn't I tell you I was in the school choir when I was young, and I was the best singer?"

"But it's 3 a.m.! You're not only keeping me awake, I'm sure all the animals in the park can hear you too."

She said she was sorry, but after a short time resumed her singing and sang every night we traveled together.

We drove to Lushoto to stay with Betty and Frank, childhood friends from the orphanage, then picked up Sister Eileen at the dentistry. My high school friend Thecla and her grandson Bairi had come to Lushoto from Nairobi by bus, and all of us piled into the Serengeti Select Safari Land Rover to spend the afternoon in Kifungilo.

We walked around the grounds of Kifungilo. The government high school was still run by a handful of Precious Blood Sisters, including Sister Monica whom I knew well. In one of the classrooms, about a hundred blue-and-white-uniformed students gathered around a single 20-inch color TV hung near the ceiling at the front of the room, mesmerized by the American soap opera *Days of Our Lives*.

Blessed Martin had been moved again! This was the fourth place I'd seen him occupy since I left Kifungilo in 1962. He was standing precariously at the edge of the same grass patch in front of the classrooms where Sister Theonesta once taught the little children and Sister Clotilda taught the big girls. He looked forlorn and neglected. I touched his weathered cement cloak and cleaned some bird poop from his arms. I was grateful that our "colored" patron was now Saint Martin de Porres, instead of just Blessed Martin. As children we were instructed to pray to him for benefactors, but we also prayed, sang, and danced in front of him, and asked him for all our possible wants, including taking us away from Kifungilo. We absolutely believed he would answer our prayers, and in my case, he did.

From Lushoto we drove to Dar, where Abdu, Fatima's husband, met us. We spent time with Fati's grandmother, a stately no-nonsense woman who once served in the Tanzanian parliament. I also visited my favorite art stores, bought items from the artists of Bagamoyo Road, and checked in on *Nyumba Ya Sanaa* (House of Art) started by the Maryknoll Sisters.

Abdu, Fati, Thecla, Bairi, and I took the ferry to Zanzibar. On board we were given preferential seats and services because Abdu was recognized as *balozi* (ambassador). He had been the Tanzanian ambassador to France under President Julius Nyerere in the early seventies. Their daughter Salma, who calls me "Auntie," was born in Paris while they were there. We stayed at the Maruhubi Villas on the sands of the Indian Ocean about a mile from Old Stone Town. I noted with interest the beds with mosquito nets near the dining tables in the main restaurant. They were for babies and little children traveling with their parents to sleep, while they finished dinner and enjoyed the evening entertainment. How would that work in America?

Besides the familiar tourist attractions, including the Sultan's Palace, a museum called the House of Wonders, I visited Mtoni where I hadn't been before. While my friends were relaxing at Mtoni Marine Hotel, I hired a taxi to drive me twenty kilometers north to Mwangapwani. My guide took me to a large natural cave with a fresh water pool. The cave had been used to hide slaves after the legal slave trade was abolished in the nineteenth century. It was a sobering, dark, moist, and depressing place. Small pools of water were connected by narrow underground passageways that led out to the ocean. People came with buckets to fetch water for their homes from the underground pools.

From the caves I went to see the five-star luxury hotel called Zamani Zanzibar Kempinski. Lush tropical gardens covered the thirty-acre grounds, interspersed with villas and spacious hotel rooms. Infinity pools disappeared into the ocean and beckoned you to swim the entire mile of oceanfront. Kuba cloth rugs and pillows accentuated the simple, clean lines of the sofas and chairs in the elongated lobby; original art from all over Africa filled every wall and niche. I was impressed by the Anantara Spa with its outdoor Thai massage pavilions, beautifully appointed treatment rooms with locally produced organic products displayed in the spa store. Despite enjoying the luxury of the moment, the memory and history of the slave caves I'd just visited lingered in my mind.

We flew back to Arusha from Zanzibar, and the next day my African brother Amani joined me. We took a small Air Tanzania plane to Mwanza. At the Mwanza airport I was surprised to see Pastor Nashoni N'gwan'gwa. He was one of the people taking care of Pastor Yegera, the bishop's assistant, when Larry and I went looking for my father in 1988. He had traveled several hours by bus to come and see me. "I longed to see our Miss Nhambu from America," he said, greeting me in Swahili. As soon as I saw him, I was taken back to that miraculous day I found my father.

Cousin Enock Kibendela, head of the Lake Region Vocational Technologies, sent his Land Rover and driver to take us to the Tilapia Hotel, where we would spend the night. He later joined us for dinner at the hotel restaurant located on the shores of Lake Victoria.

In the morning Amani and I caught the 8 a.m. ferry from Mwanza to Kamanga. The new ferry was a great improvement over the one I took twenty years ago. I wanted to take pictures so I asked the captain if I could go to the upper deck, which was unoccupied even though the lower deck was overflowing with passengers, produce, trucks, buses, and bicycles. No goats, however, and the ferry left only a half-hour late. Amani and I were allowed to sit upstairs. We were alone up there except for a few ferry employees.

The lake shimmered with crystal waves meandering ahead of us in the morning sun. The Tanzanian flag waved proudly to the people along the shores from the aft deck. Returning fishermen saluted us as they hurriedly unloaded their catch for relatives to take to market and rushed back to the lake for more fish. Dense groups of seagulls clung to the boulders, not wanting to leave their vantage points on the lake's *kopjes*. This time the crossing took only forty minutes. Then, after three hours of driving on the road that had not been improved or maintained since the visit with my children, Amani and I arrived at our father's village of Kasamwa.

70

Kasamwa Celebrates

 My favorite sister Mlekwa, my father's wife Perisi, and a whole slew of relatives were at the village to meet us. The first thing we did was gather around my father's grave, where I laid the flowers from Fatima's farm that I'd brought on the plane with me. Every one present said a personal prayer out loud, and when we were done we held hands as we sang and danced around the grave. The grave was well-maintained. A foot-tall cement enclosure surrounded it, and a new white wooden cross with the dates of Yeremia's birth and death in black letters had been installed at the head of the grave.

A goat was slaughtered, and we continued to celebrate Yeremia's life and my homecoming with song and dance as we enjoyed the meal of goat stew, plantain stew, pickled tomatoes, rice, and sweet potatoes, beer, Fanta, and Coke, prepared by Mlekwa. After eating we gathered in the living room when an unexpected question came from Perisi.

She wanted to know where my husband was, and why didn't I bring my children. It was now two years since the divorce, but I hadn't told the relatives in the village, only the few who lived in town. I told her that we were no longer together and gave her a brief explanation why. After a long silence, she stood up and announced.

"*Bwana ametuacha. Kutokana na leo, ingawapo ametuacha, tutam-wombea apate anachotafuta. Sisi kwa upande wetu, tutamwacha pia.*" (Her husband has left us. From today on, we will pray for him to find what he is searching for. Our side of the family must grant him his wish. We must let him go.)

In the silence that followed, everyone there—about twenty-five people in all—repeated what she said, one by one, beginning with the eldest. Then they sang a sad-sounding Sukuma song whose lyrics I didn't understand. It seemed like they couldn't wait to finish the sad song, because Loisi, the eldest aunt present, had already broken into a more joyful one. The song started softly and built up to a thunderous ending, with people clapping happily, drumming instant rhythms on anything they could get their hands on, and then coming up to me, one by one, to hug me and tell me that I will continue to be "the blessed one."

Whatever it was that they were doing, whether it was a tribal farewell ritual or a communal acceptance of what they couldn't change, I realized that they were taking my side. They were burying my past with my husband and giving themselves closure.

Perisi called out, *"Leteni chakula!"* (Bring the food!)

I saw that another goat had been slaughtered but this one was prepared the Sukuma way. One of the highlights of my visit came after dinner when twenty-five relatives gathered around a tiny wooden table in the living room and watched Kata and Matt's hour and forty-five-minute wedding video on the two-inch screen of my iPod! I knew they had no electricity in the village, so I brought a battery-operated, portable micro-speaker from the States. Based on the enjoyment I had as a child listening to English records on the gramophone at the orphanage and in high school, I knew that not speaking English would not deter them from fully enjoying the wedding ceremony as though they were there. I was not disappointed. When we came to the part where I gave the Swahili wedding blessing, everyone stood up and cheered! There was a lot of rejoicing, and one aunt insisted on playing that part over and over. After several repetitions, they recited the blessing along with me on the video.

A Swahili Wedding Blessing

Ukweli wa dunia ni kwamba Mwenyezi Mungu ndiye anayapanga maisha ya binadamu. Leo nisiku ya furaha kubwa kuwaona watoto wetu Katarina and Matthew wako pamoja wakiwa mume na mke, wamependeza sana kama Mungu alivyowatarajia.

Kuanzia ndoa yenu nawapeni Radhi zangu zote.

Namwomba Mola wetu aidhumishe ndoa yenu.
Aiondolee midharaba, matatizo na kuitakasa.
Akupeni nguvu na uwezo wa kustahimiliana na kuvumiliana.
Mungu aibariki ndoa yenu. Amina.

*(It is universally believed that God plans the destiny of human be-
ings. None of us can predict the future. Today is a great day, full of joy,
to see our children Katarina and Matthew as husband and wife looking
so good, as God wished.*
I pray that this marriage be everlasting.
I give you all my blessings and
*I pray that God will strengthen your marriage, keep it from trouble,
and purify it.*
*I pray that he will give you strength to persevere, to always respect
one another, and to be patient with each other.*
I pray that you will do only what is good for your new life together.
God bless this marriage. Amen.)

Only after the group had recited the blessing out loud did the
aunt allow the video to continue. They watched the mother-daughter
dance multiple times. Everyone was familiar with "Marie-José," by
Lokassa ya Mbongo, and sang along so loudly that only the old aunt
whose eyes were glued on the iPod knew when the song actually
ended. She replayed it when it finished, but the dancers continued
dancing to their own singing until they were tired. Then, taking the
iPod outside, they formed a large circle, and as Africans in the village usually do, each one went into the center and did a solo dance
with the others imitating them. Then the children entered the circle
and danced their own variations while the adults clapped and encouraged them.

The happy party would have continued, but we had more people
and places to visit that day. Perisi thanked me for bringing the wedding to Kasamwa and said that when Karl got married, she wanted
to attend the wedding in America.

After lunch we visited Chabulongo, the original family plot
where ten family members were buried. Perisi gave me a short history of their lives, and we said prayers and sang Christian songs in

Swahili at the grave sites before leaving for the ferry and the airport. I can still see my relatives outside the family compound with both arms raised overhead, waving goodbye.

We got back to Mwanza very late, but cousin Enock insisted that we go out and celebrate at a nightclub he owned called Cheers. To my surprise, it was a regular American-style club with TVs along the walls showing soccer games, potted flowers decorating cozy tables, a well-equipped bar, and even a pool table in one corner. Here, as opposed to American nightclubs, the dance floor was large. The tables and chairs close to the walls were seldom occupied because most people were dancing to the live band and stopped only when the musicians took a break.

71

The Sukuma Museum

 My father belonged to the Sukuma people, Tanzania's largest tribe. Their performing and ritualistic arts and traditions are among the richest in East Africa. We spent most of the next day in Bujora at the Sukuma Museum and Cultural Center started in 1954 by missionaries. Now it is a community-based organization that promotes and celebrates the traditional and contemporary arts of the Sukuma culture.

Schoolchildren from a nearby grade school were also at the museum that day to learn about their history from Sukuma elders. Spread over the extensive museum grounds are traditional Sukuma structures, including spaces for blacksmiths and traditional doctors, as well as a traditional community compound, a royal pavilion which housed the chief's regalia, and a dance pavilion for the Bagika and Bagalu dance societies. Most of the important art objects and artifacts in the collection—such as royal drums and regalia, costumes and accessories of the dance societies, objects of healing and devices unique to Sukuma traditional doctors, furniture, weapons, and utilitarian objects—have been donated to the museum by Sukuma elders and royal families. I entered every building and had fun beating the huge drums in the dance pavilion.

My favorite building in the museum compound is the church. The large, brilliantly colored church resembles a royal Sukuma dwelling, complete with a decorated hoe at the pinnacle, indicating the dwelling of an individual of high standing. The royal symbolism of the Sukuma church equates God with the Sukuma chief, acknowledging that the traditional Sukuma chief is the father of the village. A huge calabash holds water for baptisms; the altar has the form of a royal Sukuma throne, and the pulpit is in the shape of a horn, while the chairs around the altar are similar to those in a chief's house.

The museum provides an artistic, spiritual, intellectual, and communal focal point for Sukuma culture. I thought of my father the entire time I was at the museum. Even though he worked for white people and embraced European culture, he was very proud of his Sukuma culture and heritage. One of his wishes for Kata and Karl was for them to know and be proud of their heritage—a treasure and blessing I didn't have growing up but was now immersed in.

Because cousin Enock was a big shot in the Lake Region, I was granted permission to tour the Nile Perch Fisheries outside Mwanza. I wanted to visit the plant because the introduction to Lake Victoria of the Nile perch in the 1950s became controversial due to the negative ecological effects on the lake's indigenous fish and the surrounding area. The perch caused the extinction or near-extinction of several hundred native fish species.

The plant itself was spotless. No one was allowed in the plant with street clothes. The workers wore uniforms, tall rubber boots, hairnets, and protective mouth shields. I was told that each day this particular plant harvested eight tons of fish from the lake! Several refrigerated trucks filled with Nile perch arrived at the plant and were loaded into large, cold holding tanks and chambers. Their heads, fins, and entrails were removed as they moved along the assembly line. They were scaled, cut into fillets, boxed and labeled, and stored in gigantic metal refrigerators. On my way out of the plant, I saw three long Mack trucks being loaded with frozen fish to be whisked away to the airport for export to Europe and America.

Leaving the fish behind, I went to the home of another cousin, Isaka and his wife, for a traditional dinner of *ugali* (cornmeal), *mchicha* (spinach), and *dagaa* (tiny, salty fish). When we were there cousin Enock texted that his grandmother was waiting to see me and we should stop by her house. Ten people piled in the Land Rover and we drove the five miles to see Great-grandmother Njebele.

She smiled broadly as we approached the house. Grandmother Njebele was very, very old. She was sitting outside on a low stool, hanging on to her knobby, worn cane with bony hands disfigured by arthritis. It was obvious that she couldn't stand up by herself, but she tried. She might be old and bony, but this woman did have spunk! She spoke in Sukuma and Aunt Loisi translated. She thanked us for coming, saying she knew she would not live much longer, but she couldn't pass up this chance to see her relative from America.

She asked me about life in the States, about my husband and children, and she wanted to know if I was still dancing as in the video I had sent to my cousin and why I hadn't sent medicine against old age from America? She said that no matter how sick she got, she wouldn't go to the hospital because that place killed people. Many funny things she said weren't translated so I could understand them, but the women around her were laughing heartily!

When it was time for us to go, she called me to her, held my hands in both of hers, and told me, via a translator, that she had a secret. She told me about a dream she had that a relative from far away would come to help her die. Now she would die soon.

I inquired about her age and nobody knew. The three other women from our family started naming people in our lineage going back from my father and all the relatives who had passed, to my grandfather who would be her contemporary, and came up with an age of between 106 and 110. I was sure she was even older!

72

AIDS Orphans

After a few days' rest at the Faraji Farm in Usa River, I left for Entebbe and Kampala in Uganda to see Stefana, a childhood friend who had visited me in Florida the week after Kjell moved out. We were together in Kifungilo and junior high school in Mhonda.

Stefana met me at the Entebbe airport with her son Peter. On the way to Kampala we stopped at the compound of the world-famous artist Sanaa Gitenga, where I bought a contemporary bark cloth and papier-mâché painting. We spent the night in Kampala with Peter's family, then left for Stefana's home and school about ten kilometers from the small town of Masaka.

She and her Ugandan husband lived in rural Uganda raising their four children and a stepchild. They had purchased land in the country and were building a new house when her husband died. After his death she finished the house, kept a couple of small rooms for herself, and made the rest into a large preschool classroom for children orphaned by the AIDS epidemic. Because these children are from the poorest villages farthest away from Masaka, the children are at a disadvantage when they enter the larger, government-run primary schools. Most of the grandmothers who raise the children can't afford the monthly twenty-dollar school fees, so Stefana funds them herself.

Stefana grows her own food and supports herself by selling eggs, chicken, bananas, and honey from her beehives. She also has a few pigs in pigsties just like the German nuns built at Kifungilo.

On the way to Masaka we stood on the equator and had our picture taken with one foot in each hemisphere. We bought boxes of

Marie biscuits (cookies) at Masaka and then rode three bumpy miles on a *boda-boda* (mini-scooter) from the main road to her house and school.

After breakfast the next day we walked to the classroom where the children in their uniforms of white blouses under blue jumpers strained to see who the arriving guests were. As soon as we entered the classroom, they stood up and sang for us. Frightened little faces stared at me. Stefana introduced me as a good friend from a land far, far away called America. They reached out when we began giving away the biscuits.

It was all I could do not to burst into tears as I walked around the benches of children pleading with their eyes for a small box of biscuits. One little girl in particular broke my heart. She reminded me of a certain orphan girl in Kifungilo who didn't understand why she was alone and why her parents had left her. She looked bright but so sad and lost. Her hair was braided every which way, and her large, piercing black eyes penetrated my soul. I had to stop passing out the treats and leave the school because I was choking with emotion.

At first, I waited for Stefana in her small, spotlessly clean, well-decorated living room. But when my tears kept flowing, I hid in her bedroom. I'm sure Stefana knew what was going on with me, because when she came to the bedroom door, she said, "Rest for as long as you wish. I'll call you when the children are leaving. They want to sing for you before they go."

A little while later, Stefana returned, sat down by the bed, and wiped my tears with her bare hands. I let her wipe them, and when I looked up, she too was crying. We wiped each other's tears again and again without saying a word until we were all cried out.

"You're so hot, I think you have a fever," Stefana said.

"No. It's the heat of repressed and painful remembering."

"I remember when you were ill with malaria in Mhonda. *Mungu wangu!* (Oh my God!) Your bed was next to mine. You were shaking and I tried to hold you down, but I couldn't. Your skin was so hot, I was afraid to touch it. Mhonda was the worse place for us."

We hugged and then, putting smiles back on our faces, returned to the classroom. I watched the children file out, carrying the miniature red plastic lunch boxes that Stefana had purchased for them.

"They like to carry the boxes back and forth from school, even though they are often empty. They have nothing at home to put in them."

I clapped my hands and waved as the children walked backward toward the road, smiling and waving. Back inside Stefana's house, she told me how she had been compelled to do something when she saw the little children with no parents. "We wouldn't have had the opportunities we did if it hadn't been for the orphanage at Kifungilo," she said. "It's not much I can do, but even this small effort will make a difference for these children." I stayed with Stefana in Uganda for two more days and then flew back to Arusha.

A couple years later, when I was in Tanzania again, Stefana came to see me. I was staying with the Farajis and they invited her to spend a few days at their farm. My first book had just been published in the States, and Abdu had been one of my readers. After supper, Abdu announced that he couldn't wait to discuss *Africa's Child* and was anxious to get the perspective of another person who had also been at the orphanage.

"Seeing you today, it is impossible to believe that you had such a childhood," he began. "Tell me, Stefana, is it true that your life in Kifungilo was that hard?"

"I haven't read the book yet, but most of the time our life was hard," Stefana replied. She recounted the abuses, beatings, and hardships we had in common and some awful stories about her own experience in Kifungilo that I hadn't known about but was not surprised to hear. One of her revelations, though, surprised me.

"When we were little," she told Abdu and Fatima, "we were all afraid of Mary."

"What? You were afraid of me?" My eyes popped from their sockets and I almost fell off my chair.

"Yes, mainly in the classroom. We were frightened of you because you were so intelligent. No one came even close to you, not even the teachers."

"But why was I bullied and called horrible names?"

"We were all called names, although I never called you Piggy or Piggy Knife. But one nickname you earned. In Mhonda, *Mwalimu* Haule called you *Mwamba* because you were so smart."

I remembered my math teacher with fondness. He was my "rock" because of his encouragement and support during those tough years at Mhonda. He always called me *Mwamba* (rock) instead of "Mary Two," the name given me by the vengeful headmistress. "Rock" is slang in Swahili for "brainy."

73

Salma's Wedding

When I got back to the Faraji Farm on the last night of this trip, there was a different feeling in the air. It was very tense. I asked what had happened, but neither Abdu nor Fatima wanted to tell me. Finally, Fatima handed me a card from their daughter Salma who was living in England, and my heart skipped a beat. Dear God, please don't tell me that something happened to my beloved Salma.

I saw that it was an invitation to the wedding of Salma and her partner Claire, in Belfast, Ireland, that August. You would think there was a death in the family! Fatima refused to talk about it, and Abdu said to me, "You know how we feel about such things. There is no way that we will attend the wedding.

"I respect your feelings. You shouldn't go if you feel so strongly about it."

"This is not only against all our traditional African beliefs, but being Muslim, it's also against our religious beliefs."

"This wedding will not happen. You just wait and see. It's not going to happen!" Fatima vowed. "Nobody should attend the wedding."

"I am sorry to have to say this, especially being a guest in your house. You have always treated me like a member of your family, and as a member of the family, I will attend the wedding."

"You cannot go!" Fatima was getting angry.

"I'm not saying that a same-sex marriage is what I would wish for my children, but if that's what they wanted, I would support them. You know I will not leave Salma alone."

"It's not going to happen. I will call on all the powers I know to remove this curse!" Fatima said, raising her fists to heaven. During the rest of my stay, I tried not to mention the wedding again.

One evening we were sitting on the verandah watching a golden sunset, and I was telling stories about life in America. Once, in 1989 when their daughters Salma and Attiye were visiting me in Edina, Minnesota, we went to Southdale, the first enclosed mall in America. They had spent two weeks traveling, and they wanted to develop their photos, so we went to the mall to look for Black's Photography, a one-hour photo-processing shop.

We entered the mall at Dayton's Department Store, then the anchor store for the center. With my nonexistent sense of direction, I always used the same entrance. But everything was different at Dayton's because it was the grand opening of the newly renovated store. All sorts of festivities were going on—live piano music, hosts and hostesses greeting people with hors d'oeuvres, wine, and champagne. The three of us wandered around until I realized that I was completely turned around and couldn't find my way out of Dayton's.

Just when I was about to give up, a sweet-looking older lady with silver-blue hair approached us and asked, "Can I help you young ladies?"

"Yes, thank you," I replied. "We are looking for Black's—" Before I could finish the sentence, her demeanor changed, and she looked thoroughly confused and bewildered.

"Oh dear! Oh dear! Let see. I don't know if I can help you. I am just volunteering tonight and I don't know my way around either. But I think if you go out to the mall through that door," she said, pointing to a door only a few yards away, "you'll find some."

"Some what?" I asked her. I don't think she heard me because she had turned and appeared to be walking away from us as fast as she could.

"What did she think you were looking for?" Abdu and Fatima asked me.

"She must have thought we were looking for other Black people!"

"I bet she feared she'd have a riot on her hands because the only Black people in the store were looking for other Black people!" Fatima said.

"As it turned out, as soon as we left Dayton's, and entered the mall courtyard, we saw a Black couple who directed us to Black's Photography."

"On that note, let's toast to Minnesota Blacks. May they never scare little old white ladies!"

Abdu poured us a glass of wine and after the toast, Fatima treated us to her out-of-this-world Swahili coastal cooking, including my favorite goat pilau. After dinner their three grandchildren joined us as we danced in the living room to African music from my iPod.

This trip to Tanzania was like no other for two reasons. Traveling without my white husband showed me how far we'd come, and how far we still had to go in dealing with our perceptions of the *wazungu*. Many Africans, even educated ones in cities, still defer to the almighty *mzungu* as though he is smarter and superior to them. Personalities change in the presence of a white man, and in the villages, it is even worse.

On the other hand, it was the best trip for me because I didn't have a white man on my arm to keep my friends and relatives from being themselves. We sat on the floor and ate with our fingers. I slept in the same twin bed with my sister at the hotel when it was too late for her to take the bus home after our evening at Cheers Nightclub. I went to tiny village bars and restaurants that white people wouldn't be caught dead in and would never be invited to in the first place. The best part was that I could speak Swahili anytime. I hadn't realized how much I looked out for Kjell and catered to him because of cultural differences on our trips to Africa in the past. Now I, too, was liberated and could freely indulge in my African-ness without having to make excuses for myself or provide endless explanations.

Four months after I returned from Africa, Salma and Claire were married in a civil ceremony at the Belfast courthouse. My whole family including Kata and her husband Matt, and Karl and his fiancée Mandy, flew in from the States for the wedding. I represented Salma's family by giving the traditional Father of the Bride speech at the reception. Apart from Salma's older sister Attiye and her young daughter, also named Attiye, we were the only relatives on her side in attendance. Claire's parents and family couldn't have been nicer or more accommodating of Salma, my family, and me. I sent photos of the wedding to Abdu and Fatima and told them that I had never seen Salma happier! To my surprise, I received a beautiful letter of gratitude from them for taking care of their daughter when they couldn't.

74

Premonition

 While I was in Africa, Kjell married his woman, thus closing that chapter of my life for good! Kata and Karl did not go to the wedding. Kata wrote in an email: "I am still very heartbroken.... . I can't imagine attending the wedding. What am I supposed to say? Congratulations for destroying our family?"

Kjell has sent me emails with clippings of mutual acquaintances' obituaries and news relating to Africa or Tanzania or dancing, and I accepted the beautiful gift baskets he initially sent to the family at Christmastime. He wanted to take me out for lunch or dinner every time he had business in Florida, but I did not oblige. I wouldn't do to his wife what she did to me. No matter that he is the father of my children, my conscience would not let me have a relationship with a married man, casual as it might be!

Besides, I've moved on. Kjell moved on long before the divorce was finalized, but it became obvious that we were cut from different cloth. It took me several difficult years to let go of my marriage. The seemingly bottomless well of tears I shed in the last few years finally dried up, and I was finished with him.

Fat Mary put things into perspective for me. *I am proud that you've become reacquainted with your true self. The divorce has cleansed you from the trappings of your marriage. As Mrs. Bergh, you couldn't attain true happiness because your identity was wrapped up with that of your husband. He loved what you were, rather than who you are. He loved you for himself.*

A few months after my solo trip to Tanzania, late in 2007, I had the urge to get back to writing my memoir. It had been a long time since I'd even thought about it. In fact, I had given up the idea of writing my story. But with renewed energy and focus, I gathered my notes, travel diaries, and photo albums—all of which I had luckily kept—and got on the computer to find where I'd left off. It was a big job because my Mac computer had changed operating systems several times since I last wrote. I called on Bob, my brilliant computer guru, for help, and he brought my manuscript up to date. I decided not to reread anything but to just continue. I scrolled down to the last page of the manuscript and saw that the date of my last entry was in May of 1999.

There was something memorable about that date, but try as I might, I couldn't figure out what. I continued writing and hoped it would be revealed to me. When I was reviewing the many pages of my attorney's 2004 deposition of Kjell for the divorce chapter, I saw that my husband's out-of-wedlock child was born on the exact day I stopped writing.

Although I didn't know it at the time, that day was the beginning of the end of my married life as I knew it. Kjell had broken his vows to me and was now the father of two families. The Universe took charge and closed my manuscript, saying in effect that on that day my story changed.

I remember the day I stopped writing. I had spent several days struggling to get something, anything, on paper but ended up deleting a lot and then finally gave up. I had so many doubts. Why was I writing a memoir anyway? Who would read it? Who cared about my story when everybody has a story? With each book I read, I grew more depressed and discouraged. Other writers were so good. I couldn't even come close to their command of the English language. Compared to them, I felt that my writing skills were kindergarten level.

So here I was again, eight whole years after experiencing severe writer's block, trying to answer those same questions from long ago. I charged on, putting my insecurities on the back burner, because now my story insisted that I tell it, and it gave me no peace until I did.

I felt I had no choice, so I convinced myself that I was writing because the process of storytelling is good for the mind and can be a catalyst for enlightenment or for a change in our understanding of how we perceive our world and ourselves, and how we live our lives. I am writing my story because it is a basic human desire to connect and communicate with others through common and not-so-common experiences. But, although I tried, I didn't really believe any of the above! Then one day I got it. That day I could articulate why I felt compelled to write my story. Every cell in my body knew why I couldn't stop writing. I was writing about my life for my children and grandchildren. I wanted them to know me the way I hadn't known me. I wanted to stop the cycle of ignorance about family, roots, and culture. It is the only gift I have to give that is worthy of them.

My last summer in Norway with Kjell, when he left me in Batnfjord and returned to Minnesota, came to mind because it was one of the best summers I'd had there. I had been feeling sad, alone, and unimportant in his life for many months, but the beauty of Norway and the kindness and love of his mother, brother Einar, and sisters Berit and Ellen inspired me to try to reach out to Kjell to remind him of our good times with family in Norway.

I wrote him a long email describing the incredible beauty and serenity of our cabin overlooking the shimmering purple-velvet waters of the fjord at sunset. I told him that the only thing missing was him. It was a love letter inspired by better times in this little heaven on earth where I felt loved and accepted by everyone, including his mother. That summer I also spent a lot of time with his sister Ellen. She lived just down the road from our cabin and we enjoyed hiking, dancing, and dining together. She was always the most easygoing of the Bergh children, and my children and I adored her!

I waited several days for a reply to my love letter from Kjell, and when it came, I cursed the day I wrote it. I felt humiliated, stupid and desperate! His reply to my long letter was a one-liner: "I'm glad you have time to write the Great American Novel."

How deflating! I was simply writing my account of the trials, tribulations, and blessings that I encountered along the road I traveled, experiences that shaped who I am and the life that is mine today. Mine is a story of faith, hope, and charity, but mostly, it is a story of hope. Hope is the vehicle that transports us from present despair to the unforeseen solutions and rewards in the future. Hope keeps dreams alive and active.

75

First Grandchild

 I was on the computer in my townhome in Minneapolis in the summer of 2008 when I received an email from Kata with a strange drawing that looked like two skis, one on top of the other. I had no idea what it meant, but it wasn't the first time that I didn't get Kata's jokes or understood her emails, so I let it go and planned to have her explain it later. The next morning, she called from Stavanger, Norway, where she and her husband were visiting her uncle Einar and aunt Mary Lynne.

"Mom, did you get my email?"

"Yes, but I don't understand it."

"Go to the computer and open it up."

I opened the email and it still meant nothing to me. "I just see a couple of things that look like miniature skis."

"Mom, look closer at the little marks in the test tube."

As soon as she said test tube, my heart started beating faster.

"Are you pregnant? Oh my God!" I was so happy, I didn't wait for an answer. I started reeling around in my desk chair, screaming and laughing and crying with joy! I almost reeled the chair with me in it down the steps, three feet away. I caught myself on the railing and slid the chair back to the computer, hitting my butt on the protruding keyboard tray. I talked to Kata and Mary Lynne on the phone for a while, but all I could think of was holding my first grandbaby in my arms. After we hung up I continued my delirious celebration, running around the house, grabbing every photo of Kata, kissing it, and saying thank you, thank you, thank you!

I had seen first-time grandmothers on *America's Funniest Home Videos* lose it when they found out they would be grandmothers.

I thought they carried it a bit too far! Well, if I had a video of my performance, I think I would have won the ten-thousand-dollar first prize. I couldn't do anything for the rest of the day. I thought about Eckhart Tolle's book *The Power of Now* and let myself go. I sat down and indulged in every thought and emotion that flooded my mind and heart. I was happy for Kata and Matt too!

That year Kata came home to Florida for Christmas six months pregnant. It was wonderful to feel her belly and see her transformation to becoming a mother. The next time I saw her, the week before she delivered, she was waddling around her home in Boston. She knew it was going to be a boy and a big one at that.

She had a long and hard labor—thirty-six hours. Her doula came to the house right after she started labor in the evening and made her as comfortable as possible. Early the next morning, Matt and I drove her to the hospital where her labor continued for another fifteen hours, with her refusing any suggestion of a caesarian and me supporting her all the way. I watched the baby monitor to see if he was in distress, but everything was fine. I assisted with every aspect of the birth and was never prouder of Kata. The long and hard labor made her weak, but she pushed and bore the pain like an African!

For as long as I live, I won't forget the feeling when her baby came into the world to greet us. He had a head full of long black hair that wandered from his head, down his neck, and over his shoulders like fine silk threads. He screamed his discontent at having to leave his familiar, comfortable bubble to confront the strange florescent-lit hospital room. He especially didn't like being put on the scale that declared he weighed just over nine pounds. Tears of wonder, joy, and relief ran down my cheeks, over my red sweater, and onto Kata's arms. This was the first birth I'd witnessed. I know it has been said many times before, but everything about it was a miracle! I held my grandson in my arms for the first time when he was twenty-five minutes old.

He looked up at me with wide, open, inquisitive eyes as if to say, "Don't I know you?"

I looked down at him and replied, "Yes, we've met before!"

Kata and Matt named their son Kristian (after her grandfather)

Amani Minier, but he would go by Amani, my brother's name, which means "Peace" in Swahili.

Whenever I look at him or even just think of him, my body is caressed by the same sweetness and warmth I feel when I'm basking in the sun. Holding my grandson in my arms brings the sun indoors and turns him into my sunshine no matter what time of day or what season of the year it is. When he was three months old, he was lying on the couch in the living room of Kata and Matt's house, dressed in an aqua onesie with a bright yellow sun splashing multicolored rays all around. Under the sun were written John Denver's words from his famous song "Sunshine."

Sunshine on my shoulders makes me happy.
Sunshine in my eyes can make me cry.

I picked up Amani from the couch, put him over my shoulder, walked up and down the long hallway in Kata's home, singing the song until he slept.

Back home, I often hummed the song as I walked along the shore by my house in Delray Beach. I literally counted my blessings out loud. When I ran out of fingers and toes to count on, I continued counting them with the shells on the beach. Like the sand, my blessings were so numerous, I lost count. I would then turn to watching the ocean ebb and flow and slap against the shore. The sounds of the ocean seemed to emanate from deep within me. They brought to life the never-forgotten, long-ago rhythms I heard when I was still in the womb. With each step I took, I was aware that I was in the presence of a miracle of beauty, power, and life. During my walks, I was often overcome by an indescribable feeling of lightness of being and oneness with the Universe.

That was the same feeling I had when I held Amani in my arms for the first time.

76

A Buddhist Wedding

In August of 2010, Karl married Amanda Cameron—Mandy—in one of the most simple, beautiful, and meaningful wedding ceremonies I have ever attended. Thank God for the internet, as we were able to make the plans for the wedding—from the program, seating charts, rehearsal dinner, ceremony, and reception—online. Most of the out-of-town guests stayed downtown at the Boulderado Hotel, a beautifully furnished and restored historic hotel with Victorian grandeur.

I arrived in Boulder, Colorado, two days before the wedding and got busy making the final arrangements and putting the finishing touches together for the rehearsal dinner at the Flagstaff House Restaurant. Karl had reserved the upscale restaurant, which offered a spectacular nighttime view of the lights of Boulder spread out a thousand feet below.

The wedding ceremony was held at the Rembrandt Yard Art Gallery and Event Center just across from the Boulderado Hotel. A lone bagpiper called us to the room, and when Mandy and her father walked in, he played "Here Comes the Bride"—hauntingly beautiful on bagpipes.

For many of us, it was the first Buddhist wedding we'd attended. We were surprised by the lack of pomp and circumstance but overwhelmed by the ceremony's depth of meaning and spiritual significance. The officiate was Karl and Mandy's Buddhist teacher and monk Yangsi Rinpoche. Tall and imposing, dressed in the traditional Buddhist maroon and gold robes, he has the widest, gentlest face I've ever seen.

Yangsi Rinpoche, Mandy, Karl, the bridesmaids, and groomsmen stood at the front of the cozy room in the art gallery on either side of a small altar topped with a vase of white lilies. A large silk *thangka* of the Awakened Buddha hung on the wall above the altar.

Yangsi Rinpoche began the wedding ceremony:

Welcome to this beautiful ceremony for a very beautiful couple— beautiful inside and beautiful outside, and welcome to all of you who are here to support them.

I will now say a few words.

The wedding, from a Buddhist point of view, is basically, both of you taking Refuge in each other, but it is the trust you share that is the ultimate Refuge. Together, you will strengthen your compassion and your wisdom to benefit your family and friends. For this beautiful journey in your lives, I offer all my prayers and dedication.

I've known you a long time now. Mandy, you have a warm heart, a vast heart—full of compassion and healing power. Karl, you have a powerful wisdom that really shines to the world to benefit, liberate, and enlighten lots of sentient Beings. By the union of Mandy's compassion and Karl's wisdom, you can go further in your journey to benefit countless sentient beings.

I'd like to say a short prayer and dedication in Tibetan. The meaning of the prayer is that everything happens by cause and condition, and cause and condition have no limitation. Through this unlimited power you will grow further and further into enlightenment.

Yangsi Rinpoche then broke into a deep, guttural Buddhist chant that reverberated throughout the room, filling our minds and heart with his peace and spiritual presence.

Dzogchen Ponlop Rinpoche, Karl's Buddhist teacher from Naropa University, couldn't attend the ceremony, but he sent his assistant, Lee Worley, to deliver his blessings and special wishes for the couple. Here is that blessing:

Marriage is an excellent path to fulfilling the following Six Perfections of Life.

1. Generosity—is sharing with and caring for each other in both the joys and the sorrows of life and giving love and care to our children.

2. Discipline—means honesty, respecting and valuing your promises to each other and to your individuality, along with valuing the heart connections that have brought you together.

3. Patience—is more than forbearance. Here it means that we respect each other. It means not getting carried away by temporary conditions but cultivating an even deeper appreciation of one another.

4. Diligence—means taking delight in the marriage relationship, being joyful and positive in supporting each other's interests.

5. Concentration or Meditation—is learning to relax, learning to relax your busy minds so you can develop mindfulness and awareness in your daily lives. This is the ground for all skillful activity in family life.

6. Wisdom—is the most important one. It is the key to all success in your lives, whether spiritual or worldly. With wisdom you are able to practice the previous Five Perfections perfectly.

She then read a poem from *Rebel Buddha*, a book that Dzogchen Ponlop Rinpoche had just published and from which Karl picked the poem "Midnight" for the occasion.

After the Buddhist blessings and readings, I gave the Swahili Wedding Blessing, and Kjell conducted a short candle lighting ceremony in Norwegian.

Judy, Mandy's mother, read the Apache Wedding Prayer taken from the Hollywood movie *Broken Arrow*.

Mandy and Karl wrote their vows, which were moving and powerful. Neither they nor those of us gathered for the occasion could recite or listen to them without tearing up.

Karl invoked Dr. Martin Luther King Jr. at the start of his vows:

Today is the forty-seventh anniversary of Dr. Martin Luther King Jr.'s "I Have a Dream" speech. I'd like to set the intention of unconditional openness toward all people—Black and white, male and female, gay and straight, as the foundation for my vows....

At the dinner reception afterward, I gave a speech:

Karl was born with a head full of black curls and he was quite fat! His head sat on his shoulders with no neck in sight. I remember getting so excited when one day I realized that the folds of fat between his head and shoulders turned out to be the missing neck.

Like most boys, his teen years were full of challenges for him and for us. We now look back and wonder how we survived them.

At a time when he needed it most, Buddhism found him and claimed him lock, stock, and barrel! He embraced Buddhism with a passion, single-mindedness, and clarity that amazed us. He fell in love with his Buddhist teacher, Geshe Kungchog Kyab, who took him under his wings and guided him through some turbulent times.

With Geshe-La's help, he went to the Sera Jey Buddhist Monastery in Southern India for two months. Before returning to the States, he traveled to Dharamsala in Northern India where he attended His Holiness the Dalai Lama's annual teachings. When he returned to the States from India, he wore only the burgundy and gold robes that Buddhist monks wear. He had convinced the monk in India who took him to visit Buddhist holy sites that he needed the robes—even though we all knew he was not a monk! That summer he and I boarded a plane to Norway with his head shaved, wearing his bright robes and black sandals, and a backpack that contained only his Buddhist books and a toothbrush.

He got his bachelor's degree in Religious Studies right here in Boulder at Naropa University and then went to Portland, Oregon, where he helped found Maitripa College and where he met his beloved Mandy.

Putting the cart in front of the horse, they had their honeymoon before their wedding. For their honeymoon, they attended a two-week retreat this past July held in Seattle by their much-loved teacher Dzogchen Ponlop Rinpoche. I can't think of a better way to prepare for their future life than spending two weeks together with their spiritual guide and teacher.

When Karl was a little boy, we asked him what he wanted to be when he grew up, and his answer was "I want to be an Indian."

That answer, along with wearing monk robes and having his honeymoon before the wedding, tells us that Karl always has, and always will, march to the beat of a different drummer!

Karl is my son, and I admire him deeply. Anyone who knows him, or spends time with him, knows that he has a heart of gold. He stands up for his convictions no matter the consequences. He is who he is and is comfortable in his skin. Since elementary school he has always stood up for those who were less fortunate than him.

Choosing Buddhism has empowered him to live and share the depth, length, breadth, and wealth of his golden heart with everyone he meets.

He could be described as a "gentle bulldozer." Just like no one wants to get in the way of a moving bulldozer, no one wants to get in Karl's way once he has made up his mind to do something. Those of us who have been present, open-minded, and attentive to him have learned that what Karl leaves behind as he plows along his journey in life is a field of calm, love, compassion, beauty, and contentment.

It is said that marriage is made in heaven—but so are thunder and lightning!

Marriage might be made in heaven, but the maintenance is done on earth.

I have known Mandy for several years, and I have witnessed her commitment and determination to maintain and improve the relationship she values, regardless of the many challenges. Welcome into our family. You are precious to us, and Karl is the luckiest man in the world to call you his wife.

It has also been said that "Love is blind, but marriage restores your sight."

They know that what they see in each other is rare and worth pursuing and keeping. Hopefully over time you will prove that what you feel today is true love, and true love is endless and priceless!

I'd like to make a toast. To Mandy and Karl, may you always keep your eyes on the prize!

As spiritual and reflective as the ceremony in the museum was, the dinner and dance were filled with the joy and laughter of celebration. We danced up a storm way into the night, with Karl dancing like his life depended on it. His African heritage came out loud and strong as he covered the floor with moves and expressions I had no idea he had.

Just like Kata's wedding a few years earlier, it was indeed an inclusive, multicultural, multiracial, and interfaith wedding celebration that would have made Dr. Martin Luther King Jr. proud.

77

FONs Safari

Many, many times over the years I have lived in the United States, American friends have asked me to take them to Africa. My first trip back to Tanzania was with Kjell in 1974, about ten years after I left. We subsequently took several trips with our children and went back on average once a year as tour guides for our travel business.

Now I was planning a private safari that was special to me. My closest friends, who knew bits and pieces of my story, wanted me to lead a tour and especially to take them to the orphanage. It was now or never, so I announced that I would take them to Africa this once. I warned them that, although I was the common denominator and close to each one of them, they didn't know each other well, and I hoped we would all get along and still be friends when we returned.

On January 23, 2011, a group of FONs (Friends of Nhambu) from all over the United States met in Amsterdam for our long flight to Kilimanjaro airport in Tanzania, where we arrived late at night. Our first ritual upon arrival at Kia Lodge was to relax with a Safari beer. Each sip settled me more and more into my African side, and by the time I finished the fat brown bottle of beer I knew I was home.

The FONs included Coco and Connie, the twin daughters of renowned Black historian, author, and former *Ebony* editor Lerone Bennett Jr.; Jackie, my maid of honor and godmother to Kata and Karl; Carletta, my soul-sister friend; Rachel and Anna, both *Aerobics With Soul®* instructors, and longtime friends Bev and Oscar, and Stacey and David.

Mount Kilimanjaro took its time peeking at us from underneath the clouds in the morning but then came out in all its glory to say karibuni—welcome to Tanzania. We began our eighteen-day safari in Arusha, the hub of the tourist Northern Circuit of game reserves.

Serengeti Select Safaris, based in Arusha, booked the land portion of our trip and provided us with a Land Rover for eight passengers and a smaller one that carried four. It was heartwarming to have Sammy and Gordian whom I'd often had on previous safaris, as our drivers for the entire safari. The fact that I spoke Swahili always brought a huge smile to their faces and relieved them of some of the burden of being tour guides as well as drivers.

As we were loading the smaller vehicle, the glass in the rear door shattered. The drivers flattened a cardboard box and taped it to the door. The four friends assigned to ride in it looked at me and said, "Really?"

Using my best tour leader's voice, I explained, "Unless you don't mind missing today's safari, *hakuna matata* (no problem). Since your car has a piece of cardboard instead of a rearview mirror, our car will lead and yours will follow. This is only the beginning of what could and usually does go wrong when you're in the bush. It's part of the experience and seldom affects the quality of the safari. You might remember from *The Lion King* that *hakuna matata* is Swahili for 'no problem' and the attitude Tanzanians have when faced with any difficulty."

By the time we returned from our first drive later in the day, the tour company had a replacement Land Rover that allowed us to put five in one vehicle and the rest in the other.

I had arranged for us to visit Eunice Simonson at her beautiful African-style house up the hill at Ilboro. Her husband, Reverend David Simonson, had passed away the year before, and I hadn't seen her since. I was very saddened by David's passing. I admired him and his work tremendously while he was alive, but for me, he loomed even larger in his passing. His fifty-year missionary service to the Maasai and to Tanzania is unparalleled and legendary. He was always kind and helpful to me, especially when I was searching for my father. I felt close to David. When I heard the news of his death, I had to stop everything to be with him in prayer and remembrance. I then sat down and wrote to his widow and five children.

Dear Eunice, Steve, Naomi, Nate, Becky, and Jon,

My heart is heavy as I write this. I feel the pain of loss that you are feeling.

I cannot put into words what Dave meant to me personally because I was raised by missionaries. He was one of the few missionaries who really helped me see God. I found God not in his preaching, but in his heart. I connected with him on that level and he is living within me now, as he always has.

Just like me, I believe that most of the Tanzanian people he loved connected with him deep in their hearts, where love, gratitude, and admiration cannot be put into words. They can only be felt, because they are Sacred.

Along with my fellow Tanzanians I mourn his passing, but we know that the land he walked on and toiled in for so many years cannot and will not ever forget his precious gift of love for us.

I am so blessed to have known him and loved him in this way.

My deepest sympathy to each and every one of you, to your immediate families, and to your extended families. I am holding you all in the Light!

Poleni Sana! (So sorry)

Nhambu

As has always been her way, David's wife Eunice welcomed us with open arms, and we sat with her around the long wooden table facing Mount Meru, enjoying a cup of *chai* and biscuits. She had crafts from a women's cooperative brought to her house to promote their work to the many tourists and friends from abroad who came to see her. My friends bought several items, which delighted the African women. Before saying goodbye to her, I stopped at David's grave, which was near the road just below the hill and within sight of their house, following the African custom of burying loved ones on their property close to the house rather than in a cemetery.

From Eunice's house we drove to Arusha to get our supply of Tanzanian shillings for the rest of our safari. It was a challenge driving on the town roads because hundreds of *dala dalas* (public transport minibuses)—filled with five times more passengers than they are licensed to carry, with half their riders clinging to the outside of the bus—wove in and out of the dense traffic. Some of my friends were terrified at the spectacle and were grateful for our drivers' competence and mellowness and for their *hakuna matata* outlook on life. The scene outside our Land Rovers was chaotic, colorful, and unfamiliar to some of my friends who snapped pictures of the crazy *dala dalas* with names, usually in English, like "God Bless," "Happy People," or "Take a Chance."

The road by the market was a churning sea of everything imaginable: farm produce offered for sale in tiny mini-markets that sprung up along the edges of the road; fowl, still alive, crammed one on top of another in enormous straw crates; women walking in and around cars with large baskets of ripe bananas, roasted peanuts, or cassava on their heads, holding on to little children and carrying babies on their backs; bicycles transporting everything from huge sacks of charcoal, to plastic containers filled with water, to mounds of freshly cut green hay for cow feed; small three-wheeled scooters with six people and their luggage on board, weaving in and out of the cars, lorries, and buses.

On the verandas of the tiny huts and houses on either side of the road, tailors furiously pedaled their old-fashioned Singer Sewing machines under the ready-made, bright-colored African clothing displayed on clotheslines above their heads. Six feet in from the road, carpenters and upholsterers advertised and sold their wooden tables, beds, and chairs, multicolored sofas and armchairs. Cars and lorries featured pictures of President Obama as did many small shops. On the way out of town to Arusha National Park, we had to follow a truck at five miles an hour that was loaded ten feet high with stalks of green bananas.

At the park entrance the drivers and I went to sign in. When I looked back, I saw my friends finally exhaling, relieved to have left the chaos and confusion, dust and heat of the city behind. In the game park, there was only a narrow dirt road. No more people, traffic, or noise, only nature and the anticipation of seeing what they came to Africa for—animals in the wild.

I put on my standard game park headgear—a large black-and-fuchsia, zebra-striped cotton scarf that I always wrap over my head and tie under my chin to keep the dust off my hair—and my big sunglasses.

"Nhambu, you look just like Jackie-O with your scarf and glasses," Anna said.

"Correction," Coco volunteered. "You kind of look like Jackie-O, but to us you are Blackie-O!" And that became my nickname for the trip.

Arusha National Park is known for the beautiful, regal black-and-white colobus monkeys that live high up in the tall trees of the forest and are not easy to spot. We saw five of them, along with the more commonly seen elephants, zebras, and giraffes. I guaranteed my friends that they would be seeing even more amazing animals as our trip progressed, so they needn't take five pictures of every animal they saw.

After a few hours in the park, we went back to the main road, which was a very good one, smooth and well-maintained, nothing like the potholed, overcrowded roads of downtown Arusha. We saw few cars along this road during the two-hour trip to Tarangire Safari Lodge, my favorite place to be in Tanzania.

78

Majestic Tarangire

It was pouring rain when we arrived at Tarangire, so the lodge staff met us with umbrellas and escorted us to the reception and dining room just in time for dinner. Whenever you arrive there, be it day or night, you will be drawn to the enormous stone platform in front of the lodge that overlooks the vast, seemingly endless terrain below where the Tarangire River flows. Elephants, giraffe, zebra, impala, gazelles, dik-diks, baboons, and warthogs parade below on their way to drink from the river. Above, the sky is a deep copper canopy with thousands of brilliant stars welcoming me home to this particular spot in Tanzania, a place on earth where I can see and understand the word "millennia" and the concept of "eternity."

Tarangire has the only kind of tents that I'm not afraid to stay in. They come with solar-heated running water and self-contained flushing toilets! Trucks bring in fresh water from Arusha two hours away, because most of the water in the park has high concentrations of soda and is not fit for drinking. Inside the tents are either wood or metal twin, queen, or king-size beds. Sheets and towels are crisp, because they are sun-dried, and the soap and other bath products are locally made. Most of the tents sit under baobab trees, which, along with the elephants, are dubbed "giants" of Tarangire.

I was happy to see that my friends were as awe-struck by the place as I was. We spent several nights there to acclimate to the environment and time change. Some of the best game viewing of our safari happened at Tarangire.

Elephants in the hundreds roam the park, gracefully trudging along, sometimes hidden by the twenty-foot-high anthills scattered among the acacia, cacti, and sausage trees. They know they own the park and can wander wherever they please, often coming right up to the tents and walking with their little ones along the path, scant feet away from where we sleep, eating from the trees in between the tents. They are kind enough to let us visit and observe them, but on this trip we must have tried their patience with the endless photos we took.

Elephants like the soft pulp inside the baobab trees, so with their tusks they strip the trees of its bark and then bore holes in the trunk to get to the nutritious and delicate sap in the center of the tree, eventually destroying it. Throughout the park, we saw that many of these ancient trees, which can live up to two thousand years or more, had huge holes, even large chambers inside that stretched from one side of the thirty- to sixty-foot-wide trunks to the other side. Baobabs' huge, bottle-shaped trunks sport a small halo of leaves in small proportion to their size. One legend says this odd configuration came into being when the devil yanked the tree out of the ground and shoved it back into the earth upside down, leaving the roots in the air.

Our last evening at Tarangire we took a sunset game drive to the swamp area of Tarangire Park. As we approached the swamps we interrupted a peaceful and joyful animal convention. We saw ostrich, zebra, baboon, giraffe, warthogs, gazelles, and impalas as well as marabou storks and European long-legged, black-and-white storks. A short distance away, three young cheetah brothers peeked out of the grass, standing tall and graceful for us to snap pictures before sauntering away single file. We spent over an hour observing the animals rejoice in the setting sun, each group doing its own thing, yet acknowledging our presence and inviting us to join them in a moment that could be the definition of peace and harmony.

It was quiet in the Land Rover on the way out of the park. We were overwhelmed by what we'd just witnessed—a deep union with nature and a gift from the Universe.

The next morning before we left I took my friends on a short pilgrimage that is part of every visit I make to Tarangire National Park. We walked to the end of the row of tents toward the edge of a steep slope overlooking a bend in the river below. There, in 1994, on a ten-foot-square plywood platform under the lone acacia tree, I filmed my *Aerobics With Soul–Kilimanjaro* video. At the time, the platform stood in the direct path of baboons going to the river to drink. Unfortunately, they stopped and played on the platform, did their business, and then worked hard at ripping up the green canvas that covered the platform. I was grateful that every morning the staff at the lodge cleaned and fixed the platform for us to continue filming.

79

Wildebeests and Tsetse Flies

 We spent one of our two nights in the area at Ndutu Safari Lodge, situated in the southeastern part of the Serengeti ecosystem. Shaded by majestic acacia trees, each of the thirty-four cottages, which are built of local materials, has a private verandah facing Lake Ndutu. The lodge is surrounded by indigenous trees and shrubs, encouraging hosts of birds and mammals to come right to the front door. Giant, flat-topped acacia trees, with Lake Ndutu glittering beyond, beckon you to come closer and view the spectacle of the wildebeest migration in the calving season.

The second night we spent at Lake Masek Tented Camp, about ten minutes away from Ndutu Lodge, overlooking the small lake. Tanganyika Wildlife Camps Company built this state-of-the-art camp that I knew would amaze my friends. I made it a point not to tell them anything about the lodging in advance. The camp is eco-friendly; electric power is supplied by solar panels and water is collected during the rainy season. All products used are biodegradable in order to ensure that the environment is kept pristine.

Each of the twenty luxury tents is built on a raised wooden platform with a verandah from which guests can observe the wildlife visiting Lake Masek. Bedroom areas have large mahogany canopy beds with mosquito nets. The bathroom—with twin washbasins, a stand-alone bathtub, and an outside shower—is separated by a screen. Guests can enjoy a relaxing bath or take an outdoor shower under the stars.

The main house has a lounge, dining area, and a large verandah built around a giant tree overlooking the lake. The lounge is decorated with groupings of comfortable sofas and armchairs.

When we arrived, we headed straight to our tents. From the outside, there was nothing luxurious about this place. We walked in silence along narrow gravel paths that led to the round, rugged-looking tents set in the tall grass and spaced far from each other. One of my friends said that she felt like an explorer taking her chances in deepest Africa. This place and this view was what she had expected the entire trip to be like.

As the groups entered their tents, I heard screams of surprise, laughter, clapping and a chorus of "Thank you! Halleluiah! *Nakupenda*, Nhambu!" (I love you). Coco and Connie were like two wide-eyed kindergarteners skipping around their tent, touching and trying out everything.

"Look!" Connie exclaimed. She was thrilled with all that the tent included: a hair dryer, a phone, a bathtub, two free-standing mahogany wardrobes, canopied mahogany beds with crisp white linen and mosquito nets, floor rugs, an outside shower, dressers, ornate stereo sinks with carved wooden mirrors, even internet access! "I can't take it no more, Sista! This is way, way more than I could ever have imagined to find in the African bush!"

"Nhambu, you're the best! But why didn't you tell us about this place?" Coco asked.

"You must have noticed by now that I haven't told you about any of the places we're going to stay. I tried to pick a good mix of basic, average, and posh hotels and lodges so you could experience the variety of what is available to tourists. My only criterion was that I had to have stayed there myself, and everything had to be clean and well maintained. I don't ever have to worry about service on safari, because Africans will bend over backwards to try to accommodate your every need and your every whim."

Settling into a comfy sofa on the verandah overlooking the lake as I waited for the others to join me before dinner, I contrasted this trip with the one I took with Larry twenty-two years before when we searched for my father. I can't remember a more basic, no-frills, physically difficult trip than that one. Traveling the way locals do was a reminder that the colonizers would never have survived in Africa unless they created a semblance of their lives in Europe.

That fact opened the eyes of the now Tanzanian-run government, and consequently it embraced tourism as a necessity for

Tanzania to survive economically and compete in international markets. No modern-day tourist would travel like the locals unless it was by choice! Tourists had to feel welcome and comfortable. The government, having been almost bankrupted due to the failure and problems of *Ujamaa*, depended on foreign money and investments to develop and maintain its tourist attractions. Tourism became the single major contributor to the economy and brought international recognition because of the country's unsurpassed animal treasures. Most of the hotels, lodges, and luxury tent camps we stayed in during this trip had first-class accommodation, internet, African and European cuisine, amenities that often surpassed those in Western hotels, bars stocked with the finest wines and spirits, and superb service.

In the morning we made our own *lanchi boxis* from a buffet of fresh bread, veggies, cold meats, and fruit, because we were going to spend the entire day on the Serengeti Plains. We drove to Naabi Hill, the gateway to Serengeti, and after paying the park fees, spent three days witnessing the Great Migration.

The annual Great Migration of millions of zebra, wildebeest (gnu), and other antelope in East Africa tops almost every list of safari experiences. Each year around 1.5 million wildebeest and 300,000 zebra, along with antelope, together with their young, start their long trek from Tanzania's Serengeti Plains farther north to Kenya's Maasai Mara National Reserve. They go in search of food and water. Their journey runs in a clockwise circle and the animals cover a distance of around 1,800 miles. It's a tough journey. December through March on the Serengeti Plains and the Ngorongoro Conservation area is calving season, and calves attract predators. This is an amazing time of year to watch impressive lion kills. It's also quite spectacular to see almost half a million wildebeest offspring being born and running alongside their mothers just minutes after birth. Wildebeest are also called gnu because of the grunts they make, which sound like "gnu-gnu."

The young are almost all born during a three-week period. This overwhelming supply of potential food for predators means more of the young will survive, though it is estimated that around 250,000 wildebeest die on the migration circuit. Zebra and wildebeest graze in harmony because each prefers a different part of the grass.

It doesn't matter how often I have seen the migration, I am always filled with awe at nature's spectacle. With our Land Rovers parked anywhere in the vast plains, we were able to observe thousands of wildebeest, zebra, gazelles, with buffalo waterbucks and topis sprinkled here and there, obey the magnetic pull to migrate and live the same lives that their creator ordained long ago. Along with the majestic migration and the predators that follow them, Serengeti National Park offers the Big Five: elephant, rhino, lion, leopard, and buffalo.

Although we didn't want to interrupt our animal watching, we had to make occasional pit stops to relieve ourselves. Some friends became unglued when they realized that we had to imitate the animals and take care of business wherever we found ourselves, even in their midst, unless we were ready to hold it the entire day. By the end of the day, however, no one had trouble asking the drivers for a stop "to check the rear tire" and relieve themselves behind the car.

We stayed too long in the park, and it was getting late. Sammy the driver and I made a decision to take the *shoti-kati* (shortcut) to the lodge where we would spend the night. It was a mistake! We took the same tsetse fly-infested, thorn-covered dustbowl of a road that Larry and I had taken years earlier.

Needless to say, tsetse flies stung us, and we were tossed around like beanbags as we hit gigantic potholes. Despite the windows being rolled up to keep the thorns and flies out, we swallowed powder-fine dust that seeped in and stuck to the perspiration rolling off us. We swatted the relentless tsetse flies with hats, scarves, and T-shirts, often missing the fierce little pests but smacking each other as we shook, rattled, and rolled in the car.

After about twenty minutes of this insect-human battle, the humans lost! It was so ridiculous, it was funny. For the rest of the ride through tsetse-fly land, we laughed ourselves silly, making fun of how we looked and complaining about body parts we hoped to find intact once the vehicle came to a stop. In the meantime, Sammy, calm, cool, and collected, drove at a good clip over potholes and through thorn bushes and clouds of bloodthirsty victorious and vengeful flies without saying a word! This torturous side trip turned out to be one of the much-recounted highlights of our ill-advised *shoti-kati.*

Arriving at the Serengeti Serena Lodge late that evening became the second-most welcomed gift of the day, only because we agreed that nothing could top the Great Migration.

Set high on the saddle of a tree-covered ridge, commanding panoramic views across the Serengeti, this lodge is the ultimate fusion of traditional African architecture and world-class style. It was designed to blend completely into the living landscape. A series of traditional domed rondavels widely spaced throughout the grounds are cooled by groves of acacia trees and sparkling streams. On the very edge of the ridge, an infinity pool looks out over the Serengeti Plains, inviting guests to enjoy a swim at dusk or sip a glass of mango juice or evening cocktail.

Upon our arrival lodge staff handed us freshly squeezed orange and passion fruit juice before taking us to our well-appointed rooms. One of the amenities treasured by Americans and unique to this lodge is the "washcloth." No other place we stayed had them, and by the excitement coming from the rooms, you'd think my friends had found a bottle of champagne chilling in an ice bucket waiting for them! The interior of the lodge was designed to showcase African heritage and traditional art, best illustrated by the lavish Makonde carvings that decorated the rooms and the stunning, domed dining room. Before and after dinner, we were treated to cultural performances of African dance and acrobatics. Most of my group joined in the dancing since they were well-seasoned *Aerobics With Soul®* dancers who couldn't sit still when African drums were calling.

80

Ngorongoro Crater

We spent another full day in the Serengeti, then drove to the Ngorongoro Serena Safari Lodge. The lodge clings to the rim of the magnificent Ngorongoro Crater, the largest and most perfect volcanic crater on earth. Long and low, the lodge is built from local river stone and camouflaged with indigenous vines. Designed to blend completely into the landscape, it is invisible from the floor of the crater six hundred meters below. When it was first built, it was voted one of the best examples of an eco-hotel in the world.

Hugging the contours of the jagged crater rim, the lodge takes its inspiration from the so-called Cradle of Mankind, the prehistoric site of Olduvai Gorge close by. Linked by arched stone passages and timbered decks, the walls of the lodge are decorated with stylized prehistoric cave paintings and lit by torches. At the center of the lodge a fire is constantly kept glowing. The rooms, decorated with cave paintings, are perched on the crater rim, each with its own rock wall-enclosed balcony and wide view of the crater far below.

Known as "the eighth wonder of the world," the Ngorongoro Crater is Africa's most famous wildlife refuge. A UNESCO World Heritage Site, it offers a unique biosphere, which has remained virtually unchanged since its eruption 2.5 million years ago. Deep within the crater some 25,000 large mammals—including bull elephants, rhinos, and lions—wander the plains, lakes, and forests of "the land that time forgot."

Our two Land Rovers joined the caravan of cars descending into the crater along the narrow, precipitous dirt road. We collectively held our breath while marveling at the Maasai who had built their *manyattas* (round huts) hugging the slopes leading into the crater. We stopped at a couple of vantage points on the way down as each of my friends had a personal moment with the wonder displayed at their feet. The view below us was emotionally overwhelming!

Once inside the crater, we were amazed at the sheer number and species of animals not visible from above. Hundreds of flamingos standing in pools, kori bustards performing mating dances, crested crane couples, and lone secretary birds dazzled us while the larger mammals roamed with an assurance of their unique place and importance within the crater.

We stopped for lunch at a lush hippo pool but had to eat in our vehicles because kites and other birds, along with vervet monkeys, aggressively came after our food.

Visiting a Maasai village on the way out of the crater was another highlight of the day. As we approached the village, three Maasai elders negotiated the fee for our visit with me, and then a group of singing men, women, and children danced toward us. They were draped in their traditional red, blue, white, and black checkered cloths or blankets. The women wore intricately beaded multicolored collars, necklaces, and bracelets, while the men had magnificent ostrich-feathered headpieces and carried animal hide shields, wooden arrows, and the ever-present spears.

Known for their pride and fierceness, the Maasai are often employed as security guards in banks, hotels, private businesses, and homes in the surrounding large cities. They are nomadic pastoralists who migrated from present-day Sudan in the early seventeenth century. The majority still practice nomadic pastoralism and have no desire to farm or own land. They consider their cattle sacred, to be used only for bartering and dowries, and for their blood but not for meat.

The Maasai, who have often been exploited in the past, have developed several villages near the lodges so they can also benefit from tourism revenue. I wanted my friends to know that the Maasai *boma* we were visiting was an example of where and how most Maasai currently live. The people we were about to see did not arrive in *dala dalas* from Arusha, put on their dancing gear in order to perform for tourists, and then go back to their city lives. They actually live in the small round mud huts in their manyattas, cook over a fire inside the hut, drink curdled milk and blood from their cattle, and wear the clothing and ornamentation they have worn for centuries. Despite their ventures into tourism and the cell phones hanging from their necks and on belts next to their *rungus* (clubs) and knives, they adhere to their traditional beliefs and customs.

We entered the huts two at a time and had to practically fold ourselves in half to slide into the narrow, curved entrance. An elder Maasai told us a little about their history and explained the items inside.

The last place we visited in the village was the school. It was a one-room straw, mud, and thatched-roof building with about forty small children squeezed into several rows of narrow benches, their bare feet on the dirt floor. In front of the room hanging from the rafters, was a sheet of plywood, painted black, that served as the blackboard. On the board were written the numbers, one to one hundred, and the alphabet. After they sang for us a little boy went to the blackboard and, pointing to the letters of the alphabet with a long stick, read them out loud in English. On the way out of the village we shopped at the little kiosks of arts and crafts that each family had proudly laid out for us.

That evening we didn't hesitate to jump in and dance with the traditional dancers performing at the lodge, because we knew it would be the last chance for dancing on our trip.

In the morning we left the lodge grounds and drove along the crater rim, but when we looked down into it, we saw nothing! The entire crater was hidden under a blanket of white clouds. It was hard to believe that just yesterday we were in its depths, communing with a multitude of animals and birds, some of which never leave the crater.

81

Olduvai Gorge

 We were on our way to Gibbs Farm with a stop at Olduvai (Oldupai) Gorge. This barren landscape is historically considered the Cradle of Humankind. Louis and Mary Leakey excavated the Olduvai Gorge in the Great Rift Valley in the mid-1950s. The site, or rather group of sites, is thirty miles long and 350 feet deep and harbors remnants of almost two million years of human occupation.

Examples of at least three species of hominids have been found at Olduvai, including *Australopithecus boisei, Homo habilis*, and *Homo erectus*. In addition, the two earliest stone tool traditions have been found, along with fossil remains. Both the fossils and the tools have been important contributions to understanding human evolution.

We visited the small but informative Museum and Visitors Center that offers educational exhibits, including fossils and artifacts of our human ancestors and skeletons of many extinct animals that shared their world. A Tanzanian park guide spoke about the gorge as we sat on benches overlooking it. We didn't have time to walk into the gorge and take the guided archaeological tour of the sites, but we did stop at the handcrafts and bookshop attached to the museum.

Whenever I visit Olduvai Gorge I ponder our human origins and wonder what the world was like when we were all Africans.

Gibbs Farm, a few miles from the gorge, was nothing like any other place we'd visited. It was as green and lush, with flowers, trees, lily-filled ponds, and acres of velvet coffee fields, as the Serengeti was hot, dry, dusty, and barren. We came to this small, privately owned farm to refresh and rejuvenate after our rigorous safari on the Northern Circuit. There were no animals to see—just beautiful, individual private cottages, spacious rooms, king-sized beds, loveseats in front of a fireplace in each room, homemade organic amenities, and the freshest, softest towels anywhere in Africa. Some of us soaked in the tub before heading for a much-needed massage, while others just reclined with a cup of tea in the comfortable loungers overlooking the huge coffee plantations surrounding the farm.

At sunset we gathered around a campfire and listened to a lecture on traditional medicine given by a Maasai healer. His assistant had a cell phone in a beaded case that she wore around her neck. I convinced her to sell the case to me, although she was skeptical about whether I'd give her the whole two dollars she asked for. When I gave her five dollars, she was elated and said she would make beaded cell phone cases to sell at the Gibbs Farm store.

Our last place to visit on this stretch was the MaaSae Girls Lutheran Secondary School. The boarding school's name reflects its purpose: *Maa* for the language of the Maasai tribe and S-A-E for Speakers Advanced Education.

The school is located in Monduli, a village forty-five minutes outside of Arusha. Since the school was founded in 1995, more than 500 girls have graduated and over 150 have gone on to institutions of higher learning. Today graduates include teachers, nurses, social workers, doctors, and other professionals. Students come to the boarding school from villages that are often located in distant, isolated areas. They depend on sponsorship from abroad, mostly from America, to pay for their education. A class of around forty-five students enters the school each year. At the end of Form IV (equivalent to grade ten), students sit for the National Secondary School Exams. Some students who pass these exams then continue their education.

Traditionally, Maasai girls barely received basic elementary education. They usually married by the age of fifteen and were expected to build a home, care for children, milk cows, and fetch firewood and water. Girls had only the remotest chance to better themselves through schooling. Following many years of persuasion and negotiations with Maasai elders, some Maasai girls have finally been allowed to attend secondary school. The target population of the MaaSae school is the Maasai pastoralists who have no means or desire to have their daughters educated, often not recognizing the value of educating their daughters or the resulting benefits for the community.

The school was the vision of a former prime minister and a bishop, both Maasai, along with my friends Reverend David and Eunice Simonson, who founded Operation Bootstrap Africa, which builds primary schools in rural Tanzania.

The design of the school follows that of a traditional Maasai settlement or *engang*. The chapel, with its imposing roof in the shape of a shield, sits in the center, surrounded by two circles of buildings. In the inner circle are the dormitories, classrooms, kitchen, and dining room. In the outer circle are laboratories, a library, and an administration building, a computer lab, and teachers' houses.

Just as I did when I was in secondary school at Marian College, the girls wear uniforms of different colors depending on their grade level.

Plastic buckets of various colors were being filled with water because this time of the year water was scarce, and there was no running water in the dormitories, kitchen, or toilets. Each girl got one bucket of water a day for all her needs. The kitchen had wood-burning stoves, each with one barrel-sized pot on top.

My friends were amazed by the minimal supplies and living conditions at the school. I informed them that this school was better equipped than most government schools in Tanzania. Compared to some schools I attended fifty years ago, the MaaSae Girls Lutheran Secondary School qualified as a posh private school!

After a good night's rest at Kigongoni Lodge, which is located on an historic seventy-acre coffee farm near Arusha, we piled into our Land Rovers and left for Lushoto early in the morning. The seven-hour trip seemed extra-long because from Arusha to Mombo there was little to see except sisal plantations once owned by Greek ex-patriots.

82

Friends Visit Kifungilo

Our destination for that night was Mueller's Mountain Lodge. The only reason I brought my friends here, some 8,000 feet high in the Usambara Mountains, was because I wanted them to meet Zami, the lodge's owner. She was the cruel "big girl" who took care of me when I was at the Kifungilo orphanage twelve miles away.

Few tourists ever make it this far from the Northern Tourist Circuit. The Usambara Mountains, with their wide vistas, cool climate, winding paths, and picturesque villages, are one of northeastern Tanzania's highlights. It's possible to spend a week hiking from village to village or relaxing in one spot and exploring the area in day walks. In the olden days the forests were full of monkeys, especially the hard-to-find colobus monkey, leopards, and hundreds of species of tropical birds. Although the birds are still plentiful today, the few remaining monkeys and leopards are rarely seen.

Mueller's Mountain Lodge was built as a farmhouse in the 1930s and echoes back to when Tanzania was a German protectorate. Four half-caste children with the Mueller last name went to school with me at the orphanage and usually went home on weekends. The nuns often brought us here to the family's farm for picnics on special occasions.

Our accommodations and meals at this lodge were not on par with the other places we had stayed on the trip, so my friends focused instead on its natural beauty, isolation, and serenity.

Zami, who knew I was coming from America with a large group, made no effort to come to greet me and welcome us. We didn't see her at dinnertime either, so I took Jackie with me to visit her at her house a few yards from the main lodge. She greeted me with enthusiasm and what looked like joy at seeing me again after many years. I had gone with my husband to meet her the first time I returned to Tanzania in 1974, and now it was 2011.

As we visited I had flashbacks of her beating me because I didn't take my special Sunday bread over to her fast enough, of having to wash her monthly period cloths and then getting beaten when I didn't get all the stains out, and of her calling me "Piggy Knife." I wondered if she remembered any of that. I wondered if she could even understand the debilitating fear I felt every time I heard her yell, "Piggy Knife, come here, you dirty pig!" As a child I feared it was only a matter of time before she would take the "knife" from "piggy" and slaughter me just because she could.

You must forgive her. She doesn't remember the suffering she caused you. You're no longer a child. It's not up to you to judge or punish her. Life does that. Show her the empathy and understanding she didn't show you. She didn't know better then and still doesn't!

Fat Mary is so right!

We left Mueller's Lodge early in the morning and stopped at the dentistry in Lushoto where my beloved friends from the orphanage, Betty and Sister Eileen, were waiting to go to Kifungilo with us.

In my heart I knew this trip to Kifungilo would be my last. With every mile we drove up the rugged road, I was keenly aware of myself as a child. Wasambaa families were doing their laundry in the river below. Nearby, cows and goats drank from the river and stood among the laundry spread out on the grass to dry in the sun. The children watched the clothes so they wouldn't be stolen and to keep the cows from trampling them. I saw myself doing the same thing at the orphanage except we used large *karai*, or metal tubs, and scrubbed clothes on long, high, narrow wood tables in the laundry room while standing on a wet, cold, uneven stone floor. Then we spread them on the grass and bushes in the sun and watched them dry.

Our Land Rovers strained as they climbed up the treacherous, winding dirt road cut between mountain ranges, dense with tall trees. People carrying baskets of produce or loads of wood on their heads walked close to the edge of the road on either side of the car. My friends were quiet during the climb. They understood that this is where I was raised, and this was the place I had wanted so badly to leave. They were no longer tourists traveling in luxury and enjoying the best the country had to offer. Now they were accompanying their friend to her home located, seemingly, at the end of the world.

We came to a clearing in the road and a panoramic view of Kifungilo tucked into the slopes of a mountain pulled away the veil of commiseration from my friends and revealed an unexpected scene of brick and red-tile-roofed houses reminiscent of Germany or Switzerland. Kifungilo was indeed beautiful. It had a kind of beauty we hadn't experienced anywhere on our safari so far. Only Gibbs Farm came close. We drove down the road where, as children, we used to wait for a car coming to the orphanage to appear in the clearing and then chase it down to the convent. I could almost feel how my little fat legs hurt after running with the car.

I had promised my friends that I would take them to visit a typical rural school in a village. When I planned our itinerary, I scheduled everything based on the date, rather than the day of the week. Because of this faux pas, we found ourselves scheduled to visit Masange Primary School, a few minutes' walk from Kifungilo, on a Saturday when there was no school. When I realized the error, I frantically tried to reach Betty to ask if she could do anything to help me. I was embarrassed because I had asked my friends to bring little gifts from America for the children, and they had carried them for the entire trip. Betty called the headmistress of the school and explained my dilemma. Sister said she would do what she could, and we should visit the school at nine in the morning.

When we arrived, the children, dressed in their blue-and-white uniforms, greeted us with song and dance for almost an hour. A couple of friends asked why there were no girls before they realized that all the children, boys and girls alike, had short-cropped hair due to the heat and for convenience. The children then went to their classrooms where we visited them. As soon as we entered they stood up and sang again for us. I sang along, which surprised them. In each room I thanked the students for their warm welcome and gave a speech of encouragement in Swahili. I know that one of the highlights of the day for them was that an American tourist spoke Swahili.

We were very touched when Sister Majellis, the headmistress, told us that she sent couriers at eight that morning to knock on the children's doors and tell them they had guests from America who wanted to see them. Several hundred of the seven hundred primary school kids dressed up in their uniforms early on a Saturday morning and came to school to sing and dance for us.

Visiting the school was sobering for my friends. The majority of the students were very poor and could not even afford their school uniforms. Once they finished primary school, most would go back to working in the fields. Sister wanted to offer secondary education to those who showed potential, but she had to come up with funding herself because the little she got from the government wasn't sufficient. We left our gifts of supplies with Sister, who would take care of distributing them the following week.

In a large room with a cement floor, mattresses were piled up to the ceiling on one end and homemade desks faced a blackboard at the other. This room was used as a school during the day and housed over eighty students from distant villages who laid the mattresses on the floor to sleep at night.

The children followed us to the cars when it was time to leave. They asked us to take their pictures with our digital cameras and were so thrilled to see themselves that they innocently and lovingly kissed their images on the cameras.

Back at the convent Sister Monica greeted us and took us into the waiting room where long ago I had been shown to the *wazungu* couples who came to adopt orphans. We enjoyed some refreshments and then ate lunch in the same dining room that had fed twenty-five or more nuns during my time.

After lunch Sister Monica, Betty, and my friends toured Kifungilo grounds and school. Our first stop was the church. I beelined to the spot in the back where the Christmas Nativity scene used to be. I saw myself kneeling and talking to Baby Jesus, asking him why he was taking so long to find my mother. I couldn't find the confessional where half-deaf Father Gatang or Father Van Leer would have us shout out our sins and give us penance. I saw the same statues of the Blessed Virgin and Saint Joseph that Mother Ancilla made, but the pews were new and much improved. I went under the ivy-covered bell tower outside the church and showed my friends how hard it was to pull the thick sisal cord to ring the heavy iron bell hidden underneath.

We went to the large building where the slaughter of farm animals took place and where we made sausage, bacon, ham, cream, and butter for the Sisters and to sell in Lushoto. Several large pigs were noisily eating in the sties. From their stalls two rows of black-and-white cows stared at us. Everything looked small and compact compared to how I remembered it. We continued up the path by the turkey and chicken sheds, to the pretty irrigation stream that carried water to the vegetable and fruit plots below. As I walked along the clear stream lined with white calla lilies, my heart beat faster because we were approaching an important spot at the orphanage that I will never forget. The little pond at the end of the stream, which used to be surrounded by elegant cypress trees and beautiful multicolored daisies and lavender chrysanthemums, looked bare and neglected. There was little water in the pond, no fish, and no flowers, but the few green cypress trees still reached for the sky.

I sat on the warped wooden bench facing the pond and told my friends that this was the bench that Cathy and I had sat on some fifty years ago when she asked me if I would like to go to America with her. When I think of that day I can still feel the excitement, wonder, and magic of the miracle she brought into my life. This is the spot that gave birth to the hope that kept me going in spite of my circumstances. Hope was what helped me believe that one day I would leave the orphanage for good.

Emily Dickinson says it perfectly for me:
Hope is the thing with feathers
That perches in the soul
And sings the tunes without the words
And never stops at all.

I didn't want to linger at my miracle spot because I feared I was going to fall apart from the overwhelming memory of being chosen by Cathy.

We continued to the grotto of Our Lady of Fatima. Apart from the fact that the grotto was old and not maintained to the standard of the German nuns, it looked exactly as it did in my time. All novenas began and ended here. From the grotto we walked along the outdoor Stations of the Cross, where Sister Theonesta, who had carried me as a baby in her apron, bumped my head every time she genuflected at each of the fourteen stations.

I knew most of the nuns and priests buried in the cemetery. I said a prayer by the grave of Sister Silvestris who died in 1983, two years after I took my children to meet her. I said a prayer for Zahabu, the old woodcutter, at his grave. I realized that Sister Silvestris, who loved Zahabu, must have pulled a few strings to get him buried in the white cemetery—something not done at the time. There was a time I wanted to be buried in this cemetery too, but after Sister Silvestris died, I changed my mind, because I realized it would be a hardship for my children to take my ashes there, but mostly because it really wouldn't make a difference to me at that point.

From the cemetery we could see the children's quarters, which looked very different from how I remembered them. Kifungilo is a prestigious private secondary boarding school run by the same Order of Precious Blood Sisters as in my time, but the Sisters are now African instead of German. Despite a lot of new buildings, our old school building and sleeping room still stood, and both were being used as dormitories.

It seemed strange to be in front of the old school and not see the Blessed Martin statue. Where was he? I always looked for him each time I visited and often found that he had been moved. When I couldn't find him anywhere on this trip, I asked Sister Monica if she knew what had happened to him. She took me to a corner of the building and pointed out the statue. It was obvious that my beloved Blessed Martin had no place in this modern school now. He was leaning against a wall, facing nothing in particular, and a big chunk of cement was broken from his face. I found myself saying the same prayers we used to say when we knelt on the grass in front of him. We mostly prayed for benefactors, and I prayed to find my mother.

Blessed Martin always answered our prayers, because we never went without food or clothing, and I found my mother.

I felt so sad about the neglected and abandoned statue of Blessed Martin that I thought of asking permission to take it home to America with me. Fat Mary, who was very familiar with the role of Blessed Martin in my life, shook her head.

You don't need anything physical to remind you of him. He will always be with you. What you're seeing here is a cement statue, just as it has always been. In your heart he is the way you knew him. The students at Kifungilo now do not know him. Even if you told them they would not feel him. Set free what's left of his outward manifestation. Leave his remains at the place his statue was made.

It was late when we got to Betty's beautiful farm and home in Jaegerthal, just outside of Lushoto, for tea and samosas. She had spent the whole day with us in Kifungilo, and we reminisced about the good/bad old days at the orphanage.

On our last day in Tanzania we visited the Cultural Heritage Center in Arusha. I have known Saiffudin, "Saif," and his wife Zahra, the founders and directors of the center, for many years, and have stayed with them in their beautiful home, full of enviable art, several times. Saif, who had been traveling in Nairobi, had just flown in to meet my group. He opened the center earlier than usual and gave us a personal tour of the impressive collection of artworks in the galleries as he told us the history of the center, and then treated us to lunch.

This unique cultural center on the outskirts of Arusha represents and celebrates African cultural heritage. The original Cultural Heritage Center was started in 1994 and has grown into the impressive complex it is today. It is composed of several curio shops, a jewelry boutique that features tanzanite and other precious stones, a restaurant, bargain center, and an outstanding commercial art gallery. The African Fine Art and Antiques Collection, the only one of its kind, ranges from African antiques to contemporary and wildlife paintings, sculpture, and photography of museum quality.

The new gallery, added in 2010, is a feat of architectural engineering reminiscent of Frank Lloyd Wright's circular Guggenheim Museum in New York. The gallery's exterior is inspired by a drum, shield, and spear—well-known African objects charged with traditional meaning. The spear represents survival and strength, and is a symbol of masculinity, pride, and prestige. The shield signifies safety and shelter and represents bravery and identity. The drum is a symbol of maternity and community as well as a means of communication and celebration.

The center offers art from hundreds of tribes from Tanzania and other parts of Africa. The selection is amazing, and the curated and well-displayed art is for sale. Items can be shipped anywhere in the world from the premises. The art is not cheap but, as almost anywhere in Africa, bargaining is expected so nobody pays the stated price. We did what I would call "power shopping" for several hours, which was barely enough for my friends who wished they had days to spend in the stores and galleries.

After the shopping my friends went back to the Arumeru Hotel, where they had spent their last night in Africa, packed their bags, including the items they just purchased at the Cultural Heritage Center and the custom-made African *kitenge* outfits they had ordered from a tailor in Arusha earlier that day. On their way to the airport they stopped at Fatima's farm in Usa River for a tour of her coffee farm and a farewell meal of goat and coconut pilau.

I didn't accompany them to the airport because I was spending two more weeks in Tanzania, visiting with friends and family around the country.

83

Hurricane-Proof Statues

 I lived for thirteen years alone in the house that Kjell and I bought in 1998 when we moved to Florida, and it was a full-time job to maintain it. Kjell had been in charge of paying the bills and everything that had to do with insurance, finances, fixing and installing things when needed. When he left in 2003 I had no idea how to do anything, but he continued to pay the bills during the year and a half of our divorce process and the year of my cancer treatment.

A few months after our divorce was final in July of 2005, Hurricane Wilma hit Florida. It was the last of three successive blows in my life, and it almost took me down. In a two-year period I endured a divorce after thirty-five years of marriage, treatment for breast cancer, and a hurricane that damaged my house and completely destroyed my backyard, mangling the screen over the pool and turning the outdoor furniture into a pile of twisted metal. The power was out for two weeks, and if it hadn't been for my friend Dale who sheltered me in her home, which had hurricane-impact windows and doors, I might have succumbed to this "act of God."

When I visited the house after the hurricane, I remember sitting alone on the deck looking at the screen with its heavy beams. They had detached completely and were scattered in and around the pool like discarded metal in a junkyard. I wondered what to do first. Should I go through the house records to see if we had a contractor, find our insurance policies, find a place to keep the thawing food in the freezer, find drinking water, clean up the trees and debris in the yard, mop up the water in every room, find a roofer to fix the section of roof that had flown away—or throw myself into the pool and disappear into the tangled metal mess that the outdoor furniture had become? I do not think there was another time in my life that I felt so helpless and alone! My chest was swollen and aching, and my arms felt dead after the first of my breast reconstruction surgeries.

I sat looking at the destruction, wondering what was going to hit me next, when I felt the ancestors telling me to stand up and go to my "Mama Africa" statue on the opposite side of the pool. Mama Africa was looking right at me and she seemed to smile. As I approached her I saw that the collapsed screens and beams from the roof had completely missed her! They had fallen down and carefully placed themselves around her without touching her. She didn't even have a scratch on her beautiful granite cloak. I looked at the other three stone statues around the pool and saw that they had been similarly protected. Joy and gratitude suddenly changed my mood, and I knew that somehow, this too would pass and I would be all right!

I recalled the many nights I lay stretched out on the couch by the pool after sunset—my favorite place to relax, communing with my four statues that I had named Mama Africa, the Music Lesson, Hearts and Butterflies, and Everybody's Daughter-in-Law, as they shimmered and danced with their reflection in the pool. Would I have that again?

So many pool screens had been damaged or destroyed throughout Florida that it was eight months before I could replace mine. A family of five raccoons had a field day playing and swimming in the pool as soon as I had the debris removed. When I tried to chase them away one day they jumped out of the pool and chased me back into the house!

My property bordered a wooded sanctuary where, according to city ordinance, no one could build. At times I heard people talking near my window. When I went to see what was going on I found whole families in my backyard admiring my statues or having a picnic. They'd tell me, "We didn't know there was a park here."

84

John

In 2006, the year after the hurricane, John, Cathy's husband and my American father, was diagnosed with ALS (Amyotrophic Lateral Sclerosis) also known as Lou Gehrig's disease. The progressive neurodegenerative disease affects nerve cells in the brain and the spinal cord that are responsible for controlling voluntary muscle movement. John gradually lost his ability to move, speak, eat, and breathe, and his robust 6'3" frame slowly wasted away in front of our eyes.

We were optimistic at first because the disease progression was very slow and he continued to enjoy travel, family gatherings, and celebrations with us. I tried not to let the ominous advance of the disease and its ravaging effects dominate my mind, and for a long time I was able to put it on the back burner. We witnessed parts of his body, beginning with his arms and legs, just stop working until he was confined to a wheelchair.

John was a great cook and he really knew and loved wine. We continued to enjoy it together at most meals, but then one day, when I arrived at their house, I saw him sip wine with a straw. That was a depressing day for me, but John's face made me believe that he savored every drop he pulled through the straw as though he were holding a crystal goblet in his hand. One day when he couldn't move any part of his body anymore and was confined to his bed, he asked me to scratch his nose. At that moment I fully understood the agony and anguish he felt when his functioning brain sent messages to his damaged nerves to move his arm to scratch his nose, but his atrophied muscles could not respond. This must be worse than Alzheimer's, I said to myself. With Alzheimer's you may not totally know what's going on, but with ALS your brain is fully functioning and you're aware, but your body cannot respond.

As his illness progressed I worried about Cathy. She was the caregiver and she was beyond exhausted. I watched as her usual joy and excitement with life faded. Worry, fear, and caregiving demands filled her time as she moved from day to day as though she were in a daze. Bravely she tried to keep her spirits high and struggled to boldly face the path to her husband's death.

It was hard to leave them to return to Florida from Minnesota that summer, because I was afraid of the call telling me that John was dying and I should go and see him alive for the last time. That call came the end of February 2012, and I booked my ticket to leave the following morning.

At about 3 a.m. I suddenly woke up and found myself pacing up and down the hallway in my house, wondering who was calling me and why the phone was ringing. The physical phone made no sound, but I heard it ringing louder and louder until a very clear voice came through the noise. It was John. He held his hand out for me to hold, just like he had done so many times since he became Cathy's husband. He was lying in bed and I squeezed power and strength and joy into his hand. I continued walking around my house, now stopping to touch all the photographs of him and reliving the moments captured therein. I spoke to the photographs.

"Goodbye, John. Thank you for loving Cathy so much and for loving me."

"You know, I had no choice. You two came as a package!" he answered.

That was typical John! It felt like he was right there alive and well. I remembered the delicious food and especially fresh soups made with everything grown in his garden that he cooked for us over the years. He also made a tasty granola from scratch, which I dubbed "boom-boom food" because it encouraged my digestive system to move along when it needed extra help. I saw the many plants in the pots around my house and the beautiful flower arrangements that brought his gentleness into my home. I envisioned the fresh Christmas wreaths he made for my house in Minnesota and shipped to Florida after I moved.

I thanked him for coming to say goodbye and told him I wouldn't cry because he would be much happier and free without his useless body. I told him I was happy for him—and for Cathy and for Eleanor that his suffering had ended.

I went back to bed and slept until it was time to catch the plane for Minnesota. His funeral was in Minneapolis and he was buried in Cathy's family plot in Onamia. Eleanor sang at the funeral service with so much power, joy, and love, it was as if she were an angel of good tidings who had appeared to remind those gathered to celebrate the life John lived and to hang on to the gifts he left behind. It must have been her father hovering above, blissfully listening to her magnificent voice and telling her to rejoice that he was at peace.

A few days after the funeral I told Cathy about my visit with John in Florida the night he died, and she confirmed that it was around the time he was leaving this world.

85

Farewell to Art

One day a friend of mine who owned a condo in Delray Beach told me that her neighbors were selling their place and wouldn't I like to buy it? I hadn't even thought of moving, and when I visited the apartment, I didn't think it was big enough to hold my art. But then I saw the view and I made up my mind on the spot to buy it. On the tenth floor of an older building, it had a180-degree view of the ocean, the Intracoastal Waterway, and downtown Delray Beach.

My biggest task now that I had decided to move was figuring out what to do with my art. What to take, what to sell, and what to donate. My children took a few of their favorites, but I kept the rest of what they wanted, knowing they would eventually get those pieces. I decided to give the majority of it, especially the pieces of museum-quality, to the Children's Defense Fund for their home at Haley Farm in Tennessee. I had been to the farm for the Women's Spiritual Retreat several times and I had always imagined their big, beautiful property full of African art. Marian Wright Edelman, the founder and president of the CDF, was delighted to receive over three hundred pieces. I suggested that the art not be kept in storage, that no fee should be charged to see it, and apart from the labels, there should be no descriptive plaques. I wanted people to approach the art without being told what to see, what to feel, or what it represents. Viewers should experience the art from their own point of view, and if they wanted the tribal relevance and purpose of a piece, they could Google it or go to the Langston Hughes Library on the Farm, where a catalogue with all the descriptions could be found.

I had not anticipated how hard it would be to watch my forty-five years of collected art come down from the walls, be dismantled, packed, and crated, never to be part of my daily life again. I cried when Mama Africa's crate was being built for her. At five feet high and 2,300 pounds, getting her crated and hauled off took the moving crew almost two days. I climbed into the crate to say goodbye to her and told her that she was going to a place where many more people could admire her and feel her powerful, protective, dignified, and loving presence.

It was also very hard to say goodbye to my one-piece Nativity scene. On a visit to the Cultural Heritage Center in Arusha I noticed an artist working on a massive piece of wood with a hammer, screwdriver, knives, and some homemade tools. He was carving the Nativity scene into the trunk of a rosewood tree. The images he carved were unique. Baby Jesus was in bas relief at the center of the partly scooped-out trunk, and Mary and Joseph knelt beside him. Shepherds with their sheep draped over their shoulders were carved in various stages of walking on the sides and back of the sloping trunk, and they strained to see the little baby. The three kings bearing their gifts were the only three-dimensional figures. The expression of peace and wonder on the faces of the other observers at the scene, the asymmetrical shape of the tree trunk, and the rich rosewood color made this Nativity set one of the most beautiful and lifelike I had ever seen.

I fell in love with it. The carver eagerly told me his personal vision about the Nativity scene, which was not quite the same as mine. Just like the artist who carved the twenty-five-piece ebony Nativity set I owned, this craftsman was also Muslim. Probably because they were not restricted by the Christian version of the story, they took liberties and were very creative with the number of people and kinds of animals present at Jesus's birth. The Nativity set I kept for myself had chickens, a snake, a dog, a medicine man, a policeman, two village women carrying baskets on their heads and a nun with a painted white face!

When I discussed the tree trunk Nativity I was looking at with Saif, the owner of the Cultural Heritage Center, he agreed that it was one of a kind and could never be reproduced. He told me that when he saw the artist begin his work, he wondered if he could ever sell it because it was nothing like the other traditional Nativity sets and was too massive! I ended up buying the piece and six months later it arrived in Florida.

Before all of the art left my house I gave a "Farewell to Art Party" in my home. We dressed in African attire, wined and dined, and danced—courtesy of my friend Dymin and her live band—to give the art a proper send-off,

Two years later I was again invited to attend the Women's Spiritual Retreat at Haley Farm, so I had the opportunity to visit my art. I was so happy to see how nicely everything was displayed throughout the campus. Mama Africa welcomed visitors as they entered the chapel on a hill. The rosewood Nativity scene was in the foyer of the main house next to a huge painting of Alex Haley, the author of *Roots*.

The only plaque next to each piece says:

> *Thank you for respecting our African Art*
> *The NHAMBU Collection.*

Marian Wright Edelman and the Children's Defense Fund helped me fulfill my father's one and only request: "I want the name NHAMBU to live in America."

86

More Grandchildren

Ever since Kata left for college in Boston in 1989 we haven't lived in the same state. Karl also left for college but came back to Minnesota and Florida to live several times. It was nice to have family nearby, especially after the divorce when I lived alone. The biggest blessing of living in the same state is spending time with my grandchildren. Karl and Mandy's first child was born in 2016, a few months before *Africa's Child*, the first book in my memoir trilogy, was published.

One evening Mandy called saying she wanted to go to the hospital to be checked, and could I take her because Karl was teaching. I arrived to pick her up, but aware of my legendary non-existent sense of direction, even with GPS, she drove my car to the hospital. She was very calm, while my thoughts were all over and I was getting excited about being a grandmother again. What kind of a mother-in-law would let her daughter-in-law who was going into labor drive!

Mandy delivered a beautiful little boy, whom they named Oskar. Her instincts proved correct because his entrance into the world was not smooth. Because his heart rate kept dropping, he was delivered by cesarean, and when they pulled him out he aspirated meconium (his first poop), which caused breathing difficulties. He was in the neonatal intensive care for several days before he could go home.

At first I wasn't happy with the name Karl and Mandy gave him, because what came to mind was the "Oscar Mayer Wieners" commercial and Oscar the Grouch on *Sesame Street*; I was afraid he would be teased at school. They told me that they both liked the name, and Oscar with a "c" had been a family name for generations on Mandy's side. It was also pronounceable in both English and

Norwegian. On second thought, I remembered there was another well-known Oscar—Oscar Wilde.

When the family came to visit me in my tenth-floor condo Oskar cried the minute they got into the elevator and continued crying the entire visit. We thought maybe the elevator ride was the problem. I have been known as an "infant whisperer" because I can usually calm inconsolably crying babies, but no matter what I did, he cried even more in my arms. Was he allergic to me? I was reminded of when Karl had colic and cried continuously for the first three months of his life. The only way I could comfort Karl was to nurse him every few minutes for hours on end, and the only way I could comfort myself was to cry along with him.

When Oskar was five months old Mandy became pregnant again. I was delighted, even though I was worried about the hard work of having two kids so close together. I forgot all about that when I found out they were having a girl. The first and most selfish thing I said was, "Finally, someone to inherit my jewelry!" They named her Liv (Life) after Karl's Norwegian grandmother.

Liv had an even more traumatic entrance into the world than Oskar. She aspirated both blood from a placental abruption, and meconium, and her heart had stopped for a few seconds during labor. She was treated in the level 3 NICU for two weeks. The doctor said that if the baby had remained in the womb for five more minutes we would have lost her! It was one of the most fearful times in my life, made even worse by the fact that they had moved to Minneapolis, and I could not be with them. I was at home unable to do much, imagining the pain and discomfort Mandy was going through and picturing Karl sitting in the room, not fully comprehending what had gone wrong and wondering if his daughter would live or die. How I wanted to be with him to hug him and reassure him.

But then technology came to the rescue. The hospital had a NICU live stream that allowed me to log on to the internet and be transported from Delray Beach to the NICU in Minneapolis. I could watch baby Liv's every move and hear every whimper as she fought for life, although I couldn't make sense of the numbers and graphics on the computers and machines surrounding her incubator or the many tubes on her tiny body. It was heartbreaking and scary, and I found myself praying out loud every time I virtually visited her.

A consolation and encouragement during those first days of Liv's stay in the NICU was the picture at her station. Her incubator had a yellow giraffe on it, and on the computer screen monitoring her bodily functions was a giraffe with its neck curved, like the one on my *Aerobics With Soul®* logo. I felt the presence of the giraffe's spirit with her, and I knew in my heart that my favorite animal was protecting my grandchild. She would not only survive but may even become a dancer like her *Bibi* (Grandma).

Karl and Mandy bought a house near Minneapolis, so being a snowbird who returns to Minnesota every summer, I get to see the two grandchildren often. I cannot put into words the joy, glory, and contentment of the family bond I experience with my grandchildren when we play together. Their purity and innocence add a dimension to my priorities regarding what I choose to accomplish in the time I have left in this world. They add sweet meaning to these years and offer me the indescribable feeling of joy and love that overwhelms grandparents all over the world.

I can say that both Oskar and Liv already love to dance, but Liv takes it a step further. Of course, I play mostly African music when they are with me. While Oskar bounces and skips around to the music, holding his beloved miniature toy cars, Liv perks up when she first hears the beat, shakes her whole body to the rhythm of the drums, vigorously nods her head, and lets out excited noises and babbles as her way of singing.

Oskar and Liv are healthy, beautiful children. Once again, I am reminded of the good fortune of living in a country with such advanced medical expertise to save lives even when there is little hope. Had they been born in another place or time, I might not have my grandchildren today.

I pay homage to Kata and Matt, and Karl and Mandy, and to parents everywhere who steadfastly hold on to the hopes, joys, responsibilities, and heartbreaks of parenthood with gratitude, courage, and faith. From the moment they bring a child into the world there is nothing that will stop them from becoming the wind beneath the soaring wings of their children, to lead them and guide them along the way to taking their places in the cycle of life.

87

This One Shall Live

After my yearly safari to East Africa I usually stayed a couple weeks longer to visit with friends and family. One year, after everyone else had returned to America, I invited my father Yeremia to come and stay with me at Tarangire Safari Lodge for two weeks. It was the most relaxed and meaningful time we ever spent together.

Despite my questions, Dorothy had always refused to tell me anything about my father or her life in Africa. Ten years after her death, when I found my father, I realized he was my only resource for learning the truth about my parents. Before I left America for Africa that year I prepared a list of questions for him about my mother and their life together. I also brought a cassette recorder to record our conversation.

As he was answering my questions, it occurred to me that being able to speak with my father was the reason I worked so hard to keep my Swahili alive. I had left Africa in 1963 and did not return again until 1974. During those years I learned American English and French, and seldom spoke Swahili. On my first return trip to Africa, I was outright embarrassed that my tongue was heavy and my mind went blank when I tried to speak Swahili. I resolved then and there that I would find a way to reclaim it, even if it was just by listening to Swahili music on records and CDs or reading the few Swahili books available in America at the time.

Easier said than done. What I ended up doing was teaching Swahili for several years at Central High School in Minneapolis. Since then I have remained fluent except for contemporary Swahili. My initial embarrassment about my poor Swahili was the catalyst that made conversation with my father possible. If I had completely forgotten the language my father and I could only have communicated via a translator without the spontaneous, intimate feelings we had for each other. Swahili saved the moment that was destined for us.

I asked my father each question that I had asked Dorothy. He answered them all with candor and sincerity, and some of his recollections were full of emotion.

He said that overall, he had a good life as the Reiners' cook and house servant. He started working for them when he was seventeen years old. He lived inside the house and took care of Mrs. Reiner when her husband was away. After my birth he had to leave the house but lived in their compound, just a few yards away. They found him a wife, and he continued taking care of their house and worked for them off and on until a few years before they returned to America.

He reiterated what he had told me the day we met—he believed he and Dorothy loved each other.

"Did Dorothy ever tell you she loved you?"

"Not in words," was his reply.

"Did you tell her you loved her?"

"I couldn't." Yeremia leaned forward and looked me straight in the eye. "Don't you understand? I was not her equal. I was her servant. I did what I was told."

At that moment, their secret life became transparent and I understood everything.

My father was silent for a while but then continued telling me more. He said he was surprised that her husband, Mr. Reiner, permitted their relationship. He didn't fully understand the situation, but he thought that Mr. Reiner was no longer able to make children and might have been considerate of his wife's needs.

"He asked you to fulfill his wife's needs?"

"That's what I understood. I really didn't know for sure, but I did what I was told."

"How so?"

"Sometimes all three of us were in the bedroom together."

"Really?"

"Sometimes he was very good to me and sometimes he was not."

"What do you mean?"

"When your mother was pregnant with you, he wanted to kill me."

"But you just told me he allowed you and Dorothy to be together."

"One time he had me accompany him on a long safari. He always carried his gun in case of attack by wild animals. Without warning, he pointed it at my chest and told me to say my prayers because he was going to kill me. I just stood there trembling because no prayer came from my heart. I waited to hear the sound of the gun. He took a very, very long time, but then he slowly dragged the gun down my body, stopped at my left leg, and pulled the trigger. Look, I still have the scar."

"Oh, my God! I don't understand! That's a big scar. He must have almost blown your leg off."

"It took nearly two years to heal, but I continued working for them, hobbling around on the crutches I made from tree branches."

"I still don't understand."

"I don't understand either. As I told you, he was good to me most of the time and told me to be with his wife."

I looked at the six-inch scar on his left shin again and stroked it.

"The wound has healed, but my heart hasn't."

We looked at each other in silence.

"Was Judy the only other child you had with Dorothy?" I managed to ask.

"The only other born child, but she died. Between Judy and you, Mama was pregnant again."

"Where is the child?"

"She forced me to bring her some *dawa* (medicine) from the village to get rid of the pregnancy, and I did."

"So, you brought her some medicine from the village and she lost the child?"

"Yes."

"Do you think it was her husband who asked her to get rid of the pregnancy?"

"I don't think he even knew she was pregnant. He was away much of the time."

"So how come she did not abort me?"

"She wanted to. I was very, very afraid, but I did not bring her the medicine. 'No,' I told her. 'This one shall live.'"

"You did? You saved my life?"

"No! I did not. God saved your life." Yeremia gazed out into space as if he were watching scenes from his life. "I am happy to give you the story of the life I had with the Reiners. You and I are here only because of God. I am not sure that Mr. and Mrs. Reiner really wanted us."

"But they kind of did, didn't they? Dorothy came looking for me and found me when I was thirty-six years old, and you continued to work for them for many years."

"Yes, I worked for them all those years, but today I am telling you that I did not fully know them and they did not know me."

"Thank you for letting me be born."

We hugged and wept over our lives and destinies.

I went back to my bungalow and lay down. The weight of the story of my birth crushed me into the mattress until it felt like I was sinking into a dark place, and I would never see light again.

In the morning, though, my head was clear. Nothing was a mystery anymore now that the details of the threads in my life's tapestry had revealed themselves. I could see and follow the design made by the colors and textures that destiny chose to weave my story.

It became clear what Dorothy meant when she said she was protecting others by not giving me information about my father. She was protecting her husband, her son and family, but most of all she was protecting herself from her history.

My mother made so much sense now. For her, Africa became a place of regrets, a place that tortured her conscience. Apart from his servant duties, Yeremia was used to help solve the intimacy issues in their marriage, but unfortunately, Dorothy fell in love with the substitute husband. She tried to find peace in this world by removing me from her life, but in the end, she came looking for me to prove to herself that someone in flesh and blood embodied her exploitative love for a servant. Try as she might, she could not erase my birth. I was a loud drum beat in her head and a strong heart beat in her chest who proved what she would not admit—that she loved a Black man.

The truth brought me peace. I hope it also set Dorothy free and she is finally resting in peace.

88

Things Left Unsaid

Throughout the writing of my memoirs there were certain aspects of my story I chose not to write because I suspected that my brother Larry didn't know about them, and I couldn't bear hurting or upsetting him.

Larry loved Africa and went there every opportunity he had. His dream was to be a medical volunteer in Tanzania after he retired. I traveled there with him twice, and it was apparent that he was happiest when he was in Tanzania. He took thousands of amazing photographs, which he collected and published in *Make It a Good One,* a pictorial chronicle of his travels around the world, but especially of his life in Tanganyika. He sent me the finished but unpublished manuscript, and his love for Africa is written all over it.

I was surprised at how differently we experienced and wrote about events we shared, and I pointed out several discrepancies in what he wrote about Yeremia's time with his parents, and he said we could talk about them someday, but that was the best he could remember.

I loved Larry with my whole heart, but it was hard to be close to him. His African colonial and boarding school upbringing worked against making meaningful and lasting friendships. The white families in Africa left to go abroad for holidays, taking their children with them and frequently didn't return. Because Larry's parents lived in Tanganyika, Larry often stayed at school during breaks or had to travel alone by bus or train to his parents' home far away in small villages. The impossibility of developing lasting friendships resulted in his avoiding attachment to classmates and others to protect himself from the certainty of hurt and loneliness when they left.

He even had trouble staying in touch with me, though I always felt his love. He seldom initiated a phone conversation, but when I did, he was transported back to his happy childhood years in Tanganyika, especially when we spoke in Swahili.

I gave him a copy of *Africa's Child* and waited a whole year for his comments. None came. When I pushed him, all he said was, "It's very Catholic." I gave him *America's Daughter,* which had so much about our mother Dorothy, but he didn't read it. He kept telling me that he would start it soon, but a few months after it was published, he became ill.

I visited him in the hospital, and we stayed in touch over the phone when he moved from home into an assisted living facility. He said he was finally reading *America's Daughter,* but couldn't retain what he read, so every time he picked up the book, he started reading the first chapter. He decided to stop reading completely when he couldn't remember what he'd read at the end of each page.

"I hope your inability to retain what you read is temporary," I told him, "because there is a lot I want to discuss with you about our mother and your father."

"Go ahead, little sister. My ears are fine!"

"She was not always good to me. Sometimes she was outright cruel."

"I'm so sorry. But, Maria, that's how she was. I could tell you stories myself."

"She was mean to you too?" I asked him, surprised.

"I don't know if she meant to be."

"When I think that she gave Cathy permission to bring me to America and years later came looking for me, I can't be angry at her. I am mostly grateful."

"I let it go a long time ago. I tried my best to be closer to her towards the end of her life, but little changed." Larry paused a few moments, then repeated, "I just think that's how she was."

"It would still be nice if you could read my books. You'd discover other sides of her that you might not have known."

"If what you write is not good, I don't want to know. But I do have every intention of reading your books. I have to tell you, Sis, I am very proud of you."

A few months after this conversation, while he was still in assisted living, Larry was diagnosed with lung cancer. We talked on the phone several times. He always connected and came alive when we spoke Swahili. I tried again to discuss what my father told me about Larry's parents and their life in Tanganyika but couldn't. I didn't dare. He was very fragile, and I had the feeling that, based on what he wrote about his parents' relationship in his book, he didn't know what I planned to discuss with him. He had said that if what I wanted to tell him about our mother wasn't good, he didn't want to know. Considering that, and his condition, I made peace with the fact that we would never have that conversation. I think that was the way he wanted it.

Larry was slowly losing his connection to reality, sliding in and out of consciousness. I knew he was in emotional and psychological pain and extremely depressed because he said he no longer had a purpose in life. I listened to him and tried to comfort him as he struggled to make meaning of his impending death, but I felt inadequate. At this point, what I wanted to discuss with him about his parents was unimportant and insignificant.

A week later he took a turn for the worse. I believed he would rally as he had often done before, so I booked a flight to see him the following week, but he died a few days later.

My great consolation was the presence of my daughter Katarina, an interfaith hospital chaplain, who visited her Uncle Larry during his last year in the hospital and at the assisted living facility where he was with his three children when he died.

A few months later Kata was the officiant at a memorial service for her uncle in Boston.

My brother wanted to be cremated and have his ashes spread over the beautiful and remote Ngurdoto Crater in Tanzania. I will take him back home where he will finally rest in peace in his beloved Tanzania.

After he died I agonized about writing what I wanted to discuss with him. I came to the conclusion that he would want me to write my story as truthfully and as completely as I could. He would be the last one to stand in my way because that's who he was.

89

Reflections

Over the years I have kept up my well-known tradition of gathering friends at my place for a New Year's Eve party. After my move into the condo in Delray Beach, I inaugurated an annual Christmas Boat Parade party to replace the New Year's Eve one. From my tenth-floor balcony, we have a panoramic view of the ocean and the Intracoastal Waterway.

The day after Thanksgiving, I decorate every room in my home for Christmas, including the kitchen, bathroom, and closets. The elegantly dressed party people who come blend with the glitter and bling and become part of the precious ornaments I have carefully saved and used every Christmas since I had my first home in 1968. The festivities continue outdoors as we listen to Christmas carols coming from big and small yachts, sailboats outlined by multicolored strings of lights showcasing Christmas trees, dancing snowmen, big-bellied Santas, galloping reindeers, flying snowflakes, shining stars, and scenes of Mary and Joseph kneeling by Baby Jesus on his bed of straw. The reflection of the lighted boats gliding gracefully on the still waters of the Intracoastal and the golden colors of the setting sun makes it hard for my guests to tear themselves away from the balcony and come indoors for dinner.

Among the party people are five beautiful women—Myrna, Roz, Chris, Ketly, and Joanne—who are like sisters to me. They are my Florida family. I have no words to describe the bond we share or a way to put a price on the tender loving care with which we've held each other up in rough times. A throw blanket, given to me last year as a birthday present, has a woven image of us. Whenever I'm cold or lonely, I reach for the blanket and wrap myself in their love.

When the wining, dining, and dancing are over and everyone has left, I sit in the living room and look at the Christmas tree. All the ornaments are works of art, handmade in Tanzania by Maasai craftswomen. I walk over to a table near the window where my large carved ebony Nativity scene from Tanzania reminds me year after year what Christmas is about. As I look at these carvings telling the story of the birth of Christ, I am transported to the first Nativity scene I saw in the back of the church in Kifungilo. I had always equated the word "mother" with love because I saw how happy other children at the orphanage were when their mothers came to visit. I've come to understand that when I prayed to Baby Jesus to find my mother, I was asking him to be loved. Even as a five-year-old I knew that what I needed more than all the Christmas presents the nuns gave us was love.

I move to the balcony and stretch out on the loveseat whose cushions depict a joyful African village scene. Wrapping myself in the throw from my friends, I let them hug me. At that sweet moment I feel a pair of soft and familiar little arms around me.

"Fat Mary, I want to celebrate all that we are! From the bottom of my heart, I thank God for your attentive presence in my life. I am content, and whole, and I love who I am. You always reminded me that Baby Jesus would answer my prayers, and he has. He gave me Cathy, John and Eleanor; then my birth mother, my brother, and my father. I found my sister Judy's grave in Africa. I have my large extended family in Tanzania and have been blessed with my own children and grandchildren. Because of our Faith, Hope, and Love, they know their African family, and they know me."

You have three mothers, and each one prepared you for the kinds of love you would experience in life. Sister Silvestris, your orphanage mother, taught you about tough love. Dorothy, your birth mother, taught you about unrequited love. Cathy, your adoptive mother, taught you about unconditional love. They all showed you what love is, but on your own you discovered the most important love of all—bravely loving yourself.

Glossary

Pronunciation
In Swahili the stress of a word almost always falls on the next-to-last syllable: Tan-zan-I-a. There are only five vowels and they are always pronounced the same. All vowels are pronounced. Two vowels together are each pronounced: **Haule = Ha-U-le.**

AIMC (African Inland Mission Church) – Missionary church in Tanzania with which the Reiners were associated

Amelican gal – American girl. Little Mary couldn't pronounce "r" and some African languages do not distinguish between "r" and "l"

Amina – Amen

apartheid – South African system of racial segregation enforced by government laws to ensure the dominance of the white population

Arusha – town in northern Tanzania, headquarters for northern safari circuits

asante – thank you

asante sana – thank you very much

askari – soldier, policeman

Aunt Marion – sister of Dorothy Reiner, also a missionary

baba – father

Betty – a friend from the orphanage living in Lushoto

bibi – grandmother

biogas – gaseous fuel produced by the fermentation of organic matter

Blessed Martin – a mixed-race Dominican Brother, patron saint of people of mixed race

boma – group of Maasai dwellings including livestock enclosure; district government office

bwana – mister, sir, husband; chief, boss

Color Bar – discrimination based on color in South Africa ("Kalaba")

D&C – dilation and curettage, a brief surgical procedure in which the cervix is dilated and a special instrument is used to scrape the uterine wall

dala dala – public transport, minibus

dawa – medicine

Don Bosco Home – name of orphanage and boarding school for mixed race children, Usambara Mountains, Kifungilo.

dudu/wadudu – any insect or creepy crawly bug (singular/plural)

duka – store (Indian term)

duka-wallah – shopkeeper (Indian term)

Eleanor – Cathy and John Mamer's daughter

Elizabeth – best friend at the orphanage

far – father (Norwegian)

Father Gatang – resident priest at the orphanage

Father Kennedy – priest at Gare, nearby mission

Fatima and Abdu Faraji – friends in Arusha, Tanzania

Finca Coffee Estate – owned by the Farajis, at Usa River

Frank and Betty Humplick – well-known singer in Tanzania, married to Betty from the orphanage

fundi – skilled person, expert, foreman

Fumbwe – driver for Serengeti Select Safaris

Gare – mission station near Kifungilo

hafu-kasti – half-caste

hakuna matata – no problem

hapana – no

Imelda – childhood friend from the orphanage; Betty's younger sister

jambo – hello

Janteloven – the Law of Jante, set of social rules regarding behavior in Scandinavian countries

Jeremiah – English spelling for Yeremia, Nhambu's father

John Mamer – Catherine Murray's husband

Kalaba – Color Bar, discrimination on the basis of color

karibu – welcome, near

Karibu – title of first *Aerobics With Soul®* video

khanga – colorful cotton cloth worn by East African women and some men

kitenge – heavier, more expensive cotton fabric (often Java print) used for women's and men's shirts

Kifungilo – name of the little village where the orphanage is located. Pronounced 'key-foong-ghee-low'

kikoi – East African striped cloth with an end fringe; garment made of kikoi

kigelegele – ululation: long, high-pitched vocal sound made by rapidly moving the tongue against the roof of the mouth used to signify joy or sadness

Kilakala Girls Secondary School – name of the former Marian College

KiSambaa – language of the Sambaa tribe

KiSukuma – language of the Sukuma people

Kjell – name of Nhambu's husband. Typically pronounced 'Shell'

Kongei – African Middle School run by Precious Blood Sisters

kopjes – rock outcroppings

kuchimba dawa – slang, to relieve oneself in the bush

kusindikiza – to accompany a parting person a short way along their journey

kusonya – a sucking sound used in East Africa and the Caribbean ("steups") to show annoyance or anger

kwaheri – goodbye

lanchi-boxis – lunch boxes

Lizzy – one of the "big girl" orphans who became a nun (Sister Eileen) and a dentist

lorry – truck

Lushoto – name of the small town closest to Kifungilo

Maasai – an ethnic group of semi-nomadic people, located in Kenya and northern Tanzania.

mabladifu – bloody fools (plural form)

Marshall Reiner – Dorothy's husband and Larry's father

Mama yangu! – My goodness! (literally Oh my mother!)

manyatta – Maasai settlement composed of several small round mud huts

mapenzi – love

Marian College – high school in Morogoro run by American Maryknoll Sisters, now Kilakala Girls Secondary School

Maryknoll Sisters – order of Catholic missionary nuns founded in New York in the 1920s

Mary Rose Ryan – the name Maria used until her marriage

maskini – poor people

matajiri – rich people

matata – trouble, problems

mdogo – little one

memsahib – madam or mistress of the house (Arabic)

Merikani – America

mganga/waganga – medicine man (singular/plural)

Mhonda – Middle school near Morogoro run by Precious Blood Sisters

milele na milele – forever and ever

Miriam Makeba – South African singer usually referred to as "Mama Africa"

Mombo – town near Lushoto

mor – mother (Norwegian)

Morogoro – large town at the foot of the Uluguru Mountains

mpishi – cook

Mungu wangu wee – Oh my God!

mwalimu – teacher

Mwalimu Haule – name of supportive math teacher in Mhonda Middle School

mwenyeji/weneyji – local person (singular/plural)

mzungu/wazungu – white person (singular/plural)

Nice Biscuits – popular cookie brand

ndiyo – yes

nyumba ile – literally "that house" or "that room" where orphans gathered for various activities and where clothes were kept in cubicles

nyumba mpya – new house

Nyumba Ya Sanaa – House of Art, art and craft center started by the Maryknoll Sisters

Oldupai – Maasai name for Olduvai Gorge

Operation Bootstrap Africa – organization dedicated to increased educational and healthcare opportunities in Africa, headquartered in Minneapolis, Minnesota

pangas – large knives (machete)

Paulina – friend at Mhonda Middle School

Perisi – Yeremia's wife

pole sana – so sorry

pombe – homemade alcoholic brew

Rancho La Puerta – fitness center in Tecate, México, near San Diego

Reed, Mrs. – college professor from France

rondavel – round African hut

Rosa – big girl who first cared for Little Mary; She died after a brief marriage

Rosminian – Catholic Order of priests founded by Italian Antonio Rosmini

rungu – club

Sambaa/WaSambaa – tribe living in the Usambara Mountains (singular/plural)

Saint Mary's School – school in Nairobi where Dorothy Reiner taught

Salma – Abdu and Fatima Faraji's daughter

shamba – field

shauri ya Mungu – God's will

shenzi/washenzi – heathens, pagans (singular/plural)

Shikamoo Mzee – greeting of respect for an elder

Shikamoo Mheshimiwa – greeting of respect, lit. "I hold your feet," respected one

shoti-katis – short cuts

Simonson, Reverend David and Eunice – Lutheran Missionaries to the Maasai in Tanzania

simsim – sesame seed oil

Sister/Mother Clotilda – teacher at Kifungilo who became Mother Superior and supplied Cathy with information about Mary's mother

Sister Eileen – big girl (Lizzy) at the orphanage who became a nun and dentist

Sister Jacinta – nun at Kifungilo in charge of cooking

Sister Majellis – headmistress of Masange Primary school near Kifungilo

Sister Silvestris – nun in charge of all the orphans

Sister Theonesta – taught elementary school at the orphanage and took care of Mary as an infant

squash – non-alcoholic fruit-flavored syrup used to make drinks

Stefana – friend from orphanage and middle school

steups – (*kusonya*) sucking sound used in East Africa and the Caribbean to show annoyance or anger

Sukuma – the largest tribe in Tanzania, living around the Lake Region

Swanglish – slang (mixture of English and Swahili)

Tanga – large city on the East Coast of Tanzania, also a region

Tanganyika – name of the former British Colony which gained its independence in 1961; The country united with the Island of Zanzibar to form The United Republic of Tanzania in 1964

Tanzania – a country located on the East Coast of Africa; The name "Tanzania" is derived from two countries—the mainland of Tanganyika and the Island of Zanzibar—that united in 1964 to form the United Republic of Tanzania

Thecla – a friend from high school

tinga tinga – style of African art in Tanzania

tsetse flies – large biting flies that inhabit much of tropical Africa and feed on the blood of vertebrate animals, including humans, and in doing so, transmit the sleeping sickness parasite

Turiani – little town near Mhonda Middle School

Tussebo –home of female trolls; name of cabin in Norway

ugali – a stiff porridge used for lunch or dinner made of corn flour, water, and salt

Ujamaa – familyhood; concept that formed the basis of President Julius Nyerere's social and economic development policies after Tanzania gained independence from Britain in 1961

Uhuru – freedom

uji – soft porridge used for breakfast, made of water, corn flour and salt

ululation – (*kigelegele*) long, high-pitched vocal sound made by rapidly moving the tongue against the roof of the mouth used to signify joy or sadness

umbrella tree – acacia-type tree
Usambara Mountains – range of mountains surrounding Kifungilo
Usa River – Small town on the outskirts of Arusha; Pronounced 'ooh-sah'

yeba! – hurrah!
Yeremia – Jeremiah, Nhambu's father

Zahabu – name of the woodcutter at the orphanage
Zami – big girl in charge of Little Mary at the orphanage
zamani – long ago, old times
zawadi – gift, present
zeruzeru – albino

Acknowledgments

W ithout Catherine Murray Mamer, there would have been no hope, no love, no America, no college, no mother, no children, and a short, sad story for me to tell. How can I say thank you to someone like you? Your unconditional love has hovered above and around me and shone brightly for everyone to see since we met when I was nineteen and you were twenty-three. You have showered my children and grandchildren with the same love you gave to me. We are all indebted to you for your unwavering love, never-ending support and commitment to each one of us in your extended family. You are the spirit that flows through the generations, connecting us all with a bond that will never be broken. *Asante sana, Mama.*

Thank you, my children, Katarina and Karl. You made me a mother about the same time I discovered who my birth mother was. I knew little about motherhood, since I had no role model as a child. Despite my inadequacies, you made me feel I was a good mother. I thank you for being the catalysts that encouraged me to face the truth about my humble beginnings in Africa and for assuring me that my roots would enrich your lives. I thank you for cheering me on when I shared bits and pieces of the struggles I faced in America as a foreigner, as a mother, and as a wife. I thank you for always protecting me. I thank you for adding an unimaginable level of richness and blessing by making me a grandmother. *Nawapendeni sana!*

Jacqueline Mosio, my editor, my Best Friend Forever: When you looked at me, you saw my soul. Though we seemed oceans apart—culturally, linguistically, and ethnically—we were attracted like magnets to each other from the day we met in class at the College of Saint Catherine. You validated my uniqueness and encouraged me not to try too hard to become too American too soon. You stood by me through many years of doubt and insecurity about myself and my writing. Your brilliance in deciphering my poorly articulated thoughts and emotions along with your sensitive and sensible questions have enabled me to tell my story with courage, beauty, and even pride. I have no words to thank you for your steadfast belief in me and your insistence that my story be told. Thank you for letting me expose my vulnerability and showing me its reflection in your soul. You are my Soul Sister. *Muchas gracias!*

Asante sana kaka—many thanks to my brother Larry. He appeared late in my life, but he was worth waiting for. If I were given the choice to travel the whole wide world to find the one person I would like to have as a brother, I would pick him. He accepted me unconditionally and made my inclusion into his family smooth and worthwhile. I am forever grateful that he made time to travel to Tanzania with me in search of my father.

Thank you, Sister Eileen for your many recollections of my childhood that made it possible for me to write *Africa's Child* and for your continued storytelling that carried on to *America's Daughter*. Thank you for welcoming me and my family to the dentistry in Lushoto and for going with us to visit our childhood friends scattered around the Usambara Mountains.

Betty, thank you for sharing your little sister, Imelda, with me. She and her family have become my family in America. I value the joy and laughter you brought into my life when you visited me in my American home. No matter how many years have passed, we always pick up our stories where we left off, proving that the bond we formed in Kifungilo is alive and well. Thank you for always opening your heart and home whenever I show up at your doorstep in Tanzania.

Imelda, we were together at the orphanage, so you know my story inside out because much of it is your story too. Though you are two years younger, we latched onto each other long ago, and now all these years later we are not only the best of friends but we are family. Many thanks to you and your husband, Dallas, for your faith in me and your steadfast encouragement during the writing of my memoirs.

A special thanks to Dr. Joyce T. Jackson, former principal at Central High school, for inaugurating a Swahili and African heritage class at her school. Her concern that the curriculum be inclusive and pertinent to the lives of her students set a far-reaching model of what public education can and should be. Some of my best teaching years were those at Central High School. I have her to thank.

Thank you, Kjell Bergh, for your patience, encouragement, promotion, and support throughout the many years of my developing the *Aerobics With Soul*® Fitness Program and making the *Serengeti, Karibu,* and *Kilimanjaro* videos.

I am indebted to my *Aerobics With Soul*® instructors Yvette Trotman, Nedy Windham, Diane Gayes, Rachel Soffer, and Salma Faraji for proving that my creation could be learned and taught by instructors other than me. When I count my blessings, you five are near the top of the list. Your understanding of the meaning and essence of *Aerobics With Soul*® affirms that race and culture cannot stifle what we feel in our hearts. Tears of love and gratitude fill my eyes when I watch you teach. I am overwhelmed by your courage, commitment, joy, and exuberance for the class. My deep and sincere gratitude for all you have meant to me personally, and to *Aerobics With Soul*®. *Asanteni sana!*

Rachel Soffer: I met you when you were in your teens. As a magnet-school student, you chose to open enroll at Central High School to take my African studies class. Little did I know our paths would cross again, and that you would become an *Aerobics With Soul*® instructor and my fearless attorney. Thank you for standing by me and supporting all my endeavors. You went beyond the call of duty to provide excellent counsel to me. Your love and enthusiasm for teaching and promoting *Aerobics With Soul*® is infectious. I am overwhelmed with love and joy as I say *Merci beaucoup, mon amie, bien aimée.*

Salma Faraji: We met at your parents' farm in Usa River in Tanzania when you were thirteen years old. We danced in your parents' living room, and you have been hooked on *Aerobics With Soul*® ever since. I have no words to describe how your loyalty and admiration of my creation have touched me. You have called me Auntie from day one and made me feel as if we have always known each other. Your unwavering dedication to *Aerobics With Soul*® and love for me is multiplied several times in my love and admiration for you. *Asante sana.*

A big thank you to Jim Gayes for the expert professional medical advice that you have provided me and my family over the years as a physician and as a friend.

Merci beaucoup to Sister Marie Phillip, CSJ, my college advisor, who took a personal interest in me and did everything in her power to help me graduate with a French major.

Merci beaucoup to my French conversation professor Marie Therese Reed, who took me under her wing and made sure my French major studies were cultural as well as academic.

My deepest gratitude to Sister Rosalie, CSJ, and all the Sisters of Saint Joseph of Carondelet for enabling me to fulfill my dream of a higher education by awarding me a scholarship to the College of Saint Catherine (now Saint Catherine University). The tutelage, dedication, and commitment to women's education I received there laid the foundation for the person I am today and inspired me to "be my neighbor's keeper."

A big thank you to my readers whose comments, corrections, and suggestions have been invaluable: Katarina Nhambu Bergh, Karl Nhambu Bergh, Imelda and Dallas Browne, Anna Fitzsimmons, Diane and Jim Gayes, Catherine Murray Mamer, Carletta Smith, Rachel Soffer, Rita Speltz, Natasha Vaubel, Margaret Wong and Walter Graff, Anna Blangiado, Cassie Froese, Alicia Walker, and also to Cathy Broberg, editor.

Thank you to Barbara Cronie, Editor, Editing Par Excellence, for your professionalism, enthusiasm, and support for *Africa's Child. America's Daughter* and *Drum Beats, Heart Beats*.

As always, to my friends, thank you for your friendship, encouragement, love, and belief in me. Thank you for your patience as you nudged me along over the years saying, "We'll be dead before your books come out!" All I can say to you now is "Better late than never!"

About the Author

M aria Nhambu—educator, dancer, writer, mother, entrepreneur, and philanthropist—was raised by German missionary nuns in an orphanage for mixed-race children high in the Usambara Mountains of Tanzania. A twenty-three-year-old American woman adopted Nhambu at age nineteen and brought her to America for college. Nhambu is the creator of *Aerobics With Soul®*—the African Workout based on the dances she learned growing up in Tanzania. She prefers to be known simply as "Nhambu," which means "one who connects" or "bridge person." She is the mother of two, grandmother of three, and lives in Delray Beach, Florida, and Minneapolis, Minnesota.

Nhambu is available for speaking engagements as well as classes and demonstrations of her *Aerobics With Soul®* fitness program.

www.MariaNhambu.com

Maria@MariaNhambu.com

To purchase *Aerobics With Soul®* videos go to www.aerobicswithsoul.com.

About Dancing Soul Trilogy

The first book of Maria Nhambu's memoir trilogy, *Africa's Child* (2016), recounts her life from infancy when she was left at an orphanage for mixed race children in Tanzania to growing up under the strict discipline of German nuns to meeting the American teacher who brought her to the United States. Orphanage life was difficult and at times brutal, but her faith and deep inner resources along with a love of education and dance sustained her.

In *America's Daughter*, the second book of the trilogy (2017), she arrives in the United States in the company of American high-school teacher Catherine Murray. Her adjustment to a new culture includes shocking doses of American-style racial discrimination and her discovery that she must learn to be a Black American. She graduates from college and fulfills her dream of becoming a teacher, teaching at an inner-city Minneapolis high school. She marries, has two children, and establishes herself in the American way of life. Then a visit to Africa, especially to Tanzania, reawakens the drumbeats and dancing she carries in her soul. Upon her return home she teaches Swahili and African Studies, performs African dance at schools, and creates *Aerobics With Soul®*, a fitness workout based on African dance. She both finds and creates the family she longed for as a child and connects with her unknown background.

Drum Beats, Heart Beats (2018) opens with a challenging journey to find her father. She becomes certified as a fitness instructor and teaches *Aerobics With Soul®* in the United States and internationally. The family she longed for painfully unravels and she faces a major health crisis. Visiting Africa continues to sustain and inspire her.

Maria Nhambu's message of hope, resilience, and the importance of love for oneself is powerful and unforgettable.